THE LAW AND E[illegible]
EUROP[illegible]

Markets and the Law

Markets and the Law is concerned with the way the law interacts with the market through regulation, self-regulation and the impact of private law regimes. It looks at the impact of regional and international organizations (e.g. EC and WTO) and many of the works adopt a comparative approach and/or appeal to an international audience. Examples of subjects covered include trade laws, intellectual property, sales law, insurance, consumer law, banking, financial markets, labour law, environmental law and social regulation affecting the market as well as competition law. The series includes texts covering a broad area, monographs on focused issues, and collections of essays dealing with particular themes.

Other titles in the series

The Organizational Contract
From Exchange to Long-Term Network Cooperation in European Contract Law
Edited by Stefan Grundmann, Fabrizio Cafaggi and Giuseppe Vettori
ISBN 978 1 4724 2124 1

International Insolvency Law
Reforms and Challenges
Edited by Paul Omar
ISBN 978 07546 7482 5

International Responses to Issues of Credit and Over-indebtedness in the Wake of Crisis
Edited by Therese Wilson
ISBN 978 1 4094 5522 6

The Law and Economics of Enforcing European Consumer Law

A Comparative Analysis of Package Travel and Misleading Advertising

FRANZISKA WEBER
University of Hamburg, Germany

Routledge
Taylor & Francis Group
LONDON AND NEW YORK

First published in paperback 2024

First published 2014 by Ashgate Publishing

Published 2016 by Routledge
4 Park Square, Milton Park, Abingdon, Oxon OX14 4RN

and by Routledge
605 Third Avenue, New York, NY 10158

Routledge is an imprint of the Taylor & Francis Group, an informa business

Publisher's Note
The publisher has gone to great lengths to ensure the quality of this reprint but points out that some imperfections in the original copies may be apparent.

British Library Cataloguing in Publication Data
A catalogue record for this book is available from the British Library

The Library of Congress has cataloged the printed edition as follows:
Weber, Franziska (Law teacher)
The law and economics of enforcing European consumer law : a comparative analysis of package travel and misleading advertising / by Franziska Weber.
pages cm. -- (Markets and the law)
Includes bibliographical references and index.
ISBN 978-1-4724-1704-6 (hardback) 1. Consumer protection--Law and legislation--Economic aspects--European Union countries. 2. Package tours--Law and legislation--European Union countries. 3. Deceptive advertising--Law and legislation--European Union countries. 4. Consumer protection--Law and legislation--England. 5. Consumer protection--Law and legislation--Netherlands. 6. Consumer protection--Law and legislation--Sweden. I. Title.
KJE6577.W433 2014
343.2407'1--dc23

2013045808

ISBN: 978-1-4724-1704-6 (hbk)
ISBN: 978-1-03-292175-4 (pbk)
ISBN: 978-1-315-55627-7 (ebk)

DOI: 10.4324/9781315556277

Contents

List of Cases

Netherlands

Amsterdam Court of Appeal, 1 June 2006, NJ 2006, 461 (DES)
Amsterdam Court of Appeal, 25 January 2007, JOR 2007, 71 (Dexia)
Amsterdam Court of Appeal, 23 March 2010 (Tele 2/UPC internetten&bellen hoger beroep)
Decision *Consumentenautoriteit*, 23 April 2008, CA/NCB/17 (UPC)
Decision *Consumentenautoriteit*, 17 June 2010 CA/NB/510/30 (Celldorado)
Decision *Consumentenautoriteit*, 6 September 2010 CA/NB/527/29 (Nederlandse Energie Maatschappij/NL Energie)
Decision *Consumentenautoriteit*, 21 September 2010 CA/NB/544/10 (Garant-o-Matic B.V.)
The Hague Court of Appeal, 7 April 2009, LJN BK4880, TvC 2009 (Gold Travel)

Sweden

Bo Åberg v Kefalas Elfeterios (Case No. T 3515-03, Stockholm District Court)
Carl de Geer et al. v The Swedish Airports and Air Navigation Service (M 1931, 2007, Nacka District Court, Environmental Court)
DOM 2008:6 2008-04-11 Dnr B 2/07 (Prima Travel AB)
DOM 2009:17 2009-06-26 Dnr B 9/08 (Casa Nordica Altavista C AB)
Grupptalan mot Skandia v Försäkringsaktiebolaget Skandia (T 97, 2004, Stockholm District Court)
Konsumentombudsmannen v Kraftkommission (T 5416, 2004, Umeå District Court)
MD 1998:7 KO v Fritidsresor
Pär Wihlborg v The Swedish State through the Chancellor of Justice (T 1286, 2007, Nacka District Court)

England

British Airways v Ryanair [2001] FSR 541
Caparo Industries plc v Dickman [1990] 2 AC 605
CRE-E/26641 OFT investigation into Colin Michael Ogle t/a Swindon Decodes
Decision of the Office of Fair Trading, No. CA98/06/2003, Competition Act 1998, Price-fixing of Replica Football Kit

Director-General of Fair Trading v Tobyward Ltd [1989] 2 All ER 266
Hedley Byrne & Co Ltd v Heller and Partners Ltd [1964] AC 465
R v ASA, ex parte Charles Robertson (Developments) Ltd, The Times 26 November 1999
R v ASA, ex parte SmithKline Beecham plc [2001] EMLR 23
R v ASA, ex parte Vernons [1992] 1 WLR 1289

List of Legislation

England

ABTA Arbitration Appeal Procedure
ABTA Arbitration Scheme – rules & appeal procedure
ABTA Code of Conduct
Access to Justice Act 1990
Access to Justice Act 1999
BCAP Code
Business Protection from Misleading Marketing Regulations 2008
CAP Code
Civil Procedural Rules
Code for Crown Prosecutors
Conditional Fees Agreements Regulations 2000
Competition Act 1998
Consumer Protection Act 1987
Consumer Protection from Unfair Trading Regulations 2008
Courts and Legal Services Act 1990
Criminal Procedure & Investigations Act 1996
Enterprise Act 2002
Legal Aid, Sentencing and Punishment of Offenders Act 2012
Package Travel, Package Holidays and Package Tours Regulations S.I. 3288 of 1992
Police & Criminal Evidence Act 1984
Powers of Criminal Courts (Sentencing) Act 2000
Practice Direction 19B – Group litigation. This practice direction supplements Section III of Part 19
Regulatory Enforcement and Sanctions Act 2008
Regulation of Investigatory Powers Act 2000
Supreme Court Act 1981
The Civil Aviation (Air Travel Organisers' Licensing) Regulations 2012
Trade Descriptions Act 1968
Weights and Measures Act 1985

Germany

EG-Verbraucherschutzdurchsetzungsgesetz (EC Consumer Protection Enforcement Act)
Gesetz gegen den unlauteren Wettbewerb (Unfair Trade Practices Act)
Gesetz über Entschädigung für Strafverfolgungsmaßnahmen (Act on Compensation for Wrongful Prosecution)
Strafprozessordnung (Act on Criminal Procedure)

Netherlands

Algemene wet bestuursrecht (General Administrative Law Act)
ANVR Huishoudelijk Reglement (ANVR Rules)
ANVR algemene reisvoorwaarden (ANVR Travel Standard Contract Terms)
Besluit tarieven ambtshandelingen gerechtsdeurwaarders (Bailiff Fees Decree), Stb. 2001, 325, ammended in Stb. 2001, 600
Bijl. Handelingen II 2008/09, 31 753, no. 1
Burgerlijk Wetboek (Civil Code)
Colportagewet (Canvassing Act)
Deelnemersreglement SGR (Rules on Participation SGR)
Gerechtsdeurwaarderswet (Bailiff Act)
Garantieregeling SGR (Rules on Travel Guarantees)
Kamerstukken II 2005/06, 30 411, no. 6 (Parliamentary Minutes)
Kamerstukken II 2011/12, 33 071, no. 1–3 (Parliamentary Minutes)
Mediawet (Media Act)
Memorie van Toelichting Whc (Explanatory Memorandum Whc), Kamerstukken II 2005/06, 30 411, no. 3 (Parliamentary Minutes)
Prijzenwet (Prices Act)
Reclamecode voor Alcoholhoudende Dranken (Advertising Code for Alcoholic Beverages)
Reglement Geschillencommissie Reizen (GCR Regulations)
Reglement betreffende de Reclame Code Commissie en het College van Beroep (Regulations on Dutch Advertising Council and Board of Appeal)
SGR Statute
Uitvoeringswet Verordening Europese Procedure voor geringe Vorderingen (Law implementing the Regulation on European Small Claims Procedure)
Wetboek van Burgerlijke Rechtsvordering (Act on Civil Procedure)
Wetboek van Strafrecht (Penal Code)
Wet collectieve afwikkeling van massaschade (Collective Settlement of Mass Damage Act)
Wet handhaving consumentenbescherming (Act on Enforcement of Consumer Protection Law)
Wet oneerlijke handelspraktijken (Unfair Commercial Practices Law)

Wet op de Kansspelen (Act on the Games of Chance)
Wet op de rechtsbijstand (Act on Legal Support)
Wet griffierechten burgerlijke zaken – Bijlage behorend bij de wet (Court Fees for Civil Matters Act – Annex)
Wet prejudiciële vragen Hoge Raad (Supreme Court Preliminary Questions Act)
Wet van 25 juni 2009, Stb. 2009, 264, tot aanvulling van de Algemene wet bestuursrecht (Vierde tranche Algemene wet bestuursrecht) Stb. 2009, 266 (Amendment to the General Administrative Law Act)
Wet van 19 mei 2011 tot wijziging van de Wet op de rechterlijke organisatie, de Wet op de rechterlijke indeling, het Wetboek van Burgerlijke Rechtsvordering en enkele andere wetten naar aanleiding van de evaluatie van de modernisering van de rechterlijke organisatie en in verband met de regeling van het klachtrecht inzake gedragingen van rechterlijke ambtenaren (Evaluatiewet modernisering rechterlijke organisatie)
Wet van 28 Februari 2013, houdende regels omtrent de instelling van de Autoriteit Consument en Markt (Instellingswet Autoriteit Consument en Markt – Law establishing the ACM)
Wet verhoging griffierechten (Law on Court Fees Increase)

Sweden

Den svenska rättegångsbalken (SFS 1942:740) (Swedish Civil Procedural Code)
Förordning – Regulation (SFS 1988:208)
Förordning – Regulation (SFS 1997:9) om försöksverksamhet med grupptalan vid Allmänna reklamationsnämnden (ARN Group Litigation Regulation)
Förordning – Regulation (SFS 2002:601)
Förordning – Regulation (SFS 2007:1041) med instruktion för Allmänna reklamationsnämnden (ARN Instruction 2007)
Lag (SFS 1931:152) med vissa bestämmelser mot illojal konkurrens (Unfair Competition Act)
Lag (SFS 1962:381) om allmän försäkring (National Insurance Act)
Lag (SFS 1970:412) om otillbörlig marknadsföring (Improper Marketing Act)
Lag (SFS 1974:8) om rättegång i tvistemål om mindre värden (Small Claims Act)
Lag (SFS 1994:1512) om avtalsvillkor i konsumentförhållande (Contract Terms Act)
Lag (SFS 2002:599) om grupprättegång (Group Proceedings Act)
Lag (SFS 2011:1211) om Konsumentombudsmannens medverkan i vissa tvister (KO Representation in Certain Disputes Act)
Marknadsföringslagen (SFS 2008:486) (Marketing Act)
Proposition 1986/87:89 om ett reformerat tingsrättsförfarande
Proposition 1994/95:123 Ny marknadsföringslag Regeringen överlämnar denna proposition till riksdage
Rättshjälpslagen (SFS 1996:1619) (Legal Aid Act)

Resegarantilagen (SFS 1972:204) (Swedish Travel Guarantees Act)
Socialförsäkringsbalk (SFS 2010:110) (Social Insurance Scale)

Europe

Council Directive 90/314/EEC of 13 June 1990 on package travel, package holidays and package tours (Package Travel Directive), OJ L 158, 23.6.1990, pp. 59–64
Directive 98/27/EC of the European Parliament and of the Council of 19 May 1998 on injunctions for the protection of consumers' interests, OJ L 166, 11.6.1998, pp. 51–5
Directive 2005/29/EC of the European Parliament and of the Council of 11 May 2005 concerning unfair business-to-consumer commercial practices in the internal market and amending Council Directive 84/450/EEC, Directives 97/7/EC, 98/27/EC and 2002/65/EC of the European Parliament and of the Council and Regulation (EC) No 2006/2004 of the European Parliament and of the Council 'Unfair Commercial Practices Directive'), OJ L 149, 11.6.2005, pp. 22–39
Proposal for a Directive of the European Parliament and of the Council on alternative dispute resolution for consumer disputes and amending Regulation (EC) No 2006/2004 and Directive 2009/22/EC (Directive on Consumer ADR) Brussels, 29.11.2011 COM(2011) 793 final and proposal for a Regulation of the European Parliament and of the Council on online dispute resolution for consumer disputes (Regulation on Consumer ODR) Brussels, 29.11.2011 COM(2011) 794 final 2011/0374 (COD)
Regulation (EC) No 2006/2004 of the European Parliament and of the Council of 27 October 2004 on cooperation between national authorities responsible for the enforcement of consumer protection laws (the Regulation on Consumer Protection Cooperation [CPC]), OJ L 364, 9.12.2004, pp. 1–11
Regulation (EC) No 1896/2006 of the European Parliament and of the Council of 12 December 2006 creating a European order for payment procedure, OJ L 399, 30.12.2006, pp. 1–32
Regulation (EC) No 861/2007 of the European Parliament and of the Council of 11 July 2007 establishing a European small claims procedure (Regulation on European Small Claims Procedure), OJ L 199, 31.7.2007, pp. 1–22
White Paper Preparation of the associated countries of Central and Eastern Europe for integration into the internal market of the Union, COM 1995 163 final

Other

European Convention on Human Rights
Private Securities Litigation Reform Act 1995 (US)

List of Abbreviations

AB	Aktiebolag
ABTA	Association of British Travel Agents
ACM	Autoriteit Consument en Markt
ADR	Alternative Dispute Resolution
AITO	Association of Independent Tour Operators
ALI	American Law Institute
ANVR	Algemene Nederlandse Vereniging van Reisondernemingen
ARN	Allmänna Reklamationsnämnden
ASA	Advertising Standards Authority
Asbof	Advertising Standards Board of Finance
ATE	After-the-event (insurance)
ATOL	Air Travel Organisers' Licensing (Scheme)
ATT	Air Travel Trust
AUC	Asociación de Usuarios de la Comunicación
Awb	Algemene wet bestuursrecht
B2B	Business-to-business
B2C	Business-to-consumer
BACT	Behavioural Approaches to Contract and Tort
Basbof	Broadcast Advertising Standards Board of Finance
BCAP	Broadcast Committee of Advertising Practice
BERR	Department for Business, Enterprise and Regulatory Reform
BIS	Department of Business, Innovation and Skills
BPRs	Business Protection from Misleading Marketing Regulations
Btag	Besluit tarieven ambtshandelingen gerechtsdeurwaarders
BTE	Before-the-event (insurance)
B.V.	Besloten Vennootschap
BVL	Bundesamt für Verbraucherschutz und Lebensmittelsicherheit
BW	Burgerlijk Wetboek
CA	Consumentenautoriteit
CAA	Civil Aviation Authority
CAP	Committee of Advertising Practice
CB	Consumentenbond
CBA	Cost–benefit Analysis
CBS	Centraal Bureau voor de Statistiek
CCAS	Code of Conduct Approval Scheme
CEE	Central and Eastern European
CEPEJ	Commission Européenne pour l'Efficacité de la Justice

CFA	Conditional Fee Agreement
CLEF	Consumer Law Enforcement Forum
CMA	Competition and Markets Authority
COM	Commission
CPC	(Regulation on) Consumer Protection Cooperation
CPR	Civil Procedural Rules
CPRs	Consumer Protection from Unfair Trading Regulations
CvM	Commissariaat voor de Media
DCFR	Draft Common Frame of Reference
DG SANCO	Directorate General for 'Health and Consumers'
EASA	European Advertising Standards Alliance
EBTP	European Business Test Panel
EC	European Community
ECC-network	European Consumer Centres-network
ECHR	European Convention on Human Rights
ECLG	European Consumer Law Group
GC	Geschillencommissie
GCR	Geschillencommissie Reizen
Gdw	Gerechtsdeurwaarderswet
GGTO	Stichting Garantiefonds voor Gespecialiseerde Touroperators
GLO	Group Litigation Order
HMSO	Her/His Majesty's Stationery Office
ICC	International Chamber of Commerce
KAG	Keuringsraad Aanprijzing Gezondheidsproducten
KO	Konsumentombudsmannen
KOAG	Keuringsraad Openlijke Aanprijzing Geneesmiddelen
KOV	Konsumentverket
Kr	Swedish Kronor
LASPO	Legal Aid, Sentencing and Punishment of Offenders Act
LBRO	Local Better Regulation Office
LOG	Lag om grupprättegång
MA	Marketing Act
MKB	Brancheorganisatie voor het midden- en kleinbedrijf
MP	Member of Parliament
NAITA	National Association of Independent Travel Agents
NAO	National Audit Office
NGO	Nongovernmental Organisation
NLG	Dutch Guilders
NMa	Nederlandse Mededingingsautoriteit
NTSB	National Trading Standards Board
OCU	Organización de Consumidores y Usuarios
ODR	Online Dispute Resolution
OECD	Organisation for Economic Cooperation and Development
Ofcom	Office of Communications

OFT	Office of Fair Trading
OJ	Official Journal of the European Union
OM	Openbaar Ministerie
OPTA	Onafhankelijke Post en Telecommunicatie Autoriteit
PermRep	Permanent Representation
PTRs	Package Travel, Package Holidays and Package Tours Regulations
RA	Rational Apathy
RACC	Radio Advertising Clearance Centre
RB	Rättegångsbalken
RCC	Reclame Code Commissie
RESA	Regulatory Enforcement and Sanctions Act
RO	Reklamombudsmannen
Rv	Wetboek van Burgerlijke Rechtsvordering
RvA	Reclamecode voor Alcoholhoudende Dranken
SER	Sociaal-Economische Raad
SFS	Svensk Författningssamling
SGC	Stichting Geschillencommissies voor Consumentenzaken
SGR	Stichting Garantiefonds Reisgelden
SGST	Stichting Garantiefonds Specialistische Touroperators
SME	Small- and Medium-sized Enterprises
SRC	Stichting Reclame Code
SRF	Svenska Resebyråföreningen
Stb	Staatsblad
STIVA	Stichting Verantwoord Alcoholgebruik
StPO	Strafprozessordnung
StrEG	Gesetz über Entschädigung für Strafverfolgungsmaßnahmen
TABRS	Travel Agents' Bond Replacement Scheme
TSI	Trading Standards Institute
TSS	Trading Standards Services
UCP	Unfair Commercial Practices
UNC	Unione Nazionale Consumatori
UNIDROIT	Institut International Pour L'Unification du Droit Prive
UWG	Gesetz gegen den unlauteren Wettbewerb
VAT	Value Added Tax
VEB	Vereniging van Effectenbezitters
VKI	Verein für Konsumenteninformation
VNO-NCW	Verbond van Nederlandse Ondernemingen-Nederlands Christelijk Werkgeversverbond
VOD	Video-on-demand
VSchDG	EG-Verbraucherschutzdurchsetzungsgesetz
VvKR	Vereniging van Kleinschalige Reisorganisaties
WCAM	Wet collectieve afwikkeling van massaschade
Whc	Wet handhaving consumentenbescherming
WODC	Wetenschappelijk Onderzoeks- en Documentatiecentrum

WOHP	Wet oneerlijke handelspraktijken
Wrb	Wet op de rechtsbijstand
WvS	Wetboek van Strafrecht

Foreword

It must have been, I think, in the 1970s that I was browsing through the Annual Report on the UN Human Rights Commission. This contained National Reports from the Member States on how human rights law had developed in their jurisdiction during the last year. Now, while Western countries reported on interesting case law, as well as legislative measures, much of it trying to compromise between differing demands on the legal system, the countries of the Soviet bloc produced bland descriptions of how their laws protected citizens against human rights abuse. Clearly a travesty of what actually happened in these jurisdictions, the statements made one immediately aware that an account of what the law says is inadequate, perhaps even irrelevant, without an investigation of whether and how it is enforced.

The observation becomes of paramount importance when we are considering consumer protection law. This is not only because there is a vast network of different legal obligations, regulations, remedies and procedures. It is also because infringements of many consumer laws result in relatively modest financial losses for the victims individually, thus impairing such incentives as they might have to seek to redress; in aggregate, the welfare losses might be considerable, therefore requiring some form of collective enforcement efforts.

Note, too, that as consumer protection law has developed, so too have ideas evolved about how such efforts should be realised. At one end of the spectrum we have classical private law remedies; at the other, traditional criminal law. In between, there have emerged coordinated private group actions, administrative monitoring, procedures and sanctions, as well as industry-based self-regulatory redress and indeed mixtures of these various approaches.

Far too much of traditional legal scholarship focused on specific approaches, because the marrying of the private, administrative and criminal spheres did not fit in well with the segmented expertise within law faculties. Contemporary scholarship has largely overcome this problem, but there is still a notable reluctance to consider normatively what combinations of approaches are appropriate in what circumstances.

Hence the justification for, and importance of, Franziska Weber's study. Her task was not an easy one, particularly because she (rightly) decided to examine possible combinations from a comparative perspective. Of course, this led to an awareness that the question of what system or systems of enforcement are most desirable cannot be considered in an historical vacuum. Within different jurisdictions, the selection of appropriate legal and procedural strategies is, to some extent at least, dependent on local legal tradition and culture. In other words, as Weber affirms, path dependency must play a critical role in legal policymaking.

This does not mean, of course, that she has to abandon rational analysis in reaching conclusions about what combination of legal and procedural devices might be 'best'. But the question then arises, what criteria and methodology should be adopted for this latter goal? Here there is a risk of falling into the trap of looking for ideal, Utopian solutions which fail to acknowledge resource constraints. As Weber is quick to recognise, we cannot be interested in 'perfect' enforcement strategies; rather the aim is to postulate what is 'optimal', that is, which maximises benefits against costs. And that requires an economic appraisal.

Such an appraisal does not have to be mathematical or even precise. There is no way in which many of the crucial variables arising in the context of legal enforcement can be precisely quantified. Take the theory of deterrence, and the central question of how traders' compliance may be secured by the threat of sanctions and other enforcement procedures. Their responsiveness is likely to depend on a variety of factors. For example, as Weber points out, there is a highly significant difference between *bona fide* and *mala fide* traders. But it is very difficult to identify, prior to an infringement, in which category a particular trader is to be placed. In many areas of consumer law, it therefore makes sense to treat first offenders with lenience, since many will respond positively to an informal reprimand, particularly if that provides information as to their precise legal obligations which otherwise they might lack.

What emerges from Franziska Weber's discussion of this and equivalent sensitive issues is that the main thrust of the analysis should be based on broad predictions of the incidence of costs and benefits which are plausible. She has convincingly succeeded in this respect and the result is a study which not only provides a fascinating account of how legal and enforcement procedures have developed; it also generates important insights for policymakers on what combinations of procedures are likely to be optimal in different contexts.

Anthony Ogus

Preface

'Catch-me-if-you-can' traders, *mala fide* traders, seek to commit fraud and aim at substantially harming consumers without revealing their identity. They are on the run like Frank Abagnale, Jr in the movie *Catch Me if You Can* (2002). Whereas the movie character engages the spectators' sympathy, maybe even compassion, rogue traders and their strategic avoidance of law enforcement clearly do not. My curiosity and disapproval were first triggered years ago when I saw the dubious advertisements for ring tone downloads and the powerless outcry they led to. 'Catch-me-if-you-can' traders always find new ways to hide; the Internet is their best friend. It is therefore the other side of the coin – the enforcement side – that I wish to contribute to with my book. My analysis of European consumer law enforcement is consequently carried out with a particular view to *mala fide* and *bona fide* traders. While we want to deter the former, we have an interest in encouraging the latter.

One can look at consumer law from many different angles, one being the economic analysis of law. Law and economics provides fruitful insights for lawyers, economists and policymakers. Even though there is more to law than economic efficiency, it is essential to incorporate economic insights about enforcement of consumer protection law in the broader discussion of policy. This will improve the quality of such a discussion and indicate lines along which long-term legal reforms could be envisaged.

This book would not have been possible without Prof. Michael G. Faure and Prof. Willem H. van Boom to whom I owe enormous thanks. With regard to the country studies, I wish to thank in particular Prof. Willem H. van Boom, Prof. Antonina Bakardjieva-Engelbrekt and Prof. Christopher Hodges for sharing their knowledge of, respectively, the Dutch, the Swedish and the English legal systems. I thank as well all other members of the Erasmus School of Law, who kindly discussed my research with me and provided helpful advice. I wish to mention Prof. Klaus Heine, Prof. Roger J. van den Bergh, Prof. Luigi A. Franzoni, Prof. Anthony I. Ogus, Dr. Sonja Keske, Dr Louis Visscher, Dr Niels J. Philipsen and Henriette van Dam-Lely. To the numerous interview partners from the various countries, I also want to extend my sincere thanks for their patient help and very interesting insights.

The European Commission has recently taken a stronger stance in passing legislation concerning consumer law enforcement. This leads to opportunities and risks alike. It is among the book's objectives to provide some answers to the challenge of passing suitable legislation for the European Union and finding the desirable level of union-wide law enforcement. Some of you may remember that the criminal Frank Abagnale, Jr ended up working for the bank fraud department of the FBI. That may have been an efficient solution indeed. The long-term benefits may have justified the enormous efforts made by FBI agents – including spending Christmas at the office.

Franziska Weber

Chapter 1
Introduction

Context: The Need for Consumer Protection Laws and their Enforcement

The starting point for an economic analysis of consumer law enforcement is the existence of markets for consumer goods. Economic theory illustrates how these markets work. In perfectly working markets, no legal interventions (such as tax laws or subsidies) are necessary, as they can only lead to a reduction of economic efficiency. In economic terms, this situation is called a 'first-best solution', which is an ideal situation that does not exist in reality. The real world is full of market distortions and imperfections that necessitate legal intervention through consumer protection laws. Legal interventions are referred to as second or third-best solutions.

In the 1960s and 1970s, consumer movements strongly favoured strengthening the rights of the weak party, and pure legal literature today still includes the argument that the consumer primarily must be protected from powerful (superior) sellers. Law and economics scholars criticised this reasoning.[1] They analysed consumer protection rules in three different, consecutive streams, namely information economics, new institutional economics and behavioural economics.[2] In information economics, the consumer is regarded as exposed to certain constraints due to a lack of information. For instance, the consumer cannot appropriately perceive quality differences.[3] Imperfect information and the resulting information costs prevent the consumer from making an informed choice. This first stream shows how information affects people's ability to make choices, and, consequently, how an improvement in the information flow can solve problems in markets. Solutions do not necessarily have to come from governmental intervention, but can be achieved by internal market mechanisms.

1 See G.K. Hadfield, R. Howse and M.J. Trebilcock, 'Information-Based Principles for Rethinking Consumer Protection Policy', *Journal of Consumer Policy* 21 (1998): 131–69, p. 133.

2 See for an overview F. Rischkowsky and T. Döring, 'Consumer Policy in a Market Economy: Considerations from the Perspective of the Economics of Information, the New Institutional Economics as well as Behavioural Economics', *Journal of Consumer Policy* 31 (2008): 285–313.

3 See Rischkowsky and Döring (2008), p. 308; see J. Stiglitz, 'The Contributions of the Economics of Information to the Twentieth Century Economics', *Quarterly Journal of Economics* 114 (2000): 1441–78, G.J. Stigler, 'The Economics of Information', *Journal of Political Economy* 69 (1961): 213–25.

New institutional economics acknowledges that the pure provision of information is not sufficient and calls for regulation of certain institutions (contracts, for example). Apart from imperfect information and information costs, institutional economics is concerned with other transaction costs that impact market transparency and consumer behaviour. In addition to the requirement to provide consumers with information, regulating contract and liability law are discussed to reduce transaction costs.

Behavioural economics challenges the rational choice theory and states that the consumer – even when exposed to complete information – cannot process all this information. In a way, behavioural economics follows a similar direction as information economics: it provides insights on how consumers perceive and use available information and choice. Perception is dependent on consumers' internal constraints in the form of cognitive, emotional and situational factors.[4]

From an economic viewpoint, the general starting point for a legal intervention through consumer protection laws is the occurrence of market failures.[5] There are four types of market failure, in which the market is unable to allocate resources efficiently: information asymmetries, market power, externalities and public goods.[6] If markets do not work properly, consumer interests are assumed to be hurt.[7] A commonly occurring market failure in relation to consumer law is an information asymmetry, such as quality uncertainty.[8] Imperfect information about prices or quality affects individual decisions and the lack of information leads to inefficient negotiations and contracts. Any kind of market failure has to be cured to

4 For details, see H.A. Luth, *Behavioural Economics in Consumer Policy – The Economic Analysis of Standard Terms in Consumer Contracts Revisited* (Antwerp: Intersentia, 2010).

5 See R.J. Van den Bergh, 'Should Consumer Protection Law be Publicly Enforced?' *Collective Enforcement of Consumer Law*, eds W.H. Van Boom and M.B.M. Loos (Groningen: Europa Law Publishing, 2007) 179–203, p. 180. See also Luth (2010), pp. 1, 39 for economic rationales for consumer protection policy.

6 See Van den Bergh (2007), p. 180. According to Coase, in case of externalities, there is only a reason for governmental intervention when transaction costs are high; see R.H. Coase, 'The Problem of Social Cost', *Journal of Law and Economics* 3 (1960): 1–44; see E. Van Damme, 'Toekomst van de consument Concurrentiebeleid en consumentenbeleid', *ESB Dossier* (2007): 36–42, p. 39 about monopolies and information asymmetries.

7 See S. Issacharoff and I. Samuel, 'The Institutional Dimension of Consumer Protection', *New Frontiers of Consumer Protection – The Interplay between Private and Public Enforcement*, eds F. Cafaggi and H-W. Micklitz (Antwerp; Oxford; Portland: Intersentia, 2009) 47–62, p. 47; for a recent study on consumer detriment, see Europe Economics, An analysis of the Issue of Consumer Detriment and the Most Appropriate Methodologies to Estimate it (Final Report for DG SANCO, 2007), http://ec.europa.eu/consumers/strategy/docs/study_consumer_detriment.pdf, last accessed: 31 March 2013, p. 124.

8 See G. Akerlof, 'The Market for Lemons: Qualitative Uncertainty and the Market Mechanism', *Quarterly Journal of Economics* 84.3 (1979): 488–500; Van den Bergh (2007), p. 180.

enable the market to work and to restore competition. Therefore, well-functioning markets generally rely on government as a rule-maker and possibly as an enforcer.[9] Interventions can be more or less restrictive. Only some small, simple markets have a potential to cure themselves, for example in cases of minor distortions where a reputation mechanism might work and consumers will buy their products somewhere else.[10] An issue worth considering is that any intervention in the market will lead to costs for the producer, such as adaptation costs of a product to new standards.[11] These costs are likely to be reflected in the product's price. Thus, from an efficiency point of view, governmental intervention must be carefully designed because it forces consumers to buy 'a safe product at a higher price'.

From a legal viewpoint, consumer protection rules serve to protect (the weak) consumers; however, these laws not only protect the private interests of individual consumers, but also are indispensable for proper market functioning. It is particular to the nature of consumer problems that they lie at the borderline of private/public problems and social/commercial ones, and, therefore, a wide range of legal knowledge of different areas is necessary to successfully engage in this field of law.[12] Because substantive consumer laws encompass public and private law, redress is necessarily made to both public and private enforcement instruments. Among the options are private (civil courts) or consumer alternative dispute resolution (ADR) bodies, administrative/public agencies and criminal courts. Likewise, self-regulation is a consideration. Apart from classical, individual lawsuits, forms of group litigation are available as procedural tools. For the remainder of this book, these different ways to enforce consumer law are labelled 'enforcement mechanisms'.

The starting point for solving conflicts is private negotiation; therefore, a valid question among law and economics scholars is why formal bodies need to be involved in enforcement. According to Coase's framework, under the condition of negligible transaction costs, bargaining between parties will lead to an efficient outcome irrespective of the legal rule in place.[13] But when transaction costs exist, Coasan bargaining might not work. When these costs are high, efficient outcomes might not be reached and individuals might be prevented from entering into welfare-enhancing transactions. Therefore, starting with private or other out-of-

9 See S.D. Soderlind, *Consumer Economics – A Practical Overview* (Armonk, New York/London, England: M.E. Sharpe, 2001), p. 233.

10 See G. Howells and S. Weatherill, *Consumer Protection Law*, 2nd ed. (Aldershot: Ashgate Publishing, 2005), p. 2.

11 See Howells and Weatherill (2005), p. 39.

12 See Howells and Weatherill (2005), p. 660; I. Ramsay, 'Consumer Redress and Access to Justice', *International Perspectives on Consumers' Access to Justice*, eds C.E.F. Rickett and T.G.W. Telfer (Cambridge: Cambridge University Press, 2003) 17–45, p. 25.

13 On the notion of optimal outcomes in negotiations, see Coase (1960); Market transaction costs include searching and investigating parties, negotiations, the process of reaching an agreement.

court settlements is preferred over litigation because lower enforcement costs are assumed.[14] However, in some instances, transaction costs require the involvement of a formal dispute resolution body, like a court, to reduce these costs. Negotiations between two parties are often characterised by information asymmetries, which influence people's decision-making, particularly if one party has private, factual information. In these cases, formal litigation, lawyers, judges, public enforcers and so on serve to produce information regarding the uncertainties of a case or that may be lacking on one side or the other.[15] Furthermore, each party may have opposing prior expectations, or may engage in strategic bargaining.[16] Litigation serves to reduce uncertainty about a trading partner's reliability. An unequal distribution of information is an important reason why parties litigate before formal enforcement bodies.

Law enforcement is crucial to guarantee smooth functioning markets, as it imposes the content of substantive laws upon individuals.[17] From a legal perspective, procedural law is regarded as a serving function to substantive law (for example, in the field of private law, it provides litigants with compensation).[18] From an economic viewpoint, the threat of enforcement steers people's behaviour; more particularly their incentives to obey the law. The interplay between substantive laws and their enforcement forms the incentives and deterrents that induce law-abiding behaviour.[19]

Whereas consumer laws have been a national issue, over the last years, they have become a very complex topic.[20] The notion of consumer law cannot be fully captured anymore if states engage in purely national law-making detached from

---

14 Among the standard models of settlement is the well-known Priest-Klein model, see G.L. Priest, 'Reexamining the Selection Hypothesis: Learning from Wittman's Mistakes', *Journal of Legal Studies* 14 (1985): 215–43; G.L. Priest and B. Klein, 'The Selection of Disputes for Litigation', *Journal of Legal Studies* 13 (1984): 1–55.

15 See L.A. Bebchuk, 'Litigation and Settlement under Imperfect Information', *RAND Journal of Economics* 15 (1984): 404–15.

16 These issues were discussed in detail in presentations by G. Dari-Mattiaci during the summer school 'Access to Justice', University of Pavia, June 2010.

17 Here, the term enforcement is broader than simply the notion of enforcing a title obtained in court, but includes it.

18 This is the classical view on the purpose of civil procedure in temporary civil societies, I.N. Tzankova and M.A. Gramatikov, 'A Critical Note on two EU Principles: A Proceduralist View on the Draft CFR', *The Foundations of European Private Law*, eds R. Brownsword et al. (Oxford: Hart Publishing, 2011).

19 See C.G. Veljanovski, 'The Economics of Regulatory Enforcement', *Enforcing Regulation*, eds K. Hawkins and J.M. Thomas (Boston: Kluwer-Nijhoff Publishing, 1984) 171–91, p. 171.

20 See C.E.F. Rickett and T.G.W. Telfer, 'Consumers' Access to Justice: An Introduction', *International Perspectives on Consumers' Access to Justice*, eds C.E.F. Rickett and T.G.W. Telfer (Cambridge: Cambridge University Press, 2003) 1–16, p. 1.

European or even international developments. This interrelationship mainly applies to substantive laws,[21] but cooperation to align procedural laws also is on the rise.

Public Policy Context

At the European Consumer Summit 2013, Tonio Borg, Commissioner for Health and Consumer Policy, stated, 'This year we will focus on stepping up the enforcement of EU consumer legislation, one of the key priorities of the European Consumer Agenda that the Commission adopted in May 2012'.[22] There is current and forthcoming EU legislation concerning enforcement of consumer law. The Regulation on Consumer Protection Cooperation (CPC)[23] established an EU-wide network of national enforcement authorities with similar investigation and enforcement powers for various consumer law areas. Consultations at the EU level are on-going regarding a coherent European approach to collective redress.[24] On 12 March 2013, the European Parliament voted to support new legislation on Alternative Dispute Resolution and Online Dispute Resolution, a vote that confirmed the political agreement reached in December 2012 on the two legislative proposals the European Commission advanced in 2011.[25] The new legislation will now soon be adopted. This legislation and legislative proposals have had and will have a general impact on Member States' consumer law enforcement landscapes. The Regulation on CPC required countries that had relied purely on private law enforcement to establish a public authority, as the European Commission's explicit policy is to strengthen the role of public bodies.[26]

21 See F. Cafaggi and H-W. Micklitz, 'Administrative and Judicial Enforcement in Consumer Protection: The Way Forward', *New Frontiers of Consumer Protection – The Interplay between Private and Public Enforcement*, eds F. Cafaggi and H-W. Micklitz (Antwerp; Oxford; Portland: Intersentia, 2009) 401–45, p. 403.

22 See T. Borg, *Towards a More Efficient Enforcement of EU Consumer Rights*, 2013, http://www.european-consumer-summit.eu/index_en.html, last accessed: 31 March 2013.

23 See Regulation (EC) No 2006/2004 of the European Parliament and of the Council of 27 October 2004 on cooperation between national authorities responsible for the enforcement of consumer protection laws (the Regulation on Consumer Protection Cooperation [CPC]).

24 See European Parliament resolution of 2 February 2012 on 'Towards a Coherent European Approach to Collective Redress' (2011/2089(INI)).

25 See Legislative proposal for a Directive of the European Parliament and of the Council on alternative dispute resolution for consumer disputes and amending Regulation (EC) No 2006/2004 and Directive 2009/22/EC (Directive on Consumer ADR) Brussels, 29.11.2011 COM(2011) 793 final and proposal for a Regulation of the European Parliament and of the Council on online dispute resolution for consumer disputes (Regulation on Consumer ODR) Brussels, 29.11.2011 COM(2011) 794 final 2011/0374 (COD).

26 A change started happening subtly with the process of accession of Central and Eastern European (CEE) countries to the EU, which led to almost all accession

This book deals with the imminent questions on efficient enforcement responses, and evaluates whether economic arguments can support the shift towards more public enforcement. Likewise, insights on the value of collective actions and consumer ADR solutions can be drawn from this book and a comparative analysis reveals what kind of enforcement mechanisms can work specifically in a number of selected Member States.

Market failures have always existed and have caused losses to consumers and social welfare.[27] Over the last decade with the rise of the Internet and increased importance of online trade,[28] the relationship between the buyer and the seller has changed considerably. This change has led to new enforcement challenges, particularly because the Internet can increase one's anonymity. This is, *prima facie*, mainly a problem with traders; Internet trade seems to aggravate the existence of two classes of traders – *bona fide* and *mala fide*.[29] Internet trade seems

candidates establishing a public authority. Except for the Czech and Slovak Republic, public enforcement was recognised as an indispensable element of the overall institutional framework of consumer protection in all CEE countries; see White Paper Preparation of the associated countries of Central and Eastern Europe for integration into the internal market of the Union, COM(1995) 163 final. Then, the shift was most clear with the Regulation on CPC, A. Bakardjieva Engelbrekt, 'Public and Private Enforcement of Consumer Law in Central and Eastern Europe: Institutional Choice in the Shadow of EU Enlargement', *New Frontiers of Consumer Protection – The Interplay between Private and Public Enforcement*, eds F. Cafaggi and H-W. Micklitz (Antwerp; Oxford; Portland: Intersentia, 2009) 91–136, pp. 101, 111, 130.

27 For an elaboration on of the different forms of consumer detriments due to market failure and regulatory failure, see Europe Economics (2007).

28 Between 2004 and 2010, the percentage of individuals who ordered goods or services over the Internet in the EU-25 rose considerably, from 22 per cent to 37 per cent, in particular in the United Kingdom (UK), Luxembourg, Germany, the Netherlands, France and the Nordic countries, where 45 per cent to 65 per cent of Internet users are online buyers; see European Commission, Executive Summary of the impact assessment, accompanying the document proposal for a Directive of the European Parliament and of the Council on alternative dispute resolution for consumer disputes (Directive on Consumer ADR) and proposal for a regulation of the European Parliament and of the Council on online dispute resolution for consumer disputes (Regulation on Consumer ODR) (Commission staff working paper, Brussels, 29.11.2011, SEC(2011) 1409 final), http://ec.europa.eu/consumers/redress_cons/docs/summary_impact_assessment_adr_en.pdf, last accessed: 31 March 2013, p. 6.

29 A UK report from 2006 estimates that UK consumers lose about £3.5 billion to scams each year; see Office of Fair Trading (OFT), Research on Impact of Mass Marketed Scams, A Summary of Research into the Impact of Scams on UK Consumers (December 2006), http://www.oft.gov.uk/shared_oft/reports/consumer_protection/oft883.pdf, last accessed: 31 March 2013, p. 9; see also Expertentagung. 'Wilhelminenberg Gespräche', Sozialministerium Österreich (Austrian Ministry of Social Affairs), Catch Me if You Can/Geschäfte an der Grenze des Erlaubten, as reported in 'Die Presse', Internet-Abzocke: Ruf nach kollektiver Rechtsdurchsetzung (9 October 2011), http://diepresse.com/home/recht/rechtallgemein/699564/InternetAbzocke_Ruf-nach-kollektiver-Rechtsdurchsetzung?_vl_backlink=/home/recht/index.do, last accessed: 31 March 2013,

to facilitate illegal profits. Of course, not every trader pursues this goal – not even the majority – but the (persistent) rogue traders are capable of causing large social harm, detriment to consumers and damage to legitimate traders.[30] This potential applies to rogue traders who hide within and outside of country borders.[31]

Efficient Enforcement Designs

Major efficiency problems of consumer law in Europe lie with its enforcement;[32] in particular when it comes to rogue traders. Although substantive law is rather similar throughout the EU because of many harmonisation efforts, many different enforcement mechanisms can be found because of the important principle of procedural autonomy. The EU's legislative powers traditionally have been much wider in substantive law compared with procedural law. However, the EU is also

---

and personal communications, Gustav Stifter, Österreichisches Bundeskartellamt (Austrian cartel office).

30 See Department of Business, Innovation and Skills (BIS), Empowering and Protecting Consumers, Consultation on Institutional Changes for Provision of Consumer Information, Advice, Education, Advocacy and Enforcement (June 2011), http://www.bis.gov.uk/assets/biscore/consumer-issues/docs/e/11-970-empowering-protecting-consumers-consultation-on-institutional-changes.pdf, last accessed: 31 March 2013, p. 6; a recent National Audit Office (NAO) report has identified the costs to consumers, and hence the economy, of sharp practices as £6.6 billion in the UK; see BIS, A Better Deal for Consumers Delivering Real Help Now and Change for the Future (2009), http://webarchive.nationalarchives.gov.uk/+/http://www.bis.gov.uk/policies/consumer-issues/consumer-white-paper, last accessed: 31 March 2013, p. 54.

31 Health and Consumer Protection Commissioner (at the time) David Byrne said on the occasion of passing the Regulation on CPC, 'Catching rogue traders is hard enough in a single Member State but it becomes almost impossible when they relocate to another country', Press release RAPID, No Hiding Place for Rogue Traders: Commission Proposes EU-wide Network of National Watchdogs (22 July 2003), http://europa.eu/rapid/pressReleasesAction.do?reference=IP/03/1067&format=HTML&aged=0&language=EN&guiLanguage=en, last accessed: 31 March 2013. Cross-border problems are growing as rogue traders adapt to new technologies and opportunities. For example, the European Advertising Standards Alliance (EASA) estimates that around 63 per cent of the cross-border complaints received between 1992 and 2002 concerned rogue or peripheral traders, and this rises to about 86 per cent for direct mail.

32 See W.H. Van Boom and M.B.M. Loos, *Collective Enforcement of Consumer Law – Securing Compliance in Europe through Private Group Action and Public Authority Intervention* (Groningen: Europa Law Publishing, 2007); Howells and Weatherill (2005), pp. 50, 660; A.I. Ogus, 'Enforcing Regulation: Do we Need the Criminal Law?' *New Perspectives on Economic Crime*, eds H. Sjörgen and G. Skogh (Cheltenham: Edward Elgar, 2004) 42–56, p. 43. See speech by Commissioner T. Borg 'Building a strong political case for a consumer friendly internal market', 18 March 2013, at the European Consumer Summit; see Van den Bergh (2007), p. 179; Cafaggi and Micklitz (2009), p. 403.

beginning to have an impact on Member States' enforcement provisions, which traditionally have differed and still do. Very broadly speaking, some countries focus on public law enforcement and others on private. Economic analysis of law enforcement has shown that public and private enforcement schemes clearly each have a number of strengths and weaknesses and scholars have stated that the optimal solution might be to create a mixture of public and private enforcement that draws upon their comparative advantages[33] – the so-called 'optimal mix of public and private enforcement'. The content of such optimal mixes so far has not been defined.[34]

The allocation of enforcement between various mechanisms is only one of four crucial parameters of law enforcement, according to law and economics literature.[35] (Steven Shavell in particular has done considerable research on this topic.[36]) The other three are the optimal sanction (injunction, administrative fine, criminal fine), the optimal timing of the intervention (*ex ante* monitoring and/or *ex post* enforcement) and the optimal governmental level – either centralised or decentralised – to house the enforcement powers. The four parameters are equally important[37] and heavily interlinked. This book focuses on the first parameter; however, the 'optimal sanction' and 'optimal timing of the intervention' are discussed to the extent that they are instrumental.

33 See W.H. Van Boom, *Efficacious Enforcement in Contract and Tort* (Den Haag: Boom Juridische Uitgevers, 2006), p. 47, regarding in-between solutions: Van den Bergh (2007), R.J. Van den Bergh and L.T. Visscher, 'The Preventive Function of Collective Actions for Damages in Consumer Law', *Erasmus Law Review* 1 (2008b): 5–30, F. Cafaggi and H-W Micklitz, *New Frontiers of Consumer Protection – The Interplay between Private and Public Enforcement* (Antwerp; Oxford; Portland: Intersentia, 2009), p. 38; C. Hodges, 'Objectives, Mechanisms and Policy Choices in Collective Enforcement and Redress', *Mass Justice*, eds J. Steele and W.H. Van Boom (Cheltenham: Edward Elgar, 2011) 101–17, pp. 108.

34 See Van Boom (2006), p. 39.

35 See S. Shavell, 'The Optimal Structure of Law Enforcement', *Journal of Law and Economics* 36 (1993): 255–88, p. 257, S. Shavell, 'Liability for Harm versus Regulation of Safety', *Journal of Legal Studies* 13 (1984a): 357–74, p. 357, regarding the first three parameters.

36 See for instance Shavell (1993), S. Shavell, 'Specific versus General Enforcement of Law', *Journal of Political Economy* 99.5 (1991): 1088–108, S. Shavell, 'Criminal Law and the Optimal Use of Nonmonetary Sanctions as a Deterrent', *Columbia Law Review* (1985): 1231–62, Shavell (1984a), S. Shavell, 'The Social versus the Private Incentive to Bring Suit in a Costly Legal System', *Journal of Legal Studies* 11 (1982): 333–9. Unlike Shavell's work, this book examines the European reality rather than the American, and selects the particular case of consumer law enforcement, analysing mechanisms like ADR or self-regulation that Shavell did not examine in detail. This book sets out four particular contingencies of consumer law violations and is based on and profits from Shavell's findings.

37 See Van den Bergh (2007), pp. 182, 202; R.J. Van den Bergh and L.T. Visscher, 'Optimal Enforcement of Safety Law', *Mitigating Risk in the Context of Safety and Security. How Relevant is a Rational Approach?*, ed. R.V. de Mulder (Rotterdam: Erasmus University, 2008) 29–62, p. 33.

The central question is which role shall be given to which enforcement mechanism/player when building optimal enforcement mixes. If the goal of enforcement is optimal deterrence (outlined in the methodology section), what is the optimal mix of public and private enforcement within consumer law?

Methodology

As the title suggests, this book specifically utilises a comparative law and economics analysis.[38] The overall structure of the book establishes a theoretical set of design requirements for efficient enforcement responses – the 'optimal mixes' – in specific case studies that are then used as a benchmark for comparison with various real-life situations in European countries to reach conclusions.

Law and economics as a discipline engages in the economic analysis of the law. Therefore, it is based on economists' views that, different from lawyers', are concerned with efficiency and how to improve and optimise processes according to the overall cost–benefit ratio. Economic instruments that study human behaviour are used to predict individuals' reactions to the law. Mainstream law and economics applied in this book are based on the rational choice model.[39] Consumers have transitive preferences and seek to maximise the utility that they derive from those preferences, subject to various limitations.[40] The rationality assumption can be regarded as feasible in the context of 'white collar crimes' like in the case of breaches of consumer protection regulation.[41] When individual actors and bodies involved in law enforcement decide to pursue enforcement, we can assume they make a cost–benefit analysis (CBA). Furthermore individuals are generally assumed to be risk-averse.[42]

---

38 See G. De Geest and R.J. Van den Bergh, 'Introduction', *Comparative Law and Economics I* eds G. De Geest and R.J. Van den Bergh (Cheltenham: Edward Elgar, 2004), pp. ix–xxi. Regarding the intersection between comparative law and economics see F. Faust, 'Comparative Law and Economic Analysis of Law' *The Oxford Handbook of Comparative Law* eds M. Reimann and R. Zimmermann (Oxford: Oxford University Press, 2006), pp. 837–65.

39 See T.S. Ulen, 'Rational Choice Theory in Law and Economics', *Encyclopedia of Law and Economics*, Volume I. *The History and Methodology of Law and Economics*, eds B. Bouckaert and G. De Geest (Cheltenham: Edward Elgar, 2000) pp. 790–818. As mentioned, behavioural law and economics challenges this notion.

40 Transitive means that if a good A is preferred over a good B, and B is preferred over a good C, then A is preferred over C. Otherwise, the consumer would behave 'irrationally'.

41 See T. Gibbons, 'The Utility of Economic Analysis of Crime', *International Review of Law and Economics* 2.2 (1982): 173–91.

42 See N. Garoupa and F. Gomez-Pomar, 'Punish Once or Punish Twice: A Theory of the Use of Criminal Sanctions in Addition to Regulatory Penalties', *Harvard Law School John M. Olin Center for Law, Economics and Business Discussion Paper Series*. Paper 308 (2000): 1–30, p. 7.

Based upon these assumptions, one can describe the behaviour of players (including of potential wrongdoers) in the law enforcement process. When predicting people's behaviour, law and economics are largely based on theories that explain how people respond to incentives.[43] Therefore, rather than imposing costs and benefits on a player who faces a decision, the player's sensitivity to incentives can be ascertained and the nature of these incentives can be discussed.

There are different views on how to measure welfare: consumer surplus, producer surplus and social welfare. Consumer surplus is the difference between the value of consumption of a good for buyers (so the amount the consumer is ultimately willing to pay) and the amount the buyers must pay to get that good. Producer surplus, on the other hand, is the difference between the revenue sellers receive from the sale of a good and the minimum amount they would accept for producing it. Hence, social welfare is the sum of the consumer and the producer surpluses. Social welfare is the benchmark used in this book; because each consumer is not only a consumer, and each producer not only a producer. Rather, every individual is a combination of different attributes, which is why it would be impedingly difficult to filter out 'a distinctive consumer identity',[44] and the same is true for producers. Furthermore, consumer or producer surplus discriminates between individuals' benefits in different interest groups, whereas social welfare considers society as a whole.[45]

Legislators select the goals of a law and its enforcement, and, indeed, a policymaker can have a variety of normative goals. To start with, there is the category of non-economic considerations like the desire to compensate and distribute compensation equally (corrective justice). Distributional justice – calling for equal access to justice – is another common goal,[46] and a legislator may refer to notions of morality or fairness. These approaches are differentiated in various branches of law; goals are domain specific. For example, in tort law, the goals are compensation and deterrence,[47] and in contract law, compensation and compliance.[48] In administrative law, laws are passed with a view to fairness and compliance, and

43 See R. Cooter and T. Ulen, *Law & Economics*, 5th ed. (Boston: Pearson Addison Wesley, 2008), p. 4.

44 See J.D. Forbes, *The Consumer Interest: Dimensions and Policy Implications* (London: Croom Helm, 1987), p. 22.

45 See R.J. Van den Bergh and P. Camasasca, *European Competition Law and Economics: A Comparative Perspective*, 2nd ed. (London: Sweet & Maxwell, 2006), p. 35.

46 Regarding non-economic goals, see A.I. Ogus, 'Shifts in Governance for Compensation to Damage: A Framwork for Analysis', *Shifts in Compensation between Private and Public Systems*, eds W.H. Van Boom and M.G. Faure (Wien: Springer-Verlag, 2007) 31–42, p. 32.

47 See V. Karapanou and L.T. Visscher, 'The Magnitude of Pain and Suffering Damages from a Law and Economics and Health Economics Point of View', *RILE Working Paper No. 2009/02* (2009), p. 1.

48 See P.H. Lindblom, 'The Growing Role of the Courts and the New Functions of Judicial Process – Facts or Flummery?' *Scandinavian Studies in Law* 51 (2007): 281–310, p. 291: Reparation, that is, redress and conflict resolution as the purpose of civil procedure.

in criminal law, deterrence of crimes is desired. Other goals of criminal law might be incapacitation, punishment, retribution or social condemnation.[49]

In law and economics, deterrence prevails as the general objective of law enforcement, and, therefore, the goal is to create incentives to comply with the law.[50] The strength of this approach lies in the fact that if a wrongdoer is effectively deterred, a violation will not occur and other considerations, such as compensation, are obsolete. The larger the potential harm of violating a law and the more difficult it is to apprehend wrongdoers, the more important prevention becomes.[51]

One might be inclined to argue that the best enforcement system would be one in which all infringers are prosecuted. However, such perfect enforcement does not consider the costs. From an economic perspective, perfect enforcement is inefficient because it imposes too many costs on society and the costs ultimately outweigh the societal benefits. Given positive detection cost, society strives not for perfect, but for optimal deterrence. Consequently, 'optimal enforcement mixes', ensuring an optimal amount of litigation, are developed to deter wrongdoers.[52] From the viewpoint of social welfare, a certain amount of norm-breaking behaviour may be allowed if the costs of preventing such violations are higher than the benefits of additional deterrence.[53] Therefore, optimal enforcement also entails a correct amount of unenforced actions. Legal use of the law may never be discouraged.

Optimality can be measured at various efficiency standards. Pareto efficiency means that it is not possible to make any individual better off without making at least one other individual worse off.[54] A more common measure – and the one this book follows – is the Kaldor Hicks efficiency criterion, which states that a change is welfare improving if, in principle, those who gain from it could fully compensate the losers, with at least one gainer still being better off.[55] Deterrence leads to behavioural

---

49 See Ogus (2004), p. 45; K. Svatikova, *Economic Criteria for Criminalization: Optimizing Enforcement in Case of Environmental Violations* (Antwerp; Oxford; Portland: Intersentia, 2012), p. 23.

50 See Ogus (2004), p. 46.

51 See Shavell (1993), p. 262.

52 See G.S. Becker, 'Crime and Punishment: An Economic Approach', *Journal of Political Economy* 76 (1968): 169–217; Ogus (2004), p. 43. Costs and benefits are weighted to single out an optimal enforcement level. Therefore, unlike other research, the aim of this analysis is not to look for cost-effective solutions if a high degree of enforcement is taken as an aim and limited resources are then allocated in a way to maximise benefits arising from regulatory compliance, see A.I. Ogus, *Costs and Cautionary Tales: Economic Insights for the Law* (Oxford: Hart Publishing, 2006), p. 290.

53 For example, see A. Renda et al., *Making Antitrust Damages Actions More Effective in the EU: Welfare Impact and Potential Scenarios* (Report for the European Commission/Contract DG COMP/2006/A3/012: 2007), p. 59.

54 See V. Pareto, 'The Maximum of Utility Given by Free Competition', *Giornale degli Economisti* 67.3 (2008): 387–403.

55 See J. Hicks, 'The Foundations of Welfare Economics', *Economic Journal* 49, No. 196 (1939): 696–712 and N. Kaldor, 'Welfare Propositions in Economics

changes that promote compliance with the law.[56] Therefore, in line with the Kaldor Hicks criterion, enforcement efforts should be increased up to the point where they cease to have an additional impact on deterrence (economic benefit) that is higher than the additional enforcement costs (economic cost); in other words, the point where marginal costs equal marginal benefits must be found.[57] When determining optimal enforcement, it is crucial that neither over- nor under-enforcement occurs.[58]

According to the deterrence framework, expected liability matters to the wrongdoer *ex ante*, that is, before a wrong is committed.[59] The most important writers on deterrence theory – originally in criminal law – are Charles Montesquieu, Cesare Beccaria, Jeremy Bentham and Gary Becker.[60] The underlying assumption of their models is that (potential) wrongdoers are rational, and, therefore, weigh possible benefits against costs of their behaviour because they want to maximise their individual benefits. Wrongdoers regard crime the way that they would business. According to the deterrence hypothesis the supply of crime is elastic with respect to punishment.[61] Becker's model, which is referred to in all later writings on deterrence theory, clarifies more specifically that the offender's expected costs must outweigh the potential benefits to induce compliance with the law. The offender's expected costs consist of the probability of detection and of conviction (with the latter a dependent variable of the former) multiplied by the imposed sanction. Let the gain to the offender be labelled as 'G', the probability of detection 'Pd', the probability of conviction 'Pc' and the sanction 'S'. The probability of detection multiplied by the probability of conviction and by the

---

and Interpersonal Comparisons of Utility', *Economics Journal* 49, No. 195 (1939): 549–52.

56 For environmental law, see N. Gunningham and P. Grabowsky, *Smart Regulation: Designing Environmental Policy* (Oxford: Clarendon Press, 1998), p. 26; by guaranteeing enforcement, costs of noncompliance for (potential) wrongdoers are increased. Given the costs of law enforcement, the goal is not to induce perfect compliance, but only optimal compliance; see G.J. Stigler, 'The Optimum Enforcement of Laws', *Journal of Political Economy* 78.3 (1970): 526–36, pp. 526.

57 See A.I. Ogus, *Regulation: Legal Form and Economic Theory* (Oxford: Clarendon Press, 1994), p. 91 referring to R.A. Posner, 'The Behavior of Administrative Agencies', *Journal of Legal Studies* (1972): 305–48, pp. 305, 314.

58 See Stigler (1970), p. 528.

59 See S. Shavell, *Foundations of Economic Analysis of Law* (Cambridge, Massachusetts: The Belknap Press of Harvard University Press, 2004), p. 515. This reflects the concept of general as opposed to individual deterrence, which means that an individual wrongdoer who has already committed a wrong is deterred in the future.

60 See A.M. Polinsky and S. Shavell, 'The Theory of Public Enforcement of Law', *NBER Working Paper 11780* (2005), p. 3; in the following, it will be mainly referred to Becker's model, which is the most often cited; see Becker (1968) and previously C. Beccaria, *On Crimes and Punishments, and Other Writings*, ed. R. Bellamy (New York: Cambridge University Press, 1995), J. Bentham, 'An Introduction to the Principles of Morals and Legislation', *The Utilitarians*, ed. Garden City (New York: Anchor Books, 1789 [1973]).

61 See Cooter and Ulen (2008), p. 525.

sanction gives the expected liability of the offender (costs) that must at least equal the gain obtained from an infringement.

The very basic equation looks like this:

$$G \leq Pd \times Pc \times S$$

Variables depend on the players' actions: probability of detection varies with the effort of enforcement agencies or the reporting behaviour of individuals.[62] The expected liability for the wrongdoer depends on different remedies, resources and powers at the disposal of the various enforcement bodies. Probability of conviction may depend on procedural requirements (such as rules for burden of proof and disclosure of evidence). Therefore, in cases of low detection/conviction rates, higher sanctions must be imposed to outweigh the loss of a deterrent effect and vice versa.

Although originally developed within criminal law, deterrence theory can serve as a comprehensive framework for law enforcement in general.[63] This theory can be used to show how enforcement systems should be structured for optimal deterrence of legal breaches. Deterrence aspects can be used to deduct which institution is the optimal enforcer or which legal branches to include in the optimal enforcement mix. Factors in these choices include the investigative powers agencies may have or the sanctions that are available. For example, costs of sanctions vary between private and public law. Criminal law sanctions, because of their punishing nature, can be far more costly than private law sanctions, such as monetary compensation,[64] and these differences influence the sanctions (S) variable in the formula. Sanctions also may have various characteristics, such as fines, revocation of licenses, injunctions or damage payments. Therefore, compensation can be a means in deterrence theory. From a deterrence perspective, primarily the amount of compensation matters, not to whom or to what it is paid or how the damage amount is determined.[65]

Deterrence theory has not been accepted without criticism and it is underpinned with a number of empirical studies. In various studies, a considerable deterrent

62 See M.G. Faure, A.I. Ogus and N.J. Philipsen, 'Curbing Consumer Financial Losses: The Economics of Regulatory Enforcement', *Law & Policy* 31.2 (2009): 161–91, p. 166.

63 This is also confirmed by Calabresi for civil law, see G. Calabresi and K.S. Schartz, 'The Costs of Class Actions: Allocation and Collective Redress in the US Experience', *European Journal of Law and Economics* 32 (2011): 169–83, p. 180; H-B. Schäfer, 'The Bundling of Similar Interests in Litigation. The Incentives for Class Action and Legal Actions taken by Associations', *European Journal of Law and Economics* 9.3 (2000): 183–213, p. 184 for a rational tortfeasor.

64 For a detailed analysis of the strengths and weaknesses of various enforcement systems, see Chapter 4.

65 See A.J. Duggan, 'Consumer Access to Justice in Common Law Countries: A Survey of the Issues from a Law and Economics Perspective', *International Perspectives on Consumers' Access to Justice*, eds C.E.F. Rickett and T.G.W. Telfer (Cambridge: Cambridge University Press, 2003) 46–67, p. 56.

effect could be corroborated, and although the evidence might not always be straightforward, there is more to confirm this effect than the contrary.[66]

This book applies deterrence theory to assess the strengths and weaknesses of different enforcement mechanisms – standardised definitions – in a model world based on assumptions stemming from the common denominator of European procedural law (for example, the existence of the 'loser-pays' rule). Enforcement mechanisms are assessed against a number of established economic criteria. For two specific case studies, this analysis leads to design suggestions for 'optimal mixes', and, thus, closes the first gap in the literature.[67]

Currently, an evaluation of real-life enforcement schemes in consumer law that show different mixes of private and public enforcement is furthermore not possible, but this book makes a comparative law and economics analysis. Various selected legal systems' enforcement responses to the case studies are illustrated in detail. These illustrations are enhanced with data collected by means of semi-structured interviews with staff from various enforcement institutions. Particular attention is paid to the interrelationship between various enforcement mechanisms in the countries. In the ambit of the country studies, real-life solutions are compared with the design requirements and tentative conclusions are drawn for making welfare-enhancing changes in a country. This comparison allows for a critical perspective on legal systems. Areas are identified that may lack an optimal balance from the deterrence perspective. Although conclusions primarily concern how to improve an existing system in a particular Member State, general lessons can be learned as well for EU policymaking. Countries' structures are compared, but the efficiency of various systems cannot be directly contrasted.

Selection of the Case Studies

The strengths of the arguments in favour of public, private or mixed enforcement vary across different fields of consumer law, particularly when it comes to the amount of harm involved for the individual.[68] The content of such optimal mixes so far has not been defined.[69] This book fills this gap and illustrates the characteristics of these mixes for two case scenarios in two sectors of consumer law.

66 For various other studies, see examples mentioned in Cooter and Ulen (2008), p. 526. See also European studies, E. Eide, 'Economics of Criminal Behavior', *Encyclopedia of Law and Economics, Volume I. The History and Methodology of Law and Economics*, eds B. Bouckaert and G. De Geest (Cheltenham: Edward Elgar, 2000) 345–89, p. 355.

67 See Van Boom (2006), p. 39.

68 Van den Bergh (2007), p. 194 refers to the inherent differences in the consumers' motivation between package travel or consumer credit cases as opposed to scenarios where only very small damage is inflicted.

69 See Van Boom (2006), p. 39.

The selected case studies from two typical consumer law cases involve package travel and misleading advertising, one leading to considerable damage to one consumer and the other leading to trifling, but widespread damage. The harm for society is substantial in both cases, and, therefore, law enforcement is desirable from a social welfare point of view.[70] Because of the two types of traders' expressed considerations, the two case scenarios are split into two analyses – a *bona fide* and a *mala fide* trader – resulting in four different scenarios. The substantive law provisions of the two legal areas in the selected case studies are stipulated in two EU directives that, while harmonising the substantive law provisions, leave the Member State with the choice of enforcement bodies, a decision with which this book can assist.[71]

For all cases, a system is designed to enforce the optimal number of cases and allow for efficient breaches. Thus, society's scarce resources are allocated efficiently. The setting is outlined more specifically with some key assumptions at the beginning of each case study.

A motivation for selecting these case studies was the fact that the selected scenarios can lead to different amounts of damage to consumers, which, in turn, have different effects on people's behaviour (victims, lawyers, wrongdoers and so forth). From Cases one and two (package travel) to three and four (misleading advertising), the individual harm to the consumer becomes smaller. In the package travel scenarios, individual damage is assumed to be substantial enough to induce an individual to litigate. Regarding consumer incentives, the possibility of obtaining compensation is crucial.[72] At the other extreme, scenarios of both trifling and widespread harm are selected from misleading advertising. Whereas the damage is smaller in the misleading advertising scenarios compared with the package travel, the number of victims is greater. Likewise, the harm to competitors increases substantially, and they are more likely to take action regarding violations from misleading advertising than from violations of travel law.[73] For Cases one and two, a pure action for damages scenario is analysed. In Cases three and four, other remedies on top of compensation are considered. Furthermore, group litigation as a procedural tool is analysed and the role of 'self-regulation in the narrow sense'[74] is described with reference to misleading advertising. Intermediate solutions,

---

70 Paying for a holiday that does not fulfil the 'contracted' expectations can be regarded as a waste of resources. If consumers choose a product based on false messages in misleading advertising, their interests are hurt and resources have been misallocated, see E.R. Jordan and P.H. Rubin, 'An Economic Analysis of the Law of False Advertising', *The Journal of Legal Studies* 8.3 (1979): 527–53, p. 532.

71 See Package Travel Directive and Unfair Commercial Practices Directive.

72 See F. Weber, 'Assessing Existing Enforcement Mechanisms in Consumer Law – The Unavailability of an Allrounder', *Swedish Journal of European Law* (Europarättslig Tidskrift) 3 (2011): 536–54, which illustrates the considerations for a high-damage case in general.

73 See Jordan and Rubin (1979), p. 2: a competitor might have substantial harm from misleading advertising.

74 To be defined in Chapter 2, along with the other enforcement mechanisms.

borderlines and thresholds also are discussed implicitly throughout the analysis. A precise description of the cases is included in Chapter 5.

Selection of the Countries

Traditionally, some countries rely mainly on public law enforcement and others on private,[75] for manifold reasons.[76] Putting it very broadly, public law relates to the activities of public bodies, and private law concerns relationships among private individuals that 'vindicate' their rights under private law.[77] Public enforcement can be divided into administrative and criminal law enforcement. Various enforcement mechanisms often operate in countries' enforcement landscapes. The enforcement landscapes in the EU have partly been aligned based on European legislation,[78] still some elements are more pronounced than others in different countries.

For this book, the Netherlands, Sweden and England[79] were selected for country studies. Although the Netherlands has historically strongly relied on private enforcement, it underwent a change with the enactment of the Regulation on CPC. Consequently, at the beginning of 2007, the *Consumentenautoriteit* (Netherlands Consumer Authority, CA) was established, whose competences go further than envisaged in the regulation, namely to also cover purely national scenarios.[80] The approach of the authority is two-sided: it has its own sanctioning powers for some cases and must use the civil courts for others. The CA will become part of the newly established the *Autoriteit Consument en Markt* (Consumer and Market Authority, ACM) in April 2013.[81] In various sectors, self-regulation and

75 See Van den Bergh (2007), pp. 180, 201.

76 For more elaboration of this, see several of the contributions in Cafaggi and Micklitz (2009).

77 See C. Hodges, 'Public and Private Enforcement: The Practical Implications for Policy Architecture', *The Foundations of European Private Law*, eds R. Brownsword et al. (Oxford: Hart Publishing, 2011) 437–52, p. 1.

78 To a certain extent the EU, for instance, favoured and imposed public enforcement in consumer law with the enactment of the Regulation on CPC.

79 While the wide majority of what will be said applies to England and Wales as their legal systems are widely aligned, in the following it refers to England and the institutions that characterise its consumer law enforcement landscape.

80 See M.G. Faure, A.I. Ogus and N.J. Philipsen, 'Enforcement Practices for Breaches of Consumer Protection Legislation', *Loyola Consumer Law Review* 20.4 (2008): 361–401, p. 378.

81 The new authority will be established on 1 April 2013, according to Law establishing the ACM of 28 February 2013 (Instellingswet Autoriteit Consument en Markt) and consist of the former CA, the Nederlandse Mededingingsautoriteit (Dutch Competition Authority, NMa) and the Onafhankelijke Post en Telecommunicatie Autoriteit (Independent Post and Telecommunications Authority, OPTA). In the first phase the powers of the three authorities will, in principle, be preserved in their current form.

ADR solutions play an important role that leads to a lot of dispute resolution outside the court system.[82] This system is dependent on a very active consumer complaint structure.[83] Consumer associations, particularly the main association *Consumentenbond*, continue to play a significant role.

In Sweden, enforcement by public law institutions historically has been prevalent.[84] The country has both an ombudsman's office, which represents consumers in disputes, and a related consumer agency, which oversees consumer protection legislation.[85] In certain cases, the *Konsumentombudsmannen* (Consumer Ombudsman, KO) may take action and impose fines without involving a law court.[86] In other cases, the KO seeks actions at court or before the Swedish ADR body. Private individuals 'complement the regulatory enforcement process'.[87] The Swedish ADR body is an overarching system. There is a role for self-regulation, too, in some sectors. Consumer associations have historically been weak.

England is another country that strongly relies on public law enforcement. To a large extent, regulatory agencies handle the enforcement. The focus of the current consumer policy is described as 'consistent and expert oversight by public authorities' more than a high amount of private litigation.[88] It is special that they also rely to some extent on the criminal justice system.[89] In England, there has always been a strong liaison between regulation and self-regulation. The Office of Fair Trading (OFT) is the responsible government supervisory body and decentralised public supervisory bodies, the Trading Standards Services (TSS), play a role on the local level. Again, consumer associations have a limited role. The role of decentralised ADR bodies is increasing, although they are still not well known to consumers in some areas; litigation in the courts is considered costly.[90] In selected consumer conflicts, private solutions might prevail. Also in the UK, changes to the consumer law enforcement landscape are imminent and are referred to throughout the study.

---

82 See Faure, Ogus and Philipsen (2008), p. 382.

83 See Faure, Ogus and Philipsen (2008), p. 381.

84 See Faure, Ogus and Philipsen (2008), p. 374.

85 See interview with Gunnar Larsson, Swedish Consumer Ombudsman and Head of Consumer Authority (Stockholm, 25 August 2009).

86 See Table 3: Faure, Ogus and Philipsen (2008), p. 368 and interview with Market Court (Stockholm, 24 August 2009).

87 See Faure, Ogus and Philipsen (2008), p. 373.

88 See C. Hodges, *Global Class Actions Project, Country Report: England and Wales* (2008), p. 20.

89 See Faure, Ogus and Philipsen (2008), p. 376. Faure, Ogus and Philipsen (2009), p. 164.

90 See N. Creutzfeldt-Banda, C. Hodges and I. Benöhr, 'United Kingdom.' *Consumer ADR in Europe*, eds C. Hodges, I. Benöhr and N. Creutzfeldt-Banda (Oxford and Portland, Oregon: Hart Publishing, 2012), pp. 254, 338.

Limitations

Policymakers can have different views on the goals of consumer law enforcement, and their reasoning may differ according to the legal branch, such as criminal vs private law. The political process potentially may complicate views further. In law and economics literature, the normative goal of enforcement issues traditionally is optimal deterrence, which omits some other perspectives.

The foregoing leads to another apparent limitation. Although theory takes the deterrence perspective, in the real world this is not or not the only goal that legislators may seek from enforcement. This book takes a deterrence perspective when comparing the countries to the optimal mixes, while giving reform suggestions from an efficiency point of view. Some deviations in the countries from the suggested design can simply be explained by the fact that the policymaker had a different goal than deterrence in mind.

Legal reforms in countries are conditioned by countries' path dependencies.[91] Therefore, a set of design suggestions for creating optimal enforcement responses is presented rather than one optimal model.

The case scenarios are structured to illustrate certain features, and, in reality, they do not occur only in this clear-cut way, but also in more mixed forms. Furthermore an enforcement system must be able to deal with all types of scenarios at the same time. The case studies were chosen to exemplify certain characteristics of two typical sets of consumer law cases. But in reality, they may be interrelated, and the more they show similar features, the more enforcement responses must be aligned. Other consumer problems can occur. For instance, an angle that is left aside is substantial widespread harm.

Even if a cost–benefit analysis is intuitively very appealing, there may be serious difficulties when a value has to be attached to certain costs or benefits, especially if an optimal level is to be found that equates marginal costs and marginal benefits because the values have to be precise.[92] Here, cost–benefit goes beyond balancing effects 'by attempting to quantify all aspects of a problem and subsequently translating it into dollars'.[93] Predicting all the effects (such as social harm)[94] or giving monetary value to all effects is not always possible, and, therefore, the optimal point may be only an approximation – following the law and economics tradition of arguing

91 See P. Legrand, 'European Legal Systems are not Converging', *International and Comparative Law Quarterly* 45 (1996): 52–81; K. Heine and W. Kerber, 'European Corporate Laws, Regulatory Competition and Path Dependence', *European Journal of Law and Economics* 13 (2002): 47–71; A.I. Ogus, 'The Economic Basis of Legal Culture: Networks and Monopolization', *Oxford Journal of Legal Studies* 22.3 (2002): 419–34.

92 See A.I. Ogus, *Regulation: Legal Form and Economic Theory* (Oxford: Clarendon Press, 1994), p. 160; L.B. Lave, *The Strategy of Social Regulation: Decision Frameworks for Policy* (Washington, DC: The Brookings Institution, 1981), p. 19.

93 See Lave (1981), p. 80.

94 See Ogus (1994), p. 92.

with a rule of thumb, largely based on logic or intuition.[95] Rather than a precise arithmetical comparison of the costs and benefits of an enforcement system, 'second-best approaches' using estimation systems are employed.[96] People's responses to incentives are crucial to this analysis. As a matter of fact, comparative empirical studies in consumer protection and mechanisms to handle claims are rather limited.[97] Nevertheless, exploiting alternative methods – second-best approaches – is desirable because of the importance of approaching the topic from a broad angle.

To reach conclusions on the enforcement side of the law, the efficiency of substantive consumer law was not evaluated. The analysis relies on the assumption of rationality and insights from behavioural economics were not considered.

This book does not comment on litigation in which the consumer is the defendant.

And lastly, the *mala fide* trader's attempts to hide are discussed in a national scenario, and only a few indications are given concerning the cross-border situation.

95 See for instance: Faure, Ogus and Philipsen (2009), p. 168. This approach is used where reliable data is not available and has found broad application and acceptance in science.

96 Ogus (1994), p. 161 lists various other options of how policymakers can make approximate decisions (an impressionistic balancing of the information on impact, both quantified and unquantified; to use the data that one is able to obtain (at reasonable cost) and make reasonable guesses for what remains unknown or cost effectiveness).

97 Overall only two topics – regulatory agencies and ADR in the broad sense – are mentioned in relation to consumer enforcement in the 2010 *Oxford Handbook on Empirical Legal Research*. The author qualifies the usefulness of both types of research. Comparative empirical studies in regulatory agencies are difficult in particular because of the different structures that public agencies have and the different ways of record-keeping; see S. Meili, 'Consumer Protection', *The Oxford Handbook of Empirical Legal Research*, eds P. Cane and H.M. Kritzer (Oxford: Oxford University Press, 2010) 176–97, p. 182. Meili referred to some studies that attempt comparisons despite these limitations; K. Viitanen, 'The Baltic Model for the Settlement of Individual Consumer Disputes', *Journal of Consumer Policy* 23 (2000): 315–39 (for the Baltic States). The number of studies is overall rather limited; see Meili (2010), p. 185. ADR received the most attention in recent years (p. 184). However, the reliability of those studies is often compromised by the political and ideological agendas of their authors and/or financial underwriters (190). Furthermore it remains an 'open and contested question whether rigorous empirical studies of comparative civil (and criminal) processes are possible in widely varying local, national and legal cultures'; see C.J. Menkel-Meadow and B.G. Garth, 'Civil Procedure and Courts', *The Oxford Handbook of Empirical Legal Research*, eds P. Cane and H.M. Kritzer (Oxford: Oxford University Press, 2010) 679–704, p. 695. The weakness is repeated that studies reflect the desired results of who is paying. Likewise, regarding ADR in particular in comparative analyses, there is skepticism if statements on 'better' or 'worse' can be made at all, see C.J. Menkel-Meadow, 'Dispute Resolution', *The Oxford Handbook of Empirical Legal Research*, eds P. Cane and H.M. Kritzer (Oxford: Oxford University Press, 2010) 586–624, p. 599. There is indeed data on whether and why consumers complain about products and services they purchase or use.

The Structure of the Book

This book consists of an introduction, followed by three parts.

Introduction

In this introduction (Chapter 1), the context, relevance, methodology and limitations are established. The selection of countries and case studies is justified. It concludes with a description of the structure of the book.

I. Optimal Enforcement Mixes (Analysis)

This part includes four chapters (2–5). Chapter 2 provides a short overview of various enforcement mechanisms in consumer protection laws: private enforcement before a civil court and consumer ADR, public enforcement (administrative and criminal law), group litigation and self-regulatory bodies. A reasoned suggestion for standardising definitions of these mechanisms is made, describing the typical remedies/sanctions available.

Chapter 3 introduces the tools for the development of optimal mixes and establishes a framework for a three-stage efficiency analysis. The efficiency of an enforcement mechanism or mixes is assessed by focusing on the optimisation of risk allocation, people's incentives and administrative costs when it comes to determining the desired level of deterrence. These three stages and their various subcategories capture the notion of efficiency and facilitate subsequent analysis.

In Chapter 4, the state of the art of the economic analysis of different aspects of enforcement of consumer laws is summarised using the framework developed in Chapter 3. This chapter is by no means a pure summary. For some mechanisms – in particular, ADR, self-regulation and criminal law – the application to some of the criteria is innovative. As a result of the analyses, the efficiency, general strengths and weaknesses of various enforcement mechanisms are identified. Indeed, every enforcement system has some strengths and some weaknesses and may be inefficient in different situations, which paves the way for the discussion of 'optimal mixes' in Chapter 5. Economic efficiency considerations meet the legal boarders of different legal enforcement branches.

Finally, Chapter 5 suggests optimal mixes of public and private enforcement and hybrid solutions that would achieve efficient enforcement in the two selected cases. The refined economic insights offered in Chapter 4 regarding the strengths and weaknesses of various enforcement mechanisms are explicitly adapted to the case studies – package travel and misleading advertising/*bona fide* and *mala fide* trader – which primarily differ in the amount of harm individual consumers suffer, the number of consumers affected and the role played by competitors. Relative strengths and weaknesses of various enforcement systems for these case studies are illustrated, and suggestions are made for mixing the tools to achieve better results. The standardised definitions of the enforcement mechanisms (introduced in Chapter 2) are the starting point, but a restructure of these bodies and hybrid solutions are also discussed (for example, could the body grant a remedy that it is currently not empowered to grant?). Part I ends with suggestions for the design and characteristics of optimal enforcement mixes for the two case studies and the *bona fide* and *mala fide* trader case scenario of each. These suggestions serve as a benchmark for the country studies in Part II. Part I ends with some charts that summarise the findings on the optimal mixes.

II. Country Studies (Comparison)

The findings from the 'Europeanised' world model serve as a benchmark to assess real-life situations in three European countries: the Netherlands (Chapter 6), Sweden (Chapter 7), England (Chapter 8). These countries were selected because of the striking differences in their enforcement cultures and traditions. For each case, the current legal solutions to the consumer problem are outlined (description) and an illustration on how the real-life solutions compare to the theoretical findings is given (assessment). The goal of the book is not to find a one-size-fits-all solution. Indeed, it is the purpose of the comparative law and economics part to make clear why this cannot be expected. Tentative suggestions for welfare-enhancing changes or developments within the various legal systems are made for each country.

III. Conclusions

This book concludes with a summary of the findings and general conclusions of the study. Path dependency positively explains why enforcement landscapes in countries have developed in a particular fashion. The summary of results suggests broader conclusions for countries with similar traditions as the three investigated. Likewise, this concluding chapter allows for a direct confrontation of the solutions in the three countries for singling out some best practices for an enforcement response to consumer law in Europe. This enforcement approach is differentiated according to different case studies and different legal traditions. Findings are based on evidence provided throughout the analysis. The book concludes with lessons learned regarding EU policy advice.

Developments in legislation and publications after 31 March 2013 were not considered.

PART I
Optimal Enforcement Mixes (Analysis)

Enforcement mechanisms comprise a huge variety of forms and contingencies. The number of players involved is large and their incentives and trade-offs wide. As a result, tackling enforcement questions, particularly when they involve various branches of law, is a complex exercise. Nevertheless the importance of the topic and the need to address deficiencies demand that this challenge is met.

In this part, the most relevant enforcement mechanisms for consumer law are described, and the six most striking enforcement mechanisms, which will be analysed and used throughout this book, are classified (Chapter 2). These six mechanisms are the civil court, consumer ADR, administrative law enforcement by public agencies, criminal law enforcement, group litigation as an enforcement tool (as opposed to individual litigation) and self-regulation. Typical remedies/ sanctions also are mentioned.

The development of efficient enforcement designs is discussed in three steps. Chapter 3 establishes a framework that captures the notion of efficiency and allows discussion of the strengths and weaknesses of various enforcement systems; next (Chapter 4), the different existing enforcement mechanisms defined in Chapter 2 are tested using the established framework, and this analysis identifies their strengths and weaknesses from an economics point of view; finally, these results lead to identifying characteristics of optimal enforcement systems or mixes for efficient deterrence of (potential) wrongdoers in the specific case studies in Chapter 5.

Chapter 2
Existing Enforcement Mechanisms

In consumer law enforcement, a number of key enforcement mechanisms exist, which can be divided into private and public law enforcement. Within private law enforcement, consumer ADR solutions have become an important alternative to judicial enforcement. Public law enforcement includes administrative and criminal law enforcement. Various forms of group litigation as a procedural tool and self-regulation are other mechanisms. These mechanisms are described below and standardised definitions provided that are appropriate in the European context. These will be used throughout the book. Although the players rather than the sanctions are the core of this book, typical remedies/sanctions are linked to enforcement mechanisms.

Private Law Enforcement

Within private consumer law enforcement civil courts and consumer ADR bodies are the primary mechanisms.

Civil Procedure

For most consumer law cases, the ordinary individual procedure before the civil law courts is available, whereby impartial judges ensure the law is applied in disputes between parties and an appeal system is in place. Many countries offer special procedural rules for cases of low claim values. Since the enactment of the European Small Claim Regulation[1] that sets out the procedural rules for low-value cases involving a cross-border element, small claim courts are a widespread phenomenon in Europe; this is also true for national cases. A general characteristic of these procedures is that legal representation is not required, procedural safeguards are relaxed and litigation costs and the duration of the procedures are reduced.

A core principle in civil law is the prevalence of the principle of party presentation. Parties must bring evidence to the judge and cannot rely on judicial investigations.[2] Standing can be granted to individuals (in courts of low instances

1 See Regulation (EC) No 861/2007 of the European Parliament and of the Council of 11 July 2007 establishing a European small claims procedure.

2 See Principle 10 Party Initiative and Scope of the Proceeding, ALI/UNIDROIT Principles of Transnational Civil Procedure (Cambridge: Cambridge University

or in small claims procedures), to lawyers and to other representatives. In general, court fees do not cover the entire administrative cost, and, therefore, the state subsidises the procedures.[3]

The most common remedy granted in civil procedures is compensation,[4] for instance according to the Annex of the Draft Common Frame of Reference (DCFR) defined as 'reparation in money'. Judges may grant an 'injunction' which is an order granted by a court whereby someone is required to do or to refrain from doing a specified act. In Article 2(a) of the Injunctions Directive[5] an injunction is defined as 'an order with all due expediency, where appropriate by way of summary procedure, requiring the cessation or prohibition of any infringement'. Furthermore, various interim measures are available to the judge (such as prohibitory injunctions, interim payment orders and other mandatory injunctions).[6]

Consumer ADR

Although mediation or arbitration is common within a court procedure, ADR refers to any out-of-court mechanism for resolving disputes (arbitration, conciliation, mediation and ombudsman schemes), generally regarded as a way to avoid costly individual litigation.[7] For the purpose of consumer law enforcement, countries offer a wide variety of these possibilities that may sometimes be well structured and available as a kind of one-stop-shop for the consumer, and sometimes are dispersed throughout the country.[8] According to the explanatory memorandum of the legislative proposal for a Directive on Consumer ADR, 'these entities aim at resolving, out-of-court, disputes arising between parties, through the intervention of an entity (e.g. arbitrator, conciliator, mediator, ombudsman, complaints board)'. Consumers may complain about traders and vice versa. Compared with court procedures, ADR procedures commonly are simplified, low cost and rarely require the presence

---

Press, 2006), adopted in 2004 by the American Law Institute (ALI) and Institut International Pour L'Unification du Droit Prive (UNIDROIT).

3 See W.M. Landes and R.A. Posner, 'The Private Enforcement of Law', *Journal of Legal Studies* 4.1 (1975): 1–46, p. 31.

4 This is a non-exhaustive overview, and existing remedies will be discussed more concretely in the country studies.

5 See Directive 98/27/EC of the European Parliament and of the Council of 19 May 1998 on injunctions for the protection of consumers' interests.

6 See A. Bruns, 'Provisional Measures in European Civil Procedural Laws – Preservation of Variety or Need for Harmonisation', *Comparative Studies on Enforcement and Provisional Measures*, eds R. Stürner and M. Kawano (Tübingen: Mohr Siebeck, 2011) pp. 183–91.

7 See H-W. Micklitz, N. Reich and P. Rott, eds, *Understanding EU Consumer Law* (Antwerp: Intersentia, 2009), p. 342. Notably while the A in ADR originally stood for 'alternative', more recently it is also equated with 'appropriate', see Menkel-Meadow (2010), p. 597.

8 See C. Hodges, I. Benöhr and N. Creutzfeldt-Banda, eds, *Consumer ADR in Europe* (Oxford and Portland, Oregon: Hart Publishing, 2012).

of lawyers.[9] The vast majority of European consumer ADR schemes are free to consumers;[10] however, the legal value of the awards granted is generally viewed as weaker than a court judgment.[11] Typically, industry and the state are responsible for financing ADR mechanisms.[12] When making decisions, the ADR body is composed of the consumer and the business interest. Some bodies are capable of dealing with several individual cases about a particular issue,[13] and may be empowered to grant a number of civil law remedies. The most typical remedy is compensation.[14]

Public Law Enforcement

Public enforcement can take two forms: administrative or criminal law enforcement.

Administrative Law Enforcement

Administrative law enforcement when used in consumer law is primarily handled by governmental agents and agencies with investigative powers.[15] Actions may be initiated by private individuals, but do not necessarily have to be. Other players might be able to report or entities can work on their own motions. Public bodies can engage in monitoring.[16] The most common sanction is an administrative fine or penalty,[17] although administrative agencies also can impose injunctions. Before imposing a sanction, public agencies generally have some intermediary steps at their disposal, such as informal or formal warnings and negotiated informal agreements

---

9 See recitals 3, 19, 20 of the proposed Directive on Consumer ADR.

10 See N. Creutzfeldt-Banda, 'Empirical findings', *Consumer ADR in Europe – Civil Justice Systems*, eds C. Hodges, I. Benöhr and N. Creutzfeldt-Banda (Oxford and Portland, Oregon: Hart Publishing, 2012) 367–88, p. 380.

11 See C. Hodges, I. Benöhr and N. Creutzfeldt-Banda, 'Findings and Conclusions', *Consumer ADR in Europe – Civil Justice Systems*, eds C. Hodges, I. Benöhr and N. Creutzfeldt-Banda (Oxford and Portland, Oregon: Hart Publishing, 2012) 389–435, pp. 390, 420.

12 See Creutzfeldt-Banda (2012), p. 382.

13 According to recital 15 Directive on Consumer ADR, 'this Directive should be without prejudice to Member States maintaining or introducing ADR procedures dealing jointly with identical or similar disputes between a trader and several consumers'. Such procedures can be seen as a preliminary step to further developing collective ADR procedures within the Union.

14 See by way of example, Annual Report Geschillencommissie, 2012.

15 See A.M. Polinsky and S. Shavell, 'Economic Analysis of Law', *Discussion Papers 05-005, Stanford Institute for Economic Policy Research.* (2005) pp. 26; Polinsky and Shavell (2005a).

16 See Faure, Ogus and Philipsen (2008), p. 365. This can be proactive or reactive.

17 See European Commission, The System of Administrative and Penal Sanctions in the Member States of the European Communities (Office for Official Publications of the European Communities, Brussels, Vol. 1 and 2, 1994).

with traders.[18] An appeal, including judicial appeal in the administrative courts, to challenge a public official's decision is generally allowed, although, typically, internal appeals with the public agency must be exhausted before seeking appeal in an administrative court.[19]

A distinction should be made between bodies that can impose sanctions and those that have the power only to initiate legal proceedings or, even less, only to refer the matter to another competent institution. Often the approach is mixed.

Criminal Law Enforcement

Classical criminal law is administered by criminal courts,[20] and a central role is generally given to the public prosecution office for investigation and prosecution. The public prosecutor may involve the police force. As with the previous mechanisms, the exact structure of the procedures depends on the individual country. In criminal law proceedings, members of the court are required to act with strict impartiality.[21] The prosecutor also must consider circumstances that are beneficial to the accused and has the burden of proof. Typical sanctions may include a criminal fine or imprisonment.[22] In some jurisdictions, civil compensation claims may be enforced in criminal procedures.[23]

Standing for Group Representatives

Standing in litigation can be granted to the consumer or a lawyer, and some form of association (public or private)[24] or agency may provide representation. (Actions by

18 See Ogus, Faure and Philipsen (2006), p. 16.

19 See J. Schwarze, ed., *European Administrative Law* (London: Sweet & Maxwell, 1992), p. 97.

20 See C. Van den Wyngaert, ed. (co-editors: C. Gane, H.H. Kühne and F. Mcauley), *Criminal Procedure Systems in the European Community* (London, Brussels, Dublin, Edinburgh: Butterworths, 1993).

21 See R. Bowles, M.G. Faure and N. Garoupa, 'The Scope of Criminal Law and Criminal Sanctions: An Economic View and Policy Implications', *Journal of Law and Society* 35.3 (2008): 389–416, p. 392, regarding criminal sanctions.

22 See Faure, Ogus and Philipsen (2009), p. 180. See A. Klip, *European Criminal Law. An Integrative Approach*, 2nd ed. (Cambridge – Antwerp – Portland: Intersentia, 2012), p. 315.

23 The European country in which this is most developed seems to be Norway: J.T. Johnsen, 'Enforcement of Civil Claims in Criminal Litigation: The Norwegian Examle', *Enforcement and Enforceability – Tradition and Reform*, eds C.H. Van Rhee and A. Uzelac (Antwerp; Oxford; Portland: Intersentia, 2010), pp. 313–26; for Germany see §§ 403 – 406d Strafprozessordnung (Act on Criminal Procedure, StPO). Similar provisions exist also in Belgium, France and the Netherlands, see Ogus, Faure and Philipsen (2006), p. 37.

24 In a way publicly financed associations, like they are prevalent in Germany, are at the borderline to public agencies.

group representatives are assessed separately in this book as 'group litigation'.[25]) Common forms of group litigation are class actions and representative actions (broadly speaking, actions initiated by an association, foundation or agency for the benefit of individuals).[26] Both class and representative actions may vary considerably regarding possible claimants, representatives and the remedy sought. In terms of design, the distinction between the opt-in or opt-out nature of the action or mandatory procedures is very decisive.[27] Under an opt-in scheme, an individual is informed about the infringement and then may express the wish to participate in the case.[28] Under an opt-out scheme, the individual consumer must clarify the intention not to be bound by the outcome of the case. Basically, opting in or out is possible at all stages of the process. A third possibility is to establish mandatory procedures in which neither opting out is possible nor opting in is necessary.[29]

Class actions originated in the United States (US) and involve a lead plaintiff represented by a lawyer who files a complaint on behalf of her client and the other victims.[30] As class actions are unusual in Europe and representative actions are more widespread, this book focuses on representative actions.

Public authorities may act as representatives in these actions in various contexts (before courts or other entities), such as referring or defending cases. For instance, in Australia, the focus is strongly on the civil law system, and only the courts can impose sanctions.[31] Under some special conditions in Sweden, a public authority may represent a single consumer, as opposed to a group of consumers, before the civil court.[32] Consumer associations, business or trade organisations or other types of associations also may act as representatives. In some sectors in Germany, representation by so-called *Abmahnvereine* for instance exists. The purpose of

---

25 In other contexts referred to as aggregate litigation or collective actions.

26 See J. Stuyck et al., 'An Analysis and Evaluation of Alternative Means of Consumer Redress other than Redress through Ordinary Judicial Proceedings – Final Report', (2007), p. 12. See for an extensive discussion of different forms of group litigation in the context of competition law S. Keske, *Group Litigation in European Competition Law: A Law and Economics Perspective* (Antwerp: Intersentia, 2010), p. 39. From a procedural law point of view, test case and lead case proceedings exist, as well as different procedural ways for the judge to join claims.

27 See Van den Bergh and Visscher (2008b), p. 9, Keske (2010), p. 43.

28 See Van den Bergh and Visscher (2008b).

29 See Van den Bergh and Visscher (2008b), p. 9. These mainly exist in the US and come close to a public enforcement scheme, according to R.J. Van den Bergh, 'Enforcement of Consumer Law by Consumer Associations', *Essays in the Law and Economics of Regulation – In Honour of Anthony Ogus*, eds M.G. Faure and F.H. Stephen (Antwerp; Oxford; Portland: Intersentia, 2008) 279–306, p. 283.

30 See Van den Bergh and Visscher (2008b), p. 7. The lead plaintiff is generally only a figurehead and a lawyer does the real representative work.

31 See Faure, Ogus and Philipsen (2008), p. 376.

32 See interview with Gunnar Larsson, Swedish Consumer Ombudsman and Head of Consumer Authority (Stockholm, 25 August 2009).

these associations is to strategically oppose certain types of infringements (such as unfair commercial practices). Interestingly, the warned party has to pay the costs of the procedure.[33]

As remedies, these actions may seek injunctions or claim damages.[34] Other legal remedies include profit disgorgement,[35] pecuniary penalties, publicity orders and compliance programs.

Self-regulation

In some sectors, self-regulation is a mechanism for enforcing consumer law. Market players set up self-regulation and there may be an interface with ADR solutions that industry administers to some smaller extent and that often developed out of pure self-regulation. A recent definition of self-regulation reads: 'It is a form of regulation by a profession, trade or industry which purports to set rules for the behaviour of its members'.[36] In technical areas, responsible self-regulation is of utmost importance.[37] Industry may opt for self-regulation if it fears government regulations will be imposed.[38] Classical self-regulation is concerned less with balancing consumer and trader representation. However, these systems differ in the degree of monopolistic power, formality, legal status and participation of outsiders in rule formulation or enforcement. Compensation is usually not among the available remedies.[39] The entities can be empowered to fine members or terminate their membership in a foundation or association. Appeal options are very limited, but some boards provide for revisions.

33 For example, see http://www.wettbewerbszentrale.de/de/home, last accessed: 31 March 2013.

34 See A. Stadler, 'Group Actions as a Remedy to Enforce Consumer Interests', *New Frontiers of Consumer Protection – The Interplay between Private and Public Enforcement*, eds F. Cafaggi and H.-W. Micklitz (Antwerp; Oxford; Portland: Intersentia, 2009) pp. 305–28. Europe is in the experimental stage.

35 In German, *Gewinnabschöpfungsklagen*, to be found in § 10 Gesetz gegen den Unlauteren Wettbewerb (Unfair Trade Practices Act, UWG).

36 See E.H. Hondius, 'Self-Regulation in Consumer Matters on a European Level', *Reframing Self-Regulation in European Private Law*, ed. F. Cafaggi (The Hague: Kluwer Law International, 2006) 239–47, p. 243.

37 See J.C. Miller, 'The FTC and Voluntary Standards: Maximizing the Net Benefits of Self-Regulation', *Cato Journal* 4.3 (1985): 897–903, p. 899.

38 See R. Baggott, 'Regulatory Reform in Britain: The Changing Face of Self-Regulation', *Public Administration* 67.4 (1989): 435–54, p. 436.

39 See P. Verbruggen, *Transnational Private Regulation in the Advertising Industry – Case Study Report for the Research Project Constitutional Foundations of Transnational Private Regulation* (2011), p. 49.

Conclusion

To reduce the complexity of the topic, the following general definitions of enforcement mechanisms are deduced. Deviations from these general definitions are discussed in the country studies.

The first definition is straightforward. At the civil court, standing is granted to individuals (under special circumstances), to lawyers and to representatives. Judges are assumed to be impartial and an appeal system is in place. The principle of party presentation is prevalent rather than judicial investigations. The state subsidises the procedure.[40]

'Consumer ADR' refers to a body, unrelated to a court, which conducts less formalised procedures compared with courts. Typically, industry and the state are responsible for financing ADR institutions. When taking decisions, ADR involves the consumer and the business interest. The involvement of a legal representative is generally not required, and the awards are *prima facie* of a lower value in enforceability. In addition, the procedure involves little or no costs for the consumer who is a claimant. The most typical remedy is compensation.

'Administrative enforcement' is performed by an agency that can carry out monitoring and has some investigative powers.[41] The agency may decide the case, refer the case to a court or even defend the case in a court. There are basically no direct costs for the individual. Actions can be triggered by reporting or carried out on an own motion. Appeal along the lines of the administrative law branch is possible. Those authorities can impose various sanctions, but usually do not grant compensation.[42] There is clearly an interrelation between *ex ante* action carried out by a regulator and *ex post* action as soon as harm has occurred and is detected.

The public prosecutor is central to the functioning of the criminal process.[43] Once a crime is reported, an investigation is initiated (with the help of the police). Judges may have a role to play to authorise the use of certain investigative powers, the prosecution brings the case as the plaintiff, and the criminal court makes the judgment. A wide variety of sanctions exist, procedures may allow for dealing with compensation claims, judges are supposedly impartial and an elaborate appeal system is in place. The procedure basically does not entail administrative costs for the individual, who only reported the crime.

Group litigation refers to representative actions, rather than class actions, and captures any representative action before a court or agency that is primarily carried

40 See Landes and Posner (1975), p. 31.

41 The country studies show more specifically what is considered as investigative powers or existing public authorities.

42 Similarly characterised in Cafaggi and Micklitz (2009), p. 406.

43 See J. Hodgson and A. Roberts, 'Criminal Process and Prosecution', *The Oxford Handbook of Empirical Legal Research*, eds P. Cane and H.M. Kritzer (Oxford: Oxford University Press, 2010) 64–93, p. 80: who provide an overview of empirical work carried out regarding the role of public prosecutors, in particular their independence.

out by an association or a state authority. These representatives typically have better suited capabilities for collecting information. Group litigation subsumes different forms of bundling similar interests into one legal proceeding. The variations are manifold. Importantly, different types of remedies can be sought.

Self-regulation includes an interface with ADR solutions that to some extent are administered by industry and developed generally out of pure self-regulation; hence, for the purpose of this book, the term 'self-regulation (in the narrow sense)' is defined as codes of conduct established and enforced by members of an industry (limited regulatory powers over a certain industry). The system is financed entirely by the industry. If the code is breached, complaints may be brought free of charge. This procedure does not reflect an equal representation of consumers and traders, and damages are not usually granted.

Furthermore, this short introduction to relevant legal mechanisms in consumer law demonstrates how public and private law enforcement solutions are intertwined in various ways. For example, public bodies may sometimes enter into private transactions, and, in that sense, there is an overlap between the 'two paradigms'.[44]

44 See Hodges (2011b).

Chapter 3
Framework to Assess Enforcement Designs

The indispensable first step to analysing the efficiency of enforcement systems and combination of systems is to develop a framework for assessment. This framework includes three stages: optimal risk allocation, optimal provision of incentives and administrative costs.

In the first stage, the analysis involves verifying that the situation allows victims to initiate lawsuits, which is a precondition to enabling an optimal level of enforcement. The initiation of enforcement processes in many instances depends on private parties' actions. For this to happen, the risks of litigation must be spread efficiently. In other words, risk allocation must be optimised. Allocation is to be done, depending on people's risk attitudes, with the 'cheapest risk bearer'. Optimal risk allocation, apart from the initiation stage, is also crucial to the continuation of the process (decision on appeal and the like).

Assessing the optimal incentives for all players is the second stage of the analysis. Optimal deterrence induces an efficient number of potential wrongdoers not to violate the law. To achieve this level of deterrence, any actor in the enforcement process (individuals, enforcers and so on) must be induced with incentives to guarantee that enforcement is carried out whenever this is in society's interest. Risk allocation and optimal incentives are interlinked as risk allocation can provide solutions to some incentive problems and vice versa.

The assessment of an enforcement design seeks to balance costs and benefits; therefore, the last stage focuses on administrative costs, a very narrow category that when high can be a substantive cost factor.[1] At all three stages in the assessment framework, factors and characteristics are tested that are common to the selected enforcement systems and influence their efficiency. The factors taken (largely) from existing literature are systematised and placed in the category in which they fit best.

---

1 This framework has a similar structure to one set up by Guido Calabresi regarding liability in tort law (G. Calabresi, *The Costs of Accidents: A Legal and Economic Analysis*, 5th ed. (New Haven: Yale University Press, 1977)). Liability is to be put on the most appropriate actors: the cheapest cost avoiders. The objective function of the tort system is minimisation of the sum of the injury and injury avoidance costs associated with accidents (primary costs), risk-spreading costs (secondary costs) and administrative costs (tertiary costs). Calabresi is concerned with the question in how far an enterprise should bear the costs in a case of an accident at all; see G. Calabresi, 'Some Thoughts on Risk Distribution and the Law of Torts', *Yale Law Review* 70.4 (1961): 499–553, p. 501. The angle from which he views risk distribution and what he means by it are different from the view here, which deals with the risk involved in initiating a lawsuit.

The Three-stage Framework

Optimal Risk Allocation

Allocation of risks is important in the consumer-trader relationship at two stages: the moment of buying a product and the moment of assessing risks in a possible lawsuit. This work focuses on the latter instance. Risks, characterised by probabilities, can be calculated. Some uncertainties are unknown (possibly unknowable) probabilities.[2] Monetary values can be attributed to different risks.

Assessing how people respond to risks is crucial to predict, model or influence their behaviour in the enforcement process. Risk attitude is defined on a continuum from risk aversion to risk seeking.[3] While some people are risk lovers or risk neutral, they are the exception in society. The largest share of the population is deemed to be risk averse.[4] Risk aversion, a concept applied not only in economics, but also in finance and psychology, is defined as the reluctance of a person to accept a bargain with an uncertain payoff rather than another bargain with a more certain, but possibly lower, expected payoff.[5] A risk-averse person would pay to avoid a risk in order to have certainty of the expected value of something.[6]

For litigation to be carried out, the procedural risk must first be spread accordingly. Risk allocation is essential to efficient law enforcement. Comparative advantages in risk bearing have to be exploited. The risk should be allocated to the party best able to manage it, the party who has least risk-bearing costs. To ensure optimal law enforcement, overall risks must be allocated in such a way that a threat of successful litigation exists whenever it is desirable from a social point of view.

Public institutions or private players (one individual or a group) have different opportunities for risk spreading and pooling. When it comes to litigation, people may be 'court averse' rather than risk averse.[7] When approaching a lawyer, a client who is not an expert in legal matters may be risk averse. The lawyer is more accustomed to the risks and uncertainties in litigation, which may have become predictable factors. For the client the lawyer might serve as an information

2 See Soderlind (2001), p. 143.

3 See A. Tversky and D. Kahneman, 'Prospect Theory: An Analysis of Decision under Risk', *Econometrica* 47.2 (1979): 263–91; risk attitude is context-specific, P. Slovic, H. Kunreuther and G.F. White, 'Decision Processes, Rationality, and Adjustment to Natural Hazards', *Natural Hazards. Local, National and Global*, ed. G.F. White (New York: Oxford University Press, 1974) pp. 187–205; Z. Shapira, *Risk Taking: A Managerial Perspective* (New York: Russell Sage Foundation, 1997).

4 See Soderlind (2001), p. 147.

5 The concept of risk aversion goes largely back to M. Friedman and L.P. Savage, 'The Utility Analysis of Choices involving Risk', *Journal of Political Economy* 56 (1948): 279–304.

6 See Shavell (2004), p. 258.

7 G. Dari-Mattiac , 'Access to Justice', University of Pavia, June 2010.

generator to reduce risks. The following analysis embarks from the standard assumption of risk aversion and then includes other risk attitudes.

Three factors in risk allocation – rational apathy, free riding and funding – are assessed at this stage:

Rational apathy The 'rational apathy' problem arises from the divergence of the individual and social incentive to sue.[8] There is no systematic relation between the individual and social cost/benefit analyses. Therefore cases emerge where an individual does not have an incentive to bear the costs of court proceedings although doing so would be in the social interest. In private law enforcement, this occurs mainly in relation to small and widespread damages. However, the individual is perfectly rational in deciding not to sue.[9] Considering the costs and benefits, the private party finds that costs outweigh the benefits. As shall be seen later on, there are ways of overcoming this issue by basically aligning private and social costs and benefits. If the risk is too high for any single individual, systems must be established to allow for risk sharing or risk spreading. The 'cheapest risk bearer' must be identified. Procedural rules like reversal of the burden of proof influence risk perception.[10]

Free riding 'Free riding' can disturb risk allocation and incentives.[11] For example, when many victims suffer from a law infringement, but all stand to gain if one of them sues, it is efficient for everybody to wait for someone else to sue and then profit from the result. The individual who waits and 'free rides' does not bear any of the risks connected to the lawsuit, particularly to losing it. Taken to the extreme, if all consumers adapted a free-rider mentality, no lawsuits would be filed and consumer protection rules would not be enforced.[12] In this case, the enforcement level would not be socially optimal; therefore, optimal enforcement mixes must be found to overcome this disturbance. Again, risks must be spread to avoid free riding and to guarantee litigation in the first place. The avoidance of 'risk-free riding' is necessary to guarantee that a lawsuit is initiated as early as possible and the emanation of societal harm stopped and internalised.

Funding The amount of the monetary investment that someone makes in litigation obviously influences the degree of risk. The amount of money needed or available is decisive for the risks that one can or dares to bear. Who should

8 See Landes and Posner (1975), p. 33; Schäfer (2000), p. 195; Howells and Weatherill (2005), p. 604; N. Garoupa, 'Optimal Law Enforcement when Victims are Rational Players', *Economics of Governance* 2 (2001): 231–42, p. 233 as to the factors that motivate individuals. This category would also fit under the second stage.

9 See Van den Bergh (2007), p. 184.

10 See Renda et al. (2007), p. 175.

11 See Van den Bergh and Visscher (2008b), p. 14; Landes and Posner (1975), p. 29.

12 See Van den Bergh and Visscher (2008b), p. 16.

bear the risks in an optimal system and how can financial devices influence this?[13] Mechanisms or devices described in this section potentially can solve the risk allocation issues of rational apathy and free riding.

The two main fee-shifting rules are the 'loser-pays' rule (English rule), according to which the losing party has to pay all the costs, including the other party's costs and the 'American rule' according to which both parties may be required to pay their own expenses. These rules impact the individual's perception of the risks. There is a relation with the individuals' confidence in winning.[14] The assessment is related to people's attitudes toward risk.[15] Scholars disagree on which fee-shifting rule is efficient.[16]

Not only lawyers' fees, but also court fees influence individuals' calculations. Any procedural rule, such as a small claim track, that relieves the claimant from some of these costs decreases the claimant's financial risks. Provisions for legal aid, in which the state practically assumes part of the risk,[17] can have a decisive impact. Other ways of funding include process financing through insurers. Individuals may even find a representative in a public body, such as an ombudsman, with whom to file a complaint.[18]

The risk perception of a client's lawyer is similarly decisive. Remuneration systems can have a strong influence on lawyers' risk attitudes. Funding, and the source of the funds, available for other representatives, such as associations or public authorities, also influences these organisations' behaviour in litigation. To ensure optimal law enforcement, overall risks must be allocated in such a way that a threat of successful litigation exists whenever it is desirable from a social point of view.

As a first step, the option to enforce the law must be available. Optimal risk allocation applies not only when the lawsuit is initiated, but also in decisions regarding continuing the lawsuit (in appeal for instance).

Then, incentives for the players involved in litigation must be aligned accordingly so that they perform according to social-welfare criteria – the standardised benchmark for this analysis – throughout the entire enforcement process.

---

13 See Renda et al. (2007), p. 174 refers to factors such as one-way shifting of legal expenses, contingency fees, private or public funding instruments; increasing the prospective reward for plaintiffs, making evidence more easily available for plaintiffs at the pre-trial stage; allowing claims to be brought by way of group litigation and facilitating follow-up actions by establishing previous public decisions as *prima facie* evidence in favour of the plaintiff.

14 This is analysed in a comparative work on German and Swedish fair trading law, M. Treis, *Recht des unlauteren Wettbewerbs und Marktvertriebsrecht in Schweden* (Köln Berlin Bonn München: Carl Heymanns Verlag KG, 1991).

15 See Renda et al. (2007), p. 175.

16 See Renda et al. (2007), p. 177 in relation to private antitrust enforcement.

17 See Van den Bergh and Visscher (2008b), p. 13; also argued by Van Boom (2006), p. 48; Shavell (1982), p. 339; Stuyck et al. (2007); Howells and Weatherill (2005), p. 614. Duggan (2003) argued that among the cost-spreading measures (legal aid, contingent fee arrangements and class actions), no single measure is a complete solution; see p. 66.

18 For details, see Chapter 7 on Sweden.

Optimal Provision of Incentives

Various players take part in different law enforcement schemes and all respond to incentives.[19] When seeking to align players' performances with social-welfare criteria, obstacles and deviations may emerge. Incentives arise at different levels. While the primary goal is optimal deterrence (to induce the efficient amount of potential wrongdoers to obey the law, in other words to discipline them), the threat of enforcement to potential wrongdoers must be upheld. The broad group of people involved in law enforcement is diffuse. All players should be induced to guarantee the optimal level of enforcement that induces compliant behaviour *ex ante*. Next, the incentives for the various players and the obstacles posed to their behaviour are examined. The criteria are information asymmetries, capture, frivolous lawsuits and principal agent issues.

Information asymmetry Information asymmetries occur in relation to facts or legal rules, for instance concerning a consumer good.[20] A seller knows more about a specific product than a rival company or the consumer. These differences impact incentives for the better and worse informed parties and may impede litigation. If a faulty product is not detected, the seller may continue to offer it, and society continues to suffer harm. This asymmetry can lead to adverse selection – a market process in which differences in access to information cause 'bad' products to be selected. Akerlof, who developed important findings about this issue, argued that adverse selection ultimately leads to quality deterioration.[21]

In litigation, information asymmetries may occur between the individual claimant and the claimant's representative and between the claimant and the defendant. This section looks into information asymmetries between the two

---

19 See Cooter and Ulen (2008), p. 4.

20 See H-B. Schäfer and C. Ott, eds, *The Economic Analysis of Civil Law* (Cheltenham: Edward Elgar, 2004), p. 359. Goods are characterised in three categories: search goods, experience goods and credence goods. Search goods are those for which the consumer is able to collect information prior to purchase, thereby reducing product uncertainty. With experience goods the quality of the product is revealed only after purchase, and the quality of credence goods cannot be known (such as a visit to a doctor, a contracting with a lawyer). Whenever information about a product is highly technical or difficult to communicate, private parties may face a problem, P. Nelson, 'Information and Consumer Behavior', *Journal of Political Economy* 78 (1970): 311–29. The different types of goods are variously susceptible to information asymmetries between the seller and the buyer. Credence goods are particularly vulnerable to information asymmetries.

21 See Akerlof (1979). Taking the 'market for lemons' as an example, Akerlof illustrated how quality uncertainty can cause a process of adverse selection, which is why good quality products are ultimately driven out of the market by bad ones. If consumer cannot distinguish quality, the price will be based on average quality, and, thus, sellers of good quality products will find the price inadequate and withdraw from the market.

opposed parties (claimant and defendant), while the claimant-representative relationship is discussed below under the heading Agency Issues.

As outlined, information asymmetries are one of the core causes of litigation, and primarily refer to characteristics of products, but also may involve the characteristics of the trader. Among the most prominent consequences of information asymmetries is a low probability of detection of infringements, which can have various implications for deterrence. However, cures are available in terms of raising the amount of the sanction to compensate for those low probabilities in line with the previously mentioned equation. In some cases, detecting the wrongdoer may be too costly to incentivise a claimant to do so. For example, a landlord may have little possibility of locating a tenant who leaves a flat without paying the last two rents.

In practice, provisions that disable a lawsuit may include causality issues or prescription periods.[22] From the point of view of optimal deterrence, current laws do not necessarily strike the optimal balance between cases that should and those that should not be enforced.

Unequal distribution of information influences people's behaviour in litigation. An information asymmetry between defendant and claimant regarding the facts, their location or the law may be cured to some extent when players such as lawyers, other representatives, judges or other enforcers step in and generate information. Factors like investigative powers or skills are decisive for potentially mitigating information asymmetries always aligned with optimal deterrence.[23]

Capture Public choice theory studies the behaviour of agents in the political arena. Capture refers to the exertion of influence on public administration.[24] Collusion may take place between industry and public agencies.[25] 'Regulatory capture' may occur as groups or individuals with a high-stakes interest in certain

22 See Van Boom (2006), p. 17.

23 Van den Bergh (2007), p. 193 refers to missing investigative powers of consumer associations.

24 See G. Howells, *Evaluation of the Effectiveness and Efficiency of Collective Redress Mechanisms in the European Union – Country Report United Kingdom* (2008); See Ogus (1994), p. 57. In particular, attention has to be paid to the life cycles of agencies; C. Hood, H. Rothstein and R. Baldwin, *The Government of Risk: Understanding Risk Regulation Regimes* (New York: Oxford University Press, 2001), p. 112; Garoupa and Gomez-Pomar (2000), p. 5, 17 also dealt with the aspect of collusion in administrative agencies. For the effects of regulatory failures on consumer detriment, see Europe Economics (2007), p. 175.

25 See Bowles, Faure and Garoupa (2008), p. 407; P. Cartwright, 'Crime, Punishment, and Consumer Protection', *Journal of Consumer Policy* 30.1 (2007): 1–20, p. 7 and, for example, a discussion in Garoupa and Gomez-Pomar (2000), pp. 5, 17.

policy outcomes or regulatory decisions focus resources and energies to gain the outcomes they prefer. Like this, they may successfully 'capture' a public authority.[26]

Despite working in the public interest, public officials might be inclined to more willingly pursue other interests than their delegated tasks. Some public officials might simply be lazy. While the capture theory was developed in relation to public administration, it can be expanded to include personnel of consumer ADR bodies.[27] Opportunistic behaviour among these enforcers leads to under-enforcement, and, therefore, is undesirable from an efficiency perspective.

A remedy to these distortions may be found by triggering the desired incentives in regulation. In imposing regulations to readjust behaviour according to efficiency standards, the principles of accountability and legitimacy can be crucial to influence the incentives.[28] From a legal point of view, these concepts might also be reasons for appeal or invalidation of enforcer's decisions.

Generally, judges' degree of impartiality and independence is expected to be higher.[29] But inducing impartiality is by nature more complicated than inducing bias. Therefore, for the remainder of this book, a distinction is made between a low degree of susceptibility to capture among judges and a higher degree among public and ADR officials. Capture is inherent as to self-regulation.[30]

Frivolous lawsuits In some cases, the defendant rather than the party bringing suit turns out to be the victim – the victim of a frivolous lawsuit. In such a case, the enforcement tool might 'become a sword in the hands of plaintiffs, more than an opportunity to seek redress for harm suffered'.[31] The reason is misallocation

26 See G.J. Stigler, 'The Theory of Economic Regulation', *Bell Journal of Economics and Management Science* 3 (1971): 3–18.

27 See T.O. Main, 'ADR: The New Equity', *University of Cincinnati Law Review* 74 (2005): 329–404, p. 330; 'a certain vulnerability to capture by special interests, some consumer ADR schemes are currently not satisfactory concerning independence': Hodges, Benöhr and Creutzfeldt-Banda (2012), p. 444.

28 See for consumer associations, C. Hodges, 'Collectivism: Evaluating the Effectiveness of Public and Private Models for Regulating Consumer Protection', *Collective Enforcement of Consumer Law*, eds W.H. Van Boom and M.B.M. Loos (Groningen: Europa Law Publishing, 2007) 207–28, p. 215.

29 See A. Shleifer et al., 'Courts', *Quarterly Journal of Economics* 118.2 (2003): 453–517, p. 454; R.A. Posner, 'The Theories of Economic Regulation', *The Bell Journal of Economics and Management Science* 5.2 (1974): 335–58, p. 351; W.M. Landes and R.A. Posner, 'The Independent Judiciary in an Interest Group Perspective', *Journal of Law and Economics* 18 (1997): 875–901; R.A. Epstein, 'The Independence of Judges: The Uses and Limitations of Public Choice Theory', *BYU Law Review* (1990): 832–5. For criminal law judges, see Bowles, Faure and Garoupa (2008), p. 392.

30 See F.H. Stephen and J.H. Love, 'Regulation of the Legal Profession', *Encyclopedia of Law and Economics Volume III. The Regulation of Contracts*, eds B. Bouckaert and G. De Geest (Cheltenham: Edward Elgar, 2000), p. 990.

31 See Renda et al. (2007), p. 562.

of incentives. The danger of frivolous or unmeritorious lawsuits arises when individuals for opportunistic reasons, which may be to damage the business of a competitor, sue even though their allegations are not based on real arguments.[32] Substantial reputational harm to the defendants may result,[33] ultimately reducing social welfare. If people engage in more litigation than deemed necessary from a social viewpoint, over-deterrence may result.[34] If the producer is faced with an unmeritorious lawsuit, the defendant can decide to settle or to defend the case. In both cases, the costs incurred will be reflected in a rise in the price of the defendant's products or services. Depending on the legal system, claimants may be sanctioned for frivolous lawsuits in order to give incentives to abstain from them.

Error costs refer to courts making mistaken decisions, which are clearly undesirable.[35] Error generally consists of two types: error I costs are those that occur when an individual who is guilty might mistakenly not be found liable ('mistaken acquittal').[36] Error II costs are those that occur if an innocent individual is mistakenly found liable ('mistaken conviction'). Both errors dilute deterrence and, therefore, reduce efficiency. Two factors are at work in errors: the probability of error and the costs if an error occurs.[37] Generally, the costs of false convictions are assumed to be significantly higher than those of false acquittals.[38] The conviction of an innocent person leads to an encouragement of crime, as it reduces the marginal deterrence to its commission.[39] However, with companies, either type of error may not actually be costly unless directors can be held personally liable.[40] The concept can be expanded to any other decision-making body. Error costs aggravate the problem of frivolous lawsuits in that an undesirable case results in a wrong decision because the case is not filtered out.

Agency issues A weakness inherent in the client-lawyer relationship is that agency problems may occur between them.[41] Generally, in these relationships the client (principal) cannot fully control the quality of the lawyer's (agent's)

---

32 A formal model on incentives for frivolous suits was developed by D. Rosenberg and S. Shavell, 'A Model in which Suits are Brought for their Nuisance Value', *International Review of Law and Economics* 5 (1985): 3–13. For Europe, see Schäfer (2000).

33 See Van den Bergh and Visscher (2008b), p. 24; similarly, Schäfer (2000), p. 184.

34 See Duggan (2003), p. 47.

35 See R.A. Posner, 'An Economic Approach to Legal Procedure and Judicial Administration', *The Economic Structure of the Law: The Collected Economic Essays of Richard A. Posner*, ed. F. Parisi (Cheltenham: Edward Elgar, 2000) 290–349, p. 291.

36 See Polinsky and Shavell (2005a), p. 36.

37 See Posner (2000), p. 292.

38 See Ogus (2004), p. 51.

39 See Stigler (1970), p. 528.

40 See Ogus (2004), p. 51.

41 See S. Shavell, 'The Fundamental Divergence between the Private and the Social Motive to Use the Legal System', *Journal of Legal Studies* 16 (1997): 575–612, p. 599.

performance.[42] The basis for any principal-agent problem is an information asymmetry between two parties,[43] which can lead to moral hazard.[44] The agent uses the principal's inability to assess the value of the steps the agent takes. His motivation may be personal interests; for example, a lawyer may seek to obtain the highest remuneration rather than the best outcome for the client.

Though the problem is common in relationships between representing and represented players in the enforcement process, changing the principal yields a greater dimension. An enforcer, such as a lawyer, judge, administrator or self-enforcer, also may be considered the agent of society at large. In this case, society is the principal and the agent must work according to social-welfare criteria. The enforcement system for consumer law is characterised by the interplay between consumer and business partisans. Consequently, in courts and public authorities, decisions in line with social welfare are possible. For instance, public agents are assumed to work in the public interest and filter accordingly (unless their incentives are diluted),[45] and court rules are set up accordingly.

In this category, the remaining costs and benefits of a particular enforcement mechanism for society at large are measured that cannot be captured by any of the other categories, always with a view to the optimal level of enforcement. Looking at the scenario like this allows an assessment of costs and benefits to society at large, for example harm in the form of a duplication of enforcement costs. One can imagine various individuals' investing in obtaining the very same information to go to court, or judges' deciding various similar cases individually instead of jointly. Adaptation costs, passed on via the price mechanism, are societal costs. Likewise, particular societal benefits of certain enforcement mechanisms can be mentioned.

Administrative Costs

Administrative costs, also called system costs, comprise a very narrow category, referring only to real monetary costs for the individuals and the state from

---

42 See S. Shavell, 'Risk Sharing and Incentives in the Principal and Agent Relationship', *Bell Journal of Economics, The RAND Corporation* 10.1 (1979): 55–73; H. Collins, *Regulating Contracts* (New York: Oxford University Press, 1999), p. 236.

43 See K-G. Löfgren, T. Persson and J.W. Weibull, 'Markets with Asymmetric Information: The Contributions of George Akerlof, Michael Spence and Joseph Stiglitz', *Scandinavian Journal of Economics* 104.2 (2002): 195–211.

44 See C. Keser and M. Willinger, 'Experiments on Moral Hazard and Incentives: Reciprocity and Surplus-Sharing', The Economics of Contracts Theories and Applications, eds E. Brousseau and J-M. Glachant (Cambridge: Cambridge University Press, 2002) 293–312, in which a whole section is devoted to the principal agent problem and moral hazard. Moral hazard arises because an individual does not internalise the full consequences of actions, and, therefore, has a tendency to act less carefully than otherwise.

45 In this book, public interest and social welfare are assumed to be the same.

enforcement efforts.[46] Examples include administrative costs of judges, lawyers, public prosecutors, public officials, ADR personnel, self-enforcers, the police or other representatives.

An individual who decides to sue calculates with certain costs in the ambit of litigation and updates the decision at various stages throughout the process.[47] Costs that occur prior to initiating a trial are those of detection and investigation and of hiring a lawyer (related to litigation costs). For example, litigation costs arise at court through administration, the hearing, taking evidence and in relation to the remedies.[48] Generally costs are incurred for conduction of trial or settlement, litigation, sanctioning and evasion.[49] Some administrative costs are borne by the individuals (both parties in litigation); others are borne by the society. Systems are more or less costly to administer[50] and a point will be reached where the benefits of additional deterrence achieved are lower than the costs incurred by society.

When judging the costs of different enforcement mechanisms, attention has to be paid to the fact that any measure that induces more litigation (greater incentive to sue) leads to an increase in administrative costs. This increase has to be weighed against possible societal benefits. Elements to consider are economies of scale or outsourcing to instruments that are less costly to administer. Comparative data concerning administrative costs is barely available and the section is to give mainly some tendencies. This book pays no particular attention to the costs of setting up legislation, regulations, contracts, self-regulation and so forth.

Furthermore, error costs and administrative costs are related because providing more resources to maintain a legal system reduces error costs, but increases administrative costs.[51]

Conclusion

This chapter provides a basic introduction to the framework to assess enforcement designs, which includes three stages: optimal risk allocation, optimal provision of incentives and administrative costs. The framework captures criteria necessary

46 Again, a reference to Calabresi is appropriate: In his categorisation tertiary accident costs are the costs incurred by the legal system to establish and enforce liability – the costs of the legal system as such. See Calabresi (1977), p. 24.

47 See Polinsky and Shavell (2005b), p. 21.

48 Including time of lawyers, litigants, witnesses, judges, paper and ink, law offices and courthouse maintenance, telephone service and so on; see F. Parisi, ed., *The Economic Structure of the Law The Collected Economic Essays of Richard A. Posner*, 1 (Cheltenham: Edward Elgar, 2000), p. 290.

49 See Shavell (1984a), p. 364.

50 For example, see Renda et al. (2007), p. 569, where the authors assess the litigation costs of one scenario of their impact assessment.

51 See Posner (2000), p. 332.

to single out an efficient solution and facilitates finding optimal mixes of various mechanisms according to their relative strengths.

Therefore, the objective of this framework is to identify costs and benefits of different enforcement systems and draw conclusions regarding optimal mixes. A detailed overview of strengths and weaknesses of enforcement systems in relation to economic problems is given in the next chapter. The quest for the 'optimal mix' for various case studies is described in Chapter 5.

Chapter 4
Assessing Strengths and Weaknesses of Existing Law Enforcement Systems

This chapter provides an overview on existing literature concerning the strengths and weaknesses of different enforcement systems for consumer law and demonstrates how the previously defined enforcement mechanisms score. This discussion remains detached from remedies/sanctions as far as possible and typical remedies/sanctions are mentioned only when instrumental to the analysis. Chapter 5 then illustrates which combinations are valuable in particular case scenarios in consumer law. Importantly, the notion of being a 'typical remedy/sanction' is relaxed in Chapter 5 to some extent, which allows for new combinations and new ideas on who could provide which remedy/sanction (possibly hybrid mechanisms) to be explored.

Special attention is paid throughout this analysis to information asymmetries that were singled out as a main cause for litigation, particularly with online trade gaining in importance.

Enforcement Systems

This chapter includes an efficiency analysis of various private and public law enforcement solutions, group litigation and 'self-regulation in the narrow sense'. Private law is examined first, including civil court and consumer ADR proceedings.

Civil Court: Economic Strengths and Weaknesses

The jurisdiction, procedures and powers of a civil court or a civil court judge vary by country. Hence, for this analysis, enforcement via civil courts is defined as follows: standing is granted to individuals under special circumstances, to lawyers and to representatives. Judges are assumed to be impartial and an appeal system is in place. The prevalent principle is that of party presentation rather than judicial investigations. The state subsidises the procedures. Small claim procedures are also included under this heading.[1]

Below, the various economic characteristics of private law enforcement through individual lawsuits in civil courts are illustrated; mass litigation is discussed separately under '*Group Litigation: Economic Strengths and Weaknesses*'.

1 For a recent study on the EU, Australia, Canada and the US, see Stuyck et al. (2007).

Optimal Risk Allocation The analysis starts with an assessment of the risks involved in this type of litigation.

Rational apathy

A procedure in a civil court entails mainly court and (possibly) lawyer's fees. Depending on the cost rule, the parties incur these fees to differing extents. To start with, cases exist in which the damage is substantial and an individual is prepared to take the risk of suing in a civil court and paying the necessary fees. The individual and social costs-benefit analyses for filing a lawsuit may be different, and, therefore, the danger of under-enforcement must be considered, particularly in cases of small and widespread harm. A private person typically neglects to take into account the benefit of deterrence to society as a whole.[2] Risks involved in litigation for the individual may be high and the potential benefits may not outweigh the costs, which is a disincentive to sue. As there are costs involved in litigation – such as court fees and lawyer fees in a classical civil lawsuit – small individual harm may not be enough to trigger using this branch of law, despite extensive overall harm to society. To remedy this disincentive, the enforcement mechanism may include options for risk sharing and financing of risk costs.

Free riding

The 'specificity feature' entails[3] that courts decide cases with specific claimants and specific circumstances. Therefore, individuals must instigate each of their claims separately.[4] Free riding is not an issue in this situation; however, it may occur in cases of injunctions or reforms resulting from a judgment that provides benefits to people other than the claimant. The allocation of risks to all who profit from a remedy would have to be guaranteed to avoid a free-rider problem or the risk of inaction in such situations. The degree of free riding mentality depends on the scope procedural law leaves for other individuals to profit from clarifications on law and facts.

---

2 See Shavell (1997), p. 577. Shavell splits the analysis into three different stages in a legal process: the decision to bring a lawsuit, the decision for trial or settlement and the level of legal expenditure during the process. He ultimately concludes that the current level of litigation is not socially correct because of the divergence of the private and social incentive to sue (p. 584).

3 See Van Boom (2006), p. 13, W.H. Van Boom, 'Effectuerend Handhaven in het Privaatrecht', *Nederlands Juristenblad* 16 (2007): 982–91, p. 985.

4 See Van Boom (2006), p. 41; see F. Cafaggi, 'The Great Transformation. Administrative and Judicial Enforcement in Consumer Protection: A Remedial Perspective', *Loyola Consumer Law Review* 21 (2009): 496–539, p. 522. Coordination between injunctions and other remedies exists more for specific areas than as a general policy in Europe.

Funding

Any means of subsidising litigation costs can be a possible remedy for the rational apathy problem. For private law cases before a civil court, there are a variety of measures available such as legal aid offered by the state or insurances for both claimants and defendants.[5] Apart from these, other factors influencing the severity of rational apathy are general litigation fees (for instance, reduced by small claims courts) or allocation rules for civil procedure costs.[6] As said, there is disagreement as to which of these is the efficient remedy. Some fees can be recovered through a fee-shifting rule. The confidence about winning becomes a decisive criterion. One implication of the loser-pays rule is that the more optimistic a potential claimant is about her case, the higher the likelihood she will file the suit. In some countries, a consumer ombudsman may represent individual consumers under certain conditions in court and can assume the procedural costs.[7] In these ways, the risks involved in individual private litigation may be allocated efficiently, with the state or the defendant assuming part of the risk. This is needed more, the lower the claim value. Then again, insurers and legal aid have minimum thresholds to be applicable. Others must be excluded from profiting from the judgment to ensure there is no free riding. Rational apathy and the desire to free ride depend to some extent on the costs involved and the risk type of the individual involved. In addition, free riding may be less likely if risks to the individual are reduced. For instance, if an injunction can be achieved at low cost, the individual may be less inclined to wait for someone else to sue. Consequently, the individual would not refrain from suing. Generally, rules on the burden of proof can shift risks to the efficient bearer. The burden of proof in private individual litigation is with the party who wants to rely on a legal provision.[8] In some situations, the burden of proof for consumers may be relaxed or reversed if it is particularly burdensome to find evidence.

Generally, the more extensive the harm suffered, the more likely rational individuals will risk engaging in litigation. The lower the risks involved (reduced through funding), the greater the likelihood that an individual will engage in litigation.

5 See Shavell (1997), p. 576; L.T. Visscher and T. Schepens, 'A Law and Economics Approach to Cost Shifting, Fee Arrangements and Legal Expense Insurance', *New Trends in Financing Civil Litigation in Europe: A Legal, Empirical and Economic Analysis*, eds M.L. Tuil and L.T. Visscher (Cheltenham: Edward Elgar, 2010) 7–32.

6 See Van Boom (2006), p. 23.

7 For details, see Chapter 7 on Sweden. In a way, this is like a legal aid provision.

8 For instance, in email communications of 31 October 2011, Ulf Bernitz, Professor Emeritus of European Integration Law, University of Stockholm, stated, 'Normally, you carry the burden of proof as plaintiff. If you cannot fulfil that burden, you will normally lose the case'. For the Netherlands: 150 Wetboek van Burgerlijke Rechtsvordering (Act on Civil Procedure, Rv).

Optimal Provision of Incentives The next challenge is to trigger enforcers' optimal incentives and the latter differ depending on how the institutions within a particular legal branch are organised.

Information asymmetries

For some products, an ordinary consumer might not be able to recognise poor quality because of information asymmetry, and inefficient contracts may be the result.[9] In practice, consumer protection laws can mitigate the danger of hidden poor quality products and create a good reputation (guarantees, trademarks, licensing, truthful advertising).[10] Inefficient contracts require litigation, but information asymmetry also may prevent the consumer from discovering information about the wrongdoer, including the person's location.

Information about the other party is required for enforcement and to prove one's case. Pretrial discovery can be decisive for the amount of proof that the claimant can generate;[11] however, it is not available in most European legal systems.

The detection rate of infringements for private law enforcement is often assumed to be 100 per cent,[12] but that rate is optimistic for consumer law violations because harm often looks minor to the individual and might not be obvious. For the majority of cases in consumer law, once an infringement is detected, an individual can be assumed to have the necessary information to initiate a lawsuit.[13] Before a civil court, claimants must provide most of the evidence and may not rely on the inquisition of the judge – the core of the principle of party presentation. However, there might be cases in which the individual cannot provide this information and this asymmetry impedes the case. This impediment persists if lawyers or judges also cannot generate the information. In relation to the availability of information, trivial issues such as the identity and location of the wrongdoer that are necessary to initiate a lawsuit may be unknown and further impede litigation within private law enforcement.[14] Often neither the individual, nor the lawyer, or the judge can generate this information.

---

9 See Van den Bergh (2007), p. 186.

10 See Akerlof (1979), p. 499; Van den Bergh (2007), p. 189; Van den Bergh and Visscher (2008b), p. 15. For advertising in particular, see P. Nelson, 'Advertising as Information', *Journal of Political Economy* 82.4 (1974): 729–54.

11 It is said to lead to more costs as well, see Menkel-Meadow and Garth (2010), p. 693, confirmed for England and Wales in the Lord Justice Jackson, Review of Civil Litigation Costs, Final Report (2010).

12 R.A. Posner, ed., *Economic Analysis of Law*, 8th ed. (New York: Aspen Publishers, 2011), p. 845.

13 See Van den Bergh (2007), p. 186, for example, in traffic accidents.

14 See Van den Bergh (2007), p. 201; K.J. Cseres, 'Consumer Protection in the European Union', *Regulation and Economics* (Vol. 9, Encyclopedia of Law and Economics), eds R.J. Van den Bergh and A.M. Pacces, 2nd ed. (Cheltenham: Edward Elgar, 2012) 163–228, p. 192; for tort law scenarios, see Shavell (1993), p. 274; the hit-and-run offender is a classical example of an attempt to conceal someone's identity.

In practice, civil procedural law has restricted cases regarding prescription periods or causation issues. Efficient law enforcement is impeded when wrongdoers are able to escape a lawsuit,[15] for example because they are insolvent or judgment proof (the liability exceeds their assets), they are numerous or they are anonymous.[16] As to insolvency, the law and economics literature argues that private law generally provides only purely monetary sanctions that cannot sufficiently deter a judgment-proof offender.[17] However, a civil law injunction is different because that prospect can be a powerful deterrent for a trader.[18] Thus, even if the probability of detection is high, the probability of a wrongdoer being tried and convicted is sometimes low.

Furthermore, civil sanctions do not go above the level of harm, which is a problem in cases in which the probability of detection and conviction is low. The low probabilities would need to be outweighed by the gravity of the sanction. Injunctions can be a potential remedy. Punitive damages might be a solution, but are rarely imposed or even available in Europe; furthermore, they are criticised because they lead to over-deterrence and overcompensation.[19] However, punitive damages may be an effective method in coping with the risk of under-enforcement in instances of low probability of detecting infringements and convicting wrongdoers. Injunctions and interim measures allow putting a fast stop to a trade practice.

Capture

Capture does not apply in individual consumer law cases in civil courts because of the impartiality that courts require and the comparatively low value of consumer law claims.

Frivolous lawsuits

In general, a single lawsuit cannot generate huge reputational harm; therefore, the criteria of frivolous lawsuits are examined in detail in mass cases (see '*Group Litigation: Economic Strengths and Weaknesses*'). Things might look different if the claimant is not a consumer, but a competitor who is well equipped to detect an infringement and, importantly, could have an interest in using the law strategically.[20]

15 See Shavell (1984a), p. 360.

16 See Schäfer (2000), p. 184. In contract law, the judgment-proof problem is mitigated, according to Shavell (2004), p. 586, as people tend to know about each other.

17 See Shavell (2004), p. 473. An insolvent trader cannot be deterred by purely monetary sanctions. In practice, this is where insurances and funds come into play.

18 See Faure, Ogus and Philipsen (2009), p. 176.

19 See Van den Bergh and Visscher (2008b), p. 23. Punitive damages are an alternative to criminalisation to compensate low detection rates; see Bowles, Faure and Garoupa (2008), p. 403.

20 Compare the situation of competitors in antitrust cases, Renda et al. (2007), p. 563.

If error costs occur, they will be minor because the cost of sanctions is low.[21] Depending on the legal system, claimants can be sanctioned for frivolous lawsuits.

Agency issues

One of the most serious incentive issues in litigation is the principal-agent problem. In individual litigation, the possibilities to monitor the agent are considerable, and the possibilities are low that the agent will develop her own interests in a single damage claim. The problem is certainly aggravated in mass litigation, but may be an issue in an individual case. This issue is immediately mitigated as soon as structures such as small claims procedures emerge in which harmed individuals and defendants can represent themselves without involving lawyers.

As discussed, the focus is on the interests of society and the extent the enforcement mechanism is able to serve social welfare. The structure of private law enforcement is susceptible to creating costs to society; in particular, there could be a duplication of enforcement costs if private individuals are unable to cooperate.[22] For example, resources are wasted if two or more parties (with the help of their lawyers) spend money collecting the same information. Free riding among enforcers can occur when their litigation efforts have positive externalities.[23] In terms of social benefits, the fact that compensation is generally granted in the civil court has a positive effect in providing individuals with incentives to initiate a lawsuit. Depending on the legal system, judges induce settlements to varying extents, which can be welfare enhancing because the dispute is solved with only the threat of involving the court system as opposed to its actual involvement. The fact that in contract cases parties already have had a 'cooperative relationship' makes using the court system less likely in general.[24]

Administrative Costs The system or administrative costs are a highly relevant factor in determining optimal law enforcement:[25] is private enforcement cheaper to administer than other enforcement schemes?

In the civil court, relevant administrative costs are the time, effort and legal expenses that private parties bear, as well as the public expenses of conducting civil trials (including calculating damages).[26] Litigation costs of small claims

21 However, literature contrasting error costs in private law and criminal law is missing, which is why no firm conclusions shall be drawn regarding their overall value. It also depends on the remedy/sanction.

22 See Landes and Posner (1975), pp. 29–30.

23 See I.R. Segal and M.D. Whinston, 'Public vs Private Enforcement of Antitrust Law: A Survey', *Stanford Law and Economics Olin Working Paper No. 335* (2006), p. 12.

24 See Ogus (2007), p. 38.

25 See Becker (1968), p. 171.

26 See for instance Shavell (1984a), p. 364.

are normally lower than those of large claims.[27] Various aspects in the 'funding' category, like legal aid and insurance, may shift the administrative costs to different parties, which potentially can free a certain individual from particular costs. Small claims procedures seem to lead to overall lower administrative costs for society, because the procedure is less elaborate and a lawyer does not necessarily need to be involved. However, small claims cases still use a court structure, and may include appeals in which lawyers generally do need to be involved.

In the next sections, tentative conclusions on the administrative costs are reached when comparing administrative costs of various enforcement mechanisms. There seem to be reasons to think that administrative costs in private law are lower than with some other enforcement mechanisms.[28]

Conclusion Private individuals often litigate torts, contracts and property cases.[29] This analysis shows that by focusing on certain cases and possibly strengthening some weaknesses, the enforcement mechanism can indeed work.

From the perspective of optimal risk allocation, the risks and costs of engaging in a private lawsuit cause rational apathy to be more significant as the harm becomes smaller yet more widespread. A victim – certainly a consumer – may be even less willing to sue because there often is no monetary gain from an injunction, except possibly in follow-on damage cases. In the case of a rival, the motivation looks different. A rival company will have an interest in anything that damages the competitor's business. The burden of proof might be relaxed for the consumer depending on the legal system. No free riding is possible in relation to specific damage cases. Regarding injunctions or reforms, a free rider problem is more likely, but may be mitigated if only few resources need to be invested in obtaining these remedies.

Theoretically, there is a whole toolbox of funding possibilities, such as legal aid programmes, insurance or a shifting of legal fees for the benefit of the plaintiff, that could improve the efficiency of private law enforcement. Therefore, potential exists to resolve rational apathy and free riding issues in certain circumstances.

---

27 See Duggan (2003), p. 48.

28 In Faure, Ogus and Philipsen (2009), p. 177, the authors argued that in 'many jurisdictions, there will be significant differences in the evidentiary threshold required as between civil and criminal liability. It may also be the case that some degree of knowledge, intention or blameworthiness must be proved in the criminal context, while these conditions are not so stringent in the civil justice context. These differences normally make the preparation and adjudication of the criminal prosecution significantly more expensive than the civil claim. For most cases, that should make the civil process more cost effective than the criminal process'.

29 See Posner (2011), p. 841. On tort, see Landes and Posner (1975), p. 30. Furthermore the private and the social loss generally will be equal; for example, if a house burns down, there is a loss for society and also for the individual; see Schäfer (2000), p. 203 or Van den Bergh (2007), p. 185.

Differences in people's risk attitudes, those of the claimant and the defendant, may alter the results.

Individual private enforcement shows some strength in optimal allocation of incentives. In individual lawsuits, agency issues might be moderate, as there are wide control mechanisms and judge impartiality prevails. Moreover, some procedures may not need to involve a lawyer. In addition, frivolous lawsuits are a minor issue unless a competitor is pursuing the case. Likewise, error costs connected to private law seem to be lower than those related to criminal law, largely because sanctions are less costly. Civil lawsuits may not occur because certain information (regarding evidence or the location of the wrongdoer) cannot be generated in a private law setting. Available sanctions may not be able to compensate for all situations of low probabilities of detection, apprehension and conviction. Insolvency is a problem because sanctions other than monetary do generally not exist.

Doubling of enforcement costs can occur with private law enforcement, but, as a benefit, individuals do have a certain incentive to sue because the prospect of compensation is given. From the perspective of administrative costs, those costs seem to be lower in private law than with other enforcement mechanisms. This is certainly true regarding damage claims that fall below the threshold of a small claims provision.

In general, the biggest issue in daily consumer law problems seems to be the information asymmetry regarding a wrongdoer's whereabouts, which impedes law enforcement in various ways and for which civil procedural law usually does not provide a solution. Escaping wrongdoers can be assumed to be those that have the greatest incentive to generate substantial damage and thus the biggest losses for society. Consumer ADR mechanisms may provide a promising remedy for some of the weaknesses of ordinary private law enforcement.

Consumer ADR: Economic Strengths and Weaknesses

In this book, 'consumer ADR' refers to an enforcement body in which procedures are considerably less formalised than in a court. Typically, industry and the state finance these institutions and both consumers and businesses are involved in the decision-making. Legal representation is generally not required and the awards are *prima facie* of a lower value in terms of enforceability. Another typical characteristic is a consumer who as the claimant bears little or no costs of the procedures. The most typical remedy is compensation. In the way the ADR mechanism is currently constructed, the pre-existence of civil courts is required.[30]

Note that small claims procedures also partially fulfil characteristics of such an ADR mechanism. Therefore, the analysis of ADR and small claims may have

30 See P.H. Lindblom, 'ADR – The Opiate of the Legal System? Perspectives on Alternative Dispute Resolution Generally and in Sweden', *European Review of Private Law* 1 (2008a): 63–93, p. 72, which uses Sweden as an example.

similarities. ADR is the focus here because it stands in sharper contrast to the ordinary civil court procedure.

To my knowledge, the relationship of optimal law enforcement and an ADR body has not been described in great detail,[31] which means that this section is somewhat innovative. Below, various ADR characteristics are discussed using the analytical framework.

Optimal Risk Allocation

Rational apathy

The smaller the harm, the lower the enforcement costs must be to induce an individual to assume the risks of litigation. The ADR mechanism provides the desired lower enforcement cost for the individual because the procedures are less formal and may be subsidised by the state and/or the industry (depending on the country). However, the ADR body's decisions are less binding than a court's,[32] and if the wrongdoer is resistant, court proceedings may be initiated anyway. This procedure would demonstrate the strengths and weaknesses as outlined above.

Free riding

Generally, free riding is less of an issue in ADR because the financial risks involved in this type of litigation are much lower. If injunctions are granted by a particular consumer ADR body, the findings made in the context of court litigation above apply. The lower value of the awards may work against the strengths of the remedy injunction if granted by an ADR body. In cases of individual damage claims, the result will be specific. Outcomes of ADR procedures generally are not binding in a related court proceeding. More typically, those involved in ADR procedures profit from facts or case law established in courts.

Funding

ADR can be regarded as a funding mechanism itself because the claimant's costs are lower than private litigation before courts, which reduces rational apathy.[33] For

31 See only S. Shavell, 'Alternative Dispute Resolution: An Economic Analysis', *Journal of Legal Studies* 24 (1995): 1–28.

32 See Hodges, Benöhr and Creutzfeldt-Banda (2012), pp. 390, 420.

33 'Europeans' subjective financial thresholds for taking a complaint to court appears to be higher than for turning to alternative dispute resolution mechanisms. Around four in ten interviewees would have to lose €500 or less to go to court, compared to also four in ten who say they would have to lose only €200 to turn to an out-of-court dispute settlement body', European Commission, Special Eurobarometer n°342, Consumer Empowerment (2011), http://ec.europa.eu/consumers/consumer_empowerment/docs/report_eurobarometer_342_

example, hiring a lawyer is unnecessary. State and industry financing of the system also benefits the consumer.[34] An implication may be felt by the cost allocation rules. If the loser-pays rule applies, the loser may end up paying all the (few) costs.

Optimal Provision of Incentives

Information asymmetries

When consumer law infringements occur, an ADR body is typically more limited in remedies it can provide than a civil court, and, therefore, sanctions may not be sufficient to create a deterrent effect – even more so than in a civil court.

ADR also has limited ability to generate additional information for prosecuting and convicting a wrongdoer. Generally ADR procedures do not require lawyers and do not leave much room for inquiries, a fact that reflects the type of cases the ADR body wants to attract: the easy ones. The procedures can allow for short oral hearings or written statements.[35] As a result, the possibilities of raising further evidence are very limited. Complaints cannot be filed against wrongdoers who cannot be tracked down. In general, the trader's voluntary compliance is crucial. In various countries, traders signal their willingness to participate in the system by registering with the board. In a way, only clear-cut cases are accepted, and against a pre-defined set of defendants – those who volunteer to participate. Therefore, information required to initiate the case may be missing (such as the identity and location of the wrongdoer who has not registered with the board). And since there is no way to obtain this information, no proceedings can be initiated even if they would enhance welfare. No proceedings may be launched against traders who have not registered with the board in the first place (via trade associations or independently; see Part II). In reality, the law establishes further restrictions – causality issues or limitations in procedural law, such as prescription periods or maximum case values.

The judgment-proof problem also applies here because nonmonetary sanctions are not available, although possible injunctions may shift this balance. By and large, an ADR body cannot take up a case in which the trader is insolvent or continue a case if the trader becomes insolvent during the proceedings. However,

---

en.pdf, last accessed: 31 March 2013, p. 225. As to businesses, 'the vast majority of businesses (73 per cent) was satisfied with their experience with ADR and 82 per cent would use it again in the future. Seventy per cent would prefer to use ADR rather than going to court to settle disputes', European Business Test Panel (EBTP), Alternative Dispute Resolution (2011), http://ec.europa.eu/yourvoice/ebtp/consultations/2010/adr/report_en.pdf, last accessed: 31 March 2013, p. 2; 'According to businesses, the main advantages of ADR are that disputes are settled quickly (55 per cent) and that it allows them to maintain their reputation (25 per cent)'.

34 See Creutzfeldt-Banda (2012), p. 382.

35 See Hodges, Benöhr and Creutzfeldt-Banda (2012), p. 419. More details are included in Part II.

a closer look into some sectors reveals a strong interrelationship with trade associations and/or securities that the traders are obliged to take out, and more specifically for the package travel sector (see Chapter 5).

Capture

While capture is not a severe issue in civil courts, it can be in ADR.[36] Remedies to control for biased decision-making lie with the mixed composition of the entity, the consumer and business. Here, optimal incentives must be provided in the salary and reward structure and the source of the ADR body's financing. A neutral financer may be desirable. Accountability and appeal options are other possible cures.

Frivolous lawsuits

Individual cases before civil courts are rarely frivolous, and there is even less likelihood of frivolous cases with an ADR because the mechanism generally receives less attention from the public and has fewer possibilities for enforcing awards. In many countries, ADR does not have a specific procedure for handling mass cases.[37] However, low-cost procedures may potentially incline anyone to bring a case, including one that lacks enough merit to give it societal value.

Error costs are lower in ADR because of less costly sanctions; however, less accurate decision-making than within the court system may increase the likelihood of error.[38] Here, one must consider the setting of the ADR board, which can bundle expertise by engaging industry specialists who would not take part in court proceedings.[39] This, consequently, leads to a reduction of error on facts. However, ADR boards' means are limited if procedures are only written, investigation is excluded and due process requirements are less strictly observed. Therefore, ADR boards should not decide on issues of law.[40] Consumer ADR bodies are good for facts and courts for law.

Agency issues

Because ADR enforcement does not require the involvement of a lawyer, the principal-agent problem does not arise. An individual can opt to be represented,

36 See Main (2005), p. 330; Hodges, Benöhr and Creutzfeldt-Banda (2012), p. 444.

37 See Lindblom (2008a), p. 76: 'ADR is seldomly appropriate in group litigation'. This is discussed in Chapter 5 regarding a social welfare perspective.

38 This reasoning is analogous to that stipulated for administrative vs criminal law procedures and their differences; for those findings, see: Ogus, Faure and Philipsen (2006), p. 47.

39 See Shavell (1995), p. 2; Hodges, Benöhr and Creutzfeldt-Banda (2012), p. 441.

40 See Hodges, Benöhr and Creutzfeldt-Banda (2012), p. 415.

and the previously formulated findings in the context of the civil court apply in this case. When the ADR body, as society's agent, must produce outcomes in the interest of society, the following potential losses and benefits emerge.

The costs involved in ADR procedures for individuals are lower than in civil courts, resulting in cases being brought that would not be heard in court. Therefore, the number of cases increases. In addition, the court must check cases that the ADR could decide, although the legal grounds for doing this are generally limited. As bringing a case to the ADR does not preclude bringing it to a court (at least in certain circumstances and in some countries), enforcement efforts could be duplicated.[41] If the outcome of an ADR proceeding is regarded as only preliminary, lengthy and costly trials may ensue.[42] However, overall costs can be reduced if many cases are resolved with the ADR instead of in court, and this result could outweigh the costs of the additional cases. From an efficiency perspective, enforcement costs could be reduced by effectively coordinating the civil court and the ADR body. Certain findings could be used in the other body, a free riding of efforts that could be desirable from a social-welfare perspective. However, this coordination would find its limits with over-deterrence of the trader (the optimal sanction could not be exceeded to avoid over-deterrence). From a legal point of view, possible violations of Article 6 of the European Convention on Human Rights (ECHR) may occur, in particular if appearing before the ADR body is mandatory.[43]

Society suffers a loss when cases are decided out of court because there is no further development of the law.[44] The guidelines regarding substantive law that are achieved in a civil court cannot be formulated in ADR because of the number of non-legal players participating in the process.[45] This problem is particularly severe in legal systems in which the value of precedents is high because ADR can impair building of precedents. In civil law countries, the development of new law through case law is rare and confined to courts at the top of the judicial hierarchy. In practice, a body of case law that is consistently applied might develop with the ADR body if outcomes are publicly available.[46] To repeat, ADR bodies are good for facts and courts for the law. One advantage of ADR boards is specialists may decide a case, which could make the decision more accurate. Another point to consider is that the value of the awards can be strengthened by underlying systems

41 Regarding ADR's effectiveness, various studies have been done, but most of them proceeded from partisan perspectives and tended to draw conclusions consistent with their funders, Viitanen (2000), Meili (2010), p. 184.

42 See Lindblom (2008a), p. 86.

43 See Lindblom (2008a), p. 75.

44 See Lindblom (2008a), p. 73. G. Dari-Mattiaci, 'Access to Justice', University of Pavia, June 2010.

45 See Lindblom (2008a), p. 72.

46 For example, this is reported for the travel sector in the Netherlands; see interview with Ton Jongbloed, Professor of the Law of Enforcement and Seizure, University of Utrecht (Utrecht, 26 January 2011).

that ensure their enforceability (imaginable through courts or other players). One consideration is that the trader can pass on the costs of his voluntary participation in an ADR system to the consumer, which might ultimately put him at a disadvantage with traders who do not participate, but compete in the same market.

As a potential social benefit, ADR may induce settlement by making the defendant aware of the fact that a potential claimant is considering taking action. Whereas the goal in arbitration is generally a win-win situation, in legal proceedings a judgment is passed; one party wins and the other party loses.[47] But the outcome of an ADR decision is more of a compromise. The fact that compensation is usually granted is an incentive to initiate a lawsuit.

Administrative Costs Administrative costs for ADR procedures are lower than in the civil court because the cases are smaller and burdensome procedures like oral hearings are often not included.[48] Likewise, ADR has fewer requirements regarding evidence, and no lawyer needs to be involved. Nevertheless, as already set out under the agency issue, if coordination between this body and the civil court is unsatisfactory, costs can be duplicated. ADR body decisions may need to be checked at the court again, or the matter will be brought there independently. This duplicate effort might largely still be worthwhile, depending on how many cases the ADR body considers would otherwise be tried in civil court, and on how many new cases it triggers that would not have found a claimant in the civil court. As a last consideration regarding the optimal amount of enforcement, ADR's low costs may induce filing a complaint in situations in which the case would have been settled privately in the absence of ADR.[49] Importantly, the item administrative costs are not met entirely by the government, but also partly by traders, who might pass them on.

Conclusion ADR is beneficial to optimal allocation of risks because the costs of initiating a procedure are considerably lower than in the civil court. The procedure is fast. However, awards are generally weaker, and depending on the set-up, fewer

---

47 See B. Lindell, 'Alternative Dispute Resolution and the Administration of Justice – Basic Principles', *Scandinavian Studies in Law* 51 (2007): 311–44, p. 316.

48 See Shavell (1995), pp. 3, 12; Creutzfeldt-Banda (2012), p. 384. A recent study suggests time and cost savings in using ADR in federal government litigation for the US: L.B. Bingham et al., 'Dispute Resolution and the Vanishing Trial; Comparing Federal Government Litigation and ADR Outcomes', *Ohio State Journal on Dispute Resolution* 24.2 (2009): 225–62. In the conclusion, the authors acknowledge various limitations of the data set. The European Commission estimates that the introduction of quality ADR could lead to savings accounting for about 0.17 per cent of EU Gross Domestic Product (GDP): see European Commission, Executive Summary (2011), p. 9.

49 See Shavell (1995), p. 21.

remedies may be available than in civil court. ADR is in itself a funding mechanism. The potential for free riding essentially depends on the remedy sought.

Regarding optimal allocation of incentives, ADR cannot remedy some information asymmetries. Generally, no lawyer is involved in the procedure to generate this missing information. The ADR is not given investigative powers or the power of seizure and cases where the wrongdoer cannot be located have to be dismissed. More precisely, generally cases can be brought only against a predefined set of traders who have agreed to take part in an ADR in the first place. Law has further restricted access to the body for some cases (as to time limits). Capture is a serious issue and depends on the composition of the entity and the internal regulations. Frivolous lawsuits might be an issue because of ADR's low fees. However, the visibility of ADR decisions is lower. As lawyers are rarely involved, there are no agency issues; otherwise, the reasoning as set out for the civil court can be utilised. Duplication of enforcement efforts may occur, and, in particular, coordination with possible cases or appeals in civil courts must be handled carefully. Furthermore, and depending on the legal system and the value given to precedents, out-of-court settlements impede the further development of the law. This mechanism can also provide for compensation. ADR bodies are strong concerning expertise and less concerning a further development of the law.

Although ADR involves fewer administrative costs than courts, positive effects are generally likely, but depend on how many more cases ARD motivates, and how many of them have to be double checked by a court. Administrative costs then arise for the state and for traders.

In total, lower administrative costs suggest that remaining problems under optimal incentive and risk allocation should be solved. However, the low costs are caused in part by the ADR body's having few investigative powers. An ADR body is restricted to clear-cut cases and traceable traders, and a case cannot be taken up if more information needs to be generated. Experts involved may be strong on the facts.

Administrative Law Enforcement: Economic Strengths and Weaknesses

Turning to the realm of public law enforcement, an analysis of the costs and benefits of administrative and criminal law solutions is given.[50] The weaknesses of private law enforcement seem to suggest powerful economic arguments for enhancing public law enforcement in large parts of consumer law.[51] In instances where the market and private law fail, there may be a case for a regulatory intervention.[52] In particular, this seems to be the case where private law in its present structure

50 Any involvement of a public authority (such as an ombudsman) in court or consumer ADR procedures will be assessed under '*Group Litigation: Economic Strengths and Weaknesses*'.

51 See Van den Bergh (2007), pp. 191, 201.

52 See Ogus (1994), p. 30.

cannot generate certain information. A public law intervention may, however, be equally ineffective or too costly.

'Administrative enforcement' is law enforcement performed by an agency that can carry out monitoring and has some investigative powers. Such an agency can decide cases itself, refer cases to a court or defend cases in a court. There are basically no direct costs for the individual. Actions can be triggered by reporting or carried out on an own motion. Appeal is possible. Authorities may impose various sanctions, but usually do not grant compensation. There is clearly an interrelationship between *ex ante* action carried out by a regulator and *ex post* action as soon as harm has occurred and is detected.

Optimal Risk Allocation

Rational apathy

In general, public goods and rights relating to them should be enforced by public law.[53] Likewise, by dispersing damage over society as a whole, enforcement is basically rendered a public good, since individuals are rational when deciding not to carry out a claim.[54] With administrative law enforcement, the public as a financer assumes the risks involved in litigation. With widely dispersed harm, a case can be made for public enforcement (or also some form of group litigation) to uphold the threat of a lawsuit, as the individual clearly does not have an incentive to sue.[55]

An agency can act on its own motion, and to some extent is independent of the rational apathy problems that exist with individuals. Some form of reporting may be necessary to generate information.[56] In this instance, incentives for the individual to report need to be ensured and the related rational apathy may occur again. The benefits for individuals usually do not include compensation, which would be a strong motivating factor. The individual can calculate with the agency's superiority in generating certain information through its investigative powers. Where the individual is mainly interested in damages, incentives in this branch must be designed carefully to induce an individual to report there. Then again,

---

53 For example, see Collins (1999), p. 75, on the limits of private law in relation to public goods. Similar, attributing at least some characteristics of a public good to the provision of civil justice, see M.J. Trebilcock, 'Rethinking Consumer Protection Policy', *International Perspectives on Consumers' Access to Justice*, eds C.E.F. Rickett and T.G.W. Telfer (Cambridge: Cambridge University Press, 2003) 68–98, p. 80.

54 See Van Boom (2006), pp. 26, 29; F. Cafaggi and H-W. Micklitz, 'Collective Enforcement of Consumer Law: A Framework for Comparative Assessment', *European Review of Private Law* 16.3 (2008): 391–425, p. 398.

55 See Shavell (1984a), p. 167.

56 See M.G. Faure, *'Onbegrensd Toezicht?' Toezicht op Markt en Mededinging (Justitiele Verkenningen)*, ed. WODC (Den Haag: Boom Juridische Uitgevers, 2008) 84–104, p. 100.

there are hardly any costs involved in reporting. Monitoring may be an alternative source of information.

Free riding

In economic theory, the problem of free riding regarding public goods (for example, enforcement) can be remedied with the intervention of a public authority, provided that the nature of the action is to serve all.[57] An agency may act on its own motion, and the benefits then can be to all (apart from the defendant). If an agency is involved, free riding is rather unlikely because individuals are forced to contribute to the litigation expenses through taxes.[58] However, a discrepancy might exist in terms of who contributes and who profits from an action. Usually sanctions include fines or injunctions, but public authorities also may take cases to court to seek the remedies available there. If a competitor would reap benefits from an intervention higher than the individual consumer's benefits, the competitor might be more inclined to report and/or provide the public authority with information.

Funding

The enforcement of public law is a matter of the state's budget. The individual has fewer costs to bear because the state assumes a large part of the financing or even all of it. The state is supposedly the best risk bearer because it has numerous possibilities for pooling, more than any other player. With the fines it collects, a state may be able to finance an agency.[59] To balance enforcement costs and allocate them efficiently, some agencies require applicants or defendants to pay if their cases are lost or considered frivolous.

Optimal Provision of Incentives How can the enforcers' incentives in administrative law enforcement be optimised, and what problems are there?

Information asymmetry

If law infringements are difficult to discover, an agency's lower costs of information discovery can come in handy.[60] When information becomes highly technical, a public

57 See Ogus (1994), pp. 33.

58 See Van den Bergh (2008), p. 305.

59 See P. Sabbatini, 'Funding the Budget of a Competition Authority with Fines it Imposes' (2009).

60 See for consumer law and competition law: Van den Bergh (2007); A public enforcer has a lower cost of information discovery since it can use the power of the state – such as the threat of jail, the power of the police to conduct searches and seizures of evidence, clandestine electronic surveillance and under-cover agents, see Segal and Whinston (2006), p. 6. They refer to antitrust cases.

authority might be better equipped to gather it.[61] Technological developments such as information systems (databases) shift the efficiency arguments in favour of the public sector. Economies of scale in these situations generally support using the public law system, particularly if duplication of enforcement costs among private parties were to occur.[62] When locating wrongdoers, a public authority may have more powers and the ability to cooperate with other authorities (even increasingly with authorities across the border). Likewise, tracking online traders (digital investigation) requires certain particular investigative powers that are tools unavailable to individuals.[63] While not all authorities have the same number of powers, there is certainly a potential to equip them. Therefore, they can obtain information in a less costly way than an individual, who, for example, wants to track down a trader hiding online. The public agency has different tools at its disposal that the individual lacks. Public law enforcement allows for continuous information gathering through monitoring or market studies, which has an impact on the probabilities of detection and consequently conviction. Certain existing information asymmetries that private law cannot remedy could to some extent be outweighed by the involvement of a public agency.

These entities may lack private information (if individuals have no incentive to share it), which a reporting rule might alleviate to some extent.[64] Other ways to incentivise individuals to share their private information can be imagined. Using a decision of the public authority in a follow-on damage case in court might be one motivation. Because of the way that public agencies are typically structured, this cannot be done via the prospects of obtaining compensation directly.

Information asymmetries present in the buying situation can be reduced when pursuing monitoring and issuing warnings. In a way, the 'Akerlof scenario' – adverse selection that leads to quality deterioration – can be reduced.

Highly deterrent sanctions exist. Therefore, in cases with presumably low probabilities of detection and conviction, fines above the level of harm may

---

61 See Shavell (1993), p. 270; Hood, Rothstein and Baldwin (2001), p. 73.

62 See Landes and Posner (1975), p. 29: An example would be competition authorities that do not only have more resources, but also wide investigate powers that an individual could not make use of. Also economies of scope can speak in favour of the involvement of a public authority, see Trebilcock (2003), p. 84.

63 Future technological developments might render it indeed worthwhile to equip individuals or their lawyers with wider investigative powers. Low administrative (and other societal) costs might justify this at some point. For the time being societal costs are assumed not to outweigh the benefits of equipping every individual with wide investigative powers.

64 See W.H. Van Boom and M.B.M. Loos, 'Effective Enforcement of Consumer Law in Europe: Synchronizing Private, Public, and Collective Mechanisms', *Working Paper Series* (2008), p. 16; In competition law: leniency programs are for instance regarded as providing private information within public law enforcement structures, see Keske (2010), p. 20; Shavell (1993), pp. 259, 267. See on self-reporting: L. Kaplow and S. Shavell, 'Optimal Law Enforcement with Self-Reporting of Behavior', *The Journal of Political Economy* 102.3 (1994): 583–606.

uphold the deterring effect.[65] While there are generally not many sanctions against nonwealthy defendants, sanctions such as license revocation might be effective with regard to a judgment-proof wrongdoer.[66] A problem with fining traders is that they might anticipate these and include them upfront in the prices they calculate for consumers.[67]

Thus, unlike the manner in which private law enforcement is currently structured, administrative enforcement can be applied while no harm has yet occurred. Some actions, like market surveys or checks to determine whether a business provides accurate information on its website, can prevent certain harm and also enable the initiation of the lawsuit, which might not be possible solely by private law enforcement. This type of intervention can increase the deterrent effect because a legal response is enabled. Such a measure apparently leads to additional administrative costs.

Capture

As the name suggests, public officials work in the public interest. Social welfare is the benchmark in this analysis according to which cases have to be filtered and decisions taken. This determines the amount of consumer law enforcement that society can afford. When it comes to assessing public servants' behaviour and predictability, a rather severe issue in a public agency is the risk of capture of officials that leads to under-enforcement.[68] This is more dangerous, the more competences the agency has, and the extent to which welfare can be diluted depends on the importance of the case.[69] Regulation to separate competences either by different entities or different units may be warranted,[70] and the possibility

65 See Polinsky and Shavell (2005), p. 26. On low probabilities of detection, see also Landes and Posner (1975), p. 36. There is also the possibility to impose fines that exceed the harm.

66 See Trebilcock (2003), p. 84; Faure, Ogus and Philipsen (2009), p. 178, expand on the issue of licenses and how this can possibly have a higher deterrent effect for traders than imprisonment.

67 See Cseres (2012), p. 200 and the literature quoted there.

68 See Ogus (1994), p. 57.

69 See C. Tesauro and F. Russo, 'Unfair Commercial Practices and Misleading and Comparative Advertising: An Analysis of the Harmonization of EU Legislation in View of the Italian Implementation of the Rules', *Competition Policy International* 4.1 (2008): 192–222. See interview with Francesco Russo, Bonelli Erede and Pappalardo, Rome/Amsterdam Centre for Law and Economics (Rome, 23 April 2010). The Italian authority had not clearly defined its competences, and they were then stipulated in many appeals procedures.

70 See Cafaggi and Micklitz (2009), p. 406: 'In theory the use of public agencies to monitor and directly sanction would seem to be more effective than separating administrative monitoring from judicial enforcement. But especially in relation to cooperative enforcement, when the enforcer has to conclude agreements with the infringer,

of appeals and reviews (as generally given within administrative procedural law) may reduce the occurrence of this factor. Another measure is the case selection procedure and ways to challenge the inaction of the entity.

Frivolous lawsuits

Frivolous lawsuits are less of an issue with public law, at least in the classical sense, because individuals may at most report a behaviour without guarantees that a case will be taken up. The public official effectively filters which cases to dismiss and which cases to admit. Although the public official may be captured, this possibility can be mitigated by the appeal system.

In terms of the procedure, the danger of error costs depends on the complexity of the issues to be solved, and on the resources, expertise and experience of the public authority.[71] Capture might likewise be a reason for a wrong decision. For instance, occurrence of error costs is more likely in administrative enforcement compared with criminal law enforcement, because the decision-making process is less elaborate.[72] Therefore, naming and shaming by public authorities is regarded as dangerous. As a result, the established literature regarding criminal sanctions within the process of public administration will not be considered as a feasible option in this book.[73]

Agency issues

Principal-agent situations may occur on the side of the defendant and the defendant's lawyer.[74] According to its definition, a public authority works in the public interest. Society – again, viewed as the principal – may have costs and benefits from the work of the public officials, not least due to captured decision-making. The argument of duplication of enforcement costs through lack of coordination (discussed in the section on private law) also may be an issue with public agents if they investigate

---

the resort to an independent judiciary may ensure transparency and reduce capture. Thus the higher the use of cooperative enforcement, the more necessary it is to resort to separation between monitoring and enforcement'.

71 See Van den Bergh (2007), p. 195. See also Ogus (2004), p. 44 where he distinguished the burden of proof and procedural safeguards between criminal law and administrative law from high to low.

72 See Garoupa and Gomez-Pomar (2000), p. 5. The reason is the differently sophisticated processes that stand behind these sanctioning mechanisms; also Ogus, Faure and Philipsen (2006), pp. 47. Faure, Ogus and Philipsen (2009), p. 176, regarding the procedures at a public agency: 'Clearly, the more elaborate the procedures, the higher the administrative costs but also the lower the error costs'.

73 Another concern regarding the suitability of a public authority imposing costly (criminal) sanctions is the lack of impartial judges. The danger of capture *prima facie* does not match well with the high danger of error costs and the availability of higher (criminal) sanctions.

74 In appeal procedures, ultimately both parties might involve lawyers.

the same matter.[75] The severity of this issue clearly depends on the structure of the public sector and on the degree of coordination. Nevertheless, in the investigation and collection of information, economies of scale may prevail.[76] Duplication of costs also depends on whether all the competences are vested within the same entity or whether various entities have to coordinate the initiation of a lawsuit and adjudication.

An additional issue that does not necessarily have to be judged negatively from a social-welfare perspective is the possibility for individuals to use clarifications on law and fact by a public agency in an ADR case or in a private lawsuit in which they claim damages. However, the danger of over-deterrence is a given if a potential wrongdoer faces various responses of the legal system and should these collectively exceed the optimal sanction.[77]

An additional distinction between private and public enforcement is that the first works mainly from an *ex post* perspective.[78] However, public enforcement mainly takes an *ex ante* perspective (implying both monitoring and rule making).[79] Strictly speaking, any *ex ante* action aims at prevention rather than deterrence, although one complements the other. However, monitoring also could have an effect on deterrence because it also can lead to detection of infringements and thus be regarded as the first step in the sanctioning process. In some cases, *ex ante* actions are needed. For example, to remedy the deficiency that a consumer cannot detect harm prior to buying a product or signing a contract, public authorities must work proactively.[80] Market monitoring and measures that a public enforcer takes for society can remedy scenarios like the 'lemons market'. A public enforcer's stronger powers are an underlying threat in its customary, informal negotiations with traders, and can induce settlements.

As mentioned previously, it is not obvious that public agencies grant compensation that will influence victims' incentives. No matter how their intervention is triggered, these agencies have discretion and can take measures in the interest of society as a whole.

Administrative Costs A reason that administrative enforcement is preferred over private enforcement is the potentially lower administrative costs.[81] Again, maintenance costs as well as compliance costs are crucial.[82] Thus, unlike private enforcement, the main costs occur in the form of monitoring and detection: namely,

75 See J.Q. Wilson, *Bureaucracy – What Government Agencies Do and Why They Do It* (New York: Basic Books A division of HarperCollinsPublishers, 1989) about the working of the bureaucracy.

76 See Landes and Posner (1975), p. 29.

77 See Ogus (2004), p. 53.

78 See Van Boom (2006), p. 27.

79 See Cafaggi and Micklitz (2008), p. 417.

80 See Bowles, Faure and Garoupa (2008), p. 400.

81 Indicative: Ogus (2004), p. 49.

82 See Shavell (1984a), p. 364.

use of investigative powers.[83] Some of these costs are incurred even though no harm was inflicted, which also is different from private law enforcement. Then again, a public authority is generally not concerned with calculating and distributing damages. Regarding fines, arguments can be made for why fines are comparably less costly to administer, particularly fixed fines.[84] Administering the public entity can be more costly if various entities have to be coordinated. An appeal structure implemented internally and then via administrative courts is generally in place as well, and must be financed. While this analysis gives an indication, direct comparisons are sometimes difficult to make.

Conclusion In a certain sense, the state assumes a lot of risks regarding administrative law enforcement. The free riding mentality and rational apathy can be remedied, and only if reporting is an issue can they emerge again to a certain extent. Thought must be given to ways of incentivising people. Difficulties can arise where individuals are mainly interested in compensation that such an administrative agency cannot grant. In these situations, the individual might not be motivated to report. However, there may be ways to use the public agency's findings later on in court or other ways to induce individuals to report; it depends on the amount of damage at stake for the individual. Public agencies have other means of obtaining information regarding law violations. Public agencies have alternative sanctions that will uphold the deterrence effect when probabilities of detection and/or conviction are low. The allocation of risks is nicely solved because the state is assumed to be the best risk bearer, providing the most pooling options. Wrongdoers can be forced to contribute to the financing through fines.

The question remains how an entity selects the cases to pursue, and how to do so. Selection processes must be established in the body's governing regulations. Considering optimal incentives, many positive aspects emanate, particularly for investigative powers and information asymmetry. The danger of capture is severe. Depending on the extent of officials' discretion, frivolous lawsuits could be initiated on the agency's own motion or by individuals. Error costs in general have a high likelihood of occurring. In particular, the *ex ante* perspective leads to social-welfare benefits. Compensation is not the general goal of a public agency. Some sanctions can go against low probabilities of detection (revocation of a license or fines). Further social benefits and losses are duplication of costs because of bureaucratic procedures and lack of coordination. Additional benefits entailed in administrative law enforcement include some possibilities of naming and shaming (with qualifications) or *ex ante* involvement in monitoring and setting up regulations or guidelines.

83 See D. Wittman, 'Prior Regulation Versus Post Liability: The Choice between Input and Output Monitoring', *Journal of Legal Studies* 6 (1977): 193–212, p. 207; overall little empirical research has been done on regulatory agencies within consumer protection; see Meili (2010), p. 186.

84 See Faure, Ogus and Philipsen (2009), p. 175.

Regarding administrative costs, the picture is difficult to draw. Much depends on how many entities are set up and to what extent they use investigative powers. The degree to which a public agency engages in proactive monitoring or market surveys also has a decisive impact.

In total, compared with private law enforcement, administrative law enforcement has a high likelihood of remedying the three main weaknesses – rational apathy, free riding and information asymmetries – particularly when the individual's main interest is not compensation. Significantly, the loss of a deterrent effect, because of a low detection rate, can be remedied, and investigative powers generate considerable information to reduce information asymmetries in lawsuits, not least by *ex ante* measures. In reality, the extent of investigative powers available for an entity differ, but there is a potential to be granted these powers. These advantages have to be weighed particularly against the dangers of capture and of error costs.

Criminal Law Enforcement: Economic Strengths and Weaknesses

Some consumer law cases can amount to criminal offences (in the area of product safety, for example),[85] which is why some European legal systems rely on criminal sanctions to enforce consumer protection laws.[86] The public prosecutor is central to the functioning of the criminal process. Once a crime is reported, the matter is investigated (with the help of the police). Judges may authorise certain investigative powers, and the criminal court makes the judgment, after the prosecution brings the case as the plaintiff. A wide variety of sanctions exist (the procedure might even allow for dealing with compensation claims), judges are supposedly impartial and an elaborate appeal system is in place. The individual who reported the crime basically does not bear administrative costs.

In practice, administrative and criminal enforcement are heavily interlinked in that criminal sanctions complement most administrative sanctions (as a backup in case of noncompliance with administrative rules). Coexistence can also be found.[87]

The literature regularly discusses the criminal law system in relation to administrative law enforcement. Generally, individuals' incentives for taking part in this enforcement process are not considered and are tentatively covered in the following analysis.

Below are an analysis of the strengths and the weaknesses of criminal enforcement, possible enhancements and the interrelation with private enforcement.

85 See Cartwright (2007), p. 4.

86 See Cafaggi and Micklitz (2009), p. 408.

87 See Bowles, Faure and Garoupa (2008), p. 408.

Optimal Risk Allocation

Rational apathy

In criminal law enforcement, the state is the risk bearer, which is desirable for cases in which the individual does not have an incentive to sue, particularly those cases involving dispersed, trifling damage.[88]

Private parties are often important in reporting information to the state: namely, the police, public prosecution offices or courts.[89] In order for criminal law enforcement to be triggered, an 'initial suspicion'[90] that a crime has occurred must be reported to the police; the public prosecutor then investigates and takes action. Even if the individual does not act, the public prosecutor may initiate a case, which is important when rational apathy might exist. If the individual feels that there are no benefits from reporting – notwithstanding the legal obligation to report certain crimes – the individual's rational apathy may impede reporting. Some may even fear retaliation if they report a crime.[91] In some jurisdictions, the possibility of being granted damages via the criminal law branch (or close cooperation with other enforcement bodies to ensure compensation) may contribute to the willingness of the party to sue.

Generally, a victim who joins the prosecution as plaintiff needs a lawyer. Legal aid provisions or legal insurances may be utilised and, if found guilty, the accused must often bear all the costs.

Free riding

The effect on free riding in criminal court proceedings is unclear. Other individuals will inevitably profit if a wrongdoer is sent to prison and, therefore, is no longer able to continue wrongful business activities. However, victims need to have an 'interest' in the case in order to report. There is also the option of an own motion; thus, the system is not dependant on a reporting action. Therefore, passivity in reporting cannot lead to a lack of criminal law enforcement. Victims do not bear the majority of costs of criminal proceedings and the reasoning is similar to that involving a public agency. In practice, failure to report certain crimes may be punishable.

---

88 See Expertentagung, 'Wilhelminenberg Gespräche' (2011). Collective actions at a criminal court are discussed in particular because they reduce the individual's cost risks.

89 See Shavell (1993), p. 260.

90 Term 'reasonable suspicion' is used in Hodgson and Roberts (2010), p. 67.

91 See Shavell (1993), p. 268. However, as Van den Bergh (2007) argued (p. 190), the retributive element in consumer law applies only to a minor extent, and this also can be set in relation to the probability that the fear of retaliation is a strong disincentive to sue.

Funding

State budgets largely finance criminal law enforcement systems. The state is supposedly the best risk bearer with more possibilities for pooling than any other player. Individuals can have legal insurance for criminal law cases and funds for victim compensation exist in some countries, which is important if the victim joins the case as a plaintiff. Importantly, if found guilty, the accused must pay all the costs of the procedure; otherwise, in the event of an acquittal, the state takes financial responsibility. In some cases, the state may grant compensation to an accused who is acquitted.[92]

Optimal Provision of Incentives

Information asymmetry

To a large extent, the intervention of criminal law enforcement can remedy existing information asymmetries. Criminal law enforcement's wide investigative powers, particularly the police force, provide a number of advantages for generating information that the individual may not obtain. In particular, where other enforcement systems would be stymied, criminal law enforcement (the police) is able to locate and apprehend certain wrongdoers and initiate a case. Among the available investigative powers, those pertaining to criminal law go the furthest and include tools to which an individual does not have access. However, resources are crucial to utilise the additional investigative powers.

High sanctions are available in criminal law enforcement, which provide deterrence when probabilities of detection or conviction are low.[93] Criminal law typically deals with the cases for which the likelihood of apprehending and convicting offenders is assumed to be low.[94] An important advantage of criminal law enforcement is that the system's various available sanctions (including nonmonetary sanctions only criminal law enforcement can provide) serve to remedy the issue of a judgment-proof defendant.[95]

Criminal law sanctions often produce more private opportunity costs, which is why they have a higher deterrent effect than purely monetary sanctions.[96]

92 See for instance: Gesetz über Entschädigung für Strafverfolgungsmaßnahmen (Act on Compensation for Wrongful Prosecution, StrEG).

93 See Polinsky and Shavell (2005), p. 26. On low probabilities of detection, see also: Landes and Posner (1975), p. 36. There is also the possibility to impose fines that exceed the harm.

94 See Shavell (1993), p. 275.

95 See Bowles, Faure and Garoupa (2008), p. 402; Shavell (1985), p. 1247; Shavell (2004), p. 544.

96 See Bowles, Faure and Garoupa (2008), p. 398.

Imprisonment, for instance, is essential as a deterrent[97] and may be the adequate sanction when the probability of detection and conviction is low and the likelihood of defendants being judgment proof is high.[98] Imprisonment also is an advantageous sanction when the benefits emanating from the crime are very high.[99] The more extensive the harm, the more society values deterrence; hence, the greater willingness to bear the costs of imprisonment.[100]

Criminal procedural law differs from other procedural law in that it requires a high standard of proof that has implications for the notion of 'causality', which has positive implications for the avoidance of error costs.[101]

Capture

Because judges who impose sanctions are believed to be impartial,[102] the issue of capture does not apply here. Furthermore, adjudication and prosecution/investigation are separate in criminal law enforcement; in other words, the public prosecutor and the courts are independent of each other.[103] As stated, it is more difficult to set the optimal incentives for impartiality than to induce a bias. Regarding the public prosecutor, capture issues might well be present in the selection of cases to pursue.

Frivolous lawsuits

Frivolous lawsuits are unlikely in the criminal law enforcement system; however, damage can be inflicted if the initial suspicion is based on wrong arguments. Reputational damage occurs in apprehending someone and it is only secondary that the case may never be prosecuted because the allegations could not be confirmed. In this instance, error costs might already apply if the person is innocent.

During the procedure, error costs can be remedied to a large extent by criminal procedural law, which is more accurate compared with administrative law. Criminal procedural law involves an appeal structure, a standard of proof 'beyond reasonable

97 See Polinsky and Shavell (2005a), p. 27. However, if a person is old or dying from a disease, imprisonment cannot fulfil its full purpose; see Shavell (2004), p. 532. Here, for example, incapacitation measures are necessary and desirable.

98 See Bowles, Faure and Garoupa (2008), p. 405.

99 See for instance: Bowles, Faure and Garoupa (2008), p. 406; Polinsky and Shavell (2005), pp. 31, 60.

100 See Shavell (1985), p. 1244.

101 See G.S. Becker and G.J. Stigler, 'Law Enforcement, Malfeasance, and Compensation of Enforcers', *Journal of Legal Studies* 3 (1974): 1–18, p. 3: Becker argued that with an 'increasingly thorough and expensive investigation, one can determine with increasing precision the probable behavior of a given person'.

102 See Collins (1999), p. 82.

103 See Bowles, Faure and Garoupa (2008), p. 407.

doubt' and consideration of the mental element.[104] Because of the high standard of proof in criminal law, there is a lower probability of convicting the innocent.[105] Error costs depend on the accuracy of procedural law, and the more accurate it is, the less often errors occur. (Typically, criminal law[106] has more sophisticated procedures than administrative law[107] for standards of proof, hearings, rules on evidence and so on.) When errors do occur, the severity of costs to the accused or the victim depends on the severity of the sanctions. (Criminal law enforcement typically includes more severe sanctions than administrative law enforcement.[108]) Stigma, if it is involved in a sanctioning mechanism, leads to higher error costs. In general, the negative consequences of a wrongful conviction, particularly imprisonment, are worse than those of a wrongful acquittal.[109] Significantly, the reasons that perfect criminal law enforcement is impossible (even though it seems to make up for all the weaknesses of the previous mechanisms) has to do with these error costs, mistakes that always happen, certain people who will not respect the law, other individuals who cannot be deterred and administrative costs.[110]

Agency issues

The principal-agent relationship between accused and lawyer is assumed in criminal law enforcement and is characterised by information asymmetries. Likewise, principal-agent issues may occur if the victim joins the procedure as plaintiff with a lawyer.

Again, the idea of furthering social welfare is the measure when assessing these enforcement mechanisms. Regarding duplication of enforcement costs, criminal law might score positively because several victims can participate in one trial.

It also holds true here that in some jurisdictions there is the possibility for individuals to use clarifications on law and fact by a criminal court or by an administrative authority in a private lawsuit in which they claim damages, or that they can connect a damage claim to the criminal case. Once more, over-deterrence is a danger if the optimal sanction is exceeded. Depending on the respective legal system, another benefit may be the provision of compensation, if this can be dealt with within the criminal law branch.

---

104 See Bowles, Faure and Garoupa (2008), p. 405; R. Galbiati and N. Garoupa, 'Keeping Stigma out of Administrative Law: An Explanation of Consistent Beliefs', *Supreme Court Economic Review* 15 (2007): 273–83, 274; K.N. Hylton and V.S. Khanna, 'Toward an Economic Theory of Pro-Defendant Criminal Procedure', *Discussion Paper No. 318.3* (2001).

105 See Posner (2000), p. 201 [410].

106 See Bowles, Faure and Garoupa (2008), p. 405; Galbiati and Garoupa (2007), 274.

107 See Garoupa and Gomez-Pomar (2000), p. 5.

108 See Van den Bergh (2007), p. 196.

109 See Van den Bergh and Visscher (2008a), p. 36.

110 If an individual can be deterred by a system involving lower administrative costs, there is no need to revert to the criminal law. Administrative costs of criminal law can make up a considerable share of societal costs.

Another benefit to society of a criminal law enforcement sanction is the degree of stigma attached to it, compared with administrative sanctions.[111] People may choose not to interact with someone who has been criminally convicted. This stigma arguably serves to increase the deterrent. However, imprisonment is very costly to society because of the expense of operating prisons and the utility loss suffered by those imprisoned.[112] While the accused is responsible for paying the costs of the procedure, a prison is a burden on the state budget; an imprisoned individual contributes little to social welfare.

Because criminal law enforcement deals with punishment, the wrongdoer might have to pay damages on top of being punished.[113]

Another important distinction between criminal law and private law enforcement is that under criminal law attempts to do harm can be sanctioned, whereas under contract and tort law, legal consequences apply only where harm occurs (the breach of a contract or a tort).[114]

Administrative Costs The consensus is that criminal law enforcement involves very high administrative costs because it includes an appeal structure that supports accuracy and avoidance of error costs.[115] Therefore, conviction costs are higher and sanctions, mainly imprisonment, are expensive.[116] Furthermore, additional resources are required when the criminal law enforcement considers the mental

---

111 See E. Rasmusen, 'Stigma and Self-Fulfilling Expectations of Criminality', *Journal of Law and Economics* 39 (1996): 519–43, p. 520; however, Rasmusen argued that stigma is context-dependant: Bowles, Faure and Garoupa (2008), p. 406; Cartwright (2007), p. 13. 'Note on 'Shame, Stigma and Crime: Evaluating the Efficacy of Shaming Sanctions in Criminal Law', *Harvard Law Review* 116 (2003): 2186–207, p. 2199, putting forward a positive effect for 'career criminals'. For an elaboration on the economic criteria to use criminal law, see Svatikova (2012).

112 See Shavell (1993), p. 258. Imprisonment is more costly than the imposition of monetary sanctions, and is socially very costly; see Becker (1968), p. 180.

113 See Bowles, Faure and Garoupa (2008), p. 402; R. Cooter, 'Prices and Sanctions', *Columbia Law Review* 84 (1984): 1523–60.

114 See Shavell (2004), p. 571.

115 See S. Shavell, 'Economic Analysis of Litigation and the Legal Process', *NBER Working Papers National Bureau of Economic Research, Inc.9697* (2003), p. 49; Parisi (2000), p. 290.

116 See Becker (1968), p. 180. Costs of imprisonment include expenditures for guards, supervisory personnel, buildings, food and so on; Ogus (2004), p. 45: 'The costs increase very sharply'. See also Faure, Ogus and Philipsen (2009), p. 167: 'It is clear that some criminal penalties, such as imprisonment, are more expensive to apply than administrative or civil penalties. However, also the process costs are higher: The procedural requirements of criminal liability make it much more costly than administrative and civil procedures'.

element of the accused.[117] In addition, and depending on the legal system, compensation must be calculated and distributed.

Conclusion Considering optimal risk allocation, considerable costs and risks in a criminal procedure are allocated to the state. The allocation of risks is resolved smoothly, as the state is assumed to be the best risk bearer, providing the most pooling options. Victims can join in the procedure and there generally are provisions for suing for damages.

Criminal law enforcement offers a number of positive aspects of optimal incentives. Available investigative powers remedy many of the information asymmetry cases. Criminal law also remedies the judgment-proof problem through nonmonetary sanctions. Capture is unlikely with criminal judges and likewise the danger of frivolous lawsuits is low. Then again, the public prosecutor could be captured. However, initiating a procedure against an innocent person can inflict some damage. The danger of error costs is low, but if they occur, they may be serious because of the system's costly sanctions. Principal-agent issues occur between accused and lawyers and on the side of the victim with her lawyer as well if the victim joins the procedures. There are a number of social benefits that no other enforcement mechanism has, such as stigma or serving other objectives like incapacitation.

However, criminal law enforcement carries the highest administrative costs, and, therefore, it is hardly feasible to advocate a general use of this branch of law for optimal deterrence.

In total, in comparison to private law enforcement, criminal law enforcement is likely to rectify the three weaknesses of rational apathy, free riding and information asymmetries. Criminal law enforcement contains unique comparative advantages in that it resolves the issue of the low detection and conviction rates and is able to compensate victims. Similarly, it remedies the judgment-proof problem. The low detection rate and the insolvency risk are the most important reasons to seek sanctions such as imprisonment.

The reduction of error costs is another crucial difference with administrative law enforcement, and regarding administrative costs, those of the criminal law system are higher than those of administrative law enforcement. In addition, criminal law can be used as a threat to civil servants if they do not comply with the requirements of their tasks.

117 See Galbiati and Garoupa (2007), p. 274; Garoupa and Gomez-Pomar (2000), p. 4: An administrative agency neglects the mental states of an offender. Overall it should be left mainly as an underlying threat, according to Ogus (2004), concentrating on the relation between administrative law enforcement and criminal law enforcement.

Group Litigation: Economic Strengths and Weaknesses

Group litigation is a powerful device to enhance private law enforcement.[118] In this book, the representation by a class lawyer typical in the US is discussed only to a minor extent because the core issue in Europe is 'group litigation' by representatives.[119] 'Group litigation' is defined as any representative action before a court or agency that is primarily carried out by an association or a state authority, which typically have better suited ability to collect information. Group litigation subsumes different forms of bundling similar interests into one legal proceeding. The variations are manifold, and, importantly, different types of remedies may be sought.

In this section, the public agency's function to pursue litigation is discussed rather than its internal sanctioning powers considered in the section on administrative law enforcement. The question to consider is how does group litigation compare to the strengths and weaknesses of individual litigation?

Case management devices for a judge, such as joinder proceedings, are excluded from this theoretical exercise.[120] The judgment of such a proceeding is binding for all, but the plaintiffs still must initiate legal action individually in the first place. Test case/lead case procedures selected from a bundle of similar claims also are not considered.

Optimal Risk Allocation Initiating group litigation can be a solution for various risk allocation problems, particularly in private individual litigation.

Rational apathy

Group litigation is a potential remedy for rational apathy[121] as economies of scale are achieved and the risk of uncertainty is spread (risk sharing[122]). A group of claimants

118 See Stuyck et al. (2007).

119 The class action model is prevalent in the US, Canada, Australia and Sweden, C. Hodges, 'Collective Actions'. *The Oxford Handbook of Empirical Legal Research*, eds P. Cane and H.M. Kritzer (Oxford: Oxford University Press, 2010) 705–28, p. 707.

120 For example, see Stuyck et al. (2007), p. 263, in which the authors excluded these devices from their study on collective relief as they are to be regarded as a specific feature of individual ordinary court proceedings; case management tools for judges.

121 See Schäfer (2000), p. 186; H-W. Micklitz and A. Stadler, 'The Development of Collective Legal Actions in Europe, Especially in German Civil Procedure', *European Business Law Review* 17 (2006): 1473–503, p. 1476 or Stuyck et al. (2007); Becker and Stigler (1974), p. 13. Citizens would be more motivated to sue if they could enforce their titles together with others concerned, see European Commission, Special Eurobarometer n°195, European Union citizens and access to justice (2004), http://ec.europa.eu/consumers/redress/reports_studies/eurobarometer_11-04_en.pdf, last accessed: 31 March 2013, p. 38.

122 Risk-aversion is weighed higher than over-optimism that can also be present in litigation, see S. Keske, A. Renda and R.J. Van den Bergh, 'Financing and Group Litigation',

also has more resources to investigate more deeply and to obtain better quality legal advice.[123] As a result, the rational apathy is reduced in cases of small individual harm. However, a sufficiently high number of participants must be guaranteed,[124] or the representative or a lead plaintiff may refrain from suing. It also increases the deterrent effect. Group litigation has different structures that affect participation: In an opt-out procedure, the number of participants is usually higher than in an opt-in procedure, but the largest number can be achieved via a mandatory procedure.[125] Generally, damages increase as more victims participate and a public player or a consumer association may finance the procedural costs. Also, in a class action, attorney fees decrease on average because one joint lawsuit is pursued. In cases of very small damage claims, in which a consumer's rational apathy applies, the class action could fail, even though it is most needed here.[126] Economies of scale might not be achieved, particularly if damages have to be individually assessed and distributed. The same can happen with a representative action. This might look differently if taxpayers' money is used or the defendant can be confidently charged with the procedural costs. Alternative remedies can be striven for. In an optimal scenario, all representatives weigh the societal benefits against their costs, and then decide whether and where to bring a case (see Chapter 5).

Free riding

If those who want to benefit from an action can be required to contribute to the proceedings, group litigation can remedy the free riding problem that prevents lawsuits from being pursued.[127] By the same token, those who do not participate cannot receive the benefits of the achieved judgment. To serve this purpose, single actions can be prohibited by law or their cost can be increased to discourage them

---

New Trends in Financing Civil Litigation – A Legal, Empirical and Economic Analysis, eds M.L. Tuil and L.T. Visscher (Cheltenham: Edward Elgar, 2010) 57–91.

123 See Van den Bergh and Visscher (2008b), p. 19.

124 See R.J. Van den Bergh and S. Keske, 'Rechtsökonomische Aspekte der Sammelklage', *Auf dem Weg zu einer Europäischen Sammelklage?*, eds M. Casper et al. (München: Sellier. European Law Publishers, 2009) 17–40, p. 22.

125 For a more detailed overview of all the possible cross-effects, see Van den Bergh and Keske (2009), p. 23. See also Keske (2010). If only very few individuals drop out it will be particularly those that see a more promising result in an individual suit. These are probably the ones that suffered the highest damage and whose exit can have a detrimental effect on the remaining group, see Van den Bergh and Keske (2009), p. 25. The monopolistic nature of the mandatory procedure may generate an own efficiency loss according to Cafaggi and Micklitz (2008), p. 420; D. Rosenberg, 'Mandatory-Litigation Class Action: The Only Option for Mass Tort Actions', *Harvard Law Review* 115 (2002): 829–97, who creates a proposal for a mandatory class action.

126 See Posner (2011) regarding class actions, p. 785.

127 See Van den Bergh and Visscher (2008b), pp. 9, 18.

once group litigation is initiated.[128] If an ombudsman is in place, the public purse pays the costs, although results might not be achieved for all taxpayers. Similarly, a consumer association might achieve a judgment purely for its members who pay membership fees.[129]

However, seriousness of a free riding problem depends on the outcome of the case: if the result is an injunction, a reform or a price reduction, free riding problems will remain an issue.[130] It might not always be possible to prevent nonmembers of a consumer association from free riding. Overall the design of the case is crucial here. For instance, under an opt-out scheme, generally those who prefer to free ride must become active and leave the claim.[131]

An aspect of group litigation that mitigates free riding is that most proceedings end in an out-of-court settlement,[132] which reduces the ability to profit from the outcome if one was not party to the proceeding.

Funding

Any form of group litigation reduces the individual's financial burden, although funding the actions still can be a problem. American class actions that work via contingency fees have suffered a bad press.[133] Contingency fees have been criticised for leading to a divergence between the clients' interests and those of the lawyer because contingency fee regulations give the lawyer a personal interest. Opinions differ on the optimal fee system.[134] Contingency fees are practically nonexistent in Europe.

---

128 See Van den Bergh and Visscher (2008b), p. 21.

129 See G.J. Stigler, 'Free Riders and Collective Action: An Appendix to Theories on Economic Regulation', *The Bell Journal of Economics and Management Science* 5.2 (1974): 359–65, p. 360; see Van den Bergh (2008), p. 288.

130 See Van den Bergh and Keske (2009), p. 36: They argue that free riding is one of the biggest remaining problems with representative actions as there will be a lot of ways in which nonmembers can profit from proceedings (such as forced price reductions).

131 See Van den Bergh and Keske (2009), p. 25.

132 See Schäfer (2000), p. 192.

133 See Van den Bergh and Visscher (2008b), p. 23. A number of conditions in the US legal landscape distinguish its class actions from those of the EU, from the powers of the judiciary and its relationship to the legislature, to jury trials, to discovery rules, to attorneys' fee structure, see Calabresi and Schartz (2011), p. 170. In practice, after many years of experience with class actions many safeguards have been added to the system that do not justify classifying US class actions generically as bad, as discussed at the 5th Global Class Action Conference (The Hague, 8–9 December 2011).

134 See Stephen and Love (2000), p. 1001; Schäfer (2000): S. Issacharoff and G.P. Miller, *Will Aggregate Litigation Come to Europe?*, 2008) 1–29; L.A. Bebchuk and A. Guzman, 'How Would you Like to Pay for that? The Strategic Effects of Fee Arrangements on Settlement Terms', *Harvard Negotiation Law Review* 1 (1996): 53–65; A.M. Polinsky and D. Rubinfeld, 'A Note on Settlements under the Contingent Fee Method

Another question concerns the financing of associations because public and private financing elicit different risk-taking behaviour. With public bodies that take up cases, the decisions depend on the budget at their disposal. Then again, publicly funded bodies are generally regarded as the best risk bearer because they have several pooling options. In some countries, consumer associations are relieved of part of the court fees.[135] More developments in this area can be expected as more countries experiment with these types of actions.

The representative's cost–benefit analysis regarding litigation is crucial to determining which law enforcement avenue to pursue because these avenues have different costs (See Chapter 5).

Optimal Provision of Incentives

Information asymmetry

Group litigation can have positive effects in terms of consumers' information deficiencies in relation to the seller or producer. The role of a public authority in this regard has already been outlined. Generally speaking, consumer associations have detailed knowledge concerning consumer protection laws and can easily identify law infringements and give early warning.[136] Similar to a public entity's ability to do *ex ante* monitoring, associations may engage in certain kinds of market surveys to generate more information. The detection rate with group litigation may be higher with certain kinds of violations if consumer attention can be directed to the problem. A mass lawsuit also may attract more publicity, decreasing the chances of escaping conviction.

Group litigation's ability to remedy other information deficits, such as the location of the trader, depends on the powers of the representative authority and the body before which the action takes place. The body receiving the case may also be able to carry out investigations.

Capture

The representative authorities are exposed to all kinds of influences and interests to which they may succumb. If the representative is a consumer association, the danger of capture may be particularly high if the case involves widespread loss and members

---

of Compensating Lawyers', *International Review of Law and Economics* 22 (2002): 217–25, Shavell (2004), p. 435.

135 This is the case in Spain; see interview with Asociación de Usuarios de la Comunicación (Spanish Association of Communication Users, AUC) (Madrid, 23 November 2011). However, consumer associations must pay the costs of the other party if they lose.

136 See Van den Bergh and Visscher (2008b), p. 17.

have either little control over the association or simply no interest.[137] (Of course, consumer associations generally work in the consumers' interest to start with.)

To assess the scope of external influences, picture the association's involvement as a lengthening of the agency chain.[138] There is even a danger of fake consumer associations that are actually captured by industry group interests.[139] Lawyers might use them as vehicles as well. A public agency also may be captured (see '*Administrative Law Enforcement: Economic Strengths and Weaknesses*'). Hence, capture may be a problem for representative authorities as well as law enforcement bodies that execute the action (see Section on capture of ADR personnel or public agencies in particular).

Frivolous lawsuits

Group litigation carries the danger of frivolous or unmeritorious lawsuits[140] and the reputational harm that results may be substantial.[141] Group litigation generally causes higher damage than single lawsuits. Representative actions or class actions can be initiated to attract more media attention and recruit new members (in the case of consumer associations).

Group litigation generally leads to fewer contradictory judgments, although error costs can be aggravated. Huge error costs can occur for society, as an erroneous result will be spread to all defendants or claimants.[142]

Attention must be paid to where the action is taking place and the accuracy of the applicable procedural law. As soon as reputational issues arise, companies may be more inclined to settle than to risk litigation in court.

Agency issues

The major issue regarding disturbance of incentives is the principal-agent problem and the problem is more severe in group litigation because a large group can scarcely monitor the agent, nor do they have the knowledge. Interests within the group might also be dispersed. As a preliminary conclusion, agency problems arise regardless of who acts on behalf of consumers:[143] a lawyer, an association or a public authority (in the latter case, a lawyer receives instructions from the

137 See Van den Bergh (2008), p. 294; Schäfer (2000), p. 199.

138 See Schäfer (2000), p. 197.

139 In Italy, for instance, two associations come to mind, according to an interview with the Italian consumer association Unione Nazionale Consumatori (UNC) (Rome, 7 May 2010).

140 A formal model on incentives for frivolous suits was developed by Rosenberg and Shavell (1985). For Europe, see Schäfer (2000).

141 See Van den Bergh and Visscher (2008b), p. 24; similarly, see Schäfer (2000), p. 184.

142 See Posner (2011), p. 787.

143 See Cafaggi and Micklitz (2008), p. 401; Van den Bergh (2008), p. 290.

respective body).[144] In the end, a single person or group takes over the lead, acting on behalf of the others. In collective (class) actions, problems may arise between lead plaintiff, lawyer and passive group members; in a representative action, they may occur between the association or public authority, group members or interested parties, lawyers and possible third parties.[145] In each setting, the principal-agent problem stems from the fact that the interests of the representative and those represented may not necessarily merge because the representative may have its own interest[146] and that interest may have developed out of capture.

Generally, consumer associations may be less motivated by monetary interests,[147] which may mitigate their susceptibility to capture. Then again, they represent consumers and not necessarily the public interest. The public agency may collude with the defendant to achieve an early settlement to reduce the company's reputational damage.[148] Out-of-court solutions may be preferred to litigation because they have lower enforcement costs, but if one party is pressured into settlement, the outcome will not be optimal. Firms that enjoy an extremely solid reputation are particularly vulnerable to this scenario.[149]

The severity of agency problems rises if the number of represented people increases and their interests lack homogeneity.[150]

From a social-welfare viewpoint, group litigation provides economies of scale that mitigate possible duplication of enforcement costs.[151] However, duplication may take place if class races – various class lawyers making investments in trying to attract the same case – occur.[152] In rare cases, various consumer associations may invest in the same case. Potentially, compensation of victims can result from group litigation, which has a positive effect on incentives.

144 See Van den Bergh (2008), p. 299; Cafaggi and Micklitz (2008), p. 411, regarding consumer associations.

145 It will work out in favour of mitigating the problem if the lawyer has an interest in being hired repeatedly

146 See Van den Bergh and Visscher (2008b), p. 23, regarding class actions.

147 See Van den Bergh (2008), p. 293.

148 See A. Harel and A. Stein, 'Law and Economics at the Animal Farm: Offering a New Solution to the Class Action Agency Problem' (2001).

149 See Schäfer (2000), p. 190: The author called tendencies of meritless and opportunistic attacks on innocent parties the 'theory of capture'.

150 See Schäfer (2000), p. 199; J.C. JR Coffee, 'Class Wars: The Dilemma of the Mass Tort Class Action', *Columbia Law Review* 95.6 (1995): 1343–465, p. 1414; S.P. Koniak and G.M. Cohen, 'Under Cloak of Settlement', *Virginia Law Review* 82 (1996): 1051–270, p. 1113; Cafaggi and Micklitz (2008), p. 411.

151 See Schäfer (2000), p. 186; Micklitz and Stadler (2006), p. 1476 or Stuyck et al. (2007); Becker and Stigler (1974), p. 13. M. Olson, *The Logic of Collective Action: Public Goods and the Theory of Groups*, 2nd ed. (Cambridge, Mass.: Harvard University Press, 1971), showed that in specific circumstances individuals' uncoordinated actions may be less efficient than coordinated action.

152 See Keske (2010), p. 126.

Administrative Costs In a way, administrative enforcement costs of group litigation are comparable to costs of litigating individual cases. However, group litigation has an economic advantage over individual litigation in procedural efficiency, and, thus, lower costs.[153] If cases with the same legal and factual settings can be decided through one judgment that has a binding effect on other decisions, costs may be reduced.

However, the group litigation procedures entail more costs than individual cases. They usually require a great deal more time because additional legal control mechanisms require an increased involvement of lawyers and judges.[154] These additional costs could outweigh economies of scale. Particularly high costs are incurred in damage cases. Group litigation may guarantee cases that would otherwise not have been filed (because of rational apathy), and, thus, increase overall enforcement costs. These increased administrative costs may not be desirable, but could be outweighed by other societal benefits that emanate from group litigation. The optimal enforcement level is the benchmark.

Class actions are often costly to litigate because of high court fees (and often lawyers' fees) and costs linked to the certification of the class and the distribution of damages.[155] The preparatory work for a public agency and consumer associations also is very costly.[156] Control mechanisms – typically introduced by regulation – create additional costs that are discussed in the conclusion.

Overall, administrative costs of an enforcement procedure involving group litigation depend strongly on the court or agency before which the litigation takes place. These costs may be impeding or may need to be justified by high societal benefits, particularly if involvement in criminal cases is considered. (Some public agencies can act as prosecutors.) Furthermore, the remedy that is sought is crucial. Injunctions require less preparation and accuracy regarding the exact amount of damage suffered.[157]

---

153 See Van den Bergh and Keske (2009), p. 26.

154 See Scottish Law Commission, 'Multi-Party Actions, Report under a reference under section 3(1) (e) of the Law Commissions Act 1965', *Scottish Law Commission No. 154*, Edinburgh, HMSO (1996), p. 9; Duggan (2003), p. 55, indirect costs will be increased in particular because of the complexity of, in this case, class actions. However, it minimises other class members' indirect costs [indirect here meaning information costs, opportunity costs, emotional costs …]. This was confirmed in an interview with Organización de Consumidores y Usuarios (the Spanish consumer association, OCU) (Madrid, 16 November 2011).

155 See Renda et al. (2007), p. 570.

156 The Swedish Consumer Ombudsman reported that in the one group action that they initiated they worked approximately 300 hours before the case even started; see interview with Gunnar Larsson, Swedish Consumer Ombudsman and head of the Consumer Authority (Stockholm, 25 August 2009).

157 This was confirmed in an interview with OCU (Madrid, 16 November 2011).

Conclusion Group litigation has a number of advantages for reducing rational apathy among individuals and possibly free riding, depending on the group design and the remedy sought. The potential for free riding depends on whether the action allows only those people who contribute to profit from the proceeding (for instance membership privileges). Group litigation is a funding solution for some cases of rational apathy.

Regarding optimal risk allocation, very important arguments can be made for why an enhancement of private enforcement through group litigation may lead to considerable efficiency gains for society. Nevertheless, even if the individual is unburdened, the costs may be too high for an association or a public authority to pursue the claim. Public funding, legal aid and insurance for representatives must be guaranteed to relieve the financial burden, which is related to where the claim is brought. The representative also must weigh the costs and benefits in selecting where to pursue an action and which system to use (if there is a choice). However, there is a limit at which spreading the costs (for minor damage) is no longer worthwhile. This would depend on the remedies that are made available and on the costs needed for the preparation of the respective action.

The outcomes regarding optimal incentives are much weaker for group litigation.[158] The agency issues are most prominently severe and the interests pursued can be captured interests. The higher the monetary values at stake, the greater the capture problem. Thus, capture is typically a bigger problem with mass actions than individual actions. The danger of capture is assumed to be particularly high where the loss is widespread and represented individuals are heterogeneous and, therefore, have little control over the representative or simply no interest. In addition, group litigation's higher monetary values and potentially greater harm to the defendant increase the risk of frivolous lawsuits and their emanating damage. Importantly, as with public law enforcement, some of the information asymmetries can be remedied or mitigated, particularly if a public authority acts as a representative.[159] Market surveys and monitoring can also increase consumers' knowledge with regard to the buying stage.

There is a certain danger of fake associations. If error costs occur, they may be spread. The outcome of the assessment depends very much on the body where the case is brought, as well as on the representative. Regarding additional costs to society, class action races may pose a danger and potentially a duplication of costs among representatives. However, economies of scale may prevent duplication of enforcement costs among individuals.

In general, the involvement of a high number of players obviously poses a challenge to optimal incentives. Several of the weaknesses of individual private

158 See Keske (2010), p. 246: Neither group actions nor collective actions (class actions, in this book) are currently efficient unless they are substantially altered.

159 Apparently, if the representative is a public agency, this agency may have the powers referred to above. Also consumer associations can engage in some monitoring.

enforcement are aggravated. However, these costs may be outweighed by positive effects under the heading of optimal risk allocation.

Group litigation can reduce the individual's financial burden, but administrative costs are burdensome. A crucial determination is whether a mass of individual claims would be more costly than one collective procedure. The costs depend on the body before which the claim is brought and on the remedy that is sought. By and large, the higher administrative costs that are likely with group litigation may still be justified by the high societal benefits. The optimal level of enforcement is the benchmark.

In conclusion, substantial changes must be made to optimise group litigation as a mechanism, because it is currently imperfect in remedying the weaknesses of individual private enforcement. These obstacles can be only partially overcome. When introducing mitigating regulations, the resulting additional administrative costs must be considered – which is yet another indicator that mixing mechanisms may be a successful optimisation strategy. In the literature, optimisation attempts have been discussed for group litigation.

Public bodies must be accountable, and, therefore, administrative appeal procedures are in place. In the event of a representative action, control mechanisms are essential for the members of the association.[160] These controls may occur through government approval of the association or a permission granted by courts. Another suggestion revolves around accountability requirements.[161] If consumer associations are given quasi-regulatory functions, they must be controlled in the same way as government institutions.[162] Whereas paying attention to the group design can substantially improve group litigation, a crucial issue is who funds consumer associations. Class actions have been dealt with extensively in the literature and potential remedies include: (1) systems that allow class members to control their lawyer; (2) judicial review of the merit, terms and outcome of the case and of the contingency fees involved; and (3) auctions to determine the class lawyer.[163] However, these remedies may lead to new dangers, such as collusion or

160 Widespread actions will make it more difficult for the members to control the association; Schäfer (2000), p. 200.

161 See Van den Bergh and Visscher (2008b), p. 28: As a guiding line the truly representative character, credibility, reputability and commitment to acting in the collective interest of the consumer have to be ensured. Schäfer (2000), p. 199. Schäfer is more positive about solving this problem in relation to consumer associations than to class actions (pp. 200, 204). A class action according to him, 'creates more problems than it solves' (p. 204). The influence of the members in relation to an association is crucial (p. 197).

162 See Hodges (2007), p. 217.

163 See Van den Bergh (2008), p. 292. For a design suggestion, see Harel and Stein (2001), who evaluated the principal-agent problem in detail and presented a design that emphasised the importance of auctions, fee-forfeiture and a ban on inadequate settlements with the aim of guaranteeing payment of damages that equals at least the expected damage (of the claim); Van den Bergh and Keske (2009), p. 31. They refer to the 'Private Securities Litigation Reform Act 1995' in the US, according to which courts decide whether the lead plaintiff is able to monitor the class action and the performance of the lawyer. But there are

the defendants' acting as auction bidders themselves.[164] Also, an auction generates additional costs that can be substantial.[165]

Currently there is no consensus regarding which group litigation design is more successful and least costly,[166] although many design suggestions have been made to remedy certain weaknesses of other enforcement mechanisms. To my knowledge, an optimisation of incentives with a public agency such as the consumer ombudsman in the Scandinavian countries has received little attention in the law and economics literature.

Self-regulation: Economic Strengths and Weaknesses

In the foregoing, several examples of governmental intervention in the market were shown, such as maintaining court systems or public authorities to enforce consumer law. However, when self-regulatory entities enforce consumer rights, the market 'cures itself' and those who set up self-regulation are basically market players.[167] ADR and self-regulation may show common features and ADR often develops out of pure self-regulation. Hence, for the purpose of this book, the term 'self-regulation in the narrow sense' is defined as codes of conduct established, enforced and financed by an industry (limited regulatory powers over a certain industry). If the code is breached, complaints may be brought, generally free of charge. This procedure does not reflect an equal representation of consumers and traders and damages are not usually granted. Appeal options are very limited.

From a law and economics perspective, self-regulation is a hybrid device.[168] Private players have a regulatory role that is traditionally reserved for public officials. The approach is twofold: setting up of codes and ensuring compliance (with the codes). The latter aspect is the focus of this analysis.

---

dangers, particularly with the latter. If auctions are not properly run, they might lead to adverse selection and actually single out bad quality lawyers, see Van den Bergh (2008), p. 292. The process is comparable to that one that Akerlof outlined in relation to the 'market for lemons'.

164 See Schäfer (2000), p. 197.

165 See Schäfer (2000), p. 197.

166 See Van den Bergh (2008) who is critical about optimising group litigation involving consumer associations; Van den Bergh and Keske (2009), p. 40; in regard to favouring an adequate design of representative actions over class actions instigated by lawyers, see Van Boom (2006), p. 40; see Keske (2010), p. 246, regarding substantial changes needed in both collective and representative actions. See generally the suggestions for a workable design in CLEF (Consumer Law Enforcement Forum), prepared by G. Howells and H-W. Micklitz, *Guidelines for Consumer Associations on Enforcement and Collective Redress* (2009), p. 14.

167 See Van Boom (2006), p. 38.

168 A hybrid device is basically either of a public or private law nature, being given private or public law characteristics respectively. See Van den Bergh and Visscher (2008a), p. 44.

Whenever self-regulation does not succeed, government intervention can be considered.[169] In general, self-regulatory enforcement is a supplement rather than an alternative to other enforcement systems,[170] in particular because self-regulation is not designed to grant all the remedies that might be necessary in consumer law enforcement.

As with an ADR, the assessment of this type of self-regulation using economic factors is innovative. The strengths and weaknesses of this tool are assessed along the lines of the efficiency framework.

Optimal Risk Allocation

Rational apathy

While a self-regulatory system might work on an own motion, it is more commonly triggered by individual complaints. Therefore, the degree to which rational apathy may apply depends on the complaint system in place and the rewards and risks involved. In the business-to-business (B2B) relationship, there may be some risk of retaliation. For consumers, the typical systems entail low or no costs and little effort by the individual. Traders can be charged for their use. However, a self-regulatory entity grants only a few remedies and decisions are less binding, although the mechanisms may be well intertwined with other enforcers who uphold awards, and, therefore, strengthen their value. This reasoning obviously is similar to that of an ADR body where there are also concerns about the enforceability of its awards. Incentives for individuals to report must be ascertained. In addition to consumers, complainants may be companies who may appreciate this low-cost complaint mechanism to discipline their competitors.[171] The decision to report depends heavily on the individual, the issues at stake and whether the individual's main interest is monetary compensation. Associations or other entities might likewise report violations and a self-regulatory entity may act on its own motion. In that instance, the case does not depend on a complaint and so rational apathy problems do not prevail.

Free riding

In self-regulative cases, a 'pre-injunction step' may be taken if an activity must be interrupted or changed. As an example, a complaint may result in a change or the cessation of an advertisement, and, consequently, everyone profits. Yet the fact that everyone profits suggests that no one will complain, but will wait for others to do so instead. However, the costs involved in filing a complaint are low and various groups of individuals with different incentives are empowered to complain

169 See Van Boom (2006), p. 38.

170 For a placement of self-regulation among other instruments of regulation, see Ogus (1994), p. 107.

171 See Verbruggen (2011), p. 48 for the case of advertising.

(consumers, traders, associations and so on) thereby decreasing the likelihood of general passivity. Action on an own motion is likewise possible.

Funding

Public regulation is costly to all taxpayers, even if some do not consume the product.[172] However, the market bears the cost of applying self-regulation.[173] This is regarded as an equitable system because just as industry may profit from its misdeeds, it must also bear the costs of controlling them. Ultimately, these costs can be passed on. A self-regulatory body may consist of experts in the field who can solve issues early and at low cost. Like an ADR body, a self-regulatory organisation is in itself a funding mechanism for the previous two risk allocation problems – rational apathy and free riding.

Some self-regulation structures require a membership, and, therefore, the institution has secured funds through membership fees. In cases, in which there may be many possible members, the body could depend on donations.

Optimal Provision of Incentives

Information asymmetry

In contrast to public regulation, self-regulatory authorities have the advantage of having better information about the market they control.[174] Although a self-regulatory body may have few investigative powers, it may have greater access to private information than a public authority would have. In addition, competitors may lodge complaints and they are likely to have information about a rival's business that a consumer would not have and that can be used for the law enforcement process. Consequently, information asymmetry may be mitigated by the fact that people within the sector being regulated run the entity, and that the body can act on an own motion. Rivals can file complaints when they notice infringements. For example, a rival might realise earlier that an advertisement breaches the law simply because he must comply with the same laws.

In self-regulatory systems, the sector has the expertise to set up the regulatory codes.[175] Although the government could hire experts to track down the very same

172 See R.J. Van den Bergh, 'Towards Efficient Self-Regulation in Markets for Professional Services', *European Competition Law Annual 2004: The Relationship between Competition Law and the (Liberal) Professions*, ed. C. Ehlermann and I. Atanasiu (Oxford and Portland, Oregon, USA: Hart Publishing, 2006) 155–76, p. 159.

173 See Miller (1985), p. 898. Industry bears the costs of self-regulation: I. Ayres and J. Braithwaite, *Responsive Regulation: Transcending the Deregulation Debate* (New York: Oxford University Press, 1992), p. 114; Ogus (1994), p. 107.

174 See Van den Bergh (2007), p. 202; Miller (1985), p. 897.

175 See Hodges (2007), p. 223.

information, this process would take much longer and cost considerably more.[176] In other words, self-regulatory rules are tailored to the needs of business types and sizes, which is not possible with regulations.[177] Similarly, costs of interpretation of standards may be reduced.[178]

Self-regulation has a limited number of sanctions available, which generally do not go beyond the level of harm.[179] While this suggests less of a deterrent effect, cooperation with other sanctioning institutions may apply. When heavy sanctions are imposed, members may decide to leave the regulating organisation,[180] which would erode the deterrent effect. The extent to which businesses would choose this action could depend on how severely their reputation might be ruined and their future business opportunities affected.[181] On the other hand, termination of membership and the resulting damage to reputation could be a sanction. The fact that self-regulation includes one industry may have benefits because people know each other and wrongdoers are less likely to remain anonymous or hidden. Therefore, self-regulation may increase the probability of detection and conviction, unless the entity evolves in a cartel-like fashion, as illustrated in the next section.

Capture

Self-regulation by definition carries a risk of capture because it inherently involves the concerted actions of competitors and may be used for anticompetitive purposes. Hence, self-regulation must guard against capture,[182] both with externally and internally filed complaints. According to some authors, self-regulation risks being the 'ultimate form' of regulatory capture because of its tight link to industry.[183] However, this connection is crucial in improving the efficiency of the outcomes of industry-specific dispute resolution schemes.[184] Government may need to play an active role in monitoring self-regulatory activities.[185] The setting for pursuing complaints in the system is pivotal. The system can discipline its members.

---

176 See Howells and Weatherill (2005), p. 72.

177 See Ayres and Braithwaite (1992), p. 110.

178 See A.I. Ogus, 'Self-Regulation', *Encyclopedia of Law and Economics Volume V. The Economics of Crime and Litigation* (1999): 587–602, p. 591.

179 See Hondius (2006), p. 245.

180 See W.H. Van Boom et al., *Handelspraktijken, Reclame en Zelfregulering*, ed. WODC Ministerie van Justitie (Den Haag: Boom Juridische Uitgevers, 2009), p. 11.

181 See Faure, Ogus and Philipsen (2009), p. 172. This argument is discussed in more detail in the country studies.

182 See Van den Bergh (2006), p. 158; Miller (1985), p. 900.

183 See Stephen and Love (2000), p. 990.

184 See Duggan (2003), p. 62.

185 See Miller (1985), p. 903.

Frivolous lawsuits

Depending on the composition of such an entity, there may be reasons to believe that individuals will initiate complaints on inappropriate grounds to eliminate competitors.[186] Therefore, frivolous lawsuits could occur. Because self-regulatory systems have low costs, consumers also may simply try their luck.[187] Also, the regulatory body may initiate a frivolous complaint. If such cases yield wrong awards, error costs result. One can argue that self-regulation brings highly accurate decisions – and low error costs – because industry experts decide the cases.[188] For this statement to be true, control mechanisms over industry members' activities might be feasible. The only limited appeal options might not be of much help. However, there are underlying threats by other enforcement mechanisms.

Agency issues

Self-regulation has no principal-agent situations with complainant representatives because individuals make the complaints themselves. However, self-enforcers are set up from within the industry, which raises the suspicion that they may favour their own business interests. Then again, they work under the threat of an imposition of governmental regulation or regulatory enforcement, where the result may not be satisfactory. In terms of social welfare, self-regulation may create a duplication of costs because its outcomes are hard to enforce, and, therefore, it is difficult to make a decision binding. Hence, another enforcement mechanism may be needed. Yet, a higher degree of compliance can be assumed if the rules are set by the industry itself,[189] with an 'increased motivation',[190] and observance with a 'minimum of fuss'.[191] Self-regulatory rules also leave scope for innovation and creativity.[192] They are relatively easy to change and flexible in contrast to government regulations.[193] Therefore, the danger of outdated rules is mitigated.

186 Normally the setting up of it can also serve anticompetitive purposes for people who cannot make the standards not to be able to operate within the market.

187 See interview with AUC (Madrid, 23 November 2011). When bringing cases to the Spanish self-regulatory body autocontrol 'we do not think twice'.

188 Similar Ogus (1994), p. 107. One nevertheless has to be careful because that self-regulation often does not cover the whole market, see Hondius (2006a), p. 245. That indeed appears to be the case in consumer law. Self-regulation will be crucial particularly in misleading advertising (to be set out).

189 See Miller (1985), p. 897; Ayres and Braithwaite (1992), p. 113.

190 See Hodges (2007), p. 223.

191 See Howells and Weatherill (2005), p. 73.

192 See Miller (1985), p. 897. Hodges (2007), p. 223; also Van den Bergh (2007), p. 202 who argues that this is needed particularly where 'enforcement efforts are unsatisfactory'.

193 See Miller (1985), p. 897; Hodges (2007), p. 223; Ayres and Braithwaite (1992), p. 111. However, Hondius argued that these regulations will take time, particularly negotiated self-regulation, see Hondius (2006a), p. 244.

A social deadweight loss may occur if the industry spends resources on persuading legislators to establish regulations.[194] Self-regulation may add to tort and contract law in that it adjusts some of the vague standards in tort and contract law and thus enables easier decision-making.[195] Self-regulation may introduce legislation in sensitive areas where government otherwise would not interfere.

Administrative Costs Administrative costs depend on the structure of the self-regulatory entity, but are less than for an ADR body because self-regulation generally does not include dispute resolution to grant damages.[196] Duplication of administrative costs may be an issue, primarily if self-regulation fails and redress must be made to other mechanisms, such as when self-regulation is only a first step or if the rules are not followed and the ordinary costs of the existing enforcement system are triggered. Again, overall societal benefits are decisive for the amount of investment in administrative costs. Notably, administrative costs affect the traders' purses.

Conclusion Self-regulation has a clear advantage in optimal risk allocation because financial risks are reduced to a large extent and the industry bears the costs that emerge. However, there are limits to the cases for which it can be used. Free riding is likely with the type of interventions that self-regulation offers (for example, an advertisement that is changed), but should be only a minor problem since there are few costs involved in filing a complaint. The competitor or other actors may likewise be empowered to bring a complaint, and entities can theoretically act on their own motions.

Self-regulation is an interesting case for risk spreading because in a sense it spreads risk to industry. An individual who makes a complaint incurs few or no administrative costs.

To achieve optimal incentives, self-regulation must be designed to guard against the inherent capture of the mechanism and its susceptibility to frivolous complaints. Self-regulatory bodies rarely have consumer representatives. The enforcement mechanism has advantages in flexibility, increased innovation and compliance, and fine-tuning it with other mechanisms can strengthen the awards. As a possible danger, an increase in compliance with regulations may mean compliance with rules that are beneficial only for the industry and not necessarily for social welfare.

Information asymmetries between legislators and the industry can be remedied to a certain extent because self-regulation involves rules made from within the

194 See Ogus (1999), p. 588 who refers to G. Tullock, 'The Welfare Costs of Monopolies, Tariffs, and Theft', *Western Economic Journal* 5 (1967): 224–32.

195 See Van Boom (2006), p. 38.

196 See Faure, Ogus and Philipsen (2009), p. 171, who argued, 'If such a system is able to achieve compliance, it will typically do so at a significantly lower administrative cost than if public enforcement processes are invoked'.

industry and often complaints are brought from within the industry. There might be less scope for anonymity, reducing the possibility for escaping a procedure. Self-regulation is enhanced when there is the underlying threat of other enforcers' stepping in if self-regulation does not produce the desired results. This threat has the potential to control the players' behaviour.

The danger of duplication of administrative costs is a given in self-regulation because the mechanism cannot obtain all the remedies and might be only a first step. The mechanism is inexpensive to administer precisely because it does not grant a wide range of remedies or strict procedural rules.

As with other enforcement mechanisms, efficient self-regulation depends a great deal on the design of the measures and on the sector in which it is employed.[197] An interesting aspect is the industry itself and the competitors involved as information generators. On the flipside, self-regulation is by definition captured. The system profits from the interrelationship with systems that have higher levels of deterrence.

In practice, self-regulation exists in various forms, and there is no clear-cut line regarding co-regulation,[198] which may occur with public bodies.[199] As self-regulation does not provide for all remedies, it is not a fully fledged enforcement mechanism. Therefore it cannot be compared with other mechanisms to the full extent and should rather be considered as a supplement.

General Conclusion

This overview of various enforcement systems shows areas, in which considerable research has been conducted and where there are gaps. In particular, little research has been done regarding how enforcement systems relate to each other. Each enforcement system has its strengths and weaknesses and this analysis illustrates and confirms, that none of the systems is efficient independently and a mix is needed.[200] If mixing means coexistence, some competition will be created between

197 See for example Van Boom (2006), p. 38 who argues that the majority of writers regard self-regulation as the prime solution to private enforcement deficiencies.

198 See Hodges (2007), p. 223; F. Cafaggi, *Reframing Self-regulation in European Private Law* (The Hague: Kluwer, 2006), p. 27.

199 See Hondius (2006a), p. 243.

200 See Van den Bergh (2007); also Van Boom (2006) looked for in-between solutions (between public and private enforcement), p. 47; Cafaggi and Micklitz (2008), p. 425 listed several examples in Europe of the complex public and private divide and called for a redefinition of the boundaries. That a joint use of liability and regulation is preferable has been stressed in S. Shavell, 'A Model of the Optimal Use of Liability and Safety Regulation', *The RAND Journal of Economics* 15.2 (1984): 271–80; Cafaggi and Micklitz (2009); Duggan (2003), p. 58, also a class action or public interest suit is only a 'limited solution to the consumer access to justice problem' as other means ensuring that the costs of the lead plaintiff are spread among all have to be introduced as well. Combining

them, which has positive effects.[201] The strengths and weaknesses of enforcement systems are either more favourable or more detrimental, depending on the actual characteristics of a case. Some tools score higher than others in particular scenarios. Therefore, the analysis in the following chapter is divided into two sector studies, each with two scenarios. The common definitions of the enforcement mechanisms are the starting point for the analysis. However, some characteristics are relaxed during the discussion to assess potential hybrid and innovative solutions.

In general, consideration of the information asymmetry between claimant and defendant is crucial for efficient law enforcement, particularly in an unequal relationship involving seller and buyer. In this instance, various enforcement systems have different capabilities for generating information to remedy asymmetry. Public law enforcement in its current structure shows clear strengths in this regard. More importantly, information asymmetry does not only refer to the nature of the consumer good, but also to the characteristics of the parties – particularly those of the trader – and to the extent certain details are unknown, such as the traders' location.[202] One question is how far enforcers (individuals, lawyers, representatives, decision-makers) can go to generate missing information for the benefit of social welfare. What are the costs of producing information and in which situations can the costs be considered worthwhile?

To achieve the optimal level of enforcement – the point where marginal costs of additional enforcement efforts meet the marginal benefits of deterrence – all possible factors influencing this cost–benefit ratio must be considered.

---

public and private enforcement would enable checking the assiduousness of the public authorities, see Trebilcock (2003), p. 84. See Hodges (2011a), p. 108.

201 See Van den Bergh (2007), p. 201. Competition between enforcement mechanisms may be 'as important as competition on ordinary goods markets'.

202 While excluded from the scope of this book, consumers also could abuse information gaps.

Chapter 5
Combining Enforcement Mechanisms Efficiently for Specific Case Scenarios

Introduction

This chapter contains suggestions regarding optimal enforcement designs – 'optimal mixes' – for specific case studies, and builds upon the findings in the previous chapter regarding the general strengths and weaknesses of individual enforcement mechanisms. Economic efficiency considerations are assessed along the lines of general definitions of existing law enforcement mechanisms. However, these definitions are relaxed to some degree throughout the discussion. Some variations of the sanctions/remedies and powers available to enforcers are examined to enable the development of efficient innovative and hybrid solutions. Law might not yet have struck the optimal balance and institutions might not be set up in an efficient way. Procedural law might render lawsuits impossible in instances where they may be desirable from a social-welfare perspective. These options are discussed without affecting the core of the various existing enforcement mechanisms.

As emphasised (see Chapter 4), information asymmetry is the core problem in seller-buyer or trader-consumer interactions,[1] and consumer law enforcement mechanisms differ in their ability to mitigate this asymmetry and to generate information for the under-informed party. Information asymmetry results from unequal distribution of information concerning a product or its price between seller and buyer based on their different roles and a lack of information about the contract partner.[2] Information asymmetry is an issue at the initial buying stage, but also when litigation is considered, which is the focus of this analysis. Although the vast majority of disputes are solved out of court,[3] litigation usually occurs as a means to generate missing information and to remedy the unequal distribution. When looking for efficient solutions, a system must be able to generate the optimal amount of information. In this world, structured along the lines of basic assumptions in which these mixes are created, the different enforcement mechanisms are tools for the legislator to allocate to the scenarios to deter wrongdoers. As demonstrated in the previous chapter, each mechanism serves as a deterrent in a different way,

1 See also Van den Bergh (2007), p. 188.

2 While in general it goes both ways, for the purpose of consumer law enforcement, the analysis focuses on the lack of information on the side of the consumer as to the seller.

3 See Lindell (2007), p. 320, for civil law cases. It will also be imminent from the country studies that most cases are decided without court involvement.

and, therefore, is valuable for diverse case scenarios. Enforcement efforts may be increased as long as the marginal benefits of deterrence are higher than the marginal costs of enforcement. This will lead to the most desirable enforcement solutions: namely, the optimal level of enforcement. Within this allocation, it is efficient to mix mechanisms rather than rely on only one mechanism for enforcement of the whole of consumer law. On the basis of various case studies, a differentiation must be made in the extent, that each mechanism is able to generate benefits, and, which combination can be considered efficient.

Two case studies, each with two subcases, are discussed in this chapter. The first case study concentrates on solutions for single lawsuits and the second expands the view to mass solutions. Notably, group litigation may be carried out before any body and the various combinations are illustrated in detail in this chapter within the ambit of the second case study. As stated, the case studies were chosen to exemplify certain characteristics of two typical sets of consumer law cases. This does not mean that in reality they cannot be interrelated, and the more they show similar features, the more enforcement responses will have to be aligned.

The cases considered as typical consumer law cases involve two areas of consumer law – package travel and misleading advertising – and contingencies of a *bona fide* and a *mala fide* case scenario are considered for each. For each example, a system is designed to enforce the optimal number of cases, which would serve to allocate society's resources efficiently. The setting will be outlined more specifically with the key assumptions at the beginning of each case study. Although the market solution would be the first-best option, this chapter singles out second- and third-best solutions.

Assessment Using the Three-stage Analysis

Two contingencies of a case scenario within package travel and within misleading advertising are considered. First, here is a quick recapitulation of the reasons for selecting the case studies: the selected scenarios lead to different amounts of damage for consumers, which, in turn, have different effects on people's behaviour (victims, lawyers, wrongdoers and so forth). The harm to the individual consumer diminishes from examples one and two (package travel) to examples three and four (misleading advertising). In the package travel scenarios, individual damage is assumed to be substantial enough to induce an individual to sue and the possibility of obtaining compensation is crucial as an incentive for the consumer.[4] At the other extreme, the misleading advertising scenarios describe both trifling and widespread harm and the number of victims is larger. Likewise, the harm to competitors increases substantially and their taking action also is more likely for misleading advertising

4 See Weber (2011) for an illustration of the considerations in a high damage case.

than for violations involving travel law.[5] The travel cases involve an analysis of a pure action for damages scenario; for the misleading advertising cases, more remedies/sanctions are considered. Furthermore, aggregate solutions are raised and the role of self-regulation in the narrow sense is described with reference to misleading advertising. Intermediate solutions, borderlines and thresholds are discussed implicitly throughout the analysis.

Package Travel

Package travel is selected as a case in which individual harm may be substantial,[6] and the single individual is primarily interested in individual compensation. Internet trade is common in the travel sector.[7] In both variations of the case scenario, the consumer is assumed to have a damage of €2,000 because of the trader's contractual breach. In the first scenario, *bona fide* trader, the consumer can locate the trader; in the second, *mala fide* trader, the consumer booked the travel online and cannot locate the trader. The trader's location displayed on the Internet is incorrect; the trader is hiding.[8]

These additional key assumptions are made:

- In both cases, the consumer's case is easy to prove.

5 See Jordan and Rubin (1979), p. 2, a competitor might be substantially harmed from misleading advertising.

6 Regarding estimations of the consumer detriment within travel law, see London Economics, Study on Consumer Detriment in the area of Dynamic Packages (Final report to The European Commission – Health and Consumers DG 2009), http://ec.europa.eu/consumers/rights/docs/study_consumer_detriment_dyna_packages_en.pdf, last accessed: 31 March 2013, p. 134: The detriment suffered by consumers in the market for dynamic package travel was in terms of personal consumer detriment estimated at €1,005 million, on a yearly basis and in aggregate across the 27 EU Member States.

7 See Policy Department Economic and Scientific Policy, Study on Safety and Liability Issues Relating to Package Travel (requested by the European Parliament's Committee on Internal Market and Consumer Protection, 2008), http://www.europarl.europa.eu/meetdocs/2004_2009/documents/dv/999/999000/999000en.pdf, last accessed: 31 March 2013, p. 11. According to Internet World Statistics 2007, in Europe about 348.1 million people (43.4 per cent of the entire population) surf the Internet, with travel and tourism services among the most popular products on the Web; see Eurostat, Panorama on Tourism (2008), http://epp.eurostat.ec.europa.eu/cache/ITY_OFFPUB/KS-30-08-550/EN/KS-30-08-550-EN.PDF, last accessed: 31 March 2013, p. 18.

8 This is arguably only one of many problems, M.B.M. Loos and W.H. Van Boom, *Handhaving van het Consumentenrecht – Preadviezen Nederlandse Vereniging voor Burgerlijk Recht 2009* (Deventer: Kluwer, 2010), p. 29.

- The trader is hiding within the country, but in fact might also be hiding abroad. Where appropriate, the available cross-border enforcement mechanisms are mentioned.[9]
- The claimant prefers compensation as a remedy, which induces her to sue and the analysis focuses on this remedy. Punitive damages are excluded.
- The previously defined enforcement bodies exist for this model world. Importantly, compensation can be obtained anywhere. For instance, damage claims may be included in criminal, private and administrative proceedings (although in reality this is unusual) and in consumer ADR enforcement.
- Self-regulation in its narrow definition is excluded, same as group litigation.
- A specific damage case does not allow for any kind of profiting from the findings on law and fact for other proceedings by someone else.[10] They must be established again.
- The loser-pays rule applies to the private law proceedings because this seems feasible in the European context.[11]
- Contingency fees for lawyers are excluded, as is widely the case in Europe.[12]
- In package travel law, setting up securities for situations of bankruptcy in some form is obligatory (as set out in the Package Travel Directive,[13] Article 7).
- There is a joint liability regime within travel law for tour operators (acting in their own name, selling packages) and travel agents (intermediary,

9 Among the various examples of European legislation are the already mentioned Regulation on CPC, and the Regulation on European Small Claims Procedure, same as the Order for Payment Procedure (Regulation (EC) No 1896/2006 of the European Parliament and of the Council of 12 December 2006, creating a European order for payment procedure). Legislation is forthcoming and possibilities of tackling traders who hide behind borders are on the rise.

10 See Van Boom (2006), p. 13: Here Van Boom described the efficiency issues of deciding each case specifically with no way of profiting from it for other cases.

11 See C. Hodges, S. Vogenauer and M. Tulibacka, eds, *The Costs and Funding of Civil Litigation – A Comparative Perspective* (Oxford and Portland, Oregon: Hart Publishing, 2010), p. 28: In almost all jurisdictions the general position is that the loser pays the costs of the court, evidence and lawyer (in civil litigation). Some exceptions are possible. The rule is sometimes applied in a relaxed way, for Italy see H-W. Micklitz and C. Poncibò, *Evaluation of the Effectiveness and Efficiency of Collective Redress Mechanisms in the European Union – Country Report Italy, 2008*, p. 11.

12 Hourly fees are the rule. There is a strong cultural resistance in many states, see Hodges, Vogenauer and Tulibacka (2010), p. 25. Such arrangements are banned, for example, in the Netherlands; for an overview on rules in various countries, see M.G. Faure, F.J. Fernhout and N.J. Philipsen, *Resultaatgerelateerde Beloningssystemen voor Advocaten – Een Vergelijkende Beschrijving van Beloningssystemen voor Advocaten in een Aantal Landen van de Europese Unie en Hong Kong* (Den Haag: Boom Juridische Uitgevers, 2009).

13 Council Directive 90/314/EEC of 13 June 1990 on package travel, package holidays and package tours (Package Travel Directive).

consulting and advising travellers).[14] Therefore, the analysis generally uses the term 'trader'.

Civil Court The first branch of law that can be interesting in this setting is private law enforcement, in which the consumer pursues such a package travel case in a civil court. The damage is high enough to keep rational apathy a minor problem.[15] Free riding can be excluded, as the individual is the only one in this situation and will have to bear the procedural risk. Various factors reduce an individual's risks when engaging in litigation.[16] The threshold of €2,000 suggests that the case is included under small claims procedures, if available.[17] In addition, other features in civil law such as legal insurance and legal aid may reduce the individual's risk in both scenarios. While all this holds true for the *bona fide* trader scenario, the risks are much higher with the untraceable trader because of the uncertainty of locating the trader and of pursuing a lawsuit at all.

The information asymmetry regarding the trader's location leads to a failure of this lawsuit within the civil law court. It is too costly for the individual, her lawyer or the civil judge to generate the information and, hence, is disabled by procedural law. A *mala fide* trader potentially generates substantial societal harm (now and in the future), and, therefore, an enforcement response would be in the societal interest. As established, in a civil court, trivial issues such as lack of information regarding the wrongdoer's identity and location can hinder litigation. The information asymmetry here is likely to impede the individual's access to law. The problem persists because lawyers and civil judges are also unable to generate this information.

In the *bona fide* trader scenario, the requirement that the individual must bring the information to a civil court does not pose a problem.[18] The consumer can bring the evidence and the trader can be located. Capture, frivolous lawsuits and

14 See Article 4(3) Package Travel Directive: 'Where the consumer is prevented from proceeding with the package, he may transfer his booking, having first given the organiser or the retailer reasonable notice of his intention before departure, to a person who satisfies all the conditions applicable to the package. The transferor of the package and the transferee shall be jointly and severally liable to the organiser or retailer party to the contract for payment of the balance due and for any additional costs arising from such transfer'.

15 Across Europe, the proportion of people seeking certain levels of compensation in court is as follows: 13 per cent, €101–200; 15 per cent, €201–500; 15 per cent, €501–1,000. While these are the highest numbers, five per cent would take a business to court for €20 or less; four per cent for €21–50 and six per cent for €51–100; European Commission, Special Eurobarometer n° 342 (2011), p. 218.

16 This likewise would apply to defendants.

17 As a benchmark for maximum amounts, see Regulation on European Small Claims Procedure. The benchmark is €2,000.

18 See Van den Bergh (2007), p. 186. In contract law cases in which the contracting parties have had some contact, individuals are likely to have the necessary information to carry out a lawsuit.

error costs are minor issues for individual cases in civil litigation such as in this scenario. Legal representation is not required because the case falls under a small claims procedure. Therefore, the principal-agent problem does not apply. The threat of enforcement constrains business behaviour and traders are inclined to settle the case with the consumer out of court beforehand. The underlying threat of enforcement via the court puts the consumer in a more equal bargaining position.

Administrative costs of small claims cases are low compared with ordinary civil cases due to a simplified procedural law. Although insolvency generally poses a problem in private law, in travel law insolvency has been resolved by the legal obligation to set out securities for these cases. Such systems are an established remedy within private law enforcement regarding the lack of nonmonetary sanctions for judgment-proof offenders.

As a result, while the *bona fide* trader scenario can successfully be handled as a civil procedure, including small claims tribunals, the *mala fide* trader scenario leads to impeding problems because of the information asymmetries.

Consumer ADR Cases like these scenarios could be brought before an ADR body, which is favourable for the individual's risk assessment. As previously described, the ADR body in itself is a funding mechanism. In a clear-cut case as this, little or no additional information is needed, and the ADR's assessment can be successful. However, the ADR body provides no remedy for locating the trader. Affiliation with an ADR body and compliance with its decisions is generally voluntary and a *mala fide* trader is not likely to comply with an ADR system. As a result, the enforcement response for the second case scenario fails again. The ADR body could deal only with the *bona fide* trader case scenario. Is this preferable to the option civil court?

To start with, the degree of capture in ADR enforcement depends on whether the mixed composition of the ADR entity – the consumer and the business sides – can control against biased decision-making. Accountability is another crucial factor. Reputational harm is a minor issue with a single lawsuit and less harm is likely to emanate from an ADR body than a civil court judgment because the former is less well known and decisions often are not made public. With an ADR body, error costs might be more likely than in the civil court because of less accurate procedural laws.[19] Then again, expertise is often high with these boards, and they are to decide on facts, while courts are to decide on the law.[20] This case scenario is straightforward, an easy, clear-cut case that either an ADR body or civil court may handle.

19 Again, no authoritative assessment exists in this regard. Based on the fact that there are less procedural safeguards than in criminal law and even less than in a full private law case – if this is the decisive criterion – error costs will arguably be higher than with the previously mentioned procedures.

20 See M.L. Tuil, 'The Netherlands', *The Costs and Funding of Civil Litigation. A Comparative Perspective*, eds C. Hodges, M. Tulibacka and S. Vogenauer (Oxford: Hart Publishing, 2010) 401–19, p. 415.

As no representative is usually needed with an ADR body, agency issues are less of an issue, as with small claims procedures in a civil court. Other general societal costs and benefits of an ADR have been established in the previous chapter. The biggest loss to society stems from cases that are decided out of court because there is no further development of the law,[21] and also from a loss of the deterrent effect because enforcement is weak.[22] But these issues may pose less of a problem in clear-cut cases that deal with facts of the case and not the law. These do not affect further development of the law, unlike principle cases. Many of the effects depend on the interrelationship with the court. The question is how many cases each institution ultimately handles.

Administrative costs of the ADR body are lower than those of a civil court, irrespective of who provides financing to the ADR body.

In general, pursuing compensation in the *bona fide* trader scenario through ADR enforcement can be successful, but not in the *mala fide* trader scenario. ADR provides low-cost procedures that can be efficient for clear-cut cases in which further development of the law is no objective within a 'predefined' set of *bona fide* traders who would volunteer to it and might signal this by registering. For case scenario one, ADR is a less costly alternative from a social-welfare viewpoint compared with civil courts, primarily because of administrative costs (although this difference is less drastic for this case because it would fall under the small claims procedure in the civil court); hence, pursuing cases before an ADR body can be recommended when comparing overall societal costs and benefits. A design that makes capture less likely must be ensured. The loss of a deterrent effect because of a lower value of the awards under ADR may be mitigated in *bona fide* trader cases, which are assumed to be the ones that would voluntarily comply with the ADR system.

Administrative Law In the first case scenario, using individual private law enforcement would spread the risk effectively and, more specifically, pursuing the case through an ADR body would have comprehensive social-welfare benefits. However, public law enforcement can play a role in the second scenario, the *mala fide* trader.[23]

The following examination reviews administrative law enforcement to see if the system may have an advantage over private law, assuming there is a possibility

---

21 See Lindblom (2008a), p. 73. G. Dari-Mattiaci, 'Access to Justice', summer school session, University of Pavia, June 2010.

22 The country studies show how some countries attempt to remedy this weakness.

23 Emphasis is put on the question whether a certain necessary type of information can be produced within this enforcement branch. Then again, this theoretical assessment is not only concerned with competences as they stand in legal reality, but also with potential changes. Therefore, it is crucial to stress that the information can be produced in a less costly way or that high societal harm justifies even high administrative costs of its production (that would be the criminal law case at first sight).

for the individual to arrive at damages. Administrative law can deal with individual cases and potentially grant damages. Alternatively it can facilitate granting damages by other institutions, for instance by way of using a ruling obtained at a public agency in court

With the intervention of a public agency, the state assumes enforcement costs and the individual's rational apathy is lower than with private law enforcement. At first glance, a rational individual would be more likely to pursue this case through administrative law enforcement, if the remedies are the same, than private law enforcement because the individual's administrative costs would presumably be lower.[24] The entity could also act on its own motion. Additional factors in the risk assessment are public bodies' powers to generate information, to investigate and to monitor sectors.

Free riding, as said, is not an issue with specific individual cases; however, even on an own motion, the entity could take other measures from which society is meant to profit. From the perspective of the individual, the issue of funding is more beneficial, as the state is more involved in covering the costs.

A public authority's intervention has the advantage of less expensive generation of information, particularly with issues of Internet trade and traders who try to hide. The more powers an entity may have, the higher the administrative costs, and, importantly, societal benefits must justify the intervention. Those powers may include cross-border cooperation with other entities to locate individuals via the CPC network – the cross-border dimension is excluded in the case at hand. In the *mala fide* trader scenario, the intervention of this body could be crucial for locating the trader. As established, an authority may then lack the private information, and an individual needs incentives to share it. In this analysis, a public agency is empowered to grant compensation, and financial gain is a promising reason for an individual to intervene.[25] Therefore, if a public authority can grant or facilitate the individual's obtaining damages, individuals will certainly report and contribute their private information to the proceedings.

Although in this case scenario the individual is interested in damages, in cases with a low probability of detection and conviction, a fine may serve as a sufficient deterrent if the fine goes above the level of harm. According to deterrence theory, compensation is not a necessary requirement. However, with every remedy employed, attention must be paid to providing incentives for the individual to report. Furthermore, sanctions must not exceed the optimal level to prevent over-deterrence.

In cases, in which the claimant cannot trace the business trader, investigative powers may be used before initiating the case, in order to ensure that proceedings

24 See R.A. Posner, 'The Federal Trade Commission', *The University of Chicago Law Review* 37.1 (1969): 47–89, p. 88 suggests the power to award reparations to the Federal Trade Commission in order to motivate the consumer to bring their complaints.

25 See Shavell (1993), p. 267 – other incentives for an individual are the desire to avoid future harm, the retributive motive and possibly a fear of reprisal.

can be initiated at all. This investigation could be a moderated form of criminal law procedures that use the police force during the investigation and a similar approach can be imagined for any form of public entity. Indeed, public agencies can monitor or investigate markets or traders on an own motion. In relation to online traders, special tools may be crucial, such as the ability to detect true identities behind IP addresses. During the procedures, additional ways to raise information might be necessary. Whereas powers rest with public agencies for some *ex ante* action, judges start monitoring or looking into a case only once a case is filed. This delay may have a decisive impact on the conviction rate, as locating the trader may no longer be possible at that stage.

The risk of capture of public officials is a severe issue in administrative agencies. Regulating capture that involves administrative costs might be an efficient investment, considering the enormous strengths administrative law enforcement has in generating information and reducing individuals' burdens.

Single cases such as this scenario are unlikely to lead to frivolous lawsuits, however the public entity could also take broader measures; if the entity is captured, these measures may be frivolous. In addition, the danger of error costs is high compared with criminal law enforcement.[26] As previously stated, their occurrence is regarded as being more likely in administrative law enforcement compared with a criminal court. No assessments are available that would compare the notion of error costs with private law enforcement.

Therefore, administrative law enforcement is potentially beneficial from both the *ex ante* and the *ex post* perspective. Administrative law may provide a working enforcement solution for the second case study, particularly if the individual had an incentive to report because the public authority was able to assess or facilitate the assessment of damages. Financial gains motivate individuals the most and in particular can be envisaged in the ruined holiday scenario.

The main administrative costs that occur (which are different from those in private enforcement) are in the form of monitoring and detection, which is why monitoring must be targeted (by systems, according to which traders may signal their nature).[27] Furthermore, administrative costs depend on how many entities must be set up (such as a public agency and a connected administrative court) and any extra costs related to their maintenance and coordination. Low administrative costs depend on whether information generated can be transferred without duplication of efforts. If the administrative body is equipped to grant damages, additional administrative costs arise in calculating and distributing these. A crucial aspect of public law enforcement is that the claimant need not bear the cost of a lawyer or litigation fees, which has a decisive impact on the individual's potential rational apathy. However, as adjudication procedures become more similar to those of a civil court, additional costs may arise that the claimant would have to bear (involvement of lawyers, for instance). These costs, in turn, impact the

26 See Van den Bergh (2007), p. 195.

27 See Wittman (1977), p. 207.

individual's CBA, which will become similar to the analysis the claimant does when considering whether to involve a civil court. Thus, when restructuring existing bodies, the economic implications of changes must be considered. The conclusions include a more detailed examination of the side-effects of restructuring a public agency to allow it to grant damages (and the related need for lawyers and fees for proceedings).

Criminal Law Again in criminal law enforcement, the state bears the risk, which induces people to report wrongdoing, particularly if compensation is available via this enforcement mechanism. The criminal law branch's wide investigative powers and the intervention of the police force lead to a number of beneficial remedies for information asymmetries in litigation. No other law enforcement mechanism has such broad investigative powers and being able to track down individuals is a typical feature. It is evident that criminal law enforcement is designed to handle hard-core violations with associated substantial damages that justify the high enforcement costs due. A favourable CBA may seem less evident in consumer law, such as the case of a ruined holiday, even though here the case also may amount to fraud and lead to substantial societal harm. While a criminal law enforcement intervention is unnecessary in the first case scenario, which can be solved with less costly mechanisms, the second could profit from criminal prosecution.

An advantage of criminal law enforcement is the ability to impose other costly sanctions when the threat of having to pay compensation is not credible or insufficient and uphold the deterrent effect. The costly sanctions outweigh low probabilities of detection or conviction, such as in the second case scenario. Then again, the available investigative powers also increase the probability of being detected and convicted. The issue of a judgment-proof defendant also may be resolved with various nonmonetary sanctions available, the prime example being imprisonment.[28] Cases lacking sufficient information to launch a lawsuit may be tried under criminal law enforcement because this system has information-gathering powers, also prior to the trial, to discover the location of the trader. This ability represents the highest likelihood of the second case scenario's successful resolution.

Courts are arguably less susceptible to capture. As stated, the occurrence of error costs can be resolved to a certain extent by criminal procedural law, which, in turn, leads to high administrative costs. Criminal law leaves little scope for frivolous lawsuits. The crucial question concerns how much information is needed in a lawsuit, and who can generate it in the least costly manner. The individual claimant still must generate some information, such as the initial suspicion necessary for a criminal law case, to set a procedure in motion, but that information may not need to be complete.

Certain sanctions have a potential to function as underlying threats within a combination of enforcement mechanisms in a legal system. Hence, criminal

28 See Bowles, Faure and Garoupa (2008), p. 402.

sanctions may be necessary to punish corrupt public agents and to align their incentives with social-welfare considerations.

The high overall administrative costs of criminal law enforcement are why this enforcement mechanism is little used and not even the harm caused in scenario two of the package travel scenario is likely to trigger it. However, criminal law enforcement could be desirable for cases of mass damage involving *mala fide* traders. The availability of the mechanism as an underlying warning for very severe cases also seems desirable in the case scenarios at hand.

Conclusion When one looks at the two package travel case scenarios and the various enforcement mechanisms in consumer law, strengths and weaknesses are abundantly apparent in any of the mechanisms; therefore, mixing them could be an efficient solution. The emphasis for these scenarios is the different enforcement bodies' investigative powers.

Criminal law enforcement in consumer law cases is rare and although it would produce many positive effects, the administrative costs connected to criminal law enforcement impede its regular use. In particular, the sanction of imprisonment is very costly and some authors recommend its use only for repeat offenders.[29] Moreover, advocating perfect enforcement via criminal law is not possible, as some error costs are unavoidable and some people cannot be deterred. Criminal law may be extremely beneficial for cases involving judgment-proof offenders who will be deterred only by nonmonetary sanctions. In the package travel scenarios, the problem of judgment-proof offenders is mitigated with the obligation to set out securities for cases of insolvency. However, this provision is challenging to enforce and some traders may remain outside the system, and, therefore, qualify as judgment proof. Importantly, possible police intervention guarantees the widest investigative powers, that any enforcement mechanism could have at its disposal. This power is particularly useful if information is needed to initiate the lawsuit at all. Criminal law enforcement enables searches of individuals, which is crucial in the second case variation. In cases, in which a wrongdoer does not comply with a private or administrative order, criminal law should enter the picture and indeed the role of the underlying threat appears to be worthwhile in this regard. Criminal sanctions might be necessary to sanction corrupt public agents and to align the incentives of the enforcers. Therefore, if criminal law is considered a last and backup option, the optimal mix of enforcement mechanisms is likely to revolve around a public agency as the main player to generate information for the *mala fide* trader case scenario.

An ADR body or even a civil court may successfully handle the *bona fide* trader scenario, unless litigation fees impede the individual's cost–benefit ratio. The individual is crucial as the initiator. In the civil court, the small claims procedure and other funding mechanisms available under private law can mitigate the individual's costs. Thus, private law enforcement works well

29 See Ogus, Faure and Philipsen (2006).

in scenarios such as this when the harm is great enough for the consumer to sue, the information necessary to initiate a legal proceeding and to sustain the allegations with evidence is available and the wrongdoer can be traced. In terms of administrative costs to society, clear-cut cases should be handled by the less costly ADR mechanism rather than by civil courts.[30] The set of traders against whom a complaint can be brought are generally those who agree voluntarily to an ADR, and for other traders no deterrent effect emanates from an ADR system. ADR's mechanisms of preselection by registration can be efficient because it lacks powers to track offenders. This mechanism should target the vast number of easy cases (there may even be advantages in the assessment of facts as experts are involved at the ADR body) and traceable traders; otherwise, a case must be dismissed from the start. Therefore, in the first scenario, the necessary information for a lawsuit is available from the claimant, the ADR body, a lawyer or during the civil court procedures Private law enforcement is the cheapest way to generate this information, particularly if solved via an ADR body. From an individual and social-welfare perspective, the ADR option is favourable to the civil court in all cases that do not require a detailed assessment of the law and where there is no significant societal need for further development of the law. For these cases, the procedure leads to higher societal benefits rather than costs. Agency issues between client and representative in general are minor because there is a strong likelihood that, for the procedure, the consumer would not be interacting with a lawyer, either at the ADR level or in the civil court's small claims procedure. Capture issues in particular must be tackled to ensure that the ADR body makes decisions in the interest of social welfare.

As the *mala fide* case scenario demonstrates, information and its generation are crucial. Problems arise with this scenario, a case involving extensive enough harm to motivate the consumer to sue, but with information asymmetries (the trader's location) that impede litigation in private law. Neither the individual, nor the lawyer or the private enforcer can generate this information. Legal rules have disabled generating it (access to certain documents, registers, use of certain tools and so on). A public law investigative element is needed and possibly *ex ante* monitoring. In today's world, unlike the model world, a public authority does not generally grant damages. Therefore, in today's world, enforcement is likely to fail whenever the individual's interest is compensation and when 'information' is needed that the individual or the private law enforcement body cannot generate. Information asymmetries impede private law enforcement. Compensation cannot be granted by a public agency.

One way to provide an effective public law enforcement mechanism is to construct a public authority that can grant damages, as assumed for the model

30 'Regarding the funding of ADR, the majority of businesses (58 per cent) would be willing to contribute to the costs of setting up and running an ADR scheme by paying a fee for each case their business is involved in. On the other hand, 22 per cent is not willing to contribute financially', see EBTP (2011), p. 3.

world. From society's perspective, the prospect of having to pay compensation may be a deterrent for wrongdoers and a financial gain is a promising incentive for an individual to intervene.[31] Thus, the individual whose primary interest is compensation would certainly have incentives to report to such an authority. As a result, the private information the individual had about a violation, which might be useful for the society as a whole, could be shared with the public.

Alternatively, the investigative powers of – or their use in practice by – the civil law branch (individuals, lawyers, judges, ADR bodies and so on) could be expanded, enabling the civil law system to track down wrongdoers. As stated, this solution would provide a necessary 'public law element' to generate certain information or to monitor steadily and in a targeted way while upholding incentives for the private individual to reveal information.[32] Alternatively, an expansion of powers of lawyers or other representatives within the private law enforcement system can be envisaged.

Putting in place a public authority that grants damages would require some serious restructuring of the current situation in many countries. Restructuring a public authority to allow for compensation may require the system to become more similar to a civil court (involving lawyers and/or more procedural safeguards). This would consequently reduce the mechanism's positive effects, in particular for the individual's cost–benefit analysis (unless the state takes over a large part of the litigation costs).[33]

The question remains whether a rational consumer whose interest is compensation for damages suffered would report to a public authority that could not grant this compensation. As an alternative to extensive restructuring, the efficient flow of information between bodies could be guaranteed, which would induce them to cooperate more while adhering to their original functions. An institutional change to empower a public agency to issue damages or increase the civil court's investigative powers could be too costly. Therefore, an enforcement scenario that uses findings or information generated by a public authority within the ambit of some kind of subsequent investigation in court could preserve the institutions' original functions. The prospect of using the public authority as an information generator for later damage cases could induce the individual to report

31 See Shavell (1993), p. 267.

32 Likewise, this is an issue in competition law insofar as the exchange of information or the coordination between the European Commission and national courts can be designed to facilitate private damage claims and the incentive problems related to it. See the workshop, 'Consumers' Participation Rights in Competition Law Procedure', Amsterdam Centre for Law and Governance, Amsterdam, 8 October 2010. See also K.J.L. O'Connor et al., 'Interaction of Public and Private Enforcement', *Private Enforcement of Antitrust Law in the United States – A Handbook*, eds A.A. Foer and R.M. Stutz (Cheltenham: Edward Elgar, 2010) 280–304, p. 287.

33 See Faure, Ogus and Philipsen (2009), p. 176: As to the procedures at a public agency: 'Clearly, the more elaborate the procedures, the higher the administrative costs but also the lower the error costs'.

violations. Likewise, it could induce traders to participate in negotiations with the public authority to find solutions involving the consumer because of the underlying threat of subsequent damage claims or the like. Avoiding institutional changes also has the advantage of allowing the public authority to remain specialised and cost-effective in investigating because it abstains from doing everything, such as granting damages. There is also no danger of a spillover of weaknesses when restructuring enforcement bodies.

However, inducing enforcers to work along these lines must be guaranteed. Importantly, easy cases that do not justify high costs and that can be handled by a low-cost body must be guaranteed consideration by the ADR body. In other words, the 'public law element' must be reserved for cases such as the second scenario described here.

A public authority has the advantage of being able to take measures in the interest of social welfare, besides potentially offering the individual compensation. This function is even more applicable to cases with more widespread damage or those, in which the trader clearly intends to inflict further harm in the future, having discovered how to avoid a legal sanction. For instance, it may be worthwhile for a public authority to target traders not registered with the ADR board, as every monitoring effort certainly incurs an additional cost.

Adaptation to a country's current consumer law landscapes is crucial when suggesting welfare-enhancing changes in law enforcement systems. For instance, in countries where criminal cases regularly involve assessment and granting of damages, granting the 'public law element' by an expansion of criminal law could be considered because it would involve fewer institutional changes for those particular countries. Such countries may have less need for strong involvement of a public agency and generally may be ready to establish cooperative relationships to grant damages in these cases by the criminal court.[34]

An entity's or enforcement system's strength in resolving information asymmetries depends largely on how wide its powers can be or to what degree society considers it worthwhile to invest in this task. There will be a limit to the number of breaches for which the wrongdoer will be tracked down because the harm done may not justify the financial investment in enforcement. To put it in harsh terms, some consumers will be sacrificed.

Responding to *mala fide* case scenarios involves more administrative costs than responding to easy cases (investments in locating the offender, bringing the evidence and calculating the damage). Society cares about consumer protection only to the extent that it enhances social welfare. Additional enforcement efforts will be pursued only to the point where marginal costs equal marginal benefits of deterrence. Hence, an important aspect of these strategies is the costs, particularly

34 From a purely legal point of view, resistance to cooperation may be based on the fact that violations must fulfil different standards of proof and cannot simply be transferred from one branch of law to another. The criminal law burden of proof 'beyond reasonable doubt' is the most challenging to justify.

the administrative costs incurred. If a public agency is given both investigative powers and the ability to grant compensation, administrative costs will obviously increase. Therefore, this development can take place only if it is compensated for elsewhere in the mix.[35] Sidelining expenses through a low-cost decision-making mechanism – an ADR body – that can discuss easy, clear-cut cases seems desirable (the *bona fide* case scenario). The risk of capture must be considered in designing this body. Because this system can deal successfully with these cases, there is no need to choose more costly alternatives. However, certain pitfalls of an ADR involving other societal costs must be avoided, in particular the ADR's inability to further develop the law, which is why only clear-cut cases should be brought to the ADR. The threat of alternative enforcement responses or an appeal option when the ADR fails or produces unsatisfactory results may enhance the effective working of this mechanism (in terms of a threat to wrongdoers and of mitigation of possible error costs). For instance, competition by small claims procedures within the civil courts can be imagined and finely tuned.[36] Ways are imaginable to strengthen an ADR body's awards. Error costs are less likely in the clear-cut, easy cases that the body in this mix would focus on and with the expertise resting with the ADR body. Thus, it is clear from analysing the strengths and weaknesses of various enforcement systems that providing investigative powers and compensation for certain cases has to be cross-financed. One means for cross-financing is to filter clear-cut cases, in which the trader is identifiable and cooperative (which in practice can be solved by way of example by a preregistration with an ADR body and possibly providing some securities) to a low-cost procedure. There is, furthermore, no principal-agency issue, since representation with the body is not necessary. In the light of these strengths of ADR procedures it can be considered worthwhile to fight the danger of capture.

Societal benefits are required to justify triggering a more costly enforcement response for *mala fide* traders. Once an opportunity is detected, the *mala fide* traders act and there is considerable likelihood that they will continue to harm society. Damage may be on-going and other harmed consumers may be out there or may soon emerge. These traders are potentially harmful, also for the reputation of the sector as a whole. From society's perspective, a trader who is trying to hide is one that potentially will harm many consumers. A scenario like the *mala fide* trader described here is not likely to remain an individual €2,000-damage case. Then again, some *mala fide* traders may act only once and against one consumer. In some cases, the notion of efficient breaches becomes important, where the costs of the enforcement response are not outweighed by the benefits.

With the growth of Internet commerce, traders currently have many possibilities to hide and to generate significant benefits for themselves, which may result in extensive societal harm. An argument can be made for strengthening the

---

35 Whereas society may gain by unenforced cases and save on administrative costs, the costs of harm can be very high and the benefits in avoiding this amount of harm may outweigh enforcement costs.

36 Competition is regarded as positive, Van den Bergh (2007), p. 201.

position of the consumer through a strong public law element for cases involving fraudulent traders. This focus would target in particular the *mala fide* traders and situations where the information asymmetry between the seller and the buyer is considerable. Those traders who hide and are more difficult to catch necessitate more investigative powers (including international cooperation, which is outside the scope of this book).

In terms of the strengths and weaknesses, information costs are the decisive factor to distinguish the two different types of responses outlined. The main distinction is the severity of the information asymmetry between the buyer and the seller regarding the seller's characteristics, which can be resolved with monitoring or investigative powers (typically public enforcement powers). Societal benefits might justify an additional information generator, in particular if this can be cross-financed within the system. Ways could be devised to charge the seller with certain administrative costs incurred, which could be an additional deterrent.[37] The optimal risk allocation for consumers (and consequently society) in risky cases, is reached by introducing some kind of public law element for *mala fide* case scenarios. (These various options have been described; less restructuring, but better cooperation is warranted because it prevents an overspill of weaknesses.) Interestingly, facilitating compensation to incentivise individuals to provide the necessary private information (via reporting) could simultaneously serve compensation goals that legal scholars place at the forefront.

In general, the underlying threat of legal enforcement clearly deters wrongdoing and enhances the possibility that a satisfactory solution to any wrongdoing will be achieved with the trader in negotiations beforehand (under the threat of law enforcement), without involving courts. A trader may abstain from violating the law in the first place. The general idea is to use the comparative strengths of the different law enforcement mechanisms in relation to the related case scenarios without increasing their weaknesses through restructuring them extensively. In the main, there is a line of action ranging from dealing with only an ADR's registered traders to engaging the police to track down a wrongdoer in the most extreme case of a hiding trader. Consumer education regarding how to distinguish *bona fide* and *mala fide* traders *ex ante* can be valuable and there is a role for public authorities or consumer associations in monitoring and consumer empowerment.

The smaller the harm and/or if the case is not a single case, the more group litigation or alternative solutions (in public law) must be considered and added to this initial idea, as the next case will show. The borderline can be neat.

37 Obviously a line has to be drawn regarding frivolous lawsuits. Here, no costs should be imposed on the seller. Furthermore, the danger of over-deterrence must be avoided.

Misleading Advertising

Within misleading advertising, a *bona fide* (scenario three) and a *mala fide* (scenario four) trader scenario are described and assessed. The example of a *mala fide* trader is one, that has been prominent in the headlines in recent years, in which an advertisement for a ringtone misleads the consumer into concluding a contract instead of a one-time download. The damage to the individual is small, even trifling, but is widespread.[38] The individual damage incurred is assumed to be €15.[39] The trader calculates profits up to the moment she is fined, factors the potential sanctions into the prices, then hides and changes sectors in which to conduct business. This scenario reflects the behaviour of the profit-maximising *mala fide* trader,[40] in contrast with that of a *bona fide* trader.[41] In both cases, the competitor's damage is assumed to be €100,000.[42] Alternatively, solutions are discussed in which the competitor has no interest in the case. In the advertising sector, Internet advertising and trade are extremely common and facilitate traders' ability to hide.[43]

---

38 See Jordan and Rubin (1979), p. 530: 'No one consumer has an interest to sue'.

39 Jordan and Rubin (1979), p. 529, expressed that the role of advertising differs depending on the type of good involved. In relation to experience goods (determine the quality only by purchasing and using the goods), advertisers might have an incentive to mislead and make false claims.

40 Indeed, there is an efficiency loss if advertising cannot be believed, Jordan and Rubin (1979), p. 536; for example, in cases of credence goods, consumers are forced to rely on reputation and intermediaries. Also J.A. Moewe, 'Consumers, Class Actions and Costs: An Economic Perspective on Deceptive Advertising', *UCLA Law Review* 18 (1970): 592–615, p. 593, put forward arguments of why misleading advertising is bad for society: he sees a misallocation of resources when consumers do not engage in truthful business and said, 'Deception in advertising tends to destroy the faith of consumers in producers generally'; recent examples of rogue traders operating in the internal market include misleading and threatening clairvoyancy services, deceptive prize draws, mailings concerning unsolicited goods 'waiting' for consumers, unsolicited first aid kits accompanied by demands for payment, direct marketing of slimming products to children and misleading marketing by 'holiday clubs'. See Press release RAPID (2003). Furthermore, the Organisation for Economic Cooperation and Development (OECD) adopted a recommendation underlining the need for action, the Rogue Trader Prevention Taskforce, which decides on policy and action against the activities of rogue traders; see also Expertentagung, 'Wilhelminenberg Gespräche' (2011).

41 See Faure, Ogus and Philipsen (2009), p. 169: 'It appears that many violations of regulation are not intentional, but rather result from lack of information or knowledge'.

42 See Jordan and Rubin (1979), p. 535: competitors are harmed because sales which they would have made have been diverted to the other firm. They can be expected to lose substantially more than consumers.

43 An earlier version of the findings concerning the misleading advertisement case have been published as F. Weber, 'Abusing Loopholes in the Legal System – Efficiency Considerations of Differentiated Law Enforcement Approaches in Misleading Advertising', *Erasmus Law Review* 5.4 (2012): 289–307.

These additional assumptions about this case study are made:

- Prima facie, all cross-uses of facts and findings in one proceeding of the same claimant are possible. In particular, profiting from an injunctions case for follow-on damages is possible.[44]
- Reference is made only to representative actions, as defined previously, because of the overall strong resistance in Europe to class actions. An optimal design is assumed to be possible.[45] Any representative action before a court or agency that is primarily carried out by an association or a state authority is taken into consideration. These representatives typically have better suited abilities for collecting information in advance. Individual interests are bundled in the procedure. Opt-in, opt-out action or mandatory procedures exist.
- Any group litigation can seek actions for damages, injunctions and 'fining'. The same is true for individual actions.
- The category 'fining' is chosen artificially and covers any financial sanction that is not compensation (such as fines, profit disgorgement and the like).[46]
- Self-regulation is considered in the narrow sense. Within the ambit of misleading advertising, self-regulation means setting up codes of conduct for the advertising industry against which complaints can be brought (limited regulatory powers over a certain industry). As a consequence of the intervention, advertising may be stopped or changed.
- Again, the *mala fide* trader is hiding within the country and operates primarily via the Internet.
- For this case scenario, 'trader' stands for the defendant in general, as further questions of liability of a company or an advertiser and so on are not crucial to the general argument and are not discussed.

Civil Court For this misleading advertising case, the reasoning as to the economic strengths and weaknesses of the civil court is different because the scenario involves a case of trifling and widespread harm. As long as the advertisement continues to be public, society is harmed and interrupting emission

44 In reality this type of coordination does not exist as a general policy in Europe; see Cafaggi (2009), p. 519. The experimental character of this chapter justifies exploring these possibilities to an extent to which they are currently not available in Europe.

45 The class action model is prevalent in the US, Canada, Australia and Sweden, Hodges (2010), p. 707. Other Scandinavian countries are likewise experimenting with this. As set out previously, there are potentially optimal designs for both class actions and representative actions. This possibility is an assumption for the purposes of this book, as exploring the options in detail is beyond the scope.

46 The previous study focused on damage cases and at times referred to other remedies/sanctions where they were instrumental to achieve compensation; here, the feasibility of various remedies is assessed in more detail.

of the advertisement or changing it will benefit society. Thus, in an individual lawsuit in the civil court, rational apathy is pre-existing with only €15 of damage[47] and the individual's costs for pursuing even a small claims case are too high.[48] In some countries, civil procedural rules require a minimum threshold. From a social-welfare viewpoint, litigation costs in a civil court would justify legal aid being made available, only if stopping the advertisement were a side-effect that would therefore provide a remedy for the widespread harm.[49] For example, society would need to see an injunction issued to stop this harmful violation. According to definition, everyone profits from an injunction. However, because injunctions invite widespread free riding and no individual profit for anyone already damaged is available, the individual would be reluctant to bring forward such an action.[50] The same is true for any form of 'fining'. Any litigation results only in additional net costs for the consumer who has suffered only minor harm.

The cost–benefit analysis looks different for competitors with an interest in the case. They profit from any remedy that will harm their competitor's business or stop the considerable harm caused to them, as defined in the description of the scenario (for example, by way of an injunction combined with a claim for the lost profits). If a competitor is given standing to sue, the various sanctions under the 'fining' category could prove highly beneficial for her and her business; even if the competitor does not directly receive the proceeds, the competitor's business would be damaged. Thus, there are various possibilities for a deterrence effect.

From a rational viewpoint, this scenario would not induce an individual consumer to sue; however, the competitor is an efficient risk taker, and, therefore, the optimal provision of incentives can be analysed. The previous findings on incentives of the players before a civil court apply, but note that a competitor who is well equipped to detect an infringement and is considerably harmed may have an interest in using the law strategically. Even a competitor who is not harmed may have an incentive to sue (a frivolous lawsuit),[51] particularly if the competitor has

47 See Landes and Posner (1975), p. 33; Schäfer (2000), p. 195; Howells and Weatherill (2005), p. 604; Garoupa (2001), p. 233, regarding factors that motivate individuals; Cafaggi and Micklitz (2009). According to a recent EU study five per cent would take a business to court for €20 or less, four per cent for €21–50 and six per cent for €51–100; see European Commission, Special Eurobarometer n° 342 (2011), p. 218. This is the average data throughout Europe.

48 This holds true irrespective of the cost rule in place. This is particularly related to the preparation of such a formal procedure, expressed in contrast to an ADR procedure; see interview with Alicia Menéndez González, Spanish ADR Board (Madrid, 16 November 2011).

49 If the harm is widespread, it indeed might be worthwhile from a social-welfare perspective to make some form of funding available. There is some data available from the US that misleading advertisement cases are among small claims cases, as cited by Jordan and Rubin (1979), p. 542.

50 See Van den Bergh and Visscher (2008), p. 14; Landes and Posner (1975), p. 29.

51 Regarding the situation of competitors in antitrust cases, see Renda et al. (2007), p. 563. It can effectively become a medium used to restrict entry to new competitors and

easy access to 'fining' remedies. Potential frivolous lawsuits must be considered when designing legal provisions and procedural safeguards (where to bring a lawsuit and to whom to assign payment). For example, sanctions can be imposed upon those who bring frivolous lawsuits forward. Depending on the procedural law, some harm can be inflicted simply by an on-going investigation, even without a judgment.[52] Furthermore, the competitor may have an information advantage over a consumer concerning the business sector, and, therefore, have less need for lawyers or the civil judge to generate crucial information.[53] Regarding any low probabilities of detection and conviction, costly sanctions are available that may serve to uphold the deterrent effects of a legal response.

Concerning positive social-welfare implications, the remedies besides compensation are interesting. For society, an injunction automatically reduces harm by stopping certain behaviour for future cases; it also may reduce fact-finding cost for the same cases if follow-on damage claims can be regarded as efficient.[54] Injunctions and fining may invite free riding among consumers. They have a potential to outweigh losses in the deterrent effect. This might be even more valid for 'fining' actions than for injunctions.[55] Injunctions may be supplemented with conditional fines, which can have a furthering effect on deterrence. However, the deterrent effect of an injunction for a *mala fide* trader is generally low, since the extent of a company's profits up until the moment of the injunction might lessen deterrence. The *mala fide* trader may have already factored in a potential fine into the pricing. A crucial factor is the speed of the legal response – the availability of interim measures. Regardless of the law enforcement mechanism, these remedies generally have a potential to uphold the optimal dose of deterrence.

For this scenario, injunctions border on a collective mechanism because they always favour everyone.[56] A speedy proceeding involving interim measures to

create a net loss in social welfare; see Jordan and Rubin (1979), p. 540.

52 These might be much higher if the defendant was required to carry out costly pre-trial discovery, as in the US.

53 See Renda et al (2007), p. 77, for antitrust cases; C.B.P. Mahé, *'De Concurrent als 'Handhaver' van Consumentenbescherming', Handhaving van en door het Privaatrecht*, eds E. Engelhardt et al. (Den Haag: Boom Juridische Uitgevers, 2009) 173–89, p. 174, little or no information asymmetries exist because they know the market segment.

54 Also, various competitors might file a number of follow-on damage suits. Effects of declaratory judgments or test cases that were excluded for this research might not be too different.

55 Regarding positive assessments for disgorgement of profit claims by representations, see C. Hodges, 'Developing Approaches to Public and Private Enforcement in England and Wales', *New Frontiers of Consumer Protection – The Interplay between Private and Public Enforcement*, eds F. Cafaggi and H-W. Micklitz (Antwerp; Oxford; Portland: Intersentia, 2009) 151–69, 168 and generally Stadler (2009), pp. 305–28.

56 It can also be formulated in a negative way; see Cafaggi (2009), p. 536, 'Prohibitory injunctions have effects that reach beyond those who seek the remedies. If a product is placed out of the market or a practice declared unfair and prohibited, then little can be done

stop the advertisement immediately and during any on-going procedures is crucial, particularly regarding the *mala fide* trader scenario, in which the trader counts on a fine in the best-case scenario after making considerable profit. Importantly, if the trader wins the case, compensation might have to be paid for the lost profit caused by the interim measure in order to avoid a competitor's strategic use of this remedy.

The administrative costs for preparation and assessment of the various remedies in court depend on the elements that must be proven and thus on the extent of the investigation and the investigative powers required. Injunctions seem to be less costly than mass damage cases, in which damages must be thoroughly assessed and distributed.[57] Naturally, the same might hold true for 'fining' remedies, which also do not require an assessment of individual damages. Then again, some 'fining' remedies may require that profit be calculated. These interrelationships are less clear with individual damage cases.[58] By and large, social welfare requires avoiding over-deterrence of wrongdoing when combining remedies. The remedies are assessed according to individuals' responses to incentives as a second-best approach to assessing reliable data and remain in part unsubstantiated.

The competitor's intervention could come in handy for the individual consumer because it deters the wrongdoer's action. For example, in a proceeding that involved a connected damage claim, a consumer might use the findings from an injunctions case (if this is what the competitor opted for), and thus free ride. However, if damage is very small from the consumer's perspective, not even this effort for the connected damage claim might seem justified. A pure reliance on consumer damage claims, which might not happen due to a rational apathy problem, might lead to under-deterrence. Although an intervention from a competitor can be efficient, it is not certain, particularly in situations where one industry creates a

---

for the class of consumers interested in keeping the product in the market or the commercial practice in place'. Cafaggi distinguished it from affirmative injunctions.

57 Confirmed in interview with OCU (Madrid, 16 November 2011). In Hodges, Vogenauer and Tulibacka (2010), p. 61, regarding consumer injunctions and commercial injunctions the following is expressed: costs for the individual are extremely difficult to assess as other players can come in. For the UK, for instance, a complaint to a regulator can trigger results with minimal costs to the initiator in cases of consumer injunctions. For the Netherlands, lawyers' costs depend on the amount of work done. In various countries, injunctions among neighbours cannot be pursued as civil cases (Spain, Russia and Sweden). In the case of the commercial injunction (injunction to prevent illegal breach of intellectual property in commercial information between two substantial companies), aggregate total fees in the UK would amount to almost €80,000 because of very high lawyer fees involved. These figures provide too weak a basis for firm conclusions.

58 See Cafaggi (2009) for a summary of some literature on this topic: the elements to be proven for an injunction may differ from those necessary to recover damages. A strict liability regime operates for the former, while proof of fault is often required for the latter. No harm is necessary for the former; proof of harm is often a prerequisite for the latter. The burden of proof might likewise differ. Causation is in general stricter for actions seeking damages.

cartel-like situation in the advertising sector and there is no deterrence because no competitor will intervene.[59]

Therefore, group litigation can be a mechanism for consumers to oppose wide societal harm, and may serve as an efficient allocation of risks for consumer-initiated actions. Funding may not be worthwhile if only one individual suffers minor harm, but the situation is different if a group of individuals suffers minor harm and societal harm is extensive.

Group litigation potentially may remedy an individual's rational apathy, which is one of the main advantages over individual litigation. Free riding problems also may be mitigated. As outlined in the previous chapter, well-designed group litigation serves as a funding mechanism. However, the representative also must weigh carefully the financial consequences of pursuing a case (particularly before which body) and consequently the rationale for interventions with various law enforcement bodies are analysed.

With an injunction, everybody profits, independently of whether they contributed to the case. For instance, injunctions through group litigation can enhance welfare. Profiting from different proceedings for follow-on damage cases can be efficient. For example, an injunction issued by another court or in a different proceeding may be used as evidence. Procedural law may restrict follow-on damage claims for individuals who failed to contribute, if that were welfare enhancing. Because the injunction favours all (who are exposed to the advertisement), the risks arguably should be spread over all those; therefore, a solution may be to design the action in a way that takes this into account. A public representative using state money may be an initial idea.[60] Process insurance may play a role as well; for instance, representation by the *Abmahnvereine* exists in Germany. The purpose of these associations is to strategically oppose certain types of infringements (unfair commercial practices) Interestingly, the warned party must pay the costs of the procedure. While this requirement is very favourable to consumers, it carries risks of over-deterrence and strategic execution of frivolous lawsuits.

Group actions potentially may remedy funding issues for individuals, for instance if costs are split or assumed by another funder. However, this calculation depends on the individual amount of damage at stake. With direct damage claims, in which claims are very small and rational apathy is at play, collective action might also fail. It is highly likely that the €15 scenario falls below this threshold. (Indeed, a challenging exercise is to establish the threshold, for which collective

59 Another aspect is the question when the competitor realises a loss of profit and invests in regularly checking advertising measures of her competitors. Jordan and Rubin (1979), p. 531, argued that in a competitive industry, no firm would lose from false advertising by competitors; neither would any competitor sue in a monopolist situation, only in cases of oligopolies. Again, there would indeed be no lawsuit if all the oligopolists engaged in false advertising.

60 Reporting would possibly be the only contribution that the individual would need to make.

damage actions are no longer efficient.) Other ways of forcing the company to face a sanction must be found to guarantee deterrence in this type of situation, even if the individual does not directly profit from the sanction.

Group actions can aim at various 'fining' remedies and then everyone profits as well. An injunction might sideline 'fining'. As stated previously, bringing a group action (depending on the law enforcement body involved in judging the case) and the various remedies (their preparation and realisation) have varying costs for the representatives. Injunctions are less costly to prepare and to litigate than mass damage cases. 'Fining' remedies trigger another set of incentives, including possibly less need to thoroughly prove damage to each individual, but more need to prove the company's profits. How the representative in group litigation is funded plays a role in this analysis. Although Europe currently has a severe funding problem in this area[61] (possibly because contingency fees are generally not accepted), new forms of financing are developing.[62]

Now for the crucial point: the different degrees of information asymmetries. Necessary information must be provided to a civil court to move procedures forward because civil courts have limited investigative powers; as said, the *mala fide* scenario will fail *prima facie* in civil court. Group litigation may be a remedy to information asymmetry and in cases where harm is difficult to detect may counterbalance the missing investigative powers in private law enforcement. The representatives such as consumer associations or public agencies may be able to assist in locating wrongdoers. While consumer associations are able to generate some additional information,[63] this is particularly true if a public agency with investigative powers becomes the representative. These representatives may have

61 See G.P. Miller, 'Compensation and Deterrence in Consumer Class Actions in the US and Europe', *New Frontiers of Consumer Protection – The Interplay between Private and Public Enforcement*, eds F. Cafaggi and H-W. Micklitz (Antwerp; Oxford; Portland: Intersentia, 2009) 263–82, p. 282.

62 See Cafaggi and Micklitz (2009), p. 418. In Austria, a system of pre-financing was developed in which the Verein für Konsumenteninformation (Association of Consumer Information, VKI) concludes an agreement with a finance company that refinances the costs of the procedure. If the case is successful, they retain one third of the proceeds. This system has certain similarities with contingency fees. An advantage of several insurers is that they can compete, see H-W. Micklitz, 'Collective Private Enforcement of Consumer Law: The Key Questions', *Collective Enforcement of Consumer Law – Securing Compliance in Europe through Private Group Action and Public Authority Intervention*, eds W.H. Van Boom and M.B.M. Loos (Groningen: Europa Law Publishing, 2007) 13–33, p. 22.

63 A network or resources from membership, for instance. Then again, problems are reported in Germany in which consumer associations lack the ability to generate information regarding company profits that is necessary for the skimming-off procedures, as discussed at the conference, Borderless Consumer Protection? Effective Enforcement, Powerful Consumers (Berlin, 7 November 2011); see also F. Alleweldt et al. (Civic Consulting on behalf of IMCO), State of Play of the Implementation of the Provisions on Advertising in the Unfair Commercial Practices Legislation, 2010), p. 18.

tools to track online traders in hiding, as was previously established. Hence, there is a potential to outweigh information asymmetries, depending on which bodies are combined for the enforcement response. From a social-welfare perspective, the most crucial point, apart from improving the individual's risk ratio, is to assess which law enforcement body can generate the information necessary to pursue the *mala fide* trader scenario in the least costly way, up to the limit where society would no longer approve of generating this information. The optimal combination of entities would guarantee an efficient 'information finding'. Importantly, a public law element must be involved one way or another when it comes to *mala fide* traders. Within criminal law enforcement, police involvement has a high potential to generate information, whereas less information may be generated from procedures involving a consumer association acting in the civil court, for instance.[64] Moreover, both agencies and associations have more detailed knowledge about consumer protection laws, and therefore, can more easily identify law infringements.[65]

As indicated in the previous chapter, capture within associations or public agencies may lead to severe principal-agent problems. These problems are further aggravated as the number of players involved increases, and generally are all the more likely the higher the issues at stake. Although frivolous lawsuits are a minor threat in individual consumer cases, they are a given in group litigation.[66] Therefore, remedies that have an immediate effect must be carefully designed. Making use of interim measures is a trade-off between asking little proof and securing true statements. A careful design is likewise required for cases, in which competitors can profit considerably from potentially frivolous damage to their rival's business.

In the case scenarios discussed, a competitor or a trade association might pursue a lawsuit, and the rest of the society can free ride on their efforts. While efficient group litigation is costly to design, the benefits for risk allocation are very high and societal benefits might justify the effort. The big advantage emerging from the improved risk allocation is that the case is brought at all and is not left unenforced. This is crucial in terms of deterrence whenever the competitor has an interest in pursuing an action. Furthermore, other administrative costs vary with the remedy and the body carrying out the information search. As outlined in Chapter 4, group litigation is less costly for the individual, but, overall, the procedure is more costly. Carrying out a high number of individual lawsuits instead may be even more costly. Group litigation leads to cases being pursued that would not have been brought as individual cases.

Although in this case, the *bona fide* trader scenario can be handled through private law enforcement (for example, consumer associations as a representative in a civil court), the *mala fide* trader scenario (as with scenario two) requires

64 See Van den Bergh (2008), p. 284.

65 See Van den Bergh and Visscher (2008b), p. 17.

66 See Keske (2010), pp. 104, 111.

investigative powers of some kind. Pure private law enforcement will fail, unless another entity involved as the representative could generate this information or unless a criminal procedure were initiated. Comparably high investigative powers of public authorities are a reason for advocating their intervention in particular. Even more information could be generated within a criminal procedure, which makes the combination of a public entity acting as prosecutor in the criminal court an interesting one. The section on criminal law enforcement examines this aspect.

Consumer ADR Compensation is the most typical remedy in an ADR procedure. The smaller the individual's harm, the lower the procedural costs need to be to induce the individual consumer to invest in litigation. The ADR body can capture low-value claims to some degree, more than the civil court, but from a rational viewpoint, damage may be too small in some cases even to pursue a claim with an ADR body. This threshold is reflected in procedural rules that bar claims below a certain level from consideration (even if an optimistic individual would be inclined to bring such a case; a loser-pays rule might apply on top). This is likely to be the case for €15. Therefore, a single consumer's action before an ADR body is very unlikely in these case scenarios, but a competitor who is granted standing might bring a case. Previous findings about the 'predefined set' of defendants and the value of an ADR decision are valid and distinguish the *bona fide* trader scenario from the *mala fide*. The concerns about the value of an ADR decision make an injunction, if it can be achieved, less valuable. Changes or interruptions in advertisement are traditionally dealt with by a self-regulatory entity (to be discussed) that is highly interlinked with the market. 'Fining' remedies issued from an ADR body must be carefully considered because of concerns regarding capture and error costs, and are preferably not provided.

The analysis of group litigation in this case also is short. An ADR body has basically no investigative powers, although representatives could overcome this deficiency with their own investigations, as stated. They have a potential to outweigh this lack of power to generate information, that the individual or the ADR body cannot. Depending on the representative – a public agency more than a consumer association – the missing investigative powers can be compensated for in the case of a *mala fide* trader. At an ADR body there is often more expertise concerning questions of fact. With group litigation, capture is a large concern among the various representatives from associations or public agencies as well as employees of the ADR body. Many players involved may be likely to pursue their own interests; hence, results may be very uncertain. Therefore, involving a court in the procedure as an independent decision-maker with a strict procedural law may be advisable. Frivolous lawsuits can be an issue with group litigation, which is another argument in favour of introducing procedural safeguards. Procedural safeguards also reduce the likelihood of error costs. Error costs potentially could spread across all members of the group if mass cases were decided. These arguments speak in favour of disabling mass cases involving an ADR body. The last argument against allowing group litigation in ADR mass proceedings is the lack of a further development of case law, which is a general effect of decisions made outside of court; and a group litigation case may indeed be one, in which clarifications of law are desirable. In addition, *mala fide* traders may not cooperate in a group procedure before an ADR body, as previously outlined.

Administrative Law Administrative law enforcement may provide efficient handling of both misleading advertising scenarios. This type of enforcement means any action before a public authority, whether triggered by the authority's own motion, an individual or a representative. In these procedures, the state funds the majority of the cost and assumes a large share of the risk. The authority has the power to filter which claims to accept or to act on an own motion; therefore, the notion of who triggers a procedure is less decisive than under private law enforcement and the role of lawsuit initiator is diminished. The individual reaps the benefits when a public agency can grant damages, but the state still assumes the costs of the procedure. In comparison to private law enforcement, where initiating a lawsuit for the low individual harm in this case study is not done, these types of cases could still be brought to administrative law enforcement from the viewpoint of the individual. The public authority assumes the majority of costs. This reasoning is similar for the choice of ADR law enforcement. A public agency also has the advantage of high investigative powers (including digital investigations). The public entity's advantages and low costs to the individual are a remedy for individual rational apathy; however, for the record, although the intervention is beneficial for the individual, the authority nevertheless incurs high administrative costs. Therefore, from a social-welfare point of view, a single €15 scenario needs to be disabled.

If societal harm is extensive, but small and widespread, the public authority must be able to obtain sufficient information to take enforcement action. Individual consumers and competing traders must have incentives to transfer their private information to the public authority. Remedies such as damages, injunctions or 'fining' may play a crucial role. Not being able to obtain compensation might be a disincentive for consumers, but because the individual damage in this scenario is smaller than in the package travel scenario, the consumer may have other primary goals than just personal compensation, which may be satisfied with other remedies. Then again, having suffered only minor harm, the consumer may not be inclined to take any action at all.

Several reporting strategies can be envisaged such as cooperating with consumer advice centres where consumers may register complaints. Assuming the individual's costs may be justified in this setting because damage may not be sufficient for the individual to finance an entire procedure.

The entity's available investigative powers can then come in handy, particularly for the *mala fide* scenario (comparable to the situation in package travel). The agency's monitoring and investigations may uncover infringements that put the agency in the position to launch an action on an own motion. The speed of a reaction will be another factor in the efficiency. Thus, monitoring or *ex ante* clearing might be an effective tool, particularly to protect *bona fide* traders and to single out *mala fide* traders; however, this tool has very high administrative costs and risks societal losses through censorship.

A competitor also may be motivated to report. If a competitor stands to reap substantial financial gains (thus, avoiding rational apathy), these cases are best channelled to a civil law procedure, from a social-welfare viewpoint. However, if information asymmetry is present, the intervention of a public authority may be required, but this situation is less likely with a competitor.[67]

Despite who brings the case, the public entity must filter, accept and decide the case according to social-welfare considerations. As in the optimal mix for the package travel case, there are good reasons to increase cooperation among law enforcement mechanisms to guarantee a 'public law element', rather than restructure a public entity to grant damages.

With administrative law enforcement, the distinction between individual and group cases is blurred because the initiator is unimportant in the decision to take the case. When a group representative brings a case to the authority, the individual must only show affiliation with the group litigation and, for instance, not report. Certain findings regarding a public agency as a representative before a civil court, for instance, have already been discussed. If representative actions are brought to a public authority, advantages in risk sharing given to the individual are also present for the representative. Monitoring or investigation may be carried out either by the representative, which can be a public body, or the public body that decides the case. In contrast with private law enforcement, public entities, when they decide a case, can generate a great deal of information and this ability may be decisive for the cost–benefit analysis. From the perspective of a consumer association, these enhanced investigative powers may be advantageous in comparison with pursuing a case through a civil court (and certainly an ADR). In this sense, the procedure is superior in terms of generating more information if it includes a public authority, which is necessary for *mala fide* scenarios.

Capture is possible by the agency bringing the case or deciding a case and within associations. The more powers in the hands of the same entity, the greater the danger – for example, the same body bringing a case, and then investigating and adjudicating it. Solutions may include separate units within the entity or rules that public bodies may bring actions only to a civil court, an ADR body or specialised courts. Involving a court in the procedure may reduce the occurrence of error costs (and their spreading) and of frivolous lawsuits. This parallels developments in criminal law regarding the role of the public prosecution.

Administrative costs depend on the remedy involved and whether it concerns individual or group litigation, particularly if one assumes that damages can be granted. The number of administrative bodies involved can impact the risk of capture. Lower administrative costs depend on whether information raised

67 If B2B arbitration exists in a country, channelling it there may be efficient. The nature of B2B arbitration is not discussed further in this book.

may be transferred without duplication. Once an infringement is established, the assessment and granting of damages may be outsourced to the wrongdoer, possibly under supervision, as this would be a lesser burden on state-financed adjudication structures.

In total, particularly for the *mala fide* trader scenario, investigative powers are crucial, although perhaps not necessary for the *bona fide* trader scenario. Issues of capture, frivolous lawsuits and error costs speak in favour of involving a court element in the procedure. Public authorities also are privileged compared with pure private litigation when it comes to investigating facts about a case (such as powers to access business premises).

Competitors may have high damages at stake and, therefore, incentives to sue in civil court. Because competitors are within the same market, they are less likely to need additional investigative powers.[68] When societal harm is extensive, incentives for representatives to seek remedies such as injunctions are beneficial in cases, in which individuals would not take this step.

Criminal Law Using criminal law in these case scenarios, particularly for the *mala fide* example, guarantees the use of wide investigative powers – irrespective of the representative involved (individual or others) – as criminal procedures potentially can outweigh any of the players' lack of investigative powers. As previously established, criminal law is intended mainly to be a fallback option – an underlying threat – for consumer law cases such as these examples. The strengths and weaknesses of criminal law have been discussed above and clearly preparing litigation may be very costly because of the high burden of proof.[69] This is also true for public agencies as representatives – some public agencies may act as prosecutor (with possible police involvement). Obviously, using criminal law enforcement can be warranted for certain types of *mala fide* traders. The procedure also may serve as an underlying threat to enable exploitation of less costly mechanisms and to provide for nonmonetary sanctions where necessary.

In a collective criminal proceeding, error costs – which arguably rarely occur – may be very high for the wrongly convicted (pay for all), as well as for the victims if a wrongdoer goes free (no money for anyone and potentially a repeat offence). Therefore, a high degree of accuracy, typically attributed to criminal law procedures, can be very valuable in mass cases.

Self-regulation The definition of self-regulation is narrow and for advertising is a code of conduct that must be observed. In the event of a successful case and a compliant trader, changes are made to the advertisement and, consequently,

68 Little or no information asymmetries are present because they know the market segment, Mahé (2009), p. 174.

69 See interview with Gunnar Larsson, Swedish Consumer Ombudsman and Head of Consumer Authority (Stockholm, 25 August 2009) who expressed this for the Swedish legal system.

everyone profits. All other remedies are excluded from self-regulatory enforcement. In fact, the result is similar to an injunction. In the advertising sector, self-regulation rather than an ADR body can be found.

Again, rational apathy may be an issue in reporting and individuals (consumers, traders) or representatives need motivation to act. Costs are borne by the market in which the self-regulation is applied.[70] A self-regulatory system contains a lot of information about the market to be controlled, including the ability to trace wrongdoers. Also, individuals may need information only about the ad and not the wrongdoer to file a complaint. However, some traders – particularly *mala fide* traders – will not participate in self-regulation.[71]

The advantage in terms of information must be weighed against the risk of capture, which is a given in self-regulation. Consumer involvement may potentially mitigate capture, however. In addition, self-regulation does not pose an agency problem because no representative is needed.

Despite its limited scope, self-regulation can have considerable benefits if traders are compliant (the *bona fide* trader scenario). However, in the case of a *mala fide* trader who is unwilling to comply and reluctant to join the sector's self-regulatory organisation, self-regulation is unable to force the trader to comply with its decision. Cooperation of media owners may be weak when it comes to Internet media because there is no legal obligation to cooperate,[72] which aggravates matters in the scenario in which a *mala fide* trader hides online. Self-regulation has another advantage in *bona fide* trader cases: the possibilities of *ex ante* advice or voluntary preclearing,[73] which allow an advertisement to be checked before being put on the market. Voluntary preclearing can signal if a trader is *bona fide* and would allow some targeted monitoring in cooperation with other enforcers, for example. Furthermore, considerations regarding efficiency may include allowing the findings of a self-regulatory body to be used in other judicial proceedings, such as damage cases.

While generally one single complaint is sufficient, collective actions may exert needed pressure. It may be desirable if individuals are disinclined to complain because of low damages and little interest in curbing the trader's future actions. In some cases, such as when a sector acts like a cartel, the competitor also may have no monetary interest in intervening. Here, the self-regulatory body also will not act on its own motion. A representative in group litigation may be inclined to file a complaint with the self-regulatory body first due to its low procedural costs.

---

70 See Miller (1985), p. 898. Industry bears the costs of self-regulation: Ayres and Braithwaite (1992), p. 114; Ogus (1994), p. 107. Also traders have an interest to bring about regulation that improves the working of the economic system, see R.H. Coase, 'Advertising and Free Speech', *Journal of Legal Studies* 6.1 (1977): 1–34, p. 6, but it has to be looked at with suspicion.

71 See Alleweldt et al. (2010), p. 22.

72 See Verbruggen (2011), p. 125.

73 See ibid., pp. 19, 47, 114.

Intervention by a body as representative with investigative powers can enhance efficiency by generating more comprehensive information within the system. As stated previously, self-regulators generally have considerable information about their own sector and its participants. Depending upon who brings the case, there may be capture issues and agency problems. As mentioned, the underlying threat of other enforcement systems is crucial.

Administrative costs of self-regulation costs are low compared with public enforcement, for instance.[74] Because no damages are granted, administrative costs are presumably even lower than those involving an ADR body. However, the prevention of other societal costs has to be assured in the self-regulatory body's design. Then again, if a preclearance system is in place, its financing must be considered. Nevertheless, the way this mechanism can be used in this case scenario is not to assess damage, order an injunction or 'fining' remedies, but to take a preliminary step toward changing a misleading advertisement, in other words a less binding 'injunction'. Consequently, while self-regulation often may be only a first step, its lower administrative costs may justify implementing this mechanism for the few cases that risk duplication of costs. The exact extent of the administrative costs depends on what the self-regulatory entity precisely looks like and how it coordinates with other entities in the enforcement mix. It is dependent on a 'stick'. Efficiency considerations may support funding for these tasks, rather than induce self-regulatory bodies to engage in preparing collective actions. Some monitoring effort may be imaginable, but only regarding the code of conduct.

The value of self-regulation is its being a potential low-cost cross-financer for more costly procedures and its providing some *ex ante* action. The results of the self-regulatory body must be monitored carefully for social-welfare interests because self-regulation inherently is inclined to pursue industry's interests.

Conclusion Relevant new law enforcement tools for these case studies are any form of group litigation and self-regulation. In terms of design suggestions, consideration revolves around the competitor's incentives. A competitor who has suffered substantial individual damages will have high interests at stake and can profit from remedies such as injunctions or 'fining' – anything that may damage the competitor's business. In general, the findings in the package travel case study apply here. Apart from civil court, a particular country may offer B2B arbitration options that may follow different procedural rules than the consumer ADR procedure outlined. Notably, in relation to a trader, a competitor generally suffers from a lower information asymmetry than does a consumer. Therefore, in terms of optimising responses, it is useful if the competitor presents the evidence without a costly investigation. Unless the information asymmetry is high, most cases may be handled in private law bodies rather than a public authority or criminal

74 See Faure, Ogus and Philipsen (2009), p. 171, if such a system is able to achieve compliance, it will typically do so at a significantly lower administrative cost than if public enforcement processes are invoked.

court. A trader's interest in damaging a competitor's business frivolously must be considered. Although the competitor's intervention may benefit social welfare, the competitor may not have an incentive to sue in every situation, such as in the 'cartel situation'.

When a case has small, but widespread harm, the calculation and distribution of compensation to individuals may not be worthwhile from an economic point of view. Therefore, to prevent loss of deterrence, other possible remedies must be included in the assessment. Injunction or 'fining' remedies are other sanctions/ remedies that may deter the wrongdoer. It is essential to realise that *mala fide* traders count on the fact that the individual will not sue because of the minor harm suffered; therefore, the challenge is to design an optimal response that involves alternative remedies and players, notably forms of group litigation and interventions by public authorities to uphold deterrent effects. This response is particularly crucial in situations in which there is no free riding on the competitor's efforts because the competitor has no incentive to sue. The initiation of lawsuits via other players, like consumers or their representatives, must be guaranteed. Competition between various initiators can be beneficial.

An optimal mix of law enforcement mechanisms can centre on some main questions. It can be discussed which bodies should play a role in the mix, particularly regarding ability to generate information and the danger of diluted incentives by capture or principal-agent problems. Based on the previous analysis, there are good reasons why a public law element is necessary for *mala fide* trader scenarios. The way in which this information enters the enforcement response is less decisive. It could enter via a public authority that acts as a representative or likewise a public authority that adjudicates a case. As established earlier, coordination of law enforcement bodies is preferable to restructuring them. Only for *bona fide* trader scenarios can a response without a public authority be effective, such as relying purely on a consumer association's actions before a civil court. Also associations may engage in monitoring for certain types of case scenarios. Generally, to maintain the lowest-cost deterrence, enforcement methods must be fine tuned to produce necessary information. One way or the other, if information asymmetry is high, then the enforcement response must include the means to introduce the necessary information, whether that information concerns the nature of the trader or other characteristics of a case. Furthermore, the underlying threat of a strong enforcement response can be useful when trying to solve matters out of court. Likewise, a deal may result from informal negotiations at an agency in which the trader commits to compensating the consumers. By the same token, enabling follow-on damage claims may be efficient as long as over-deterrence does not result.

Capture, frivolous lawsuits and error costs regarding decision-making by public authorities, are reasons to favour involving a court element in mass procedures early on. The problem with error costs in group litigation is that these costs are spread over the group. Decisions must be challengeable, such as the taking of no action on behalf of a public agency if a case is reported must be justified. Group litigation has benefits if the entity making the judgment is independent of the one that initiated the lawsuit and carried out the investigation. This separates powers and prevents capture. Adjudication could be undertaken by a civil court or by a different, independent public entity. No matter who initiates the case at a public entity, cases must be filtered according to social-welfare criteria; therefore, capture and any pursuit of individual interests counter to society's interests must be excluded. As established previously, the social costs of mass cases handled by an ADR body exceed the benefits, which is why this option should be excluded. The ADR's role is basically not given in these scenarios regarding mass cases and likewise ADR is not recommended for individual damage cases of €15. When it comes to other remedies, self-regulation for advertising cases is, in practice, more prominent than ADR.

An optimal design for any representative action is possible. Ingredients such as opt-in, opt-out or mandatory procedures must be taken into account, same as the remedy sought. Free riding can largely be remedied through the design and choice of remedy. Furthermore, in terms of an association's accountability, regulation can be considered. In practice, financing these entities, particularly in mass damage cases, needs improvement in Europe, but certain innovative solutions have been referred to throughout this chapter.

In addition to seeking the least costly remedy for any information asymmetry (particularly for the *mala fide* trader scenario), representatives must decide where they can afford to bring a claim as they conduct their individual CBAs. Self-regulation may be a good low-cost choice.

As demonstrated in the first case, the criminal court acts only as an underlying threat and not as a regular addressee of mass claims.[75] A case could be transferred to the criminal court if the investigative powers of the public agency do not suffice to adjudicate and deter. Or, depending on the approach, the public agency could involve the police when acting as the prosecution. Again, in cases in which a wrongdoer does not comply with a private or administrative order, criminal law may enter the picture. Also, any case brought to a criminal court will benefit from improved access to information. Likewise, criminal courts have the advantage of accurate procedures, which lower error costs; in mass scenarios, error costs are spread across everyone. In addition, any case involving a public authority as adjudicator or claimant has a high potential of generating information, although not as high as in a criminal investigation. Therefore, a consumer association may report a crime and the public prosecutor can pursue it further, at society's expense. A procedure involving both a public authority and a criminal court has very high potential for generating information *prima facie*. As is usual, criminal law is meant to be only an underlying threat in optimal mixes for the *mala fide* trader. For a

75 In very exceptional cases (severe widespread harm in product safety cases) one can think of use being made of this. Expertentagung, 'Wilhelminenberg Gespräche' (2011): collective actions at a criminal court are discussed in particular because they reduce the individual's cost risks.

representative empowered to act as a prosecutor, the preparation of a case in the criminal court could be costly, primarily because of the high burden of proof.

Regarding information seeking, various remedies come into play that may require different degrees of investigative powers; for instance, profit disgorgement requires a great deal of investigation if profits need to be measured exactly.

To a large extent, the seriousness of capture, frivolous lawsuits and principal-agent issues depend on the remedy and how much is at stake. The same is true for administrative costs. For example, in a damages case, proving exact harm and then distributing damages is more costly than proving some harm may occur in an injunctions case, which also requires no distribution of damages. In addition, opt-in/opt-out may be decisive, and 'fining' usually excludes distribution of proceeds.

When fine-tuning design, attention must be paid to guaranteeing that impartial entities make the final decisions because, for instance, representatives argue in the consumers' interests. Optimal responses differ for *bona fide* and *mala fide* trader scenarios. They are arguably often difficult to distinguish and signalling strategies must be employed. While repeat offences are a comparatively clear sign that the company at stake is a *mala fide* trader, the company also could find ways to avoid this signalling effect, such as by changing its name. The *mala fide* trader, the repeat offender, the one who deliberately calculates sanctions into fees charged to consumers, must be deterred, possibly by criminal law (personal liability). However, the *bona fide* trader, who may inadvertently place misleading advertising and intends no harm, must be treated differently.

The pivotal question is how high must a sanction be to deter a profit-maximiser from abusing the slow response – or no response – of the legal system and from calculating existing sanctions into business fees? A speedy proceeding, such as an interim measure to stop behaviour or injunctions, may be crucial. Any type of subsidies for injunction procedures, such as relief of court fees and the like, may be helpful. However, with frivolous lawsuits, fast remedies may be abused for anticompetitive purposes, resulting in a social loss. Therefore, particular attention must be given to the competitors' incentives to file suits or seek other remedies with a high potential of harming a trader's business. Taken together, these are further reasons for adding a court element to the procedures to provide more accurate procedural safeguards. Likewise, some strategic use by consumers or consumer associations is possible and these incentives must be monitored.

When thinking along these lines, the 'fastest reaction' is some kind of *ex ante* action that possibly prevents the misleading advertisement from ever appearing. Therefore, despite very high administrative costs, *ex ante* control can add value in both *bona fide* and *mala fide* trader scenarios, in that the consumer is protected from the *mala fide* trader and the *bona fide* trader is protected from legal consequences. One wonders whether the only way to protect society from *mala fide* traders' violations is to bar them access to the advertising market altogether. Such a prevention argument can be put forward if societal harm would be extensive and should be prevented from occurring in the first place;[76] and obligatory preclearance of advertising may be considered for certain products that may cause considerable societal harm. Perhaps this could be differentiated through various advertising sectors, for instance those that have the potential to cause substantial harm and those that do not.[77] This policy could potentially reduce administrative costs.

The first addressee to implement a preclearance policy seems to be a public agency that has wide monitoring powers and fines at its disposal in cases of noncompliance. Moreover, self-regulation also can provide preclearance of advertisements before they become public. In the real world, a differentiation can be suggested regarding countries where self-regulation is successful and those where it is not.[78] In countries where self-regulation is strong, such a system may work for *bona fide* traders, but *mala fide* traders will not respond. Having said that, harsh sanctions would lead to over-deterrence for even *bona fide* traders. In general, cooperation between self-regulation and a public authority may be helpful; however, legal considerations against censorship and freedom of speech issues arise and it is impossible to justify the administrative cost of checking every advertisement. An indiscriminate application of preventive enforcement risks wasting society's resources to prevent desirable violations.[79] A voluntary system may be favoured. It may allow traders to signal that they are *bona fide* and would allow for a certain degree of targeted monitoring, in cooperation with other enforcers. This system could contribute to social welfare.

Regarding the notion of efficient breaches, some *bona fide* infringements can be tolerated. As a side issue, individual cases of harm of €15 must be disabled, since the enforcement response is too costly regardless of the body involved. These low harm cases likewise may be considered efficient breaches because enforcement is too costly in terms of social welfare.

Furthermore, the self-regulatory body is the cross-financing mechanism for other strong information asymmetry cases that need a more costly enforcement response, which is comparable to the reasoning in the package travel cases. While self-regulation places some emphasis on *ex ante* action, the other bodies primarily work *ex post*. A sound connection between self-regulation and court proceedings that provides ways to use findings established by the self-regulatory body in courts can be beneficial.

76 See T. Friehe and A. Tabbach, 'Preventive Enforcement', *International Review of Law and Economics* 35 (2013): 1–12, for example terrorism.

77 If all advertising is scrutinised, even accurate advertising must run the risk of a charge of being misleading. This puts a high burden on advertisers, see Jordan and Rubin (1979), p. 552.

78 The Netherlands is a successful example, see Faure, Ogus and Philipsen (2008), p. 374.

79 See Friehe and Tabbach (2013), p. 2.

Criminal law enforcement should be open to cases in which offenders do not view the public authority's interventions as a threat and do not comply. Cooperation between the police and public agencies as prosecutors can be warranted.

The analysis clearly indicates that the issue of thresholds is a crucial one. The first threshold concerns the point, at which the damage is high enough for an individual to use an ADR body but not a civil court or to use public enforcement – if damages are granted there – but not a civil court. The second threshold is the point at which a group action for damages is justified, but not an individual action, assuming that it is possible to adequately design the group action. Another question is when actions for damages fail, and only actions for injunctions or 'fining' remain the last option. Obviously, as with the package travel case, which was designed in a specific way in order to clarify that the victim was the only consumer who was affected, a different case scenario could occur in which a group of consumers would seek a large amount of compensation because of a breach in contractual obligation. Likewise, competitors might want to bundle their damage claims.

General Conclusion

Optimality is related to institutional settings. Countries have different attributes: some have strong private consumer associations while others rely on a public authority for law enforcement. The powers of these authorities can vary. Self-regulation also is not effective in every context. Some jurisdictions are more ready than others to assess damages within criminal law proceedings and rely on criminal law in general.

In the following part, three country studies will further clarify these differences through the importance given to various players. The selected countries are then compared to the suggestions in this research and potential improvements are described as well as instances in which the right balance for optimal deterrence has been struck. Apparently, when changes are suggested, change-related costs (of reforms) must be outweighed by the accordingly high benefits.

One approach might be to construct completely new legal institutions, but, instead, this study takes the core of existing enforcement bodies, discusses possible changes in remedies or competences and places them in optimal mixes according to their strengths and weaknesses. For overall social-welfare considerations, the weakness of one body may be compensated by the strengths of another. While the model world reflects the key features of the European legal reality, the country studies are more specific regarding individual legal systems.

Charts (summary)

Case 1 – Package Travel, Version 1 and *2*
(Only damage claims and only individual law enforcement)
Version 1: Bona fide trader
Version 2: Mala fide trader

Table 5.1 Main findings for package travel scenarios

	Private Law Enforcement	**Public Law Enforcement**	**Assessment**
Rational Apathy (RA)	In court: low because damage considerable → (+) Particularly low with an ADR, as the mechanism is even less costly for individual → (++) *In court: RA impeding because lack of information causes difficulties in starting the case → (-)* *ADR: Generally only 'predefined' set of traders who volunteer → (--)*	RA even lower because state assumes majority of costs and investigative powers are given (under the condition that damages are obtained) → (+++) Criminal law even more extreme → (++++) *Unlike in version 1, here investigative powers are necessary → (+++) Criminal law → (++++)*	For version 1, private law enforcement, even an ADR suffices (one might think of securities for the award system). *For version 2, investigative powers are needed; thus a public law element in some form;* while the first type of case should be disabled from being brought to a public body, *for type 2 cases, the incentives for the individual to bring a lawsuit have to be guaranteed → by providing for compensation; follow-on damage claims and so on (preference is indeed on closer coordination rather than restructuring).*
Free-Riding	Specific cases (*both versions*) → (+) no issue.	Specific cases (*both versions*) → (+) no issue.	

Funding	There are many mechanisms facilitating access to law (legal aid etc.); case would fall under small claims procedure→ (+) ADR is a remedy for a civil court itself → (++) *Initiation of lawsuit impeded at both→ (--)/(--)*	For *both*: State assumes agency and court fees; potentially no costs for a lawyer or litigation necessary (if not restructured); procedures less costly for the individual → (+)	Version 1 is safe with an ADR or possibly the civil court. *Version 2 must be handled within public law, mainly because of need for investigative powers;* Importantly, if the public authority is not restructured (aligned with civil court by involving lawyers and so on) to grant damages, the findings are true; otherwise more administrative costs might be involved for the individual.
Information Asymmetry	Case is clear; trader traceable → (+) With ADR → OK if within predefined set of traders → (+) *Initiation of the lawsuit impeded and there is no remedy because the bodies do not provide for investigative powers to initiate litigation at all → (-)/(-)*	Powers to investigate would be given, but are not needed → (+) For cases of insolvency, additionally criminal law, sanctions are available (for those that avoid the legal requirements to provide for a security). *Initiations of the lawsuit can possibly be facilitated through the investigative powers → (++); criminal law has the most investigative powers among the law enforcers → (+++)*	For version 1, private law enforcement is sufficient. *Version 2 requires investigative powers that can be guaranteed with administrative enforcement and even more criminal law enforcement; sanctions might also be adequate.*
Capture	For *both*: in civil court: → (+) less of an issue than with ADR → (-)	For *both*: in criminal court: → (+) less of an issue than with public officials → (-) Doubtful as to public prosecutor → (-)	Independent of version 1 or *2*; courts have advantage over agencies.

Table 5.1 Concluded

	Private Law Enforcement	Public Law Enforcement	Assessment
Frivolous Lawsuits	For *both*: no danger with a single case → (+); even less with ADR whose decisions are less public → (++)	For *both*: (even preliminary) investigations (investigations into business premises, arrests) can look bad → (+/-)	This category would be more important if the study explicitly considered mass cases as well (see the second set of case scenarios).
	Rate of error costs, particularly in unclear cases, likely to be higher with ADR body due to less accurate procedural law than civil court → (-), ultimately depends on degree of specialisation and experts involved → ADR can be (+) regarding facts.	Error costs more of an issue with public agency → (-)	Experts are available within ADR body; case at hand is a clear-cut case.
Principal Agent	For *both*: little involvement of lawyers needed and, if so, chances to monitor are higher than with mass cases → (+)	For *both*: either no lawyer or chances of monitoring likely to be higher than with mass cases → (+/+)	In most procedures, no lawyer is involved and if so, the principal agent issue is to be neglected for single cases.
	Note that there is no further development of the law with the ADR body → loss to society; ADR award is generally weaker than a title granted in court, but systems to put security are imaginable.	*Criminal law provides the adequate sanctions for judgment-proof wrongdoers (imprisonment) if one assumes that there is a likelihood that mala fide traders do not provide for required securities for insolvencies → (+)*	Only clear-cut cases filtered to the ADR body; the rest, rather with court procedure and safeguards. Value of ADR awards *prima facie* lower, but can potentially be increased.
Administrative Costs	In fact, only version 1 can be dealt with, for *both* it is true: At civil court → (+/-); for small claims procedure (+) Low at ADR → (++) However, it would depend on how many more cases an ADR body triggers that would not be enforced otherwise, and on the interplay between the two bodies.	For *both*: administrative agency that makes use of investigative powers and particularly if damages have to be calculated in addition; costly → (-) Criminal court → (--) (practically excluded, due to substantial costs for investigative powers, high standards of proof and so on).	Costs of public enforcement impeding and thus only use if strictly necessary, particularly if lawyer involved and damages have to be assessed and distributed also here → rather fine-tune interaction? → An ADR should be favoured for clear-cut cases; only otherwise make use of better procedural rules and more costly maintenance of either civil court or agency or even criminal court. Some efficient breaches may be allowed.

Case 2 –Scattered Damage Due to Misleading Advertising
(Damages, injunctions and 'fining' – implicitly)
Version 3: Bona fide trader
Version 4: Mala fide trader

New mechanisms:
<u>Group litigation</u>
Self-regulation

Table 5.2 Main findings for misleading advertising scenarios

	Private Law Enforcement	Public Law Enforcement	Assessment
Rational Apathy	For *both*: individual consumer action ruled out → (--) ADR has a potential to capture lower values than civil court; still €15 too low → (-) → Case looks different for the competitor → (+) <u>Group litigation can be a remedy → (+) up to some minimum limit of damage; injunction/ fining only if individuals do not have to contribute to the costs</u>; competitor might even finance it (unless there are no real competitors because the whole sector acts the same).	For *both*: if reporting suffices, individual (particularly competitors) could indicate such a case → (+) Body can act on an own motion → (+) provided that they grant damages or facilitate obtaining them in follow-on cases; like this, injunctions and fining actions would also be financed by the state; some of these actions favour all. <u>Also a form of group litigation if association or public entity comes to (another) public entity to sue/report; at some point distributing damage is no longer worthwhile, but injunctions or fining may be (remedies are the same regardless of who triggers the action; some will have more incentives than others to do so)→(+)</u> Reporting of a crime can be incentivised, as state takes over the costs of the procedure → (+)	<u>Group litigation</u> potentially remedies rational apathy; reporting to the public entity can be incentivised, same as reporting a crime; individual cases within the private law enforcement fail most probably; for the competitors, high stakes may justify taking action within private law enforcement.
Free Riding	Per definition from an injunction; also in cases of 'fining' all profit; follow-on damage claims could incentivise individuals; alternative initiators become important.	Per definition from an injunction; also in cases of 'fining' all profit; follow-on damage claims could incentivise individuals; alternative initiators become important.	Version independent can potentially be a problem if no one consumer has a greater interest than the others. Danger of over-deterrence has to be considered if both competitors and consumers take action.

Table 5.2 Continued

	Private Law Enforcement	Public Law Enforcement	Assessment
Funding	Group litigation is the remedy in individual cases (unless competitor). In group litigation, the entity would determine the least costly avenue to bring an action – before which body to bring it (group litigation with the ADR body is excluded; see below). The extent to which group litigation arises depends on where the proceeds go, for example, in cases of 'fining'.	Group litigation, representatives taking over the reporting or pure reporting by individuals all likely to lead to a state-financed action (including public agency acting as prosecutor itself). Again, the entity to bring the case would weigh where it is more costly to do so and which remedy is worthwhile; the extent to which group litigation arises depends on where the proceeds go, for example, in cases of fining.	Group litigation or a strong involvement of a public law enforcement body (public agency or criminal law) generates cases; whether an action is brought is remedy dependant: for example, proving the exact harm in a damages case and then distributing it is more costly than proving that some harm could occur in an injunctions case, where no distribution is necessary afterwards; opt-in/out can be decisive; 'fining' usually excludes distribution of proceeds. For private enforcement, only group litigation can be dealt with, unless competitors step in; for public enforcement, incentives for only a reporting action can be provided and individual litigation may happen. Note: the extent to which the public agency procedure remains at a low cost for the individual depends on whether the procedure needs to be restructured and aligned with a civil court, because new remedies like damages shall be granted; there is reason to believe that restructuring entails dangers/costs and a cooperation between existing bodies providing for the typical remedies can be favoured instead.

Information Asymmetry	In group litigation, some investigation is possible by all representative bodies; more investigative powers rest with public authorities (and even more within criminal law) than with consumer associations; *for scenario 2, in one way or the other, a public law element has to be used (either as representative body or adjudicative body (see next column)).* Within civil law bodies, little investigation is possible → (--), particularly by ADR → (--); the representative would need to remedy this.	In group litigation, some investigation is possible by all those bodies, though less by consumer associations than by public agencies. A number of investigative powers are given to the administrative agency (*particularly necessary for case scenario 4*)→ (+) and even more in the criminal process → (++) → so there is no need to outweigh these by involving in the procedure a representative that has strong investigative powers (consumer association as representative would be OK/pure reporting). *Deterrence by criminal sanctions might be necessary for the mala fide traders*; *bona fide* traders should not be affected negatively by this; a twofold approach appears necessary. Monitoring or *ex ante* clearing might be an effective tool, particularly to protect *bona fide* traders and to single out *mala fide* traders. If voluntary, potentially only *bona fide* traders will use this service and will be singled out (**for example, in interrelation with self-regulation).**	Case 3 can be solved for instance by a consumer association acting in the civil court. *In particular for scenario 4, some investigative powers are necessary, so in one way or another a public law element has to be used (either as representative body or adjudicative body); a consumer association as representative within a private law setting does not generate sufficient overall information; the criminal law element should be reserved in particular for the mala fide traders.* **Possible effect of self-regulation: people within the industry are known.**

Note: In terms of discussing mass solutions, the possibilities to bring cases to an ADR body or a civil court are discussed in the column private law enforcement and the possibilities of bringing a case to the public agency or the criminal court in the column on public law enforcement independently of the player bringing the action.

Table 5.2 Concluded

	Private Law Enforcement	Public Law Enforcement	Assessment
Capture	More an issue with an ADR and within representing bodies (like a consumer association; a public body) → (-) Civil court OK → (+) If a captured representative were to bring a case to the ADR body, there is a danger of many captured bodies being involved. → (--) → reason 1 why group litigation with ADR body is disabled.	More an issue with public agency → (-) than with court → (+) A particular danger would be one public agency starting a mass case and also deciding it → (--) Some separation of powers should be provided for (either different entities, or public entity an bring case to court only and so on); overall more problematic if decision is to affect a group of people rather than only one person. The public prosecutor might be captured.	The next three categories depend on the remedy in the sense that the more there is at stake, the more serious the issues of capture, frivolous lawsuits and principal agent become. There are generally more issues with the personnel of ADR bodies or public agencies, and group litigation speaks in favour of involving a 'court element' or at least some separation of powers within public entities. **Self-regulatory bodies are by definition captured and need underlying threats-control mechanisms to have deterrence value in this setting.**
Frivolous Lawsuits	Severe issue with group litigation → (-); more with more publicity: civil court → (--) [ADR only → (-)] Error costs more severe at ADR concerning law (less concerning facts because of experts)→ (-) → reason 2 why group litigation at ADR is disabled (would be spread over the group); with civil court less serious problem → (+)	Severe issue with group litigation → (-); error costs more severe at administrative agency → (-); less at criminal court due to increased accuracy → (+)	Generally higher likelihood of frivolous lawsuits with group litigation; error costs in mass cases are spread across all and a court element can thus reduce the likelihood of their occurrence (if error within criminal law procedure occurred, the consequences would be very costly for the involved parties).
Principal-Agent	The more players are involved, the more dangerous this issue becomes (associations, lawyers, individuals, lobbies) → (-) Group litigation with ADR likely to be a case where clarification of law is important → reason 3 why group litigation with ADR is disabled; some free riding on the competitor's efforts can be possible and efficient.	The more players are involved, the more dangerous this issue becomes → (-) In cases where individuals only report, this danger is eliminated → (+) If captured, decisions of public agency might differ from social welfare as outlined above; some free riding on the competitor's efforts can be possible and efficient.	As soon as representation is involved, principal-agent situations are automatically incurred. In terms of their role as agents of society, the enforcement mechanisms lead to some costs and benefits, particularly if incentives are diluted.

Administrative Costs	Group litigation is always very costly and very high administrative costs are incurred when damages have to be closely assessed→ (-)	Group litigation is always very costly, presumably a bit less so with the public agency → (+) than in the criminal court → (-) Would depend on how many administrative bodies are set up (for instance to separate powers). Monitoring leads to extra costs → (-) This is particularly true for version 3; *for version 4, lawsuits with costly sanctions are much more likely and presumably efficient.*	Costs depend on the number of bodies involved and whether, for instance, damages are calculated and distributed within the setting of a public authority, amount of monitoring carried out; administrative costs depend on the remedy granted. Criminal law enforcement again scores highest. **Self-regulation is overall less costly to administer, but may be only a first step;** ***ex ante*** **action incurs administrative costs:** **Before an advertisement is made public, it could obtain clearance from such an entity, which would prevent social costs (in certain cases);** ***if this were possible only on a voluntary basis, mala fide traders potentially would avoid this and it could be a way of separating the bona fide from the mala fide traders.*** **Once the misleading advertisement has been released, self-regulation also could be a low-cost solution to make changes to it** (rather than ADR in reality); **again, traders' cooperation would be crucial, and is more likely for bona fide traders.**
			Note: Group litigation with ADR body disabled; the *mala fide* trader would not cooperate either way. Along the lines of the notion of efficient breaches, some *bona fide* infringements can be tolerated by providing only for a voluntary *ex ante* control. Another consideration is that individual cases of harm of €15 must be disabled, as the enforcement response is too costly, no matter which body is involved.

PART II
Country Studies (Comparison)

Part I describes economic insights in optimal enforcement designs for specific case studies and formulates suggestions for mixing enforcement mechanisms; Part II assesses real-life situations in some selected countries using findings from the aforementioned case studies as a benchmark. The Netherlands, Sweden and England were selected because of their different enforcement traditions.

For each case, the following steps are applied:

1. The legal solutions to the consumer problem are outlined (description);
2. The country's real-life solutions are compared with the optimal solutions and tentative suggestions for future developments are given (assessment and conclusion).

Areas in which the optimal balance of deterrence has not yet been struck in the legal setting are identified. Tentative suggestions are made regarding the design of optimal enforcement mixes that would enhance social welfare, with the precondition that changes must be Kaldor-Hicks efficient, that is, those who are worse off could be compensated by those who are better off so that there is an improvement overall.

Solutions for individual lawsuits/cases are primarily described in the first part of each country study and aggregate solutions and self-regulation in the second part.

Chapter 6
The Netherlands

Introduction

The Netherlands has a strong private law enforcement tradition. With the enactment of the Regulation on CPC, the *Consumentenautoriteit* (Netherlands Consumer Authority, CA), a public authority for consumer law enforcement was introduced in 2007. The CA, which becomes part of the *Autoriteit Consument en Markt* (Consumer and Market Authority, ACM) in 2013, acts when a collective violation (*collectieve inbreuken*) occurs and consumers' collective interests are at stake.[1] The CA also may act if a large group of consumers may be affected by a violation in the future (such as by losing trust in the workings of the market).[2] Consumer empowerment is done via the website platform, *ConsuWijzer*.[3]

The CA has both private and public law enforcement powers. The authority cannot act in individual cases and does not grant damages. It complements private law enforcement and individuals' general responses via the private law branch remain in place.[4] For cases that are not of a collective interest, private law remains the only option.

Among the traditional players in private law enforcement are consumer associations. *Consumentenbond* (CB), the most representative consumer association, plays a rather strong role in the Netherlands. Like the CA, CB may carry out various forms of group litigation, which will be illustrated.

For the majority of sectors in the Netherlands, an out-of-court mechanism for consumer redress exists: consumer complaint boards, or *Geschillencommissies* (GCs), which operate under the auspices of the Foundation for Consumer Complaints or *Stichting Geschillencommissies voor Consumentenzaken* (SGC).[5] Currently, such consumer boards are available in 53 sectors, including the travel sector.

---

1 See Article 3(k) Regulation on CPC 'collective interests of consumers' means the interests of a number of consumers that have been harmed or are likely to be harmed by an infringement. See definition in *Wet handhaving consumentenbescherming* (Act on enforcement of consumer protection law, Whc); *Kamerstukken* (Parliamentary Minutes) II 2005/06, 30 411, no. 6, pp. 4–5.

2 See Loos and Van Boom (2010), p. 137. Van Boom refers to the example of the following decision of the CA: Decision Consumentenautoriteit 23 April 2008, CA/NCB/17 (UPC).

3 See http://www.consuwijzer.nl/, last accessed: 31 March 2013. It registers every complaint and is a channel from the citizen to the public enforcement authorities.

4 See Faure, Ogus and Philipsen (2008), p. 378.

5 See http://www.degeschillencommissie.nl, last accessed: 31 March 2013.

The advertising sector entertains strong self-regulation. The prominent player is the Dutch Advertising Council or *Reclame Code Commissie* (RCC), which is part of the Dutch Advertising Code Foundation or *Stichting Reclame Code* (SRC). This body checks to see that advertising conforms to the Dutch Advertising Code.

Traditionally, the so-called 'Dutch *polder* model' (consociational politics)[6] is crucial. The Netherlands is a small country in which lots of discussions and negotiations are the rule. The *Sociaal-Economische Raad* (Social and Economic Council, SER), under the Ministry of Economic Affairs, facilitates meetings between consumer representatives and members of VNO-NCW/MKB,[7] the trade association, to develop two-sided standard contract terms, for instance.

Case 1 – Package Travel

How would the package travel case be handled in the Netherlands (damage of €2,000; a *bona fide* trader scenario [1] and a *mala fide* trader scenario [2])? Particular attention is paid to the *mala fide* trader, an online merchant who tries to hide his identity.

Online trade is common in the Netherlands, and in 2010, Dutch consumers invested approximately €3.5 billion in online holiday bookings.[8] The Netherlands has been a trading nation for many centuries,[9] and most traders are interested

6 See F. Weber and C. Hodges, 'Netherlands', *Consumer ADR in Europe*, eds C. Hodges, I. Benöhr and N. Creutzfeldt-Banda (Oxford and Portland, Oregon: Hart Publishing, 2012) 129–65, p. 133, referring to N. Huls, 'Consumer Bankruptcy: A Third Way between Autonomy and Paternalism in Private Law', *Erasmus Law Review* 3.1 (2010): 7–21, p. 19.

7 Verbond van Nederlandse Ondernemingen-Nederlands Christelijk Werkgeversverbond (Confederation of Netherlands Industry and Employers, VNO-NCW) and Brancheorganisatie voor het midden- en kleinbedrijf (SME lobby organisation, MKB) are both central/umbrella business organisations in the Netherlands. The main members of both organisations are sector organisations, but also individual companies. Both are representative, although MKB has a slightly more SME character. VNO-NCW is a central employers' organisation in the Netherlands. With 130 affiliated (sectoral) associations, it represents more than 115,000 Dutch companies. MKB-Nederland is also a central employers' organisation in the Netherlands. It represents 150 sectoral organisations covering more than 186,000 enterprises, see Response by the Confederation of Netherlands Industry and Employers (VNO-NCW) and the SME lobby organisation MKB-Nederland to the European Commission's consultation document dated 18 January 2011 on the use of Alternative Dispute Resolution, http://ec.europa.eu/consumers/redress_cons/adr_responses/Confederation_Netherlands_Industry_Employers_en.pdf, last accessed: 31 March 2013.

8 See Consumentenautoriteit, Agenda 2012/2013, http://www.consumentenautoriteit.nl/sites/default/files/redactie/consumentenautoriteit-agenda-2012-2013.pdf, last accessed: 31 March 2013, p. 12. This is the biggest share within online investments by consumers.

9 See interview with VNO-NCW/MKB (The Hague, 7 March 2011).

in long-term profit maximising and want to stay in business; indeed, some are interested in securing short-term profits and will change sector and/or country. Travel agencies are no exception, and most are legitimate businesses that benefit from being known to consumers.[10]

Summary of Legal Rules

As a first step, a consumer can always resort to the courts. In most cases, the consumer complaint board, the *Geschillencommissie Reizen* (GCR), is an alternative addressee. A special insolvency fund exists for the travel sector, as required in European travel legislation[11] and the CA has undertaken some action in the Dutch travel sector.

At the Civil Court The package travel provisions, including the right to obtain compensation, are set out in the civil code (Article 7:500 *Burgerlijk Wetboek* [BW]). For consumer law cases, the ordinary rules of civil procedure are available, even though there are some modifications because the consumer is generally the weaker party. Small claims cases are decided by the subdistrict judge.[12]

As a general principle in Dutch procedural law, the claimant has the burden of proof (Article 150 Rv, '*wie eist bewijs*').[13] Investigative powers of the civil court may include limited ability to obtain documents and various other court orders to generate information.[14] There is an agreement that in principle the individual must take the initiative in civil law cases.[15] There is much less agreement on how wide the discrepancy may be between the judge's legal ability to investigate and the

10 See personal email communications with CA (15 December 2011).

11 The legal provisions to provide for securities for insolvency situations are set out in Article 7:512 BW and Article 8.7 Whc.

12 See A.W. Jongbloed, 'Burgerlijk Procesrecht voor de Individuele Consument', *Handboek Consumentenrecht*, eds E.H. Hondius and G.J. Rijken, 3rd ed. (Zutphen: Uitgeverij Paris, 2011) 509–34; M.M. Van Campen, 'Privaatrechtelijke Handhaving door de Consumentenautoriteit', *Privaatrecht Ondersteund – Doelen, Baten, Kosten en Effecten van Bijzondere Ondersteuning door de Overheid van Privaatrechtlijke Handhaving*, eds W.H. Van Boom, S.D. Lindenbergh and S.B. Pape (Den Haag: Boom Juridische Uitgevers, 2007) 35–60, p. 57.

13 Problems sometimes occur for the consumer regarding this burden of proof, as illustrated in M.Y. Schaub, 'Handhaving van Consumentenrecht', *Handhaven van en door het Privaatrecht*, eds E. Engelhardt et al. (Den Haag: Boom Juridische Uitgevers, 2009) 149–71.

14 See I.N. Tzankova, 'Class Actions, Group Litigation and Other Forms of Collective Litigation Dutch Report (Memorandum in the ambit of the Global Class Action Exchange Project), Report Part 1' (2007), p. 2. See also Articles 22 Rv.

15 See R. Verkerk, 'The Netherlands', *European Traditions in Civil Procedure*, ed. C.H. van Rhee (Antwerp – Oxford: Intersentia, 2005) 281–90. Competences with respect to fact-finding have expanded and judges also started using them more frequently.

factual situation. A lot depends on the judge.[16] There are procedural particularities that mitigate the defendant's refusal to cooperate, such as a reversal of the burden of proof.

A civil judge has no ability to locate a trader who provides the wrong or no address on the Internet (case scenario 2), and, therefore, recourse via the civil court is practically impeded.[17] Generally, if a claimant does not have the defendant's address, the writ of summons cannot be served because the name of the defendant and the address have to be provided and verified by the lawyer. Normally this information is available to a claimant through the trade register or online registers, but these are useless in the case of the hiding trader.[18] Then again, a claimant who cannot trace the trader could potentially come to a favourable judgment and be granted a title against the defendant. However, this title is equally useless,[19] even if passed on to a bailiff office that takes over the enforcement, if the trader does not cooperate.[20]

In Dutch law there are no special sanctions for frivolous lawsuits[21] and the consequence is simply that those suits are turned down. Furthermore, rarely is the claimant ordered to pay the full defendant's costs.

Most proceedings involving consumer law are initiated via a procedure before the subdistrict judge.[22] Before 1 July 2011, the subdistrict judge dealt with all cases of a value below €5,000 and with disputes concerning rent and labour contracts (irrespective of the amount).[23] That limit has been increased to €25,000

According to Articles 23 and 24 Rv the judge's decision should be based only upon issues raised by the parties.

16 That opinions on this differ a lot was the essence of a discussion followed by a presentation of the research in the Behavioural Approaches to Contract and Tort (BACT) seminar at the Erasmus University Rotterdam (Rotterdam 10 December 2010).

17 See interview with Professor Ton Jongbloed, Professor of the Law of Enforcement and Seizure, University of Utrecht (Utrecht, 26 January 2011).

18 In terms of tracing traders behind websites, special licenses are needed to obtain this information. These are for instance available to public authorities, private investigators, bailiffs or lawyers. The information that an individual can obtain from websites like www.sidn.nl/nc/over-nl/whois', last accessed: 31 March 2013 or www.whois.net/ip-address-lookup, last accessed: 31 March 2013 is very limited due to data protection requirements. The same is true for the international website http://cqcounter.com/siteinfo/, last accessed: 31 March 2013. A *mala fide* trader can be assumed to provide wrong information to such websites.

19 See personal communications with Professor Willem H.W. Van Boom, Erasmus University Rotterdam (Rotterdam, 2 December 2012).

20 See *Gerechtsdeurwaarderswet* (Bailiff Act, Gdw).

21 See personal communications with Professor Willem H.W. Van Boom, Erasmus University Rotterdam (Rotterdam, 2 December 2012).

22 See Loos and Van Boom (2010), p. 26.

23 See E.H. Hondius, *Netherlands National Report – Study: An Analysis and Evaluation of Alternative Means of Consumer Redress other than Redress through Ordinary Judicial Proceedings* (2006), p. 1.

and the judge is now competent in all cases of consumer credit (such as loans up to €40,000) and all consumer sales contracts.[24] The case scenarios described here fall under this threshold.

The subdistrict judge is a single judge who must have six years of experience in the legal profession and be selected by a special commission and nominated by the Queen.[25] Claimants may argue their case without a lawyer. The procedure and the language are less formal compared with an ordinary procedure.[26] All types of evidence are allowed. Equally all civil remedies are available. An appeal is possible, but only if the claim concerns a value higher than €1,750. In this case, legal representation is mandatory.[27]

Only 66 per cent of consumers know of the existence of this subdistrict judge.[28] While there is thus no requirement to have a lawyer, not having one in practice can be disadvantageous because the less experienced party may end up in an unequal position against the represented party. The subdistrict judge is active and helpful in these types of procedures.[29] However, *mala fide* traders cannot be dealt with in this procedure. Consumers suing individually can resort to consumer associations for help, such as advice on how to present evidence.[30] Before 2000, the CB could even take up civil cases for its members through its legal service, but that proved to be too expensive.[31]

For the record, as soon as a cross-border element is involved, the European rules on the Small Claims Procedure apply.[32] As a precondition, at least one of the parties must be domiciled or habitually resident in a Member State other than the one of the court seized. However, a case may not be taken up if a claimant who completes the application for this procedure is unable to supply the address of the

---

24 See *Evaluatiewet modernisering rechterlijke organisatie*, Stb. 2011, 255, Act, of 19 May 2011. This may reduce the barrier to sue in court for a new set of cases, see M.B.M. Loos, 'Individuele Handhaving van het Consumentenrecht bij de Burgerlijke Rechter', *Tijdschrift voor Consumentenrecht* 1 (2011): 1–11, p. 4.

25 See Hondius (2006b), p. 7.

26 See Loos and Van Boom (2019), p. 30.

27 See Hondius (2006b), p. 7.

28 See L. Nikkels et al., *Kennen Consumenten hun Rechten en Plichten? Onderzoek naar het Kennisniveau vanConsumenten* (2008), p. 29.

29 See interview with CB (The Hague, 3 December 2010).

30 Ibid.

31 See Faure, Ogus and Philipsen (2008), p. 393, based on interviews with employees of the consumer association.

32 See X.E. Kramer, 'Vereenvoudiging van de Geschillenbeslechting in Consumentenzaken: De Europese Small Claims Procedure en Nationale Initiatieven', *Tijdschrift voor Consumentenrecht* 4 (2007): 111–21, p. 118. See *Uitvoeringswet verordening Europese procedure voor geringe vorderingen* (Law implementing the Regulation on European Small Claims Procedure).

trader.[33] Some exceptions may provide the claimant an opportunity to complete the application document.[34] In practice, this procedure is not widely used.[35] The contact point in the Netherlands of the European Consumers Centre (ECC) network furthermore provides information and advice in cross-border situations.[36]

Litigation costs can take various forms: court charges, bailiff's services (either in starting the procedure or in enforcing a judgment), witness' costs and expert's costs.[37] A rather accurate prediction of the costs involved in Dutch civil litigation is possible because most are calculated on the basis of a tariff.[38] The fee for a procedure before the subdistrict judge is €75 for natural persons (€112 for legal persons) for cases with no clear monetary value or in which an amount of less than €500 is claimed.[39] If the value exceeds €500, but stays below €12,500, natural persons incur a fee of €213 (€448 for legal persons). This would be applicable for the case at hand in 2013. For case values in between €12,500 and €25,000, the fees are €448 for natural persons (€896 for legal persons). By way of example, for case values exceeding €100,000, the fees are €1,474 for natural persons (€3,715 for legal persons). In addition, bailiff's services currently amount to €76.71 (see Article 2 a *Btag*).[40] A bill to substantially increase court fees – basically, to introduce a user-pays rule – was withdrawn in April 2012.[41]

Dutch lawyers' rules of conduct forbid no-win-no-fee arrangements (in which the lawyer receives no payment if the case is lost) and *quotum pars litis* arrangements (in which the lawyer receives a percentage of the claim).[42] In the Netherlands, there is a strong resistance to contingency fees. Hourly rates for lawyers are at least €150.

The loser-pays rule is applicable in Dutch Civil Procedural Law,[43] although, in practice, it is applied with some flexibility. The judge can lower excessive costs and

33 See presentation by R. Terryn, *The Loopholes of Consumer Law, Ius Commune Conference* (Leuven 25 November 2010).

34 See Loos and Van Boom (2010), p. 56.

35 See interview with Professor Ton Jongbloed, Professor of the Law of Enforcement and Seizure, University of Utrecht (Utrecht, 26 January 2011).

36 See http://www.eccnl.eu/, last accessed: 31 March 2013.

37 See Loos (2011), p. 5.

38 See Tuil (2010), p. 409.

39 See *Wet griffierechten burgerlijke zaken – Bijlage behorend bij de wet* (Court Fees for Civil Matters Act – Annex).

40 See for all tariffs: *Besluit tarieven ambtshandelingen gerechtsdeurwaarders* (Bailiff Fees Decree, Btag)), Stb. 2001, 325, ammended in Stb. 2001, 600.

41 See *Wet verhoging griffierechten* (Law on Court Fees Increase) (*Kamerstukken* (Parliamentary Minutes) II 2011/12, 33 071, nos 1–3).

42 See Tuil (2010), p. 402. He also mentions some exceptions to this prohibition.

43 See Article 237 Rv.

divide costs between the two parties.[44] This concept has been further developed in case law.[45] It is mitigated in the sense that only a 'liquidated rate' is shifted.

Some consumers have insurance for certain types of lawsuits and claimants without financial resources may obtain legal aid (with a varying contribution by the claimant).[46] Legal expenses insurance covers approximately 47.8 per cent of the households and these insurers are rather powerful in deciding the direction a claim may take.[47] There is no apparent reason why legal aid and insurance would not be given in cases of package travel.[48] Legal aid may apply when the minimum case value is €500.[49] Legal aid is relatively widely available in the Netherlands,[50] although it is expected to decrease over the coming years with economisations.[51]

In fact, in the travel sector consumers (or traders) rarely revert to court procedure).[52] Rather, almost all disputes in the travel sector are solved via the GCR. The ordinary courts may be necessary in particular in cases involving foreign traders or Dutch traders who are not registered at the ADR body.

The overall case numbers in 2011 were 609,640 judgments in the small claims procedure (661,600 in 2010; 650,550 in 2009; 561,900 in 2008)[53] and 115,750 in the ordinary civil procedure, in the first instance (118,420 in 2010; 111,740 in 2009; 102,010 in 2008).[54] Consumer cases are not singled out specifically in these statistics and therefore, conclusions may not be drawn.

---

44 See Hondius (2006), p. 8; the rule is for instance only applicable for lawyer costs according to the court-approved scale of costs, see Loos (2011), p. 5.

45 See I.N. Tzankova, 'Global Class Action Project Country Report the Netherlands – Part 2' (2008), p. 2. It is also called a 'mitigated loser-pays rule', see Tuil (2010), p. 415.

46 See M.B.M. Loos, 'Evaluation of the Effectiveness and Efficiency of Collective Redress Mechanisms in the European Union – Country Report Netherlands' (2008), p. 39.

47 See Tuil (2010), p. 407.

48 See interview with CB (The Hague, 3 December 2010).

49 See *Wet op de rechtsbijstand* (Act on Legal Support, Wrb) as of 1 July 2011. Certain maximum income limits are valid as well.

50 See Tuil (2010), p. 406.

51 See Loos and Van Boom (2010), p. 44.

52 See interview with Professor Ton Jongbloed, Professor of the Law of Enforcement and Seizure, University of Utrecht (Utrecht, 26 January 2011).

53 See Annual report Rechtspraak 2011, p. 78. Data from the *Centraal Bureau voor de Statistiek* (Central Bureau for Statistics, CBS) differ: for the small claims procedure 452,400 in 2008; 519,800 for 2009; 550,300 in 2010 and 509,500 in 2011 (preliminary result), and for ordinary civil procedures 31,100 in 2008; 35,500 in 2009; 36,700 in 2010 and 28,300 in 2011. See Statline, Rechtspraak; kerncijfers, http://statline.cbs.nl/StatWeb/publication/?VW=T&DM=SLNL&PA=70229ned&D1=a&D2=a&HD=090416-1648&HDR=G1&STB=T, last accessed: 31 March 2013. Despite the increase in the jurisdiction of the subdistrict judge on 1 July 2011 no increase can be seen. There might be other influential factors.

54 See Annual report Rechtspraak 2011, p. 73.

The Dutch Consumer ADR Board Consumer ADR plays a very strong role in the Netherlands.[55] The foundations of the various GCs are established by standard contract term negotiations conducted under the auspices of the SER. These negotiations are conducted by trade and industry associations on the one hand and consumer organisations on the other.[56] On the consumer side, the CB and sectoral consumer organisations, if they exist, conduct the negotiations. As a consequence, competition in the market may occur purely along the lines of price and quality and not conditions. The GCs are the dispute resolution organisms in these contract terms.[57] The ADR body applies private law; equity is generally more important than a strict adherence to procedural law standards.

Currently, 53 different consumer boards issue awards in the form of 'binding advice', which is regarded as a settlement agreement.[58] As a precondition to bringing a claim to the ADR board, the trader must be registered with the board. Traders may register in two ways: as members of the registered sector organisations or independently (but still must comply with the standard terms). The consent of both parties is necessary to initiate the procedure.[59] The business' consent is given through its membership in a national trade organisation or its registration at the GC and it waives its right to go to a civil court. The consumer gives consent in each individual case and may choose court proceedings as an alternative.[60]

One of the ADR boards deals with travel and is empowered in the standard contract terms of the *Algemene Nederlandse Vereniging van Reisondernemingen* (Dutch travel association, ANVR) – the '*ANVR-reisvoorwaarden*' – in Article 17[3]. The procedure goes as follows:[61] as a precondition to a proceeding before the board, the consumer is obligated to contact the trader directly and try to resolve the dispute. If the consumer does not comply with this provision, the trader can ask the GC to refuse a complaint. In practice, sometimes it is difficult to prove that contact with the trader was established.[62] The obligation to attempt to settle beforehand leads to very high numbers of cases being solved at that stage, especially since the

55 See interview with Professor Ton Jongbloed, Professor of the Law of Enforcement and Seizure, University of Utrecht (Utrecht, 26 January 2011).

56 See Weber and Hodges (2012), pp. 135 for more details.

57 See Annual report Geschillencommissie 2009, p. 7.

58 See Tuil (2010), p. 403.

59 See Hondius (2006b), p. 3.

60 See Loos (2008), p. 21. The so-called 'geschillenartikel' gives the consumers the possibility to go to the ADR body; no obligation emanates from this provision in line with Article 6:236 (n) BW, personal email communications with SGC (10 November 2011).

61 See Weber and Hodges (2012), p. 141 for more details.

62 See Loos and Van Boom (2010), p. 32. See interview with Professor Ton Jongbloed, Professor of the Law of Enforcement and Seizure, University of Utrecht (Utrecht, 26 January 2011). He agrees, and repeats the notion that no written proof is always a big disadvantage.

GC procedure acts as an underlying threat.[63] To start the procedure, a questionnaire is completed to explain the claim and propose a possible solution; evidence is attached. A lawyer's involvement is not required.[64] If a claim is accepted, the documents are sent to the other party for a response. A date for a hearing, which is rather informal, can be fixed. Both the consumer and the trader are free to join or not join this short hearing and present their claim orally. The procedure involves witnesses and experts.[65] The decision is in writing. Cases of traders not being registered with the board are inadmissible, which amount to three per cent of the cases in 2011 and four per cent in 2012.[66] Therefore, a dispute with a *mala fide* trader clearly cannot be handled at a GC.

Some other cases are generally excluded, such as disputes that pertain to death, physical injury or illness and those already pending before a court.[67]

The GCR Board includes three members: a chairman nominated by the board, a member nominated by the CB and a member nominated by the ANVR. None is to represent his respective side. The wide majority of the chairpersons are subdistrict court judges.

Both consumers and traders can initiate the procedure. Within two months, either party may appeal the case in court on limited grounds (for instance, if the Board decision is unacceptably unfair and unreasonable, a violation of the right to be heard).[68] In an appeal procedure, a lawyer may be required because a judge hears the case,[69] often the subdistrict judge. Between January 2005 and July 2008, for instance, 13 cases came before the courts, of which the 'binding advice' was nullified in five cases.

The notion of 'binding advice' entails *prima facie* that the award cannot be enforced against an unwilling debtor. However, trade and industry guarantee the enforcement of awards by all traders who are registered with the trade association, vouching for their members' compliance with the board decisions. The business guarantee is available for up to three months after the 'binding advice' has been

63 See interview with VNO-NCW/MKB (The Hague, 7 March 2011). The Dutch are tough negotiators; also the consumers generally know their rights very well. If a lawyer is nonetheless involved, this is done at own expenses.

64 See Hondius (2006b), p. 5; personal email communications with SGC (10 November 2011): The procedure is purposely arranged in a way that the consumer can defend himself.

65 See Hondius (2006b), p. 5.

66 See Annual report Geschillencommissie 2011, p. 22 and annual report Geschillencommissie 2012, p.16.

67 See Hondius (2006b), p. 3.

68 See Article 25 *Reglement Geschillencommissie Reizen* (GCR regulations). Until 14 days after the decision spelling mistakes of miscalculation and so on can be corrected. See Article 7:904 BW and Article 25 *Reglement Geschillencommissie Reizen* (GCR Regulations).

69 See A. Klapwijk and M. Ter Voert, *Evaluatie De Geschillencommissie 2009* (Den Haag: Van Boom Juridische Uitgevers, 2009), p. 76.

rendered.[70] In 2010, this business guarantee was restricted in all sectors to €10,000 to avoid special rules applicable for insurers (such as having a license with a Dutch bank).[71] If a member does not pay the compensation, the consumer may refer the claim to the association (ANVR) and the association would pay and then recoup the money from the trader.[72] It is very rare that members would refuse to pay a GC award, but some members may object as a matter of principle.[73] ANVR may kick out noncompliers. In terms of guaranteeing solvency of the members, all are screened when they join the association, but not subsequently.[74] ANVR may fine members and loss of membership is an alternative sanction.[75]

Furthermore, for security, the 'deposit payment' system applies. A consumer who disputes a trader's bill must remit the outstanding sum to the appeal board for safekeeping before the complaint will be handled. For independently

70 See Article 17(5) 5 ANVR algemene reisvoorwaarden (ANVR Travel Standard Contract Terms). There is generally a very high compliance rate in the GCs, see Loos and Van Boom (2010), p. 98 who cite the Klapwijk and Ter Voert (2009), p. 80: Overall traders comply with 82 per cent of the awards.

71 As explained by SER, http://www.ser.nl/nl/taken/zelfregulering/consumentenvoorwaarden/meer%20weten/nakomingsgarantie.aspx, last accessed: 31 March 2013.

72 See interview with thuiswinkel (The Hague, 13 April 2011).

73 See Weber and Hodges (2012), p. 151; see also interview with ANVR (The Hague, 13 April 2011).

74 See interview with ANVR (The Hague, 13 April 2011).

75 See Article 12 Huishoudelijk Reglement ANVR (ANVR Rules). The maximum fine is €5,000. According to personal email communications with ANVR (14 October 2011), the loss of membership is a serious fear for traders. The ANVR is also very tough in terms of sanctioning members internally, even though only very few cases have been reported. The underlying threat of criminal law is of no issue in the Netherlands. As to the behaviour that the ANVR reports, this is confirmed in an interview with the CA (The Hague, 23 March 2011). The CB in personal email communications (25 October 2011) expresses: 'Why I do think the traders obey? I think the main reason is that being part of ANVR in Holland is important for travel associations. A lot of Dutch consumers do not book a trip with travel agencies who are not member of the ANVR. So in fact it is a marketing-instrument. Also the Consumentenbond advises to only book with a travel agency that is part of ANVR. Getting into the insolvency fund is also possible if you are not a member of ANVR, so that is no explanation. Loss of membership is a serious fear for traders, not only because of the loss, but also because of the possibility of the loss being communicated in the newspapers. The underlying threat of administrative law (not criminal!) is maybe also starting to work, but is quite unknown yet, I think'. In other sectors there is a comparably lower fear of losing membership, which is why it is more difficult in those sectors to have the traders obey; 'In paragraph 22 it is suggested amongst other things that the availability of public enforcement by regulators can act as a strong incentive for parties to use ADR. This is certainly not the case for the Netherlands, as we already had an extensive ADR system long before a consumer authority was set up', see Response by the Confederation of Netherlands Industry and Employers (VNO-NCW) and the SME lobby organisation MKB-Nederland (2011).

registered traders, a system of deposit or bank guarantees for individual disputes is likewise applicable.

Consumers may check if a trader participates in the GC system, which may indicate if the trader at hand is *bona fide*; therefore, negotiations with possible *mala fide* traders may be avoided in the first place.

In 2010, members of the trade association ANVR included 1,426 travel agencies, 126 flight agencies and 220 tour operators.[76] Approximately 90 per cent of all package tours booked in the Netherlands annually were made through ANVR members, covering around 6.5 million people. While it is not the general policy of the SGC, in the travel area, all decisions of the GCR are sent to the ANVR.[77] This is how a dispute with a *bona fide* trader would most likely go. By way of illustration, if several complainants raised the same issue, this board normally sets the hearing for those cases on the same day to reach the same decision for all.[78]

Consumers' costs connected to the GCR procedure depend on the costs of the trip: €76.26 for travel costs up to €500; €101.68 for travel costs from €500 to €1,500 and €127.10 for costs of more than €1,500.[79] The registration fee includes the services of the arbitrators and any expert visit and report. In the case study, €127.10 applies. The overall costs for the consumer usually amount to less than €100 and only in one out of twenty cases does the consumer pay more than €500.[80] The GCR costs are clearly attractive when compared with court cost.[81] This statement may need to be qualified for cases of a lower value than €500 in which case a natural person would pay court fess of €75. When the case is decided, the losing party pays the fee; however, a losing party may not be charged with the lawyer's costs. In very exceptional cases, the losing party may be required to reimburse other costs. No legal aid is provided for a GC proceeding.[82]

76 See Annual report ANVR 2010, p. 3. From here on they will be referred to by the general term 'trader'.

77 See personal email communications with ANVR (14 October 2011).

78 See interview with Professor Ton Jongbloed, Professor of the Law of Enforcement and Seizure, University of Utrecht (Utrecht, 26 January 2011). This seems to be a particularity of the GCR. The general policy of the SGC is a so-called 'on hold' procedure; whenever there are many identical or widely identical disputes, only one case is decided and applied to all cases that were left 'on hold'. Another mediation possibility is given in the light of the outcome of this one case, personal email communications with SGC (10 November 2011).

79 See Annual report Geschillencommissie 2012, p. 20.

80 The costs entail: travelling, phone calls, copies, printing and collection of information, see Klapwijk and Ter Voert (2009), p. 12. Note that this data comes from a study on the SGC in general, and not just the GCR. Furthermore, the fees for the GCR have recently been increased.

81 See Tuil (2010).

82 See interview with CB (The Hague, 23 March 2011).

Traders currently pay the biggest share to maintain the board, with the state funding the remainder.[83] Over the years, the ministry subsidised between 15 per cent and 20 per cent and business between 80 and 85 per cent of the costs.[84] The total annual costs fluctuate between €5.5 million and €6.5 million. ANVR pays the annual costs for handling the caseload to the SGC, part of which is paid on account and then subject to adjustment at the end of the year when the GC's total usage is known.[85] Individual traders do not pay case fees to the SGC for each case, so the associations must fund the bill and either have a reserve or a means of collecting quickly from members.[86] ANVR members who lose a GC case must pay €500 to ANVR plus the consumer's fee and the compensation (if so decided).[87] Companies that register individually with the SGC – usually because they are not members of a registered trade association – pay a fee on registration, subsequent annual fees and a fee per case. A 2007 survey found that the range of overall costs incurred by individual companies for that particular year varied from under €100 to over €20,000.[88]

The average duration of GC cases was generally 3.6 months in 2012 (3.5 months in 2011; 4.4 months in 2010; 4.7 months in 2009).[89] In 2012, 530 complaints were made before the GCR and 299 were decided; in 2011, these numbers were 716 and 410, respectively.[90] Claims that concerned the quality of accommodation were the biggest group, representing 34 per cent of the claims; overbooking of accommodation represented seven per cent. The average travel costs were €3,392. The consumer was present in the hearing in 82 per cent of the cases, the trader joined in 84 per cent of the cases. The consumer used legal assistance in 12 per cent of the cases, the trader in one per cent of the cases. The average amount of compensation in all founded or partially founded claims was €830. The board

83 See Klapwijk and Ter Voert (2009), p. 26.

84 See Weber and Hodges (2012), p. 138.

85 See ibid.; see interview with Professor Ton Jongbloed, Professor of the Law of Enforcement and Seizure, University of Utrecht (Utrecht, 26 January 2011). The ANVR finds that the sum initially budgeted can vary against the final account by 50 per cent or 60 per cent.

86 See Article 20(2) of the *ANVR algemene reisvoorwaarden* (ANVR Travel Standard Contract Terms).

87 See interview with ANVR (The Hague, 13 April 2011). In a previous system there was a penalty for traders that took too many cases to the GCR, which has now been replaced by the user-pays principle. A fee of €150 for ANVR members that won a case has likewise been abolished, as this practice was reported to provide an incentive for traders to reduce the number of claims.

88 See Klapwijk and Ter Voert (2009), p. 92. The total sum consequently includes costs for travelling, telephone calls, collection of information, contact with lawyers, consumers and the GC. These are general numbers.

89 See Annual report Geschillencommissie 2012, p. 17; annual report Geschillencommissie 2011, p. 8 and annual report Geschillencommissie 2010, pp 8, 114.

90 See Annual report Geschillencommissie 2012, p. 108.

reported handling the caseload very well.[91] The number of traders bringing a case in the travel sector was almost zero.[92] The number of complaints overall at the GC have been decreasing.[93] Fifty-one per cent of complaints were filed digitally.

A comparison of the various procedures suggests that pursuing cases in court is theoretically possible, but unfeasible in practice, particularly for financial reasons.[94] This is a disincentive for filing cases that cannot be handled at the GCR. The Dutch government planned to require consumers to pay more of their own costs if they decided to pursue a case before an ordinary judge when a GC case is possible.[95] This was consequently abolished.

GCR cases have the advantage of being decided by experts with 15 to 20 years of experience in travel law.[96] The body has developed a wide amount of case law and many cases would never have been brought to an ordinary court.[97] Whereas the ANVR ensures the enforcement of the GCR's 'binding advices', this is not guaranteed with judgments obtained in the civil court.[98] Therefore, the originally weaker award at an ADR body is considerably strengthened. The subdistrict judge does not seem to be a competitor to the board,[99] because a judge never can be specialised enough, would have to be up-to-date on many issues and the judgments come at a high risk factor for traders (in particular, regarding open norms).[100] Overall very few awards are appealed in the courts and in the traders' perception judges are very unlikely to squash the findings of the ADR body.[101]

---

91 See interview with Professor Ton Jongbloed, Professor of the Law of Enforcement and Seizure, University of Utrecht (Utrecht, 26 January 2011).

92 See ibid.

93 See Annual report Geschillencommissie 2012, p. 5.

94 See interview with Professor Ton Jongbloed, Professor of the Law of Enforcement and Seizure, University of Utrecht (Utrecht, 26 January 2011).

95 See Loos and Van Boom (2010), p. 46 who refer to Bijl. Handelingen II 2008/09, 31 753, no. 1, p. 16.

96 See interview with Professor Ton Jongbloed, Professor of the Law of Enforcement and Seizure, University of Utrecht (Utrecht, 26 January 2011).

97 See E.H. Hondius, 'Public and Private Enforcement in Consumer Protection – A Dutch Perspective', *New Frontiers of Consumer Protection – The Interplay between Private and Public Enforcement*, eds F. Cafaggi and H-W. Micklitz (Antwerp; Oxford; Portland: Intersentia, 2009) 235–59, p. 239.

98 See interview with CB (The Hague, 3 December 2010).

99 See interview with Professor Ton Jongbloed, Professor of the Law of Enforcement and Seizure, University of Utrecht (Utrecht, 26 January 2011). Compare also the figures in the Oxford study, Hodges, Vogenauer and Tulibacka (2010), p. 33. In a case scenario concerning the repayment of €200 to a consumer, for a product not delivered in the Netherlands, a claimant would not incur fees for a lawyer but court fees of approximately €230 instead.

100 See interview with thuiswinkel (The Hague, 13 April 2011).

101 See interview with VNO-NCW/MKB (The Hague, 7 March 2011). There have been successful appeals in energy and bank cases, according to personal email communications with Professor Willem H.W. Van Boom, Erasmus University Rotterdam.

The complexity of the matters heard at the SGC is restricted because the body has a more limited procedure compared with civil litigation. Courts are required for mass cases in particular.[102] This perception might be related to the limited given appeal option.

Government funding is decreasing which may be a partial cause for a drop in cases. Traders may be more inclined to settle issues beforehand because of the high maintenance costs of the system.

A related question that came up in an interview with the CB is whether traders are willing to finance the SGC when it is increasingly becoming the default system.[103] Indeed traders feel the increase in costs and would prefer more government subsidy.[104] The GC is firmly embedded in the Dutch enforcement system.[105]

According to CB the gap in marketing practices between responses to those traders under a scheme and those who are not under a scheme is becoming increasingly wider and consumers' responsibility is increasing.[106] Participation in the GCR and even more so participation in the SGR (an insolvency fund that is outlined in the next section) are considered as strong quality labels.[107]

According to a recent European study, 21 per cent of surveyed consumers had a consumer problem within the past 12 months with a legitimate cause for complaint.[108] In terms of the estimated financial loss, 39 per cent of the consumers had none and 14 per cent had zero to €20, summing to an overall average of €402.[109] With 84 per cent of consumers having a problem leading to a complaint, the Netherlands scored highest. Regarding the financial threshold needed to trigger a lawsuit, the highest number of people (22 per cent) opted for €501–1,000 as the threshold.[110] Then again, four per cent would also go for cases of €20 or less and 14 per cent for cases ranging between €201 and €500. The financial threshold for involving an ADR body was also €501–1,000 for the top 19 per cent in the Netherlands. In terms of small claims of less than €20, the amount is five per cent and also the percentages for claims for up to €100 is slightly higher than in the court. Thus, there is only a small difference in threshold. This data is cited as it presents results for the Netherlands, Sweden and England. However, no strong results may be drawn from it. A Dutch study showed that consumers refrain from

---

102 See interview with CB (The Hague, 23 March 2011).

103 See ibid. The continuous decrease in complaints can be explained by various factors, one of which is the reasoning that traders value their contributions as too high and prefer a settlement. For various explanations, see P. Kisjes 'Geschillencommissie Reizen, minder klachten, meer betalen', View, August 2011, p. 15

104 See interview with ANVR (The Hague, 13 April 2011).

105 See interview with CA (The Hague, 23 March 2011).

106 See ibid.

107 See interview with SGR (Rotterdam, 3 November 2011).

108 See European Commission, Special Eurobarometer n°342 (2011), p. 170.

109 See ibid., p. 179.

110 See ibid., p. 2[illegible]7.

seeking redress through the SGC where the claim is below €100–200 (depending on the admission fee).[111]

Travel Compensation Fund Traders who are members of the ANVR are connected to two funds, the Catastrophe Fund (*Calamiteitenfonds*) and the Travel Compensation Fund (*Stichting Garantiefonds Reisgelden* [SGR]), an insolvency fund for tour operators and travel agents.[112] While the first fund is for catastrophes, the second is designed to compensate consumers if the trader goes bankrupt before or during their journey[113] and could be interesting for the case scenarios at hand. If the consumer cannot go on the holiday in the first place, she will be compensated and if the journey must be interrupted, the fund also will pay repatriation costs and other losses. The SGR structure administers both funds. For all Member States, the Package Travel Directive clearly states that security provided by retailers/organisers 'for cases of insolvency must cover the total refund of money paid over and the full repatriation costs'.[114] Most of the travel operators participate in the SGR (via ANVR or independently). SGR is in charge of 95 per cent of advance-paid travel sums, which means about five per cent of travel sector operations are not secured through the fund.[115] Five per cent refers to the turnover that the sector makes, and, therefore, is still substantial, considering the high amount of money that is moved in the package travel sector.

Travel operators are legally obligated to provide for securities in cases of bankruptcies, for example by insurance or bank guarantee. Therefore, traders who are not members of the ANVR or are not registered independently with the SGR must provide for an equivalent security.

The SGR fund is primarily designed for situations mentioned above. Aside for general damage claims, the insolvency fund could step in to remedy a judgment-proof trader problem before the ADR body. The fund is also available in cases of insolvency if the consumer has already acquired 'binding advice' from the GCR (or a final and conclusive title in court).[116] In these cases, the consumer must file a written application to the SGR. On the other hand, if the GCR procedures are

111 See Loos (2008), p. 42.

112 See L.J.H. Mölenberg, 'Reisovereenkomst', *Handboek Consumentenrecht*, ed. E.H. Hondius and G.J. Rijken (Zutphen: Uitgeverij Paris, 2011) 233–56, p. 255.

113 The SGR is a non-profit organisation that came about for historical reasons. It is not in its interest, yet it has almost a monopoly as a consequence of this. See interview with SGR (Rotterdam, 3 November 2011).

114 See Article 7 of the Package Travel Directive. A revision of the Package Travel Directive is ongoing.

115 See personal email communications with SGR (24 January 2011 and 17 August 2011). Note: likewise, these companies may, according to the rules of the ANVR, not become an ANVR member. From data of the CBS one can deduce that the total amount of advance travel payments is €4.5 billion.

116 See personal email communications with SGR (24 January 2011). See Article 2.2.d. Garantieregeling SGR (Rules on Travel Guarantees).

on-going and the 'binding advice' has not been issued, the consumer cannot turn to the SGR.[117] Some have suggested that in cases of insolvency, the GCR may at times use its discretion to render a decision anyway, but the extent that this actually happens is unclear.

A company that faces financial problems must signal this to the SGR, which then disseminates this information to the sector.[118] The insolvent company will usually provide an overview of the bookings that have to be compensated. While consumers are often grateful, some feel unfairly treated. There is no internal appeal procedure available to consumers. However, there are cases before the civil court and even criminal cases that involve consumer claims regarding unfair treatment by the SGR.[119] When a trader who is not a participant in the fund becomes insolvent, the ordinary insolvency procedure is initiated.[120]

Therefore, the interrelationship between the fund and the GCR is a remedy for certain insolvency situations plausible in the case studies, but leaves a gap if the consumer has not already acquired 'binding advice'. Likewise, some traders remain outside the system.

Anyone who is not a SGR participant cannot become an ANVR member, in accordance with the rules of this sector organisation.[121] Operators that have their seat outside the Netherlands are obliged to comply with the insolvency regulations in their country.

What if a trader who is an SGR participant 'disappears'? In these cases, the SGR may unilaterally declare insolvency, end the trader's participation in the SGR and compensate consumers for all bookings cases made during the time of the respective trader's SGR participation. If the trader loses SGR participation, she also loses ANVR membership.[122] SGR has the ability to fine participants between €250 and €10,000 if they do not provide annual reports.[123] The ultimate threat is termination of participation.[124] Thus, this is a rather strong safety net for consumers that does not apply to traders not participating in the fund in the first place.

---

117 See personal email communications with SGR (17 August 2011): The cases in which a consumer with a binding advice turns to the SGR are very rare and do not make out a substantial financial factor.

118 See personal email communications with SGR (17 August 2011).

119 See interview with SGR (Rotterdam, 3 November 2011).

120 The so-called curator, appointed by the court, administers the bankruptcy situation and has to be contacted by the consumer.

121 See interview with SGR (Rotterdam, 3 November 2011). In particular, there can be exceptions for foreign traders who are members of ANVR, but are exempted from being a member of the SGR because they already fulfil the security requirements abroad.

122 See interview with ANVR (The Hague, 13 April 2011).

123 See personal email communications with SGR (17 August 2011).

124 See interview with SGR (Rotterdam, 3 November 2011), the termination of membership entails the possibility of losing clients: Those who cancel their participation themselves often want to get back into the fund; where the participation is cancelled

All compensations made from the SGR guarantees fund are based on consumers' contributions.[125] This fund was established in 1983 (before the EC Directive), and until 1 April 1999 consumers contributed to this fund each time they booked with an SGR participant. For many years, this contribution was 10 Dutch Guilders (NLG) or about €4.50 and later 15 NLG (about €6.80). Since 1 April 1999, the SGR guarantee has been free to consumers and compensation is paid purely from capital gain from assets. For the Catastrophe Fund, contributions of €2.50 per booking must be made.[126]

Traders do not have to provide for other traders' defects because they are not financially affected by 'bailing out someone', but rather the SGR is financed by capital gains from contributions made by previous consumers. Having said that, participating traders must pay fees, which include a registration fee of €550 (with which the assessment of the solvency/liquidity of the company is carried out and the administration of SGR is financed) and an annual contribution fee of between €270 and €1,356 (depending on the turnover). There is a yearly check on companies' finances.[127] If such finances are not sufficient, companies may continue to participate in the fund if a high bank guarantee is provided. Otherwise companies must leave the fund.

Criminal law can be used where fraud occurs.[128] A consumer might consider himself to be dealing with a *bona fide* trader, who in fact is only connected to SGR on paper. The SGR refers these cases to the public prosecutor. Also, in the case of a nonparticipating trader, a trial could be instigated via criminal law.

Some small companies are excluded from the ambit of the SGR.[129] Since 2012, a specialised fund has existed for smaller tour operators (*Stichting Garantiefonds Voor Gespecialiseerde Touroperators* [GGTO]).[130] A new travel association was likewise founded: *Vereniging van Kleinschalige Reisorganisaties* (VvKR). Also two additional funds, the *Stichting Garantiefonds Specialistische Touroperators* (SGST) and *het Nederlands Garantiefonds*, have recently been set up.[131]

Involvement of the Consumer Authority The Dutch CA, which has been granted a special mandate in enforcement, has various competences. First, the CA engages

through the SGR this is much less the case. Lastly, companies that went insolvent generally disappear from the market as such.

125 See personal email communications with SGR (24 January 2011).

126 See interview with thuiswinkel (The Hague, 13 April 2011); see interview with Professor Ton Jongbloed, Professor of the Law of Enforcement and Seizure, University of Utrecht (Utrecht, 26 January 2011).

127 See personal email communications with SGR (17 August 2011).

128 See ibid.

129 See for statute and rules on participation (deelnemersreglement): http://www.sgr.nl/index.asp?uid=6, last accessed: 31 March 2013 and related rules for becoming a member of ANVR its 'Huishoudelijk Reglement'.

130 See http://www.stichting-ggto.nl/, last accessed: 31 March 2013.

131 See Annual report CA 2012, p. 22.

in monitoring (*toezicht*). This unit acts as a filter; it carries out investigations in the market and writes a report for the legal unit, which decides whether to initiate civil or administrative law enforcement procedures.[132] Furthermore, input regarding possible interventions may be instigated by the media or on the website platform *ConsuWijzer*, where consumers may file complaints.[133] The CA's decisions are based on its priorities, which are set according to the impact of the violations (mainly the amount of damage to consumers, the impact on consumers' confidence and market disruption). The CA will intervene in the package travel scenario only if these requirements are fulfilled. Therefore, the authority cannot act in individual cases and does not grant damages; it acts if a violation harms the collective interest of consumers. Among the priorities for 2007 were cases related to the travel sector and for 2008 security mechanisms in the travel sector.[134] Although the CA allocates most resources to these fields, resources are left for *ad hoc* interventions in severe cases in other thematic areas.

Generally, the CA has the power to initiate proceedings for contraventions of specific statutes,[135] particularly provisions in the BW.[136] The CA has both civil and administrative enforcement powers.[137] Civil law enforcement is applicable to open norms and administrative law enforcement to closed ones. For civil law enforcement, the exclusive competence is with the court of appeal in The Hague. Closed norms are enforced via administrative law enforcement because they do not require interpretation (for example, the blacklist in unfair commercial practices).[138] Using both powers in parallel could potentially be burdensome for traders because of the need for various specialised lawyers, but, in practice, this has not happened.[139]

The CA first initiated an investigation in the travel sector in 2007 (in total 107 investigations). As a result, in 2008 the authority ordered more than 100 traders in

132 See interview with CA (The Hague, 26 May 2009).

133 See ibid.

134 See Kwink Groep BV, *Eindrapport Evaluatie Consumentenautoriteit op grond van de Whc* (2011), http://www.consumentenautoriteit.nl/sites/default/files/redactie/eindrapport-evaluatie-consumentenautoriteit.pdf, last accessed: 31 March 2013, p. 48.

135 See *Prijzenwet* (Prices Act) and *Colportagewet* (Canvassing Act).

136 For instance distance selling Article 7:46 BW, unfair contract terms in consumer contracts Articles 6: 231–47 BW.

137 See Van Campen (2007), p. 41.

138 The precise competences are set out in annex a (private law enforcement) and b (administrative law enforcement) to the *Wet Oneerlijke Handelspraktijken* (Law on Unfair Commercial Practices, WOHP).

139 See pro facto (M.J. Schol, J. Nagtegaal and H.B. Winter), *Evaluatie Wet Handhaving Consumentenbescherming – Ervaringen met het Duale Handhavingsstelsel en de Handhavingsbevoegdheid Inzake Massaschade* (2010), p. 36; see Kwink Groep BV (2011), p. 71: in the roughly 40 cases where this issue was at stake, the CA has each time opted for only one procedural avenue: The administrative law procedure. In the ambit of establishing the ACM, it is discussed to give the CA purely administrative law enforcement powers. This is not to happen directly, see personal email communications with CA.

the sector to provide for securities in cases of insolvencies, as required.[140] While many of the traders complied, the CA had to use its private law enforcement powers in some cases (primarily Article 3:305d BW in conjunction with Article 2.5. Whc – *verzoekschriftprocedure*).[141] With this procedure the CA can ask the court to impose certain orders. The court may request to end a violation and impose an order with incremental payment in case of noncompliance. The CA furthermore can seek remedies such as injunctions or declaratory judgments via Article 3:303a BW.[142] The CA is not empowered to file an action for monetary relief.

The CA has brought 14 cases to the court of appeal in The Hague via Article 3:303d BW in the period since its establishment until today. All the cases in which the CA has used its civil law enforcement powers so far have concerned securities for package travel in case of insolvencies. Cases have taken on average 15 months from the initial investigation to handing the petition to the court,[143] and the court has taken on average five months to pronounce a judgment.

In particular, the CA scrutinises companies that are not members of the SGR and asks them to show how they have organised their securities. The judges order the companies to provide for securities immediately or to stop offering package deals and also may impose orders for incremental payments.[144] The latter may amount to €500 per day, with a maximum of €100,000.

An example is the Gold Travel case, which the CA won (28 April 2009).[145] Because the trader had not fulfilled the obligation to provide securities for cases of insolvency, the court ordered the company to stop offering package deals under penalty of a fine. Overall, some traders established securities and others left the package travel market. The court regarded various alternatives to the SGR as insufficient to comply with the legal obligation. Additionally, the CA promoted security mechanisms for the travel sector in the media.[146] The CA reported some difficulties in assessing whether alternative security measures to the fund are lawful, and, therefore, which cases to take to court. In the proceedings, the CA used its investigative powers and the judge made a marginal test. For example, the CA has the ability to make digital investigations to track IP addresses, even though

140 See Annual report CA 2008, p. 14.

141 With the introduction of Article 3:305d BW for the CA, this article was also made available to the CB. It is an easier procedure than version 3:305a BW, but the CB has not made use of it yet.

142 See R.W. De Vrey, 'Handelspraktijken', *Handboek Consumentenrecht*, eds E.H. Hondius and G.J. Rijken, 3rd ed. (Zutphen: Uitgeverij Paris, 2011) 421–40, p. 431.

143 See Kwink Groep BV (2011), p. 9.

144 See Annual report CA 2010/11, p. 18. Byblos Reizen Amsterdam, Akwaaba Tours Maastricht, 4WB Travel Club Groenekan, Club Travel Breda, Jero Reizen Bemmel, Cimarron Eindhoven, Best of Britain Delft, Dynamic Holland, Harlem and Opvakantie Rotterdam in January and March 2010.

145 See Loos and Van Boom (2010), p. 141. The Hague Court of Appeal 7 April 2009, LJN BK4880, TvC 2009 (Gold Travel), p. 265.

146 See Kwink Groep BV (2011), p. 32.

these powers are generally not necessary with travel companies.[147] (These powers are outlined in more detail in the next case study.) Confidentiality requirements apply to the information the CA generates. However, information stemming from a closed (rather than on-going) case before the CA theoretically could be used in an individual case.

The CA regards the ANVR as a very well-operated trade association.[148] ANVR proactively contacts traders and reports those who do not provide the required security to the CA in order for the latter to assess if it is necessary to take action.

In the end, the Dutch travel sector includes almost no traders who do not provide any kind of security mechanism.[149] Also, for a trader to disappear is rather difficult because of the net of control mechanisms relating to payments to the insolvency funds and membership in the ANVR. Potential *mala fide* traders may be singled out because they are those who are not *prima facie* members of the ANVR. Further potential *mala fide* traders are the ones not registered with GCR, SGR or the other available insolvency funds. Over the last four to five years, there were some instances involving *mala fide* traders who expropriated advance payments, in particular Turkish travel companies.[150] But this incident harmed the assets of the SGR and not consumers.

The SGR does not see a role for the CA in cases before the SGR in which a company stopped paying and cannot be tracked down.[151] This scenario in fact does not exist according to the SGR: only traders who are registered with the chamber of commerce may register with the SGR. Registration does not necessarily prevent a trader from disappearing later.

The trade association has an interest in closing the remaining gaps for rogue traders. The *signaleringslijst*, a kind of blacklist initiated by the ANVR to warn consumers against nonmembers, has provoked mixed reactions.[152] Some traders seem to have been put on the list even though the CA had assessed them as compliant; these errors were consequently corrected.[153]

In its first years, the CA has been very active regarding these security mechanisms for insolvencies.[154] In 2011, the CA contacted an additional 60 traders because it appeared from market surveys and complaints that they were not members of the SGR fund and some did not provide for an alternative. Twenty-three traders

147 See personal email communications with CA (15 December 2011).

148 See Kwink Groep BV (2011), p. 38.

149 See interview with Professor Ton Jongbloed, Professor of the Law of Enforcement and Seizure, University of Utrecht (Utrecht, 26 January 2011).

150 See interview with ANVR (The Hague 13 April 2011).

151 See personal email communications with SGR (24 January 2011).

152 See 'De ANVR op de stoel van de rechter?' (14 January 2011), http://www.reishonger.nl/reisnieuws/anvr-op-de-stoel-van-de-rechter, last accessed: 31 March 2013.

153 See personal email communications with ANVR (14 October 2011).

154 'Consumentenautoriteit: Na actie meer reisaanbieders met garantiestelling' (15 June 2011), http://www.consumentenautoriteit.nl/nieuws/2011/consumentenautoriteit-na-actie-meer-reisaanbieders-met-garantiestelling, last accessed: 31 March 2013.

either adapted the securities or stopped offering package deals and 26 committed to adjusting the securities and informing their customers about the situation on their websites. No legal action was taken. The CA displayed the traders' names and the complaint on the Internet, therefore providing some 'naming and shaming' action. Among the CA's current priorities is the topic of nontransparent prices in the travel sector.[155]

Criminal Law Enforcement in the Travel Sector Finally, if fraud or deception were at stake, a package travel case could be tried under criminal law, in exceptional circumstances. For example, provision of wrong information may fall under laws against forgery (Article 225 *Wetboek van Strafrecht*, Penal Code – WvS). Also, a simplified procedure in the subdistrict court is available that might be relevant in a package travel scenario.[156] The subdistrict judge deals with only minor offences, typically ones in which the accused has refused a proposed settlement from the police or the public prosecutor. The subdistrict judge usually delivers an oral judgment right after the session. In practice, criminal law enforcement in the Netherlands does not prioritise consumer law cases,[157] and there is hardly any role for criminal law to play in package travel cases.[158] Victims may link a damage claim to the criminal process; however, in practice, the possibilities are limited.[159] In interviews for this study, criminal law was mentioned in relation to fraudulent uses of the logo of the SGR or consumers' dissatisfaction with SGR rulings.[160] There is no separate compensation fund in Dutch criminal law.[161]

The Dutch concept of corporate liability proffers the liability of the legal person to natural persons (individuals), which extends to directors and employees (Article 51 (2) WvS).[162]

Assessment and Conclusion

The first part of this chapter illustrates the law enforcement mechanisms in the Netherlands that could handle the package travel case scenarios, elaborating on the general definitions described in Part I. The SGC, the Netherlands' ADR body,

155 See Consumentenautoriteit, Agenda 2012/2013.

156 See B.F. Keulen and G. Knigge, eds, *Strafprocesrecht*, 12th ed. (Deventer: Kluwer, 2010), pp. 10, 125.

157 See Faure, Ogus and Philipsen (2008), p. 388 according to interviews carried out with enforcers in 2006.

158 See interview with Professor Ton Jongbloed, Professor of the Law of Enforcement and Seizure, University of Utrecht (Utrecht, 26 January 2011).

159 See Ogus, Faure and Philipsen (2006), p. 37; Keulen and Knigge (2010), p. 229. The importance of the role of the victim in criminal law is increasing.

160 See personal email communications with SGR (17 August 2011).

161 See ibid.

162 See B.F. Keulen and E. Gritter, 'Corporate Criminal Liability in the Netherlands', *Electronic Journal of Comparative Law* 14.3 (2010): 1–12, p. 3.

could successfully handle the *bona fide* trader scenario. For travel law, the ADR system seems to be a clear win, certainly from the consumers' viewpoint.

The GCR includes both the consumer and business sides, a desirable feature. GCR procedural rules set out that consumer and trader representatives must be involved. Consumer associations and trade associations are involved in setting up two-sided standard contract terms. The fees for the individual complainant are low to induce cases of a rather low value and these fees are reimbursed if the case is won. Administrative costs also seem to be rather low. Traders can register either via their sector organisation or independently. The compliance rate is high because of the sophisticated system of underlying business guarantees that disciplines the traders. This system strengthens the awards offered (the 'binding advice') considerably and seems to make these awards more favourable than a judgment in civil court. Also, precautionary deposits are required for traders registered independently at the board. Likewise, traders' interests are secured because consumers must deposit money as well. Furthermore, the SGR pays an award granted by the GCR if the trader is insolvent. Some discretion is available regarding on-going procedures. However, these cases involving an SGR award constitute a low percentage of the overall damage payments that have to be made by the fund. The fund is applicable if insolvency occurs before the consumer goes on holiday or while on holiday.

The number of traders who can be tried is limited because traders must be registered with the GCR for a case to be brought, thus restricting cases to *bona fide* traders. A strong point of ADR in the Netherlands is that the procedure is not simply written, but also includes a hearing. There are limits in complexity of cases brought to the GCR. Oral hearings last only about 30 minutes, which limits the evidence that can be submitted. Here, a civil court would offer more possibilities. Also, traders may bring claims to the GCR, but in fact they do not. They waive their rights to bring a case to the ordinary court via the two-sided standard contract terms, a welcome situation from an efficiency perspective.[163] The requirement to establish contact with the trader before a case can be brought to the GCR induces settlement before any action is taken and the potential procedure before the GCR works as an underlying threat in these negotiations. Likewise the procedure, as such, facilitates the settling of complaints. This threat applies only to the registered traders; unregistered traders may not fear a consumer action at the civil court because the rational apathy problem prevails. However, in the €2,000 case, in which the small claims procedure applies, a consumer may indeed seek court action because the current fee for such a case is roughly €213. The proposed increase in court fees would not have been desirable from this point of view. Legal aid and insurance would be available to facilitate a civil court procedure in the case scenarios as outlined. A main problem in the civil court would be the inability to locate the *mala fide* trader and initiate a procedure at all.

163 Traders regard this as practical. There are legal concerns to oblige the consumer to do the same.

The GCR has developed a vast amount of case law. For the consumer, the right to go to civil court can never be precluded, but the current system renders this path unattractive and only very few cases end up there. Civil court judges may even lack the expertise. Expertise in travel law rests with the ADR body, despite a less sophisticated procedural law and the case law generated is regarded as valuable. There is a danger in foregoing a court's case law in terms of long-term social costs. This effect is a problem with the ADR approach. In terms of administrative costs it can be welcomed that an appeal of the 'binding advice' is possible in court only on limited grounds. In terms of accuracy this may not be problematic for the clear-cut cases that the ADR body is to attract.

The governmental financial support of consumer complaint boards is constantly being reduced and the traders' high contributions, temporarily even if they won a case, have possibly resulted in a decrease in cases (at least in the travel sector). The financial structure potentially provides an incentive for each branch association to reduce the number of claims in its sector, maybe below an optimal level in the overall enforcement balance because a 'user pays' system prevails.[164]

The Dutch market relies on reputation mechanisms and signalling (belonging to the ANVR, the SGR or the newly established funds). A large number of traders belong to trade associations, and, therefore, cases would safely fall within the GCR system. Participation in the SGR is crucial for insolvency situations. In the rare occasion that a SGR participant disappears (the case of the Turkish companies), the trader's participation will be terminated and the harmed consumers compensated. Therefore, likely *mala fide* traders may be suspected among those with no membership at ANVR and SGR and who are not registered independently at the GCR. Responsibility is partly placed on the consumer to select the business partner well. Within ANVR the Code of Conduct is observed basically in the form of self-regulation.

The subdistrict judge is not regarded as a competing enforcement mechanism to the GCR. *Mala fide* traders will not be registered with the board in the first place and a civil court cannot handle those cases. Overall, the ADR body filters out clear-cut cases with compliant traders and serves as a cross-financing mechanism for a more costly system for *mala fide* trader scenarios. The business guarantee appears to be an even stronger compliance guarantee than the enforcement in a civil law procedure. Signalling in various ways is possible. While a civil court procedure in many respects generates more information than ADR, a case against an untraceable trader likewise fails in a pure private law procedure. The appropriate investigative powers are not available within the system. The set of design requirements suggests that, for this case, a 'public law element' needs to be added to the procedure in some form.

164 This was suggested. It was confirmed by traders that they ask their members to coordinate with the ANVR regarding which cases to take to court, as the association wants to consider the long-term situation.

The Dutch CA has indeed undertaken quite some action in the package travel market, taking traders who do not provide for securities for insolvencies to court on various occasions. They cooperate with the ANVR who reports on nonmembers suspected of noncompliance with the legal provision to the CA. In this way, a targeted approach can be followed. As mentioned, there are other ways to signal in the market. Furthermore, the CA has carried out its own investigation into the market and subsequently launched various actions. Since 2007, a persistent monitoring of the sector has taken place and securing the traders' compliance to the securitisation agreement ensures their visibility in the market. This approach provides a public law element to the market through *ex ante* action to ensure that occurrences of *mala fide* trader scenarios are limited. More societal resources are spent on these traders who have a higher potential of causing substantial societal harm in line with the design suggestions. The situation of an untraceable trader is basically prevented in the first place. As a reaction to the CA's action, various traders have left the market and stopped offering package travel deals. To scrutinise the market, the CA apparently uses a range of investigative powers to reduce the information asymmetries in the sector. They can use them within their investigations and relieve the judges to some extent from making them. The CA effectively goes through the civil court for enforcement in the cases undertaken. In this way the public law element is added to the procedure. (These powers are set out in more detail in the next case study.)

ANVR's insider knowledge of the business sector reduces the information asymmetries, which also aligns with the design suggestions. The consumer has a responsibility to check if the trader is adhering to the ANVR and the SGR (or the newly established funds). According to the consumer association, these signals are important to decrease the number of business done with *mala fide* traders.

Indeed, the Dutch enforcement responses as to package travel align with the design suggestions for an optimal model. To start with there is almost no role for criminal law within the sector and hardly any use of criminal law enforcement was reported. Looking at the wide action that the CA undertook, one might want to argue that there is now in fact no need to revert to this underlying threat as the CA action was sufficient for the time being. In general, criminal enforcement is available in the Netherlands and the CA also closely cooperates with the prosecution office. Therefore, the threat is still credible. Criminal law enforcement must ensure that it is ready to take cases if the CA enforcement fails.

Regarding the cooperation between CA and CB, the CB does not focus on the travel sector in terms of taking legal action, but does provide information on package travel deals to consumers.

One suggested improvement in the system has to do with speed. As the CA has confirmed, there can be a rather long time lapse between an investigation and the judge's final decision, which risks leaving *mala fide* traders to operate in the market. The matter 'speed' could still be fine-tuned. The administrative procedure at the CA, available for other sectors, is currently not necessarily faster,[165] basically because of possibly long administrative appeal procedures. On average, CA took 15 months to come to its administrative decision. Informal enforcement by the CA led to faster results.

As the 2011 action shows, the CA employs some 'naming and shaming' of traders (online) who do not respond to their investigation. Likewise traders who commit to complying with the security requirements must display intent on their own websites to clearly signal the current situation to consumers. Some concerns have been expressed in economic literature about 'naming and shaming' among public agencies. The implications of the integration of the CA in the ACM have yet to be seen.

It appears, furthermore, that a trade association can play a role in enforcement by signalling, disciplining members and financing the ADR system for its own breaches. In fact, trade associations play this role in the Netherlands and their insider knowledge is tapped.

Although the current subdistrict judge is not considered to be a competitor to the GCR, the increase in the competences of the subdistrict judge may change the situation; however, the data on the caseload in 2011 did not show such a trend. The average amount of the cases at the GCR (€3,392) may indicate that the limit of €2,000 was indeed too low. Court fees are (slightly) higher than fees with the ADR board. The loser-pays rule applies at both bodies.

It stands out that the public law element is used in an *ex ante* way, taking action before insolvency situations occur and as a side-effect securing the identity of the trader for any future actions. For cases in which harm already has happened and consumers have been harmed, the public law element could be increased, for example through an official procedure to enable follow-on damage claims after an intervention of the CA. Thus, full advantage could be taken of the threat of public authority's actions to induce negotiations between traders and consumers. However, there may be no necessity in the market for this suggestion because the prevention approach renders a low likelihood that a market player can hide.

Case 2 – Misleading Advertising

Within misleading advertising, a *bona fide* (scenario 3) and a *mala fide* (scenario 4) trader scenario are assessed. This time, the damage to any individual is small, even trifling (€15), but widespread. This case includes a new actor – the competitor – whose damage from a misleading advertisement can amount to €100,000. Alternatively, solutions are discussed in which the competitor has no interest in the case. Again, a particular focus is on the behaviour of the *mala fide* trader in online transactions.

165 See Kwink Groep BV (2011), p. 53. The exact measure of when violations were effectively rectified is often difficult to establish with the various procedures.

Summary of Legal Rules

With implementation of the EU Directive on Unfair Commercial Practices[166] in 2008, the Netherlands introduced the WOHP, which includes misleading advertising. The enforcement of this act is purely administrative. The WOHP empowers the CA in various ways to deal with collective consumer matters.[167]

This rather new WOHP does not change the fact that matters may be settled between the consumer and the trader or between traders privately. Likewise, self-regulatory solutions are available in the advertising sector.

Individual Civil Litigation

The consumer

In many sectors where a misleading advertising case may arise, a consumer may seek to cover damages through the GCs, whose functions were outlined more specifically in the package travel cases. (Of course, the advertisement for a package travel also might be misleading.) In addition, the consumer may pursue the case in court (also outlined above).

The WOHP leads to changes in the BW: most importantly, the tort law provisions on unfair commercial practices are inserted (Articles 6:193a–j BW).[168] In these cases, the consumer profits from a reversal of the burden of proof.[169] In addition, there is a link to so-called absence of intention (*wilsgebreken*) set out (Book 3 BW). If a contract were concluded on the basis of a misleading or aggressive commercial practice, the consumer may argue deception or mistake (*bedrog or dwaling*) and may be granted a rescission.[170] The consumer can get rid of the contract because of a mistake (Article 6:228 BW).[171] The provisions on legal

166 See Directive 2005/29/EC of the European Parliament and of the Council of 11 May 2005 concerning unfair business-to-consumer commercial practices in the internal market and amending Council Directive 84/450/EEC, Directives 97/7/EC, 98/27/EC and 2002/65/EC of the European Parliament and of the Council and Regulation (EC) No 2006/2004 of the European Parliament and of the Council (Unfair Commercial Practices Directive).

167 Generally see W.H. Van Boom, ed., *Handhaving Consumentenbescherming – Een Toelichting op de Wet Handhaving Consumentenbescherming* (Zutphen: Uitgeverij Paris, 2010), p. 51: The possibility for the consumer to make use of civil or criminal law enforcement is not impeded; W.H. Van Boom, 'Inpassing en Handhaving van de Wet Oneerlijke Handelspraktijken', *Tijdschrift voor Consumentenrecht en Handelspraktijken* 1 (2008): 4–24.

168 See P.G.F.A. Geerts and E.R. Vollebregt, eds, *Oneerlijke Handelspraktijken, Misleidende en Vergelijkende Reclame – Een Bespreking van ee Art. 6:193a-6:196 BW* (Deventer: Kluwer, 2009), p. 39.

169 See Article 6 193j BW.

170 See Schaub (2009), p. 153.

171 See Schaub (2009), p. 153.

aid apply as of a minimum amount of case value that is currently fixed at €500.[172] In this case scenario, the damage is too small to justify an individual consumer lawsuit for damages through these routes and the individual's interest in making a substantial investment in any other remedy is low. However, if individual victims only have to complain to trigger action, they are more likely to do so, as some of the upcoming sections show.

Generally, it is difficult to prove someone has suffered damage from a particular misleading advertisement or the level of the damage suffered.[173] For many years, the CB lobbied for having an unfair commercial practice automatically trigger rescission of the contract, but it did not succeed.

The competitor

A competitor also may face damage because of misleading advertising and the damage can potentially be much higher than a consumer's. In fact, competitors initiate the majority of civil cases concerning unfair commercial practices.[174] Competitors are protected whenever they suffer a detriment due to B2C (Business-to-consumer) or B2B (Business-to-business) advertising.[175] Here little or no information asymmetries are present because competing businesses know the market well.[176] Furthermore, bargaining powers are more aligned. Therefore, a competitor's intervention can be very beneficial for the consumer and could be a deterrent. In fact, in a court case between UPC and Tele2, the issue of advertising came up.[177]

Competitors, unlike individuals, generally have not had a contractual relation with the trader. The deterrent effect depends upon the remedies a trader may seek. In the ordinary civil court, there are not many damage cases with traders because it is very difficult to fulfil the requirement to show the advertisement caused damage and to prove the amount of damage.[178] The same is true for skimming off illegally gained profits.[179] More likely actions are for injunctions, to publish verdicts or to publish rectifications. A related category of cases involving damages are trademark

172 See interview with Professor Ton Jongbloed, Professor of the Law of Enforcement and Seizure, University of Utrecht (Utrecht, 26 January 2011).

173 See interview with CB (The Hague, 3 December 2010).

174 See Mahé (2009), p. 174.

175 See ibid., p. 180. The empowerment of the competitor is justified as to the notion of *reflexwerking*.

176 See ibid., p. 174; a majority of authors seems to assume that the competitor has a right to sue, see Geerts and Vollebregt (2009), pp. 8, 41.

177 See Amsterdam Court of Appeal, 23 March 2010 (Tele 2/UPC internetten&bellen hoger beroep).

178 See interview with Professor Jan Kabel, Institute for Information Law, Amsterdam/Consultant RCC (Bloemendaal, 3 December 2010).

179 See Article 6:104 BW.

look-alike cases. Associations of traders, unlike individual traders, do not become active in the Netherlands.[180]

Group Litigation The CA and consumer associations may pursue group litigation. The most important development was the introduction of Articles 3:305 a–c BW in 1994 that authorise representative organisations to initiate a collective action with the following objectives:

- seeking a declaratory judgment to the benefit of interested parties, holding that the defendant has acted wrongfully against the interested parties and is legally obliged to do something or to abstain from doing something vis-á-vis these interested parties;
- seeking injunctive relief, holding the defendant to perform a legal duty owed to interested parties (positive mandatory injunction) or to abstain from acting (prohibitory injunction);
- seeking performance of contractual duty of the defendant owed to multiple interested parties;
- ordering the termination of contract between the defendant and multiple interested parties;
- ordering the rescission of contract between the defendant and multiple interested parties.

Actions for damages as such are excluded. The *Wet Collectieve Afwikkeling van Massaschade* (Collective Settlement of Mass Damage Act, WCAM) stipulates some special provisions.

Involvement of the CA

In 2009 and 2010–11, misleading advertising was among the CA's priorities. Through its administrative enforcement powers, the CA is the enforcer of the WOHP. Previous legislation regarding misleading advertising, such as transparency requirements, remains in force.[181]

The administrative sanctioning powers of the CA cover a whole spectrum, ranging from pure warnings or negotiation techniques to fines. Eighty-five per cent of cases are solved by informal means.[182] For example, the CA may request a violator to refrain from the violations and will publish this commitment and take further action only if the trader does not stick to the commitment.[183]

180 They could make use of Article 3:305d BW.

181 The provisions are all codified in the BW. The code contains regulations on transparency, e-commerce, distant selling, pricing canvassing and so on.

182 See interview with CA (The Hague, 23 March 2011).

183 See interview with CA (The Hague, 26 May 2009).

Alternatively, the CA may take direct formal measures such as administrative penalties. The maximum penalty is €74,000.[184] In cases of unfair commercial practices, such as a misleading advertisement, the CA can issue a penalty of a maximum of €450,000 per violation. A crucial factor is that the fine is per violation, which means the amount may increase if several violations can be proven.[185] Another remedy is an order to end the violation subject to an incremental penalty for each day of continual infringement. Both remedies may be combined. The last remedy also may be used to prevent violations that are imminent. In July 2009, an expedient administrative order under penalty was introduced and has been increasingly used since. This remedy does not require a proven infringement, but only a suspicion.[186] Once the infringement is detected, action can be undertaken within two weeks. Except to await the trader's response, there are no other special requirements.

The CA has the discretion to act upon complaints. Competitors can also complain to the CA aside of consumers,[187] which they rarely do.[188] As to the choice of instruments and the amount of the penalty, the decision of the CA depends on the circumstances, manner and severity of the violation. The ordinary administrative appeals are available, first internally and then in the courts. Appeals are indeed common.[189] These are the administrative enforcement competences. The CA's civil enforcement powers were outlined in some detail in the case study on package travel. The CA cannot compensate consumers.

---

184 Before 1 January 2008 it was 67,000. The change occurred as the criminal code was changed, too.

185 In one case, ring tone advertisers were fined with €1.2 million in total (see Decision *Consumentenautoriteit* 17 June 2010 CA/NB/510/30 (Celldorado)). High fines were also imposed in the energy sector, which is why CB thinks that traders are deterred by this, see interview with CB (The Hague, 3 December 2010). Perceptions seem to be changing. In interviews carried out in 2006 for a study by Ogus, Faure and Philipsen (2006), the perception by officials from the Ministry of Economic Affairs, Directorate for Consumer Affairs was that the deterrence of '*mala fide*' traders was inadequate.

186 See interview with CA (The Hague, 23 March 2011); see *Wet van 25 juni 2009, Stb. 2009, 264, tot aanvulling van de Algemene wet bestuursrecht* (Vierde tranche Algemene wet bestuursrecht) Stb. 2009, 266 (Amendment to the General Administrative Law Act), 5.3.2. *Last onder dwangsom.*

187 See for example 'Besluit op bezwaar handhavingsverzoek Tele2, Atlantic Telecom Business, Pretium Telecom tegen KPN' (31 July 2009), http://www.consumentenautoriteit.nl/besluiten/besluiten-bezwaar/besluit-bezwaar-handhavingsverzoek-tele2-atlantic-telecom-business-preti, last accessed: 31 March 2013.

188 See interview with VNO-NCW/MKB (The Hague, 7 March 2011).

189 See regarding the appeal procedures, http://www.consumentenautoriteit.nl/besluiten/beroepszaken, last accessed: 31 March 2013. See also Kwink Groep BV (2011), p. 49.

Wide investigative powers of the enforcement entity are a precondition for success against *mala fide* traders and the CA has various investigative powers;[190] the approach is comparable to that of the police, according to the CB.[191] For example, the CA can access business premises with the help of the police (Article 5:15 Awb). Other competences include access to information and documents (Article 5:16, 5:17 Awb) or requests for identification (Article 5:16a Awb). There is an obligation to cooperate with the CA (Article 5:20 Awb) and people or companies risk a fine if they are noncompliant (Article 2.10 Whc). Digital investigations are carried out.[192] When the CA publishes its findings, almost 100 per cent of the traders react with an injunctions procedure.[193]

The Regulation on CPC established minimum investigative powers that all 'competent authorities' must have, but differences among countries remain. With rogue traders, remedies like requesting transcripts from call centres may be effective.[194] Here, the CA can act faster than a civil judge. With Internet trade, digital investigations such as tracking IP addresses may be crucial. Also, cross-border cooperation with other public authorities in the CPC network is possible.

Regarding capture issues, the CA follows a concept called 'Chinese wall' that heavily restricts the ability of monitoring and legal units to work together when fining.[195] The divide concerns persons in charge and not the unit as such. The CB has a very positive view of the separation of powers within the CA, noting that there are many possibilities for appeal on law and facts.[196]

A proposal to introduce skimming-off actions for the CA has been abandoned in light of the merger plans.[197] These could have been interesting as an alternative remedy.

190 To be found in Articles 5.15–5.19 of the *Algemene wet bestuursrecht* (General Administrative Law Act, Awb).

191 See interview with CB (The Hague, 3 December 2010).

192 See personal email communications with CA (15 December 2011).

193 See Van Buchem, B. (Director, CA), 'More state influence for the enforcement of consumer law? The path the Netherlands has taken', presentation, Borderless consumer protection!? Effective enforcement, powerful consumers (Berlin 7 November 2011).

194 See personal email communications with CA (3 November 2011).

195 Ibid.

196 See interview with CB (The Hague, 3 December 2010). An even more independent entity could be independent of the Ministry of Economic Affairs, but is currently not regarded as necessary. Kwink Groep BV (2011) judges the CA's performance as 'very good', also considering stakeholders' points of view, p. 46.

197 See interview with CB (The Hague, 3 December 2010). The suggestion resulted from the study: Van Boom, W.H., B.J. Drijber, J.H. Lembstra, V.C.A. Lindijer and T. Novakovski, *Strooischade: Een verkennend (rechtsvergelijkend) onderzoek naar de mogelijkheden tot optreden tegen strooischade* (2009), see https://zoek.officielebekendmakingen.nl/blg-82770.pdf, last accessed: 31 March 2013. They actually suggest empowering the CB with this remedy rather than the CA.

Overall in 2012, the CA made one penalty decision, seven administrative appeal decisions, seven other appeal decisions and one order subject to a penalty.[198] In the area of unfair commercial practices in 2010, the CA levied a fine of €120,000 against Garant-o-Matic[199] for misleading mails and one of €1,020,000 against Nederlandse Energie Maatschappij for misleading advertising over the telephone.[200] Artiq Mobile B.V. and Blinck International B.V. were fined €1,190,000 in June 2010 for misleading SMS services.[201] For 2012–13, misleading and aggressive telemarketing are mentioned as CA priorities.[202]

The large amount of cases that reached the CA when it was newly introduced is regarded as an indicator of the apparent need of such an entity.[203] At CB and the Dutch Advertising Council RCC, positive remarks were made about the CA.[204] CA and CB are close allies and the CB informs the CA during the informal phase if it plans to intervene. As to clientele, CB is the pure, independent consumer representative, while CA is a governmental organisation. The CB reported that it is often very helpful in their negotiations with traders to threaten CA intervention. CB and CA meet once a month to plan jointly. The CB also may make an enforcement request at the CA. The CA apparently allows more cases to be resolved outside of the courtroom. The CA and the RCC are official partners, too, and their cooperation (outlined in the section on self-regulation) seems to be fruitful. There is some criticism on the appropriateness of an administrative appeal procedure,[205] which some traders regard as discouraging.

The CA solves most of its cases informally, which is desirable for *bona fide* traders. *Mala fide* traders also may operate within unfair commercial practices. As an example, the SMS sector used these informal negotiations to delay proceedings. Ultimately the ministry intervened to encourage a code threatening that otherwise legislation would be imposed. In addition, the CA fined the biggest players heavily.

More *ex ante* intervention by the CA in the advertising market would be difficult because of respect for fundamental rights and questions of censorship.[206] Mainly, the CA wants the private apparatus to work properly.

The WCAM established provisions for settlements (*sluiten vaststellingsovereenkomst*) in a mass damage claim to be declared binding in

198 See Annual report CA 2012, p. 27.

199 See Decision Consumentenautoriteit 21 September 2010 CA/NB/544/10 (Garant-o-Matic B.V.).

200 See Decision Consumentenautoriteit 6 September 2010 CA/NB/527/29 (Nederlandse Energie Maatschappij/NL Energie).

201 See Decision Consumentenautoriteit 17 June 2010 CA/NB/510/30 (Celldorado).

202 See Consumentenautoriteit, Agenda 2012/2013.

203 See interview with CA (The Hague, 23 March 2011).

204 See interview with CB (The Hague, 3 December 2010) and interview with Professor Jan Kabel, Institute for Information Law, Amsterdam/Consultant RCC (Bloemendaal, 3 December 2010).

205 See interview with thuiswinkel (The Hague, 13 April 2011).

206 See interview with CA (The Hague, 23 March 2011).

court.[207] Either consumer organisations (primarily) or the CA can use this provision (Article 2.6 Whc).[208] The CA has the official duty to restrain itself as to this option and no case has happened or is planned so far.[209] Therefore, procedural details are outlined in the discussion of consumer associations.

Enforcement by consumer associations

Traditionally, enforcement of consumer law has depended heavily on consumer associations.[210] There is no official list of these organisations. The most important consumer association is the CB with its 550,000 members.[211] The CB is a representative consumer organisation according to Dutch Civil Law and also a 'qualified entity' as defined in Article 3 Injunctions Directive.[212] Other organisations that are considered consumer organisations are the association 'Own House' (*Vereniging Eigen Huis*), the foundation 'Consumer and Safety' (*Stichting Consument en Veiligheid*) and the shareholders association VEB (*Vereniging van Effectenbezitters*). While one role of consumer associations is lobbying and consumer empowerment, another important task is involvement in law enforcement. They may take legal actions, but their first step is to negotiate with the trader to cease the contravention.[213] All remedies except damages may be pursued. As said, consumer associations can be involved in the WCAM procedure, which is a special procedure to obtain damages. 'Collective action' was introduced in the BW in 1994 for consumer associations, codifying case law that had granted these organisations the ability to file actions even before this date.[214] Article 3: 305a BW is the main legal basis to go to court in the general interest of consumers.[215] Preconditions to use this act are that 'the interests of consumers in the case must be similar'. There are formal restrictions in relation to the organisations that can put forward a legal claim (for example, the claim must fit the goals described

207 See for details F. Weber and W.H. Van Boom, 'Dutch Treat: The Dutch Collective Settlement of Mass Damage Act (WCAM 2005)', *Contratto e impresa/Europa* 1 (2011): 69–79.

208 On the basis of the WCAM; see also Article 7:907 BW.

209 See pro facto (2010), p. 28, referring to Memorie van toelichting (Explanatory Memorandum) Whc, *Kamerstukken* (Parliamentary Minutes) II 2005/06, 30 411, no. 3, pp. 38–9.

210 CB could carry out mass claims in relation to package travel laws, but is in fact predominantly concerned with consumer education in travel law.

211 See http://www.consumentenbond.nl, last accessed: 31 March 2013.

212 Directive 98/27/EC of the European Parliament and of the Council of 19 May 1998 on injunctions for the protection of consumers' interests.

213 See interview with CB (The Hague, 3 December 2010).

214 See for instance: T. Arons and W.H. Van Boom, 'Beyond Tulips and Cheese: Exporting Mass Securities Claim Settlements from the Netherlands', *European Business Law Review* (2010): 857–83, p. 861.

215 See Article 6: 240 BW concerning unfair contract terms. See Van Campen (2007), p. 44.

in the statutes). A representative organisation may be created on an *ad hoc* basis, provided the objectives described in the articles of association coincide with the interest the organisation seeks to protect. This renders it theoretically possible that two or more organisations can bring separate collective actions for the same issue.[216] Most commonly, the CB seeks an injunction, which may be ordered with the threat of a penalty payment for noncompliance or a declaratory judgment, which asks the court to declare the trader's liability in the interest of various consumers who joined the claim.[217] In the latter case, the amount of damages must be assessed in a follow-on procedure at the costs of the consumer. In litigation the CB seeks to prepare follow-on damage cases as far as possible, for example by already establishing facts like a reversal of the burden of proof for follow-on damage claims. The main criterion for cases that the CB takes is the existence of various claims.

Before initiating a proceeding, the plaintiff has an obligation to negotiate with the other party first, which imposes a heavy burden on the plaintiff (in terms of capacity), at least in the CB's experience. The CB has achieved declaratory judgments or recalls.[218] In the *Legionellazaak*, an important mass tort case, CB successfully filed for a declaratory judgment for the benefit of victims.[219] In this procedure, the CB could indirectly facilitate follow-on claims. Unlawfulness and reversal of the burden of proof was already set in this procedure for follow-on procedures; only the damage still had to be measured. Litigation, especially in complex cases, is expensive. The CB estimated that the *Legionellazaak* cost them more than €300,000 in lawyers' fees.[220] Overall, a proceeding in the first instance is very costly and even more so if it is appealed,[221] which is why the number of cases is limited. The *wet op de rechtsbijstand* (Act on legal support, Wrb) allows for public support for consumer organisations only under very limited circumstances (see Article 12).[222]

Dutch procedural law offers a special settlement procedure regarding mass damages in the WCAM for which a primary right of initiative is granted to consumer associations.[223] The procedure goes as follows: first, an association representing the victims and the party (or parties) compensating the damage drafts a contract on compensation. This contract is concluded on the basis of an amicable settlement agreement concerning payment of compensation between

216 See Tzankova (2008), p. 5.

217 See Faure, Ogus and Philipsen (2008), p. 394.

218 See Schaub (2009), p. 157.

219 See interview with CB (The Hague, 3 December 2010).

220 See Loos (2008).

221 See Hondius (2006b), p. 2.

222 See Loos (2008), p. 19.

223 See Hondius (2006b), p. 9. See also Arons and Van Boom (2010), p. 867; W.H. Van Boom, 'Collective Settlement of Mass Claims in The Netherlands', *Auf dem Weg zu einer europäischen Sammelklage?*, eds M. Casper et al. (München: Sellier, 2009) 171–92, p. 177. As said the CA uses this provision with caution, no case has happened or is planned.

the allegedly liable party (or parties) and the foundation or association acting in the aligned common interest of individuals involved (and injured).[224] Then, the parties to the agreement jointly petition the Amsterdam Court of Appeals to declare the settlement binding on all persons to whom damage was caused;[225] interested persons are not summoned in this procedure, but are notified by post or by newspaper announcement.[226] The court hears the arguments of all interested parties, considers several points concerning the substantive and procedural fairness and efficiency of the settlement (amount of compensation, adequate representation of interested parties and so on) and makes a judgment. If the court rules in favour of the settlement, it declares the settlement binding upon all persons to whom damage was caused and who are accommodated by the settlement. Unwilling parties have the opportunity to opt out within a certain period, after which the opt-out option lapses. The association representing the victims must have full legal capacity to act in court and must mention the protection of the victims' interest as a main goal in its articles.

A weakness of this process is that the party that caused the damage is under no legal obligation to cooperate in a settlement agreement. In addition, the court cannot declare the contract binding unless it includes a description of the group that will benefit from the settlement (the victims), the approximate number of victims, how compensation will be rewarded, on what grounds and how it will be calculated.[227] Other reasons for a court to annul the contract include: the compensation is not reasonable; the compensating party does not have sufficient securities; the victims' interests are insufficiently guaranteed; the association does not have a sufficient representative character; or the group's size is too small to justify a settlement.

Once the contract is declared binding, all victims (mentioned in the contract) become party to the settlement. Victims unknown to the organisation also may benefit from the settlement.[228] Individuals may be heard during the court hearing.[229] They can also oppose the settlement. While the court may give parties the opportunity to modify the settlement during the procedure, it has no power to oblige them to make certain modifications (Article 7:907 (4) BW).[230] During

224 See Weber and Van Boom (2011), p. 69.

225 See Article 1013(3) Rv for the exclusive competence of the Amsterdam Court of Appeal in WCAM cases. See Loos (2008), p. 3: an advantage of this exclusive competence for the Amsterdam Court of Appeal is that the Court can develop case management expertise. Another advantage of assigning the Amsterdam Court of Appeal was thought to be its broad financial expertise due to its Enterprise Section (*Ondernemingskamer*).

226 In normal petition procedures, the interested parties are given notice by a registered letter (Article 272 Rv). However, this was considered too burdensome a requirement in WCAM petitions.

227 See Hondius (2006b), p. 10.

228 Ibid., p. 11.

229 See Weber and Van Boom (2011), p. 75.

230 See Hondius (2006b), p. 10.

the petition procedure, interested third parties also may be given notice to appear at the hearing. The individuals have the opportunity to oppose – at their own expense – the settlement. Nevertheless, the position of individual claimants during the court procedure seems to be weak. Should individuals want to intervene in the procedure, they are responsible for their own costs.[231] If the court decides that the settlement is of general benefit and it consequently declares the settlement binding, the only solution for individuals who do not want to be bound to the settlement is to opt out.

The procedure in court is an ordinary civil procedure in which the contract has to be attached to the written application and ordinary means of execution are available to the parties.[232] Other on-going proceedings against the company (or companies) are stayed during the settlement procedure. All contracting parties together have to appeal to the Supreme Court (*Hoge Raad*) if they do not agree with the court's decision (Article 1018 Rv).[233]

The parties themselves bear the initial procedural costs of negotiations.[234] Ultimately the court will assign them to one party. Consumer associations have limited financial means and may be wrung dry in the negotiations process itself. Associations are hardly ever eligible for public legal aid; therefore, membership fees finance the expenses.[235] Moreover, according to Dutch rules on cost shifting, the prevailing party can only partially shift court fees and attorney fees to the losing party.[236] Consequently, the financial incentives for consumer associations are geared towards a responsive, amicable settlement. Although the procedure is relatively short, the negotiation of the contract can take several years, depending on the contracting parties' attitudes. Traders still face the risk that consumers who opted out will sue. CB sees a gap in law enforcement when the parties are not willing to negotiate.[237] The cases that came up were for large damages; cases with trifle damages have low chances because there is no underlying threat that individual consumers would start a lawsuit.[238]

231 See ibid., p. 11.

232 See ibid., p. 11. 'When the compensation is a sum of money, the compensating party pays the entire sum. If the total amount does not suffice to pay all victims (because the number of victims was underestimated), the individual amounts of compensation will be reduced from the moment the deficiency becomes apparent'.

233 See ibid., p. 10: 'The procedural rules differ very little from a normal declarative procedure. Only the application's content requires certain specific data.'; 'Victims or a group representing certain victims can intervene during the procedure. They can state why the Court should not declare the contract binding.'; 'The Court can fix a time period after the publication of the settlement during which victims can seek their compensation (min.1 year)'.

234 See Weber and Van Boom (2011), p. 74.

235 See Loos (2008), p. 38.

236 See Tuil (2010), pp. 401–20.

237 See European Consumer Law Group (ECLG), report 2003/4, p. 13.

238 See Loos (2008), p. 16.

Among the six cases as of 2013 that were carried out, the DES case stands out, which concerned product liability for medicines. The case ended in an agreement in 2000 with establishment of a DES fund of €35 million.[239] In a misleading advertising case against Dexia (regarding share-lease contracts), many investors ended up with residual debts because the remaining value of the shares was insufficient to cover their loans. The settlement sum was €1 billion and Belgian consumers were also compensated.[240]

Although not perfect, the WCAM of 2005 is described as a 'meaningful step forward' when it comes to improving legal responses for compensating victims of mass damage cases.[241] The Dutch lawmaker is considering amendments to the law.[242] In the current design, the behavioural incentives of three main players are at stake: first, the incentives for the individual to opt out; second, the incentives for the consumer association to negotiate in the first place; and third, the incentives for the tort-feasor to cooperate in the settlement negotiations. The current design shows inherent limitations and those incentives can be easily diluted.[243] The WCAM does not explicitly address the issue of widespread scattered losses, which apply to this study's case scenario.[244]

The Supreme Court Preliminary Questions Act (*Wet prejudiciële vragen Hoge Raad*) of 1 July 2012 made it furthermore possible for lower courts to ask the Supreme Court for a ruling on a question of law under special conditions, granted that it is relevant for various cases. This new procedure aims to improve the basis of any subsequent settlement by enabling parties to obtain swift clarifications on questions of law.

There is no official mass procedure at the Dutch GC. If a lot of equal cases come up they are dealt with in the frame of an 'on-hold procedure',[245] which is not a real official procedure.

Overall in the Dutch legal system, there is currently no way to deal with small and widespread harm if the goal is to compensate the actual victims – a disadvantage for the case scenarios at hand. Financing problems and a difficulty in

---

239 Amsterdam Court of Appeal 1 June 2006, NJ 2006, 461 (DES). Some for more details, Loos (2008).

240 Amsterdam Court of Appeal 25 January 2007, JOR 2007, 71 (Dexia).

241 See Weber and Van Boom (2011), p. 77.

242 See http://www.parlementairemonitor.nl/9353000/1/j9vvij5epmj1ey0/vivie6xp2swk, last accessed: 31 March 2013.

243 See Weber and Van Boom (2011), p. 74 for details on the assessment of the incentives.

244 On this type of damage, see for instance W.H. Van Boom, 'De Minimis Curat Praetor: Redress for Dispersed Trifle Losses', *Journal of Comparative Law* 4.2 (2009): 169–83.

245 See personal email communications with SGC (12 January 2011). As outlined, the practice of the GCR is somewhat different in this regard. The procedure has not been officially formalised.

incentivising the other side to cooperate are the main obstacles. However, there are possibilities to go against wrongdoers with the help of injunctions or fines.

Apart from individual action and these special procedures, a common feature of Dutch law is the pooling of interests (*bundeling van belangen*). An association (or anyone) can collect and then exercise individual claims through assignment of the claim or as an agent for the claimants (having obtained their explicit consent).

The Role of Self-regulation The Dutch Advertising Code Foundation SRC is the Dutch self-regulatory organisation introduced in 1963 that covers companies making about 80–90 per cent of the profits in the advertising sector.[246] Self-regulatory claims more specifically must be filed with the Dutch Advertising Council, RCC. The institution is based on a voluntary agreement of the advertising industry. For well-founded complaints, the industry is obliged to retract the advertisement.[247] SRC's activities cover primarily misleading advertising matters, but may go wider to include questions of taste and decency.[248] SRC is a member of the European Advertising Standards Alliance (EASA), which harmonised advertising codes in Europe to a large extent. Apart from the general code of conduct, there are also various sectoral codes.[249] The role of the CB in negotiations of the codes differs compared with negotiations on the two-sided terms and conditions.[250] For instance, a code may state explicitly that the CB does not agree with certain aspects of it.[251]

The RCC and the Board of Appeal adjudicate complaints and the RCC primarily evaluates advertising based on complaints. Generally, the complaints concern

246 For an overview of the associations associated with the SRC, see http://www.reclamecode.nl/bijlagen/20110920_NRC_Engels.pdf, last accessed: 23 February 2011, p. 4. VNO-NCW/MKB are involved in the Dutch Advertising Code Foundation only as auditors. Pursuant to the Mediawet (Media Act), all media institutions producing advertising messages are compulsorily affiliated with the Dutch Advertising Code Foundation.

247 See Van Boom (2006), p. 37; see http://www.reclamecode.nl/, last accessed: 31 March 2013.

248 See interview with RCC (The Hague, 17 March 2011); interview with Professor Jan Kabel, Institute for Information Law, Amsterdam/Consultant RCC (Bloemendaal, 3 December 2010). According to the annual report of the RCC 2010, p. 23 the highest number of claims is 429 (misleading advertising), 309 (issues of taste and decency), 173 (sectoral codes) and so on.

249 See Van Boom et al. (2009a), p. 18.

250 See interview with CB (The Hague, 23 March 2011); see interview with RCC (The Hague, 7 July 2011): the CB's vote weighs more heavily than just one official vote. A CB member used to be in every committee, but this had to be changed as the CB also wanted to file complaints.

251 See personal communications with RCC (27 October 2011). An example is the advertising code for food products, in which the CB is stated as not agreeing with regards to questions of: age limit, the exclusion of packaging material, point of sale material

misleading advertisements.[252] Most of the claims are initiated by consumers, some by organisations and some by traders.[253] However, traders may hide at times behind private individuals to save costs. Complaints are made via an online form or by mail. Once received, the supplier of the advertisement has 14 days to react to the allegations. A public hearing follows in which experts or witnesses can be called. The procedure ends with a written recommendation. All decisions are published and alert decisions appear in press releases. The RCC can issue recommendations (99 per cent) and so-called *vrijblijvend advies* (1 per cent).[254] In essence, all cases end with recommendations that may include stopping a certain advertisement. All broadcast ads are then directly stopped (withdrawn or amended) and the recommendations monitored. With some sector organisations, the SRC has concluded agreements with financial sanctions (for example, in relation to alcohol, agreements between the SRC and *Stichting Verantwoord Alcoholgebruik* [Foundation for the Responsible Use of Alcohol, STIVA]).[255]

The president of the RCC can under particular circumstances decide not to take up a case right away.[256] The Board of Appeal can confirm, annul or change the RCC's decision or send the matter back to the RCC.[257]

There is no possibility for mass claims, but a change in a misleading advertisement will automatically benefit everyone. There is also no necessity for mass claims because the RCC can act upon one single complaint.

The *Commissariaat voor de Media* (Dutch Media Authority, CvM) administers the Dutch media licenses according to the *Mediawet* (Media Act).[258] Apart from complaints by the addressees of the advertising or competitors, there is also a role for broadcasters. They have the possibility to block the broadcasting of ads, as they express in their standard contract terms that respect the Advertising Code. If

and the absence of a distinction between healthy and unhealthy food. This is called a mediation procedure.

252 See interview RCC (The Hague, 17 March 2011); interview with Professor Jan Kabel, Institute for Information Law, Amsterdam/Consultant RCC (Bloemendaal, 3 December 2010).

253 For 2012, 2,304 claims were initiated by consumers, 23 by traders, four by the CB, ten by EASA and five by NGOs, see Annual report RCC 2012, p. 23.

254 In 2012 for instance, there was one 'vrijblijvend advies', see Annual report RCC 2012, p. 17.

255 See Van Boom et al. (2009a), pp. 60, 66. See *Reclamecode voor Alcoholhoudende Dranken* (Advertising Code for Alcoholic Beverages, RvA). This fine can amount up to a maximum of €50,000.

256 See Article 11 of the *Reglement betreffende de Reclame Code Commissie en het College van Beroep* (Regulations on Dutch Advertising Council and Board of Appeal).

257 See Article 26(b) of the *Reglement betreffende de Reclame Code Commissie en het College van Beroep* (Regulations on Dutch Advertising Council and Board of Appeal).

258 See interview with RCC (The Hague, 7 July 2011).

they seek to refuse an act, there is a special procedure to get a ruling of the RCC,[259] although broadcasters may be very reluctant to engage in this procedure.[260] The cooperation of Internet media owners is likewise difficult to assure.

Since 2006, RCC has had a monitoring and compliance unit, which basically checks the rate of compliance with decisions. Approximately one trader is estimated to be noncompliant per month.[261] Noncompliance cases are published on the website and the CA is informed. The standard procedure for checking compliance is to send a letter regarding the decision to monitor compliance. Various actions are judged as compliance: in cases of TV advertising, media blocking is judged as compliance because the commercial is withdrawn.[262] For print media, withdrawing an ad is more difficult, especially if the ad is old and printed samples are in circulation; therefore, monitoring depends on the compliance cooperation with the RCC. The time for compliance must be reasonable.[263] Compliance is not regarded as a problematic issue at the RCC; the compliance rate in 2012 was 96 per cent.[264]

Preclearance of advertisements is obligatory for medicine and health products and alcohol and is done by KOAG/KAG (*Keuringsraad Openlijke Aanprijzing Geneesmiddelen* and *Keuringsraad Aanprijzing Gezondheidsproducten*) and by STIVA (regarding alcohol).[265] For alcohol, preclearing is only done for advertisements that appear on television, radio and in the cinema. Broadcasters furthermore also have an obligation to check ads.[266] In August 2011, a generic copy advice procedure was initiated and experiences are currently being gathered.[267] Users of this voluntary service are charged €500 and the result is nonbinding.[268] No distinction is made between broadcast and other advertising. Complaints and their contents cannot be predicted at this stage and only the RCC or the Board of

259 See RCC, The Dutch Advertising Code – Information about the working procedures of the Advertising Code Committee and the Board of Appeal (2011), http://www.reclamecode.nl/ bijlagen/20110920_NRC_Engels.pdf, last accessed: 31 March 2013, p. 9. 'If a media-institution considers an advertising offered to it impermissible under the Dutch Advertising Code for broadcasting or distribution, it should bring this decision in writing, giving reasons, to the attention of the advertiser with due speed and no later than within two weeks after receipt of the advertising. The advertiser can lodge an objection to such a decision, in writing and giving reasons, to the Committee. The sum of €500 is charged for handling the objection'.

260 See personal communications with RCC (7 December 2011).

261 See interview with RCC (The Hague, 17 March 2011).

262 See ibid.

263 A month is judged as long.

264 See Annual report RCC 2012, p. 26.

265 See interview with RCC (The Hague, 17 March 2011).

266 There is no way to fine the broadcasters if they do not comply.

267 See www.checksrc.nl, last accessed: 31 March 2013.

268 See personal communications with RCC (7 December 2011).

Appeal can decide whether an ad breaches the Dutch Advertising Code.[269] The basis check is carried out according to restrictions in the codes and the previous case law of the RCC. Therefore, in this case study, the *bona fide* trader could check his own advertisement.

In 2012, 1,675 complaints led to an award (1,528 in 2011).[270] The president of the RCC directly declined the complaint in 691 of the cases.

The CA and the RCC are official partners and their cooperation is considered fruitful.[271] The CA allows the RCC to handle any infringement in the field of misleading advertising that falls within its remit without prejudicing its right to take action itself. Of course, the CA adds to the enforcement procedure with formal sanctions only if there is a collective issue at stake. If the self-regulatory code does not apply, an advertiser does not comply or there are repeated violations, the CA can act.[272] The RCC passes on files of noncompliant traders to the CA. It appears that the existence of the CA can aid the RCC process in terms of inducing traders to comply.[273] For example, in the cases of noncompliant traders, the CA is not bound by the RCC's judgment.[274] Even if a case were appealed at the RCC, the CA would reckon with it, but could still take action. The CA also may hand in claims to the RCC. As the monitoring and compliance unit is rather recent, no suggestions on the effectiveness of the involvement of the CA can be derived. At times, investigations by both the RCC and CA may occur in parallel.[275]

RCC ruling can be used (even though not binding) at the GC in the various sectors. The CB has asked the RCC for its decision recently in two cases: *Schweissbänder* and TV-on-demand KPN (a program was advertised that could not be watched) to prepare a consumer damage case.[276] Theoretically, a trader may first turn to the RCC and then use these findings in the court to be granted damage.

---

269 Between the monitoring and compliance department and the adjudicative body, the concept of the Chinese Wall applies.

270 See respective annual reports.

271 See interview with Professor Jan Kabel, Institute for Information Law, Amsterdam/Consultant RCC (Bloemendaal, 3 December 2010).

272 See protocol Consumentenautoriteit – Stichting Reclame Code, http://www.consumentenautoriteit.nl/sites/default/files/redactie/Samenwerkingsovereenkomst%20Consumentenautoriteit-Stichting%20Reclame%20Code.pdf, last accessed: 31 March 2013; pro facto (2009), p. 8.

273 See interview with CB (The Hague, 3 December 2010) and interview with VNO-NCW/MKB (The Hague, 7 March 2011). The high enforcement rate at the RCC is confirmed. In personal communications RCC (7 December 2011) underlines that the roles of CA and RCC are very different.

274 See interview with RCC (The Hague, 17 March 2011). For instance in the sms sector, there were very few complaints at the RCC, but still the CA imposed a big fine because they regarded the code of conduct as generally breaching the law. This is regarded as an exception.

275 See personal communications with RCC (7 December 2011).

276 See interview with RCC (The Hague, 17 March 2011).

Using the RCC body is generally free. The RCC president decides not to take up the case. In that case, the claimant may appeal the decision for €15. If an appeal is launched in the ordinary procedure, €30 is incurred. Traders generally pay €1,000 to bring a case, but sometimes may pay nothing or a reduced fee of €250. Appeals lead to fees of €500 or €250.

The RCC is funded via advertisers' contributions based on their advertising volume.[277] Advertisers contribute 0.025 per cent of their gross media spending to the RCC (system drawn up by *Nielsen*), €250 per €1 million. This means that for advertisers with a gross media spending of more than €1 million a contribution is obligatory. Advertisers that do not reach this threshold do not pay.[278] Pursuant to Article 19 of the Dutch Advertising Code an advertising organisation or institution shall, at request of the chairman of the committee, produce a valid proof of payment of the financial contribution as stipulated each year by the RCC. If advertisers refuse to pay, which is a violation of the code, negotiations will be initiated internally at the RCC.[279] A financial chamber handles these cases, and 'media blocking' (all types of media) may be considered as a sanction, which has not been imposed to date. While the minimum contribution is €250, the highest contributions are capped at €30,000.[280]

RCC intervention is relatively quick, particularly blocking TV advertisements.[281] A decision at the RCC is generally reached within a short time.[282] Compliance is often immediate: TV and radio advertisement are blocked right away.

The RCC has expressed satisfaction with handling cross-border issues.[283]

Criminal Law Enforcement in Advertising A case of misleading advertising might amount to a criminal law violation (violating the WvS), but these instances are rare[284] and would depend on the advertising sector. Food law or medicines come to mind where specific legislation exists,[285] but then, self-regulation and co-regulation is prevalent in those industries. A recent case that was settled concerned

277 See Van Boom et al. (2009a), p. 57.

278 See www.srcbijdrage.nl, last accessed: 31 March 2013.

279 See interview with RCC (The Hague, 17 March 2011).

280 See interview with RCC (The Hague, 7 July 2011).

281 See interview with RCC (The Hague, 17 March 2011).

282 According to Article 8(1) of the procedural rules of the RCC with regards to urgent cases, the meeting is held within 14 days. The Annual report RCC 2010 states on p. 22 that 459 complaints were dealt with in less than one month, 303 in 1–2 months, 327, 2–4 months and 12 in 4–6 months.

283 See interview with RCC (The Hague, 7 July 2011).

284 See interview with CB (The Hague, 3 December 2010).

285 See personal email communications with Professor Jan Kabel, Institute for Information Law, Amsterdam/Consultant RCC. An attempt to regulate misleading advertising by criminal law apparently failed (Article 328 (2) WvS – still existing).

fraudulent gambling shows on TV.[286] The criminal law at stake concerned the Act on the Games of Chance (*Wet op de Kansspelen*). Therefore, criminal law enforcement might indeed be an option under Dutch law for the category of cases involving *mala fide* traders in exceptional circumstances. As mentioned previously, corporate criminal liability can be extended to natural persons.

A behaviour may violate the unfair commercial practices law (WOHP) and the WvS. The CA transfers these cases to the Public Prosecution Office (*Openbaar Ministerie* [OM]). The cooperation protocol[287] between the CA and the OM requires the bodies to discuss cases in periodic meetings or when a particular case comes up, to decide who will pursue the case if the behaviour falls under both competences. Generally the CA takes up these cases because consumer law cases are not a priority for criminal law enforcement.[288]

Assessment and Conclusion

Public law enforcement, through the introduction of the CA with its investigative powers, is an historical change in the Netherlands and adds a public law element to various law enforcement scenarios. As seen with the package travel scenarios, CA may play a role regarding *mala fide* traders who do not provide the required securities for insolvency situations. Also in this case scenario, CA intervention primarily concerned *mala fide* traders.

The enforcement response for this scenario includes interplay between the RCC and the CA. Furthermore, consumer associations are involved in collective procedures. The WCAM is not apt for small and widespread damage, and, therefore, the compensation path cannot deter traders. However, there are various ways of fining or reprimanding the traders and inducing them not to violate the law. There is an *ex ante* and an *ex post* side to the system in line with the design suggestions for this case scenario and criminal law enforcement is possible for exceptional circumstances.

Considering an efficient design, no official procedure for collective proceedings currently exists at the ADR body, which is desirable. In practice an 'on-hold' procedure may be used, as explained above. Information regarding frequency is not available.

In misleading advertising cases, self-regulation plays a role, which has traditionally worked rather well in the Netherlands. Anyone can complain to the RCC and the procedure is low cost. A high compliance rate by traders has been reported. A weakness to this system is that the effect of advertising can be fast and

286 See interview with Professor Jan Kabel, Institute for Information Law, Amsterdam/Consultant RCC (Bloemendaal, 3 December 2010).

287 See protocol Consumentenautoriteit – OM, http://www.consumentenautoriteit.nl/sites/default/files/redactie/samenwerkingsprotocol-procureurs-generaal-consumentenautoriteit.pdf, last accessed: 31 March 2013.

288 See personal email communications with CA (15 December 2011).

even a short airing may lead to profits. Traders finance the RCC system. From a deterrence perspective, the CA can be an underlying threat for the RCC. In addition to signalling cases to the RCC, the CA may also fine companies and RCC decisions may be used as evidence in individual proceedings for damages in the civil court or the GC. Among applicable suggestions for the 'optimal enforcement mix' is the preclearance of advertising content, which may be used by *bona fide* traders. However, in the Netherlands this advice is nonbinding and is a rather new development. Preclearance is available for any type of advertising independent of the medium where it is broadcast. Some advertising sectors have a system of obligatory preclearance in place.

There are no real possibilities of damage claims for consumer associations. The WCAM currently still poses some incentive and financing problems and is intended for cases of mass personal injuries rather than small and widespread damage. From a deterrence perspective, any intervention that deters the wrongdoer is sufficient and there is no need for the sanctions to include damage payments. There are indeed some alternative remedies to compensation available in the Netherlands. Consumer associations may bring actions for injunctions or declaratory judgments and they have done so on various occasions. The representative bodies may achieve all remedies except for monetary relief. For example, when taking legal action, consumer associations may try to prepare possible follow-on claims for consumers (already establish unlawfulness or a reversal of the burden of proof) to leave only the calculation of the actual damage to the individual case.

The CA has competences and sanctions available to deter *mala fide* traders. The CA acts based on complaints or its market surveys. Over the last years, some form of misleading market practices have frequently been among the CA's priorities. The mere fact that this body exists may induce some *mala fide* traders to comply with the decisions of the self-regulatory body or with the law in the first place. The CA's investigative powers, outlined throughout the chapter, are crucial in tracking traders, particularly those that place Internet ads. The broadcasters that likewise adhere to the advertising code and can signal or refuse misleading advertisements are an additional monitoring body for TV advertising. The cooperation among Internet media owners still shows some weaknesses.

When it comes to the incentive structures of representing bodies, the consumer association apparently works in the interest of consumers, rather than operating according to society's interest. Concerns have been expressed in the literature about capture of consumer associations consequently . It may therefore be desirable that a court is involved in the decision-making.

With the CA, as outlined before, there are ways to separate powers and the administrative appeal system is in place. The importance of a 'court element' for mass cases has been established in Part I. This element is certainly granted if a consumer association takes up a case in the civil court. The CA has very powerful internal sanctioning powers, which are more critical in terms of an accurate procedure and reducing risks of capture. Then again, appeals are possible. CA fines may be considerable, particularly for unfair commercial practices and they are calculated per violation. The CA has powers to track hiding traders and the RCC also reduces the occurrence of hiding traders within the market because of the first-hand information it has. Not all traders in the advertising market are participants in the RCC and these may potentially be the *mala fide* traders.

The RCC's intervention (which works for *bona fide* traders) can be considerably speedy and the fastest sanction available at the CA is the expedient administrative order under penalty.

Individuals with a damage of only €15 are not induced to bring a damage claim in the civil court and likewise cases do not come up in the GC. If the consumer expects to win and recoup this investment, the cost–benefit ratio might still change. Then again, it might not be in the societal interest to allow individual €15 claims because the costs of handling the claim outweigh the benefits (certainly if no injunction is achieved simultaneously).

Competitors can file actions as well and for competitors and consumers alike, establishing the causal link between damage incurred and the misleading advertising can be a challenge. Competitors' strategic interests need to be disciplined. The competitor also may opt to go to the RCC body first, although fees for competitors are higher here than for consumers. Therefore, at times, traders may vest in the cloth of a consumer to avoid some fees. Overall, 'official' traders bring few complaints to the RCC. In terms of restricting the strategic use of the self-regulatory body, the fact that traders have to pay for using the body can be approved in the light of the design suggestions; the Dutch rule is exceptional in Europe.

Criminal law is a fallback option. For the optimal design, the underlying threat of the criminal law enforcement is certainly desirable for deterrence of *mala fide* traders.

Considering improvements, the Dutch system already involves all possible players and, to a certain degree, the sanctions may be adapted to the type of trader. If the RCC does not work, there are various underlying threats in the system, the CA's action or the criminal law. Consumer associations are another potential player. While action in the package travel market by the CA is mainly on an *ex ante* level, here it comes *ex post. Ex ante* action mainly emanates from the RCC. This allows to a certain degree for signalling. The emphasis of a voluntary system can be beneficial in terms of very high administrative costs that one would incur if the aim were to check all advertising. From a legal perspective, 'freedom of speech' is a basic right that must be ensured.

Some fine-tuning can still be suggested. Regarding the trader who obtains a 'clearance' at the RCC, a stronger value and degree of 'binding' in a later judgment may be considered.

The CA and the CB must cooperate carefully and there are a lot of consultations that occur to ensure no duplication of enforcement efforts. (In some respects, both bodies could bring overlapping actions.) The ability for one body to challenge the inaction of the other may be advisable.

The CA may currently first bring a case to the RCC and independent of its decision still may decide to fine the trader. This situation may lead to an unnecessary duplication of costs and amount to over-deterrence of traders.

The advantage of a consumer association's taking action is the court element in the procedure. This is not the case if the CA uses its administrative enforcement powers. An administrative court may be involved at some stage.

The CA's competences in relation to advertising are basically administrative. In terms of deterrence, there are a number of available sanctions. There may even be situations of over-deterrence. The expedient administrative order under penalty is powerful in interrupting a violation quickly. The administrative procedure may generally take a long time.

Mass damage actions when damage is small and widespread are currently not possible and may be introduced. Likewise, the idea of introducing 'skimming-off' procedures with the CA may be an interesting way to enhance deterrence. This sanction might not differ very much from fines that the CA may currently impose. In the end, what counts is that the sanction is a threat to the trader's finances. A *mala fide* trader also may profit from a complicated enforcement regime.

General Conclusion

The two case studies cover various typical contingencies of consumer law problems and allow for a description of a large variety of players who potentially may be involved in consumer law enforcement in the Netherlands.

Overall, adding the CA to the enforcement landscape in the Netherlands aligns well with the optimal enforcement designs, particularly in terms of providing a public law element in both types of case scenarios. Particularly in negotiations of two-sided standard contract terms, consumer associations have reduced anonymity in some sectors and emphasised the importance of having strong trade associations that may discipline members or report nonmembers. *Mala fide* traders generally do not participate in those schemes. Before the introduction of the CA, the CB was involved in court cases. However, consumer associations are more limited in their investigative powers, which may be crucial for some emerging case scenarios. In this instance, the CA (and newly available sanctions) has certainly changed the enforcement response, which is particularly important because there is currently no working format for a collective mass action for small and widespread damage available. Resources of the institutions as such will always be an issue that must be solved. The cooperation between the CA and CB seems to be fruitful. A lot of experimenting still goes on, including decisions regarding further sanctions like skimming-off profits that the CA could potentially be empowered to grant.

The CA and the RCC both engage in *ex ante* and *ex post* actions in different circumstances. The RCC's knowledge of the sector is exploited. Regarding the importance of underlying threats, the CA has positive effects for the RCC.

Overall, the GC has the mandate that the optimal mix would suggest: disable some very small individual damage cases and not provide for an official mass procedure. In some, but few, instances, criminal law may be used, which aligns with the efficient mixes as well. Most information asymmetries can be cured by an intervention of the CA.

In various mass procedures a court element is present, as the optimal mix design suggests. For individual consumer cases, the court option is rare, even with the subdistrict judge. This seems to exclude the body as competition or an underlying threat to the GC system. An action could not be filed there instead.

The RCC and the GC provide for cross-financing of the public law element for cases with high information asymmetry, that arise in part from the challenges of Internet trade. Interestingly, traders and trade associations ultimately finance the RCC and the GC (except for a small share of public funding), which means costs are possibly passed on to consumers. Still both bodies – the RCC and the SGC – are different in the degree to which they involve consumers in their decision-making and the remedies that they grant. To a certain extent, self-regulation also plays a role with the trade associations in the travel sector and not only regarding advertising.

Generally, the Netherlands follows its tradition when widening the definition of private law enforcement to include hybrid mechanisms like self-regulation or out-of-court dispute resolution (the classification of the two is not always clear-cut). Certainly, the expertise in the travel sector seems to be with the ADR body rather than civil court.

On 1 April 2013, a merger between the CA, OPTA and NMa into the ACM is planned. Despite a discussion, this merger upholds the two-sided enforcement response (civil and administrative law) instead of changing to pure administrative law enforcement. While this is a result of budget cuts, the impact on overall deterrence of consumer law violations is unclear. Less funding may be available, but the merger could increase the investigative powers of the CA and facilitate cooperation with OPTA and NMa, which may increase efficiency. Currently only for a few competences a change is envisaged,[289] and the practical impact remains to be seen.

289 See Law establishing the ACM of 28 February 2013 (Instellingswet Autoriteit Consument en Markt).

Chapter 7
Sweden

Introduction

Specific consumer protection laws have existed in Sweden since the end of the 1960s, although rules on competition laws and legislation on consumer information date even earlier.[1] Reforms to introduce class actions in the 1980s and 1990s culminated in the *Lag om grupprättegång* SFS 2002:599 (Group Proceedings Act, LOG).[2] The Market Court, with special competence for cases related to the Swedish Competition Act and the Swedish Marketing Act[3] and other consumer and marketing legislation dates to 1970, and the *Allmänna reklamationsnämnden* (ARN), a central board for out-of-court settlement of consumer-to-business disputes, dates to 1968. Basically, any consumer dispute may be brought to the ARN, which functions as an independent public authority financed by the state budget.[4]

Scandinavia's typical focus on public law enforcement[5] is evident in both the *Konsumentombudsmannen* (Consumer Ombudsman's office, KO), which takes legal action on behalf of collective consumer interests, and the related *Konsumentverket* (Swedish Consumer Agency, KOV),[6] two bodies that merged in 1975. Since 1976, the Director General of KOV is also the KO.[7] KO/KOV is concerned with consumer

---

1 See U. Bernitz, 'Consumer Protection: Aims, Methods, and Trends in Swedish Consumer Law', *Scandinavian Studies in Law* 20 (1976): 11–36, p. 16.

2 See M. Kohler, *Die Entwicklung des schwedischen Zivilprozeßrechts* (Tübingen: Mohr Siebeck, 2002) 598, p. 440 for more details on the reasons underpinning these developments.

3 See *Marknadsföringslagen* (SFS 2008:486) (Marketing Act).

4 See A. Bakardjieva Engelbrekt, *Sweden National Report – Study: An Analysis and Evaluation of Alternative Means of Consumer Redress other than Redress through Ordinary Judicial Proceedings*, 2006, p. 1; see for a follow-up contribution to this report A. Bakardjieva Engelbrekt, 'Från Materiella Regler till Genomföranderegler: En Ny Fas i det Europeiska Rättssamarbetet på Konsumentskyddsområdet?' *Europarättslig Tidskrift* 3 (2007): 568–97; see also Viitanen (2000), p. 315. Its legal mandate is established in *Förordning – Regulation (SFS 2007:1041) med instruktion för Allmänna reklamationsnämnden* (ARN Instruction 2007).

5 See Faure, Ogus and Philipsen (2008), p. 374.

6 See interview with Gunnar Larsson, Swedish Consumer Ombudsman and Head of Consumer Authority (Stockholm, 25 August 2009). The KO is also the Director General of the Consumer Agency.

7 See A. Bakardjieva Engelbrekt, *Fair Trading Law in Flux? National Legacies, Institutional Choice and the Process of Europeanisation*, US-AB, Stockholm

empowerment. The institution is the competent authority designated as a result of the Regulation on CPC.[8] KO/KOV is responsible for the supervision of consumer protection legislation and, in this context, engages in monitoring and various types of legal action (for individuals or groups of consumers).

Consumer associations do not play an important role in law enforcement in Sweden.[9] Individuals complement the regulatory enforcement process.[10] There are two lines of courts: one starting with the district court and one starting with the administrative court. District courts hear both criminal and civil cases.[11] Unlike other European countries' procedural laws, the Swedish penal procedural law is not codified separately from the civil procedural law, not even after significant law reform of 1942 (*Nya Rättegangsbalk*). Rather, laws are taken together under a common heading for civil and criminal procedural law.[12] Swedish courts traditionally have had little influence in civil matters.[13] However, since the 1990s, this has been changing.

Self-regulation is important in some of the consumer law disciplines as well and an Advertising Ombudsman, or *Reklamombudsmannen* (RO), was established in 2009.

Sweden does not perfectly fit as either a common law country (like England) or a civil law country (like the Netherlands).[14] But based on the limited role Sweden gives to courts for interpreting the law,[15] the country is closer to a civil law country.

Below, the institutional law enforcement in Sweden is analysed for the two case studies, package travel and misleading advertising.

(2003), p. 186. It was analysed recently to see if this was still a successful concept: Departementsserien 2009:14 Konsumentombudsmannen – en översyn. As of yet no legal action has followed from this.

8 See § 3 (4), *Förordning* – Regulation (SFS 2009:607).

9 Since 1993/4 the KO/KOV decides on the funding of the associations, 12kr million in 2009.

10 See Faure, Ogus and Philipsen (2008), p. 373.

11 See 'The Swedish National Courts Administration', *Scandinavian Studies in Law* 51 (2007): 629–50.

12 The Act on Swedish Judicial Procedure was last amended in 2009. Nowadays Swedish criminal procedural law is supplemented by provisions outside of the act (for instance the Penal Code), see L. Carlson, *Fundamentals of Swedish Law* (Lund: Studentlitteratur AB, 2009), p. 111.

13 See P.H. Lindblom, 'Group Litigation in Scandinavia', *ERA Forum* 10 (2009): 7–35, p. 8; Lindblom (2007), p. 282.

14 See Carlson (2009), p. 36. It is said not to be a typical civil law country because it does not have a complete codification like the German Civil Code. When it comes to security interests in chattels for instance, it has relied almost purely on case-law. It is at times regarded as a third way in between.

15 See Carlson (2009), pp. 38, 42. The value of legislative preparatory documents is almost as high as that of the legislation itself.

Case 1 – Package Travel

How would the package travel case be handled in Sweden (damage of €2,000; a *bona fide* trader scenario [1] and a *mala fide* trader scenario [2])? Particular attention is paid to the *mala fide* trader, an online merchant who tries to hide his identity.

Summary of Legal Rules

The provisions on package travel in Sweden were introduced as a result of an EC directive governing package travel law in 1993 and amended in 1995.[16] Prior to this, there was no such legislation. Sweden's consumer protection in this field worked via general agreements on package travel negotiated by KOV with the major Swedish travel organisations. In cases of a violation of these agreements, a claimant could resort to the provisions on unfair contract terms.[17] Today, two types of institutions can handle package travel cases involving payments of compensation – the district court and the ARN.

Generally, a consumer may get assistance from consumer advisors (*konsumentvägledare*). In 2007, more than 118,000 consumers used these advisors,[18] who in most cases are municipal public officials.[19] Their assistance is free of charge and easily accessible.[20] In addition to advising consumers on their rights and the best forum to bring a claim, consumer advisors mediate between consumers and traders. Mediation is very informal and may lead to various remedies, including conduct and monetary remedies, but enforcement is not guaranteed. While some consumer advisors only give advice, others contact the trader on behalf of consumers.[21] The satisfaction with the quality of the work of these advisors varies throughout the municipalities.[22] This mechanism may be an option for the package travel case or at least help to identify the body with which to pursue action.[23]

Konsument Europa (part of KOV), the Swedish partner in the ECC network, facilitates information on any consumer query on cross-border purchasing.[24]

---

16 See H. Schulte-Nölke 'EC consumer law compendium – Comparative analysis' (Bielefeld: University of Bielefeld, 2007), p. 161.

17 See Schulte-Nölke (2007), p. 220.

18 See Motion 2008/09:C390 Konsumentpolitik, Section 5.

19 See Bakardjieva Engelbrekt (2006), p. 12.

20 See Bakardjieva Engelbrekt (2006), p. 2.

21 See personal email communications Konsument Europa/ECC Sweden (29 November 2010).

22 See Bakardjieva Engelbrekt (2006), p. 12.

23 Confirmed by interview with Professor Ulf Bernitz, Professor Emeritus of European Integration Law, University of Stockholm (Stockholm, 11 November 2010).

24 See http://www.konsumenteuropa.se/en/About-us/, last accessed: 31 March 2013.

At the District Court The district court deals with civil cases (*tvistemål*) and criminal ones. A judge at the district court is competent to act as both a civil or criminal law judge,[25] and both types of cases are set out in the Swedish Civil Procedural Code (RB) (*Den svenska Rättegångsbalken* [*SFS 1942:740*]). There are two types of civil proceedings: those that are amenable to out-of-court settlement (*dispositiva tvistemål*) and those that are not (*indispositiva tvistemål*).[26] In the latter, the parties cannot formally reach a settlement and cannot 'dispose' of the matter because society also has interest in the outcome.

Generally a consumer law case will be dealt with as a *dispositiva tvistemål*,[27] which, for example, would apply to the package travel scenario. Traditionally, Swedish civil procedural law has provided a strong principle of party presentation (also called party disposition)[28] and the power of the judge is limited.[29] Today, this still holds true; however, the principle of investigation is anchored more firmly now with its limits on the impartiality of the judge. The principle of party disposition allows for the judge's active participation within the substantive boundaries drawn up by the parties.[30] The civil judge does not have wide investigative powers.[31] There is no discovery or disclosure and if the consumer cannot locate the trader, the claim cannot be initiated.[32] In summons applications, the defendant's personal identity numbers and her postal address must be stated.[33] The court handles the service of summons. Furthermore, if the claimant does not have the address or

25 See personal email communications with Professor Per Henrik Lindblom, Professor Emeritus of Civil and Criminal Procedure, University of Uppsala (7 November 2010).

26 Examples are adoption or division of marital property.

27 Almost all disputes pertaining to the Law of Obligations figure in the category 'Dispositive tvistemål' Some consumer law issues can be 'indispositiva tvistemål', for instance in marketing practices law, unfair terms in consumer contracts and the like, where KO has standing, see personal email communications with Professor Antonina Bakardjieva-Engelbrekt, Professor of European Law, University of Stockholm (14 February 2012).

28 See B. Lindell, *Civil Procedure in Sweden* (Uppsala: Iustus Förlag, 2004), p. 30. Only what is alleged by the parties can be considered by the judge. There are some cases that do not constitute dispositive cases such as custody issues in family law.

29 See Kohler (2002), p. 348.

30 See Lindblom (2009), p. 10. According to personal email communications with Market Court judge (1[illegible] October 2011) the process according to RB is adversarial, even though there are some inquisitorial elements with regard to criminal cases and 'indispositiva civil cases'.

31 See personal email communications with Professor Per Henrik Lindblom, Professor Emeritus of Civil and Criminal Procedure, University of Uppsala (7 November 2010); See similar personal email communications with Stockholm District Court judge (7 October 2011).

32 See personal email communications with Professor Per Henrik Lindblom, Professor Emeritus of Civil and Criminal Procedure, University of Uppsala (7 November 2010). Also see interview with Professor Ulf Bernitz, Professor Emeritus of European Integration Law, University of Stockholm (Stockholm, 11 November 2010). In his point of view the civil judge could not take up the case.

33 See Lindell (2004), p. 102.

has a wrong address for the trader, the title she will receive will be useless.[34] The situation is comparable to the one in the Netherlands and renders the *mala fide* trader case (scenario 2) impossible within a private law setting.[35]

Sweden is characterised as a defendant-friendly forum because of the definitiveness of pleadings, limited opportunities to amend pleadings and limited discovery mechanisms to the parties.[36] Judges have taken an increasingly active role in promoting settlements and nowadays about 60 per cent of all cases that reach a court end in settlement (often confirmed in a judgment).[37]

Generally, the burden of proof rests with the plaintiff.[38] Legal representation in the district court is not required, which can reduce the parties' costs,[39] but often a lawyer is present. There are no fixed lawyer fees and fees tend to be substantial.[40] Lawyer fees are calculated on the basis of estimated time spent and the quality of the service rather than the value discussed in the dispute. The English rule on costs applies,[41] except for small claims cases, where the American rule applies.[42] The general court fee in Sweden is 450kr. Sweden generally does not impose court fees on claimants who initiate proceedings as a 'matter of principle'.[43]

For claimants who are unable to pay for a legal representative, the Swedish government offers legal aid to cover part of the costs for a lawyer and expenses related to evidence and other matters. All costs are not necessarily covered. The underlying assumption is that the claimant should contribute to the cost to the extent that she can afford it. There are six levels of applicant fees and contributions vary between 10 per cent and 40 per cent.[44] To save state funding, Section 9 of the Legal Aid Act (*Rättshjälpslagen* [*SFS 1996:1619*]) made legal aid subsidiary to

34 See interview with Professor Ulf Bernitz, Professor Emeritus of European Integration Law, University of Stockholm (Stockholm, 11 November 2010).

35 Online registries, such as InfoTorg or Bolagsregistrets (http://www.bolagsregistret.se/, last accessed: 31 March 2013) can be accessed. The same weaknesses as in the Netherlands apply.

36 See Carlson (2009), p. 115.

37 See Lindblom (2008a), p. 84.

38 See personal email communications with Professor Ulf Bernitz, Professor Emeritus of European Integration Law, University of Stockholm (31 October 2011).

39 See Lindell (2004), p. 56. According to personal email communications with Stockholm District Court judge (18 February 2011), the court is obliged to help the parties in clarifying the dispute (Chapter 42 § 8 II RB). Therefore it is indeed not always necessary for an individual to hire a lawyer.

40 See personal email communications with Professor Ulf Bernitz, Professor Emeritus of European Integration Law, University of Stockholm (31 October 2011).

41 See Lindblom (2009), p. 10. See Chapter 18:1 RB.

42 Ibid., p. 11.

43 See http://www.domstol.se/Ladda-ner--bestall/Avgifter/, last accessed: 31 March 2013; Hodges, Vogenauer and Tulibacka (2010), p. 13.

44 See Carlson (2009), p. 122.

private legal insurance.[45] Rather recently public legal aid was cut considerably and replaced by private litigation insurance.[46] Note that 'subsidiary' means that legal aid cannot be granted in cases in which the applicant should have obtained legal insurance, but did not do so. Insurance for litigation costs is usually a maximum of five 'base amounts' which is 220,000kr. The base amount for 2012 was 44,000kr[47] and is generally limited to lawyer's fees for about 100 hours of work or 120,000kr.[48] This might thus be available for a package travel case in the courts. For instance, legal aid is not granted in cases of small economic value in comparison with the legal cost,[49] which applies to the next case scenario. Legal insurance is another option generally available under this scenario for financing law claims.[50] Ninety-seven per cent of the Swedish population has legal insurance, as it is an add-on compulsory insurance to normal household insurance.[51]

Regarding fighting vexatious litigation, there is no prohibition against instituting any kind of claims.[52] However, there is a way for the court to refrain from serving the summons if no legal reason for the claim is provided or if it is otherwise obvious that the claim is unfounded. In such a case, the claim cannot be dismissed, but is disapproved. Likewise, there is a provision, by which claims that conflict with common moral views may be dismissed.[53] Possible consequences are fines, requirements to pay the other parties' legal costs in cases of careless obstructions

45 See Lindell (2004), p. 155. Legal aid in 1994/95 amounted to 870kr million. The guidelines of how to apply legal aid are to be found in the preparatory works (Proposition 1972:4).

46 See Lindblom (2009), p. 10. He refers to the legal aid system as a 'disgrace' in Lindblom (2007), p. 288.

47 See personal email communications with Svenska Resebyråföreningen (Swedish Travel Association, SRF) (1 November 2011). The base amount is decided according to the Socialförsäkringsbalk (SFS 2010:110) (Social Insurance Scale).

48 See P.H. Lindblom, *The Globalization of Class Actions Oxford Conference*, 12–14 December (2007), p. 17. The same is true for legal aid.

49 See Lindell (2004), p. 156 referring to Proposition 1972:4; see also Bakardjieva Engelbrekt (2006), p. 29.

50 See personal email communications with Professor Ulf Bernitz, Professor Emeritus of European Integration Law, University of Stockholm (31 October 2011). The insurance policies contain a number of restrictions and thresholds. Normally, certain types of cases are excluded.

51 Legal protection is automatically included in virtually all Swedish home and contents, home and residential, leisure home insurances, comprehensive insurance of boats and comprehensive/partial motor car insurance, see M.G. Faure and J.P.B. De Mot, 'Comparing Third Party Financing of Litigation and Legal Expenses Insurance', *Journal of Law, Economics and Policy* 8.3 (2012): 743–78, p. 752. In 2004 the number was 95 per cent, see Lindell (2004), p. 155.

52 See Lindell (2004), p. 86, referring to Chapter 42:5 RB.

53 See Chapter 13:11 RB.

and the preclusion from introducing new legal facts and new evidence.[54] As fines for frivolous cases are extremely rare, they are disregarded here.[55]

In Sweden the state spends some €4 billion on courts on an annual basis,[56] and parties pay some one per cent of the total on applications.[57] Users pay only a negligible amount of the court maintenance.

In 2006, rules on a simplified judicial procedure for claims of low value (small claims – *FT-mål*[58]) were integrated in the RB (Proposition 1986/87:89).[59] The procedure is not specifically designed for consumer disputes, but can apply where the value of the claim does not exceed half of the base amount, according to the National Insurance Act.[60] Currently, the base amount is 44,000kr, and, therefore, half of the base amount is 22,000kr.[61] This would apply for the case scenarios. The differences to an ordinary court procedure are in the composition of the bench, special rules on litigation costs, lack of legal representation for at least one of the parties (see Proposition 1986/87:89) and other simplified rules of procedure.[62] This mechanism has not substantially contributed to consumer access to courts[63] for reasons that include the limited opportunities to use legal aid or be reimbursed for lawyer's fees.[64] In both ordinary and the small claims procedures, lawyers are not required, but consumers usually do not feel comfortable representing themselves.[65] Another difference between the two procedures is that two different cost rules apply, one meant to encourage not hiring a lawyer (who would have to be paid at one's own expense). Under the American rule for small claims, the winning party has a right to reimbursement only for the cost of a maximum of one hour of legal

54 See Chapters 9: 1–3, 18:6, 42:15 RB.

55 See personal email communications with Professor Ulf Bernitz, Professor Emeritus of European Integration Law, University of Stockholm (31 October 2011).

56 See E. Dubois, C. Schurrer and M. Velicogna, *The functioning of judicial systems and the situation of the economy in the European Union Member States, Report prepared for the European Commission by CEPEJ (Commission Européenne pour l'Efficacité de la Justice)* (2013), p. 546.

57 See Hodges, Vogenauer and Tulibacka (2010), p. 13 for the 2012 amount.

58 'FT-mål' means förenklat tvistemål = simplified contentious case; see personal email communications with SRF (1 November 2011).

59 Previously there was a separate Act: Lag (SFS 1974:8) om rättegång i tvistemål om mindre värden (Small Claims Act).

60 See Lag (SFS 1962:381) om allmän försäkring (National Insurance Act), see 1:3d RB.

61 See personal email communications with SRF (1 November 2011).

62 See Bakardjieva Engelbrekt (2006), p. 26.

63 See ibid., pp. 5, 26.

64 See ibid., (2006), p. 29. The court fee is equal to the general one, namely 450kr.

65 See Lindblom (2008a), p. 81.

advice, the court fee, translation costs and travel expenses of the party, an attorney or witness.[66] In all other cases, the full reimbursement of attorney fees is the rule.[67]

So far, this mechanism has mainly been used by traders as a debt-collection instrument.[68] In 2012, as many as 22,952 cases were filed as FT-mål (21,222 in 2011).[69] If a procedure is initiated as an ordinary civil law procedure, it cannot later be changed into a small claim procedure, for example if the claim value is reduced.[70] For cross-border cases, the European Small Claims procedure applies. The average net cost of a small claims case initiated for the public purse was estimated at 2,874kr in 2004.[71]

A recent Eurobarometer study showed that 30 per cent of Swedish consumers over the past 12 months had a legitimate cause to complain.[72] The average financial losses were €208, with, for example, 44 per cent claiming none and 17 per cent claiming €1–20. Therefore, for a certain percentage of small consumer claims matters, special low-cost devices are needed to incentivise consumers to sue. Ninety-one per cent of the Swedish interviewees said they would make complaints in the event of a problem, the highest percentage in the study. Among Swedish interviewees, 22 per cent said the range of €500–1,000 was the financial threshold for involving a court[73] a result that is comparable to the trend in the Netherlands. Twenty per cent set the threshold at €1,001–2,500, 13 per cent at €201–500 and three per cent at €20 or less. Financial thresholds for pursuing a case with the ADR were 17 per cent at €201–500, 17 per cent at €101–200, 12 per cent at €51–100, six per cent at €21–51 and eight per cent at €20 or less.

The Swedish ADR Board The main addressee of package travel cases is the publicly financed ARN.[74] In contrast to the situation in the Netherlands, traders do not contribute. The ARN currently examines complaints in 13 divisions: general (miscellaneous), banking services, housing, boats, electricity, real estate agents, insurance, motor vehicles, furniture, travel, footwear, textiles and cleaning/laundry. It has a particular division for 'travel'. A case can be brought against any trader and there is no need for traders to be registered with the ARN.

Consumer, labour, industry and other interested organisations nominate people with relevant expertise to the different boards; the board chairman then makes the

66 See M. Sunnqvist, 'Loser pays – But only a reasonable Amount – Cost and Fee Allocation in Sweden' *Cost and Fee Allocation in Civil Procedure*, ed. M. Reimann (Dordrecht; Heidelberg London; New York: Springer, 2012) pp. 267–73; Chapter 8, § 8A, Section 1–5 RB.

67 See Chapter 18 § 8 RB.

68 See Lindblom (2008a), p. 81.

69 See Court Statistics: Official Statistics of Sweden 2012, p. 9, Table 1.1.

70 See Bakardjieva Engelbrekt (2006), p. 25.

71 ibid., p. 29.

72 See European Commission, Special Eurobarometer n°342 (2011), p. 170.

73 ibid., p. 217.

74 See Bakardjieva Engelbrekt (2006), p. 1. See also Viitanen (2000), p. 315.

appointments for a limited time. Experts can be especially appointed (§ 19 ARN Instruction 2007). Consumer interests also are represented by KOVs officials. The Swedish consumer association approves of the public financing because it increases the perception of loyalty.[75]

Proceedings can be initiated by an individual consumer against a trader, by the KO on behalf of a group of consumers or by an association of consumers or wage earners on behalf of a group of consumers. The KO has a primary right of initiative.[76] For this case study, only individual cases are assessed.

Within the ARN, consumer matters are centralised and 'transparency and uniformity of the decisions of the board' are ensured.[77] The procedure is purely written and evidence is not seized, which automatically limits the complexity of cases. The consumer can complain without a representative at no charge, and cases are dealt with quickly, which also means low costs for the consumer. If the board takes up a consumer complaint, the trader is asked to comment on the consumer's claims.[78] In turn, the consumer has an opportunity to see and comment on the trader's response. Both parties may submit written evidence, such as contracts or certificates of inspection. The dispute is then usually solved at a meeting of the board competent for the matter and the parties may not be present. A department may make a decision when the chairperson and four other members are present.[79] The chairperson is a lawyer and has experience as a judge. The other members come from various consumer and trade organisations. All members act impartially in the meeting. The secretariat may deal alone with simple matters or those in which the trader does not respond, which is about 50 per cent of the cases.[80] The system is now completely electronic.

In its decisions, the board refers to Supreme Court cases and preparatory works. Normally cases considered are straightforward and the board does not deal with claims of 'insignificant value'.[81] For matters before the travel board, a general

75 See Sveriges Konsumenter, The Swedish Consumer Association, response to the European Commission's consultation document dated 18 January 2011 on the use of Alternative Dispute Resolution, p. 1.

76 The board is furthermore accessible for foreign consumers in cross-border disputes, in particular in view of the information activity carried out by the Swedish unit in ECC-Net, Konsument Europa. See personal email communications with KO/KOV (22 November 2011): Whenever the KO decides not to represent consumers in a group action at the ARN, the KO makes a (formal) decision so that the consumer organisation can take action instead.

77 See Bakardjieva Engelbrekt (2006), p. 8.

78 See personal email communications with ARN (26 January 2011).

79 Likewise a department may take a decision with a chairperson and two other members, unless one of the members requests that four members participate.

80 See F. Weber, C. Hodges and N. Creutzfeldt-Banda, 'Sweden', *Consumer ADR in Europe*, eds C. Hodges, I. Benöhr and N. Creutzfeldt-Banda (Oxford and Portland, Oregon: Hart Publishing, 2012), 229–52, p. 242.

81 See Bakardjieva Engelbrekt (2006), p. 2.

threshold of 1,000kr applies.[82] The board's recommendations are generally limited to issues of contractual liability[83] and the most typical remedy is compensation for damages because of breach of a contract, which would apply in the package travel case study. The board may also recommend a price reduction.[84] Besides monetary remedies, conduct remedies (such as obligation to perform, change and termination of contractual agreements) may be issued. Damages are calculated on a case-by-case basis as circumstances differ.[85] Therefore, no easy scheme or formula applies, apart from the board's earlier rulings. Similar cases are treated in the same way. Package travel cases are dealt with at the ARN rather than the district court.[86] In general, far more consumer law cases are decided at the ARN than in the courts,[87] which traders regard as unfortunate.[88]

The ARN's recommendations are not binding on the parties, which may raise doubts regarding their effectiveness. However, in practice, most businesses respect the board's recommendations.[89] According to the ARN's website, the rate of trader compliance with ARN decisions was 71 per cent in 2011 and 76 per cent in 2012.[90] The compliance rate varies between sectors and in the travel sector compliance was above average at 72 per cent in 2011 and 80 per cent in 2012. For package travel cases, the rate is reportedly almost 100 per cent. Traders who do not comply with the board's decision may be published on a blacklist in the consumer magazine *Råd & Rön*, which is issued by *Sveriges Konsumenter*, a Swedish consumer organisation. This list is cited widely in the media. Overall, this is significantly different from the system in the Netherlands.

The board deals only with contracts concluded in Sweden and does not handle complaints against foreign traders. The Internet is a particular challenge here. The board's investigative powers are limited, and, therefore, if a trader cannot be traced, the board has to dismiss the case.[91] Further limitations to the ARN's

---

82 See Weber, Hodges and Creutzfeldt-Banda (2012), p. 241.

83 See A.H. Persson, 'Evaluation of the Effectiveness and Efficiency of Collective Redress Mechanisms in the European Union – Country Report Sweden' (2008), p. 11.

84 See interview with Lotty Nordling, at the time director of the ARN (Stockholm, 24 August 2009).

85 See personal email communications with ARN (26 January 2011).

86 See personal email communications, KOV (2 September 2009).

87 See Lindblom (2008a), p. 81.

88 See personal email communications with SRF (13 September 2011).

89 See also Lindblom (2008a), p. 81. See personal email communications with SRF (13 September 2011). Based on sales, SRF currently represents 85 per cent of Sweden's travel agencies and nearly 50 per cent of the tour operators (excluding the big charter tour operators). There are a great number of small or very small tour operators who are not members. The only way to punish those members, if any, who do not comply with their rules and code of conduct, is to expel them from the association.

90 The percentages are preliminary numbers.

91 See personal email communications with ARN (26 January 2011). There is no legal possibility to transfer a case to a district court. Overall the board dismisses many

jurisdiction are that it cannot deal with disputes between individual consumers or between producers or traders.[92] Unlike in the Netherlands, Swedish traders do not have to be registered with the board in order to be the defendants in these proceedings; any Swedish trader may be addressed.[93] The board may accept a case only if the consumer has previously sought voluntary settlement of the claim with the trader, but was rejected, as in the Netherlands. A complaint must be lodged no later than six months after the trader has turned down a consumer complaint.[94]

The (former) director's overall impression is that although board members come from certain industries, they make very fair decisions; the fact that they do not always decide in the consumer's interest indicates that the mechanism really works,[95] a view that the business side supports.[96] Frivolous complaints are not regarded as a problem.[97]

ARN decisions in principle are not subject to appeal.[98] However, under certain narrowly defined circumstances there may be a possibility for the board to review a decision.[99] The board does not have the competence to decide matters already decided by ordinary courts, pending before courts or that are within the jurisdiction of other public bodies; however, ARN cases may be referred to these entities.[100] An ARN decision may not be granted if one has already been issued in the same matter.[101] Resorting to the district court is always possible. An individual may start a new

cases, but when asked about frivolous lawsuits, it was reported that it is impossible to know why consumers in dismissed cases turned to the board in the first place.

92 See Bakardjieva Engelbrekt (2006), p. 2.

93 See interview with Professor Ulf Bernitz, Professor Emeritus of European Integration Law, University of Stockholm (Stockholm, 11 November 2010); see personal email communications with ARN (26 January 2011).

94 See § 5 of the ARN Instruction 2007.

95 See interview with Lotty Nordling, at the time director of the ARN (Stockholm, 24 August 2009).

96 See personal email communications with SRF (13 September 2011). He 'would not agree that it is too easy for the consumers. I have no statistics, but I think that not even half of the cases are won by the consumers'.

97 See interview with Professor Ulf Bernitz, Professor Emeritus of European Integration Law, University of Stockholm (Stockholm, 11 November 2010). See personal email communications with SRF (13 September 2011).

98 See § 29 of the ARN Instruction 2007.

99 For instance, these reasons can include new evidence and circumstances that have not been referred to earlier and that could lead to a substantially different outcome and should the party prove it probable that this could not have been done earlier, or the fact that the decision is manifestly wrong due to a mistake or omission on the part of the Board. The request for review shall be made in writing within two months after a decision on a dispute.

100 See Bakardjieva Engelbrekt (2006), p. 2. See § 6 of the ARN Instruction 2007; see Persson (2008), p. 10. See interview with Lotty Nordling, at the time director of the ARN (Stockholm, 24 August 2009). She even mentions that courts were previously obliged to notify ARN if ARN cases came to court. This system was abolished.

101 See Persson (2008), p. 10.

procedure in the court where she can use ARN's decision as evidence to support her case. This possibility mitigates to some extent the lack of enforceability of ARN decisions, but also leads to additional costs. For example, in court, witnesses may be heard that might prove to be favourable to the case. The use of the ARN is never a prerequisite for allowing consumers or traders a regular court procedure,[102] which differs from the Netherlands where traders waived their right to go to court. ARN also may give an advisory opinion in consumer disputes, at the request of a court of law.

The ARN board is evaluated in a very positive way, particularly because of the low-cost procedures combined with a relatively high rate of compliance. Limits concern the quality of the proceedings, such as the inability to collect evidence and the weak safeguards for due process. A thorough assessment of the law can be provided only through the district court. The ARN board – and this is the reason why case scenario two fails – can be active only if the trader is located in Sweden and if her location is known.

Although the case scenario assumes only one damaged consumer, mass damage cases are certainly possible. Only so much shall be said in this case study because group litigation is assessed in the next case study. In short, the KO may apply to the ARN if a group of consumers have similar claims on the same grounds.

Boards and ombudsmen exist as an alternative means to administer justice.[103] However, it is unlikely that the courts could manage all the disputes that arise. In 2012, ARN dealt with 11,531 incoming cases of which 1,691 were in the travel sector; in 2011, the number was 9,342, with 1,668 in the travel sector.[104] The proportion of cases decided in favour of the consumers was 43 per cent in 2012 and 59 per cent in 2011, which clearly indicates that by no means does the ARN always decided in favour of the consumer.

The whole ARN body is financed exclusively by taxpayers' money, 32.2kr million in 2012.[105] In 2012, the duration of the proceedings was 191 days in general and 176 days for the travel board. The duration of a revision is 32 days. The average net cost per case in 2012 was 3,174kr. The ARN is firmly embedded in the Swedish culture.[106]

The Swedish Travel Guarantees Act Anyone who arranges or sells travel arrangements regulated in the Travel Guarantees Act[107] must lodge security with

---

102 See Sveriges Konsumenter (2011), p.1; see Swedish Ministry of Justice, response to the European Commission's consultation document dated 18 January 2011 on the use of Alternative Dispute Resolution, p. 3.

103 See Lindell (2007), p. 340.

104 See http://www.arn.se/Om-oss/Statistik/, last accessed: 31 March 2013 and the Annual report of ARN 2012.

105 See Annual report ARN 2012, pp. 16, 24.

106 See personal email communications with Konsument Europa/ECC Sweden (29 November 2010).

107 See *Resegarantilagen* (SFS 1972:204) (Swedish Travel Guarantees Act).

the Legal, Financial and Administrative Services Agency (*Kammarkollegiet*) prior to selling or marketing these arrangements.[108] In Sweden there is no fund for insolvencies; instead, each operator must lodge its own security.

The amount to be secured by each trader is determined individually, based on reported business activities.[109] Every operator must declare such activities according to forms that can be found on the website. Most operators declare once a year, but some more often. If this is not the first time that the operator applies, the follow-up form also must be submitted stating the actual results of the last season. Failure to provide correct numbers may lead to monetary fines or imprisonment. (not imposed by *Kammarkollegiet* directly)[110]

A travel company's economic responsibility is calculated monthly. The amount needed in a specific month is determined by adding the income of that month, any advance payments for future travel arrangements not yet fully paid and the repatriation costs for the passengers travelling that particular month. To calculate the amount that has to be paid, the following factors are considered: the number of passengers per month, the cost of the travel arrangements, advance payments and cancellation fees, length of time before departure that payments must be made and repatriation costs. The sum is increased by 10 per cent and rounded off. All traders must have a valid security that covers at least six months out of a year. If this security is not enough for the entire year because there are one or more peak seasons, the security must be complemented with additional securities valid only for these months. If profits are made during only a certain time of year, it may be possible to lodge low security during most of the year and complement this with high ones during peak times. *Kammarkollegiet* asks travel companies to notify them in case of an increase of the reported numbers by more than 10 per cent, as the lodged security might then be too low.

The agency's first step is to determine the amounts that must be secured. Next, the operator has to contact her bank, insurance company or credit market company to arrange the security. This guarantee is then kept at the authority.[111] If compensation is necessary, *Kammarkollegiet* notifies the guarantee issuer to pay the consumers.

108 See § 1 Travel Guarantees Act.

109 See personal email communications with Kammarkollegiet (13 January 2011). See § 2 Travel Guarantees Act.

110 See §§ 4a, 5, 14 Travel Guarantees Act: 'Anyone who intentionally sells or markets travel without having lodged security as laid down in this act shall be sentenced to a fine or imprisonment for not more than one year (…). Criminal charges for offences against this act may only be brought with the consent of the Swedish Legal, Financial and Administrative Services Agency (Förordning – Regulation (SFS 2002:601))'.

111 See personal email communications with Kammarkollegiet (13 January 2011). They hold roughly 2,000 guarantees at present.

If a travel deal is interrupted or cancelled, the consumer may apply to the Travel Guarantee Board, a separate governmental board for those specific cases.[112] The consumer must apply no later than three months after returning from the trip.[113] The amount secured in the guarantee may be used to compensate the costs of advance payment, full payment or value of the benefits that were included in the travel agreement, as well as possible costs of repatriation[114] and other expenses related to incomplete tours.[115] Compensation is exclusively provided for in this limited number of cases. In the case scenario in which the consumer takes the tour, but is dissatisfied, the consumer cannot claim reimbursement from the Travel Guarantees Board.[116] Unlike in the Netherlands, there is a more restrictive interpretation of insolvency situations. The insolvency situations as mentioned in the European Directive are covered.

This system exists in addition to the possibility of suing at the district court.[117] However, the ARN procedure cannot be initiated if a company is insolvent.

Kammarkollegiet cannot forbid operators from marketing, and there are reports of companies that evade their obligation by refusing to acknowledge the authority's decisions. *Kammarkollegiet* can refer cases to the KO or involve the police.[118]

Involvement of the KO/KOV The competences of the KO/KOV include carrying out comprehensive market surveys, setting up guidelines and taking legal action. The KO/KOV reviews and archives complaints, but is under no obligation to investigate all complaints. Since 2012, KOV has had a Department for Consumer Protection (*Avdelning för konsumentskydd*), which consists of the Secretariat of the KO (*KO-sek*), two legal sections/units (*Rättsenheter*) and a section/unit for product safety. The head of the department is also the deputy KO. The KO's legal tasks, litigation and case management are executed by the Secretariat of the KO consisting of the deputy and four legal advisors.[119] The legal units consist of about 25 legal advisers

112 See § 9 Travel Guarantees Act. According to § 10 Travel Guarantees Act: 'This board consists of a chairperson and four other members, two nominees who can be considered to represent the interests of consumers and two who represent commercial interests. Each member shall have an adequate number of deputies. The chairperson and deputy chairperson are to hold or have held the office of judge'. The chairperson, other members of the board and their deputies are to be appointed by the government (*Förordning* – Regulation (SFS 1988:208)).

113 See § 8 Travel Guarantees Act.

114 See § 6 Travel Guarantees Act.

115 See personal email communications with Kammarkollegiet (13 January 2011).

116 See ibid.

117 See interview with Professor Ulf Bernitz, Professor Emeritus of European Integration Law, University of Stockholm (Stockholm, 11 November 2010). See personal email communications with ARN (26 January 2011): The proceedings are not connected. The Consumer Complaints Board does not refer to the fund in its judgments.

118 See personal email communications with Kammarkollegiet (13 January 2011).

119 See personal email communications with KO/KOV (22 November 2011).

working *inter alia* with surveillance of market practices, consumer complaints and projects. The KO has three different roles: it can act as legal counsel for the individual, take legal action in the consumers' interest or act as a prosecutor. It may act at the ARN (only for groups of consumers), the Market Court, the District Court, Courts of Appeal and the Supreme Court. Besides involvement in court litigation, the KO may be a mediator and has quasi-adjudicative competences, given that the traders accept these to issue prohibition or information orders, both combined with a conditional fine.[120] When a trader has breached a prohibition or information order, the KO may act as a prosecutor to bring proceedings for imposition of conditional fines as a criminal case at the District Court.

A trader's failure to lodge the necessary securities as required by the package travel law is considered a contravention of the Marketing Act (MA) and the KO is empowered to take legal action in the consumers' interest. The KO can take these disputes to the Market Court, a special court for fair-trading disputes (among others). *Kammarkollegiet* is appreciative of this involvement. In such a case, the civil servants of *Kammarkollegiet* send their file to KOV/KO and provide any extra information. Otherwise, the case is handled independently by KO/KOV.[121] As an example, in a case against Prima Travel AB, the company was forbidden to market tours without the necessary securities under a conditional financial penalty of 750,000kr.[122] A similar issue was at stake in a 2009 case called 'Casa Nordica Altavista C AB' which was dismissed in the Stockholm District Court because of the company's bankruptcy.[123] This involvement is comparable to that of the Dutch CA. Again, the trader's accountability is guaranteed. In the course of these investigations, the KO may use investigative powers as set out in the MA. Section 42 of the MA specifically sets out that parties must give statements and provide necessary information at the request of the KO, such as documents or samples of goods. The KO/KOV does not have the competence to enter premises or seize documents, but it can visit businesses if it informs them in advance. Traders may be asked to make available for inspection such premises or corresponding locations, with the exception of dwellings, where the business activities are conducted (Section 44 MA).[124] The powers are more limited than criminal powers; they may involve 'sweeps'. The KO may search for traders online (IP addresses) to locate the trader's whereabouts and to use this information in the courts (Sections 42 and 45 MA).[125] In an investigation in 2011, for example,

120 See Section 28 MA.

121 See personal email communications with Kammarkollegiet (13 January 2011).

122 See personal email communications with Kammarkollegiet (10 October 2011), DOM 2008:6, 2008-04-11 Dnr B 2/07.

123 See DOM 2009:17, 2009-06-26 Dnr B 9/08.

124 Other enforcement powers of the KO are set for instance in §§ 8 and 8a in the *Lag (SFS 1994:1512) om avtalsvillkor i konsumentförhållande* (Contract Terms Act). Part of the competences are set out in the ARN Instruction 2007.

125 See personal email communications with KO/KOV (22 November 2011).

it was determined that companies selling goods on the Web must display their email addresses.[126] These investigations are generally initiated if there is reason to suspect something and mainly concern problems with the identity of traders. Despite this involvement, there is room for criminal law enforcement to prevent traders' wrongdoing on the Internet.

As with the analysis of Dutch law enforcement, these case studies may be interrelated. Misleading marketing related to package travel is challengeable via the MA and allows for the involvement of the KO. The possibilities are described in detail in the second case study concerning misleading advertising.

The KO may represent one individual consumer in the ordinary court. In case of an intervention of the KO, the consumer profits not only from the KO's free legal representation, but also from other privileges ensured by Legal Aid Act (§§ 16–20 *rättshjälpslagen*). For example, the state bears the cost of any evidence necessary, for expert opinions, mediation and so on. The state pays for the litigation costs if the case is lost. The involvement of the KO is possible under special conditions.[127] The preconditions for an intervention are that 'the dispute shall either be significant for the application of the law, i.e. to clarify the legal situation within a certain area, or the dispute shall be of common consumer interest, i.e. concern a great number of consumers'.[128] This is also the benchmark for the possible involvement in a package travel case. The scheme is used regularly and demand for it is on the rise. The law was introduced primarily to promote the formation of precedent in the financial field, issues in the law had to be clarified, and consequently expanded.[129] The intervention aims at a clarification in the law, which is why these cases do not end up in settlement. Once the KO intervenes, the case cannot be tried under the rules of the small claims procedure.[130] Furthermore, the KO's decision not to intervene may not be appealed.[131] This broad margin of discretion is judged critically.[132] As in other administrative cases, the denied applicant may turn to the Ombudsman of Justice (*Justitieombudsman*) and complain about the handling of the case.[133] The popularity of the ombudsman procedure is on the rise, with

126 See personal email communications with KO/KOV (25 October 2011).

127 See § 2 of SFS 2011:1211.

128 Translation available online at: http://www.konsumentverket.se/otherlanguages/English/This-is-how-you-apply-for-KO-support-/, last accessed: 31 March 2013.

129 Originally the KO could only represent consumers in disputes concerning financial services, then the scheme was extended to all kind of consumer disputes. See Persson (2008), p. 8. This amendment was done in the form of a trial period in 2006 (SFS 2006:1021) which came into effect on 1 January 2007. The law is permanent as of 1 January 2012 *Lag (SFS 2011:1211) om Konsumentombudsmannens medverkan i vissa tvister* (KO Representation in Certain Disputes Act).

130 See 4 § SFS 2011:1211.

131 See § 7 SFS 2011:1211.

132 See Bakardjieva Engelbrekt (2006), p. 31; the KO himself reports that he has never been approached by any lobby groups and thus takes his decisions independently.

133 See personal email communications with KO/KOV (5 March 2012).

a growing number of applications from consumers seeking the KO's assistance. However, representation happens in only a fraction of those cases. In 2012, three cases were selected out of 106 applications; in 2011 three out of 39 were selected.[134] Interestingly, for a case with a travel package bought online where the trader cannot be located, it would be crucial for the KO to use its monitoring or wider investigative powers. Are its investigative powers any different from those of an ordinary lawyer representing a consumer? If KO steps in for an individual, the use of investigative powers spelled out in the MA is precluded because the case is considered a 'common case' and not a 'market case'. The KO may, however, already have acquired the knowledge through a former surveillance investigation in one of the legal sections/units (*rättsenheterna*), in which case, the information can be used for the common case. While rather indirect, this is or could potentially be crucial for cases involving a *mala fide* trader.

Criminal Law Enforcement in the Travel Sector An individual consumer law issue may give rise to a criminal proceeding. For instance, noncompliance with the obligation to provide financial securities for cases of insolvencies can lead to criminal prosecutions, as discussed above.

Civil and criminal law cases in Sweden take place before a district court. If the crime is not very serious, the prosecutor may decide to issue a 'summary penalty order', which comes down to an assessment of fines without a trial. A precondition for this order is the suspect's confession. In addition to punishment in a criminal proceeding, the accused may be obliged to pay damages, which may be considered in conjunction with the criminal trial.[135] Compensation from crimes may be obtained in four ways: court-ordered restitutions, a lawsuit for damages, compensation through private insurances or government compensation plans. With these four possibilities, there is basically a sequence that the victim can follow. First, a victim must claim damages according to tort law in a civil law lawsuit or connect this civil claim for compensation with the criminal trial. The public prosecutor prepares and presents the claim for damages in conjunction with the prosecution in the criminal trial assessed in court. If a crime was committed, the victim is entitled to compensation for any kind of injury. Generally, Swedes purchase insurance, as part of their home insurance, for losses or injuries resulting from crimes. The government compensation fund steps in if the wrongdoer is unknown or unable to pay damages or if the victim does not have private insurance.[136] This route could be interesting in a consumer case with *mala fide* traders in which a crime was committed. The compensation fund is secondary to damages and insurances. The state has accepted a great responsibility for victims of crimes and public law is said to have influenced civil law in a way

134 See Annual report KO/KOV 2012, p. 22.

135 See R. Mannelqvist, 'Compensation for Victims in Public Legislation and as a Civil Right', *Scandinavian Studies in Law* 50 (2007): 423–34, p. 424.

136 So-called 'Criminal Injuries Compensation'.

that has led to increases in compensation levels. On the other hand, criminal law compensation is very similar to tort law. For a victim, this variety of options may be confusing; conflicts between the schemes can arise.[137] It is also common for the public prosecutor to bring forward a damage claim for a victim in a criminal case and in some cases she is obliged to do so.[138] Importantly, the impartiality of the prosecutor is disputable when it comes to claiming damages on behalf of a victim.[139] In this case, the prosecutor's position is similar to that of the legal representative in civil law cases. In a criminal case prosecuted by the state, the state brings forward the criminal action and the victim's claim for damages in the same litigation.[140] This means that the criminal law standard of 'beyond reasonable doubt' is applied to the tort law claims and actually means that the defendant may be more easily exempted from paying damages, which is why it is advisable for the prosecutor to also allege damages based on negligence.

Criminal law plays a limited role in consumer protection.[141] Criminal proceedings are mainly used in fraud cases, which in a very severe case can be imaginable in a package travel scenario (particularly scenario 2).[142] *Kammarkollegiet* occasionally reports traders. The trade association likewise expresses that if they find out about these companies, they report them to KOV and/or *Kammarkollegiet* or even the police.[143] In addition, consumers may report to the police. Also in Sweden, the corporate veil may be pierced when it comes to individual's liability for crimes (see Chapter 36, Section 7 of the Swedish Penal Code). An 'entrepreneur' shall be ordered to pay a 'corporate fine' for a 'crime committed in the exercise of business activities', if (1) the crime has entailed gross disregard for the special obligations associated with the business activities or is otherwise of a serious kind, and (2) the entrepreneur has not done what could reasonably be required of him for prevention of the crime.

The KO can in certain cases act as a prosecutor in the court (for instance, regarding the imposition of a fine due to a violation of an order/injunction issued by the KO or due to a judgment by the Market Court), in which case the burden of proof rests upon it.

---

137 See Mannelqvist (2007), p. 433.

138 See Chapter 35 RB, evidence in general. See personal email communications with Stockholm District Court judge (7 October 2011). It depends on the case in how far a judge will accept facts that were established in a different legal institution.

139 See L. Heuman, 'Objectivity in Swedish Criminal Proceedings', *Scandinavian Studies in Law* 51 (2007): 213–28, p. 227.

140 See Carlson (2009), p. 147.

141 See, for instance, personal email communications Professor Antonina Bakardjieva-Engelbrekt, Professor of European Law, University of Stockholm (1 March 2012).

142 Their rare, but nevertheless occasional occurrence, was confirmed by personal email communications with SRF (13 September 2011).

143 See personal email communications with SRF (13 September 2011).

Assessment and Conclusion

Comparing the Swedish enforcement system with the optimal design suggestions for the two case studies, the following statements can be made: the *bona fide* trader case scenario can be handled successfully at the ARN, if not in some form of mediation. The system of local consumer advisors that in some cases also carry out mediation might potentially keep cases from going to the ARN or further. The compliance in package travel cases with the ARN-issued recommendations is very high, higher than the average compliance rate, because traders appreciate the procedures of the board and wish to avoid blacklisting. Industry compliance may depend a lot on the competitiveness of a market:[144] the higher the concentration of industry and the more established the players, the greater is the compliance (for instance insurance companies and banks). Both, consumer and trader representatives are involved in the procedure. Expertise is concentrated at the ADR body. Decisions favouring either party may be taken and at least half have been made against consumers. An appeal on limited grounds is possible within the ARN. A court procedure is always possible, even if a recommendation was obtained, which potentially entails duplication of enforcement costs. The procedure in Sweden is exclusively in the written form. Some cases are dismissed as too complex. The Supreme Court must have decided applicable case law in order for the ARN to handle less clear-cut cases. 'Frivolous complaints', which may be connected to a doubtful composition, are not considered a problem. This mechanism is not very costly to administer, with a net cost per case of 3,174kr in 2012. The ARN is entirely financed by the state, which can arguably prevent diluted incentives on either the consumer or the trader side because neither contributes directly to the funding and both may use the ARN at no cost.

An underlying threat is that a civil case at the district court is never precluded by an ARN decision, but this threat might really only be present if the claim value exceeds a certain minimum. A €2,000 scenario falls under the small claims provisions and relieves the consumer of certain procedural aspects. Then again, in both ordinary court procedures (widely) and small claims procedures, legal representation is not necessary, although the cost rules differ. Therefore, in some ordinary court procedures (the small claims procedure), and before the ARN, individual costs are reduced. The American rule on costs applies in small claims cases.[145]

Broad insurance coverage exists as an add-on to general household insurance and some legal aid. From the consumers' point of view, the small claims track has not been very successful. The limits of the effectiveness of the ARN relate to *mala fide* traders.[146] Unlike in the Netherlands, Swedish traders do not have to be registered

144 See personal email communications Professor Antonina Bakardjieva-Engelbrekt, Professor of European Law, University of Stockholm (1 March 2012).

145 This was in fact not considered in the model world.

146 See Bakardjieva Engelbrekt (2006), p. 5.

with the board in order to be the defendant in these proceedings.[147] There is no underlying system to guarantee compliance. Both facts suggest a lower likelihood of compliance with such a system. Indeed the compliance rate in the Netherlands is higher, but direct comparisons are not possible. In 2012, overall compliance rates at the ARN averaged 76 per cent and with package travel the rate was up to 80 per cent. Cases of noncompliance can be traced to issues of insolvency or the fact that companies 'disappeared',[148] which is indeed the main characteristic of a *mala fide* trader. Given the low costs of district court litigation, one could expect travel cases there, but this is not the case in reality. The formal nature of court proceedings might act as a deterrent after all. On a side-note, the Swedish state subsidises civil litigation as much as 99 per cent, in stark contrast to the Netherlands where court fees are charged and even a user-pays system for the court structure was considered.

Insolvency may be an issue – 'a surprise' – in any kind of proceeding. Traders that want to offer package travel deals are obliged by law to provide securities, kept at *Kammarkollegiet*, for cases of insolvency. Claimants may seek compensation from these securities alongside the judicial means.

Bona fide trader case scenarios may be handled in line with the suggested optimal enforcement mix and the ARN may potentially serve as a cross-financing mechanism for a *mala fide* trader. In scenario 2, which deals with a *mala fide* trader, a certain degree of investigative powers would be needed to track the online trader. Cases where traders cannot be tracked down have to be dismissed at the ARN. Likewise in the district court, procedures are impeded if traders cannot be located. In such a case, the consumer would most likely try to involve the KO.[149]

A public law element could be added to the procedure, which can be done in various ways, for instance by involving the KO. KO intervention allows two features suggested in the optimal mix for an individual damages case: investigative powers and granting damages In rare cases, the KO would accept an individual application for court defense if the required criteria were fulfilled by the case involving the *mala fide* trader. This brings huge benefits in terms of litigation costs for the claimant.[150] Judging from the selection procedure that the KO follows, complicated cases could be taken up, which could potentially involve package travel. KO intervention would be particularly beneficial if the KO could use investigative powers for this procedure. Currently, the KO's role is like that of a lawyer intervening in a case and

147 See interview with Professor Ulf Bernitz, Professor Emeritus of European Integration Law, University of Stockholm (Stockholm, 11 November 2010); see personal email communications with ARN (26 January 2011).

148 See interview with Lotty Nordling, at that time director of the ARN (Stockholm, 24 August 2009).

149 See interview with Professor Ulf Bernitz, Professor Emeritus of European Integration Law, University of Stockholm (Stockholm, 11 November 2010). He also regards it as likely that the ARN could in these cases ask the KO.

150 Also changing the legal aid or insurance system would have an effect on the cost ratio, though not on the amount of available investigative powers.

it cannot make use of the investigative powers as set out in the MA. However, if the KO possesses information resulting from an on-going investigation of the KO/KOV, this information can also be used in this individual civil case. Therefore, the route to combine investigative powers and an action for damages is indirect, but possible.

Then, comparable to the action of the CA in the Netherlands, the KO monitors the obligation to provide for securities with *Kammarkollegiet* and files cases against companies that do not comply. *Kammarkollegiet* refers the cases to the KO. Occasionally, *Kammarkollegiet* or the trade associations may report to the police, but rarely do so because consumers generally have already reported them.[151] Also, to protect against the risk that a trader has not provided securities, consumers may inquire in advance if the trader has registered securities with *Kammarkollegiet*.

When investigating a trader (such as related to marketing matters), the KO may use various investigative powers.[152] Therefore, there is potential to remedy information asymmetries regarding a trader's whereabouts. Similar to the approach in the Netherlands, the KO elicits a trader's identity with the requirement to adhere to the security scheme (and this information is generally available). This protection is on an *ex ante* level. Involvement of a public player on behalf of one single consumer is more unusual.

The ARN procedure comes to mind as another possible way for information to enter the enforcement response. However, the KOV officials who are part of the ARN board are not supposed to act as party representatives. Thus, KOV's investigative powers may not enter the procedure in that way. When a KOV employee sits on ARN and there is a 'case' against a trader that the KOV employee has directly/indirectly investigated, the employee may not take part in making the ARN recommendation.[153]

If criminal law is involved, wide investigative powers are guaranteed to tackle cases of *mala fide* traders. Furthermore, various ways are possible for individuals to be compensated. The KO may act as a prosecutor in certain cases, but then must satisfy the standard.

Regarding the alignment with the optimal mix, the Swedish law enforcement scores positively in terms of players involved. ARN (and potentially the local consumer advisors) basically serves as a cross-financing actor for cases that would require the involvement of a public law element. The public law element is given in various ways, including involvement of the KO or even by criminal procedures. In terms of improvements, a suggestion is to facilitate use of the KO's investigative powers for cases in which the KO represents an individual in court. Currently this investigative power cannot be used directly, but only if the information were already available from a previous investigation. An improvement could be to better

151 See personal email communications with SRF (13 September 2011).

152 As an underlying threat to these actions, if orders are violated, the KO can pursue these violations as a criminal case (as a prosecutor). This involves the court element again, but delays the process to some extent.

153 See personal email communications with Gabriella Fenger-Krog, litigator KO/KOV (22 November 2011).

secure the public law element in relation to *mala fide* traders. KO representation of consumers in individual cases at first was available only for financial services matters, but has expanded to any type of consumer disputes. Therefore, another expansion is not a far-fetched idea. In cases involving a rogue trader who may inflict further damage, efficiency is served when the complainant's costs are relieved and compensation may be granted through the district court.

Problems might include the danger of capture. An automatic safeguard is in place in the system where the KO has to defend the cases in court. Only with cases of minor importance may the KO take internal action and, again, only under the precondition that the trader accepts. The availability of the court element can be judged very positively in terms of securing incentives and outcomes in the interest of social welfare.

Regarding the low-cost, cross-financed ARN, systems that secure compliance could be strengthened (such as, underlying business guarantee, involvement of trade associations, registration requirements and deposits). For package travel cases in particular, strengthening the system is less of a concern because compliance rates are high. Traders can potentially be pressured into compliance by the underlying threat of a court procedure, indeed also a rather low-cost procedure or some competition. The extent that the courts are used is unclear, but a figure from 2004 suggests that the small claims procedure cost the public purse 2,874kr per case, an expense that today might not be so different from the cost of cases handled by the ARN; therefore, promoting small claims procedures could be encouraged further. Costs for individuals may be low in both procedures as well. There might not be an immediate need given rather high compliance rates. Also, the restriction of the ARN to straightforward cases is desirable for social-welfare considerations.

Case 2 – Misleading Advertising

The misleading advertisement case includes a *bona fide* trader (scenario 3) and a *mala fide* trader (scenario 4), but this time, the damage to the individual is small, even trifling (€15), but widespread. On the other hand, damage to the competitor, a new actor in this case, may amount to €100,000. Alternatively, solutions are discussed in which the competitor has no interest in the case. Again, particular focus is on the behaviour of the *mala fide* trader in online transactions.

Summary of Legal Rules

In 1919, an attempt was made to introduce an act against unfair competition (*Lag mot illojal konkurrens*),[154] similar to the *Gesetz gegen den unlauteren Wettbewerb* (Unfair Trade Practices Act, UWG), which used a criminal law sanctioning

---

154 See *Lag (SFS 1931:152) med vissa bestämmelser mot illojal konkurrens* (Unfair Competition Act).

system.[155] However, the act never gained importance in practice because the reality was characterised by industry internal self-regulation. Since 1970, the provisions on advertising have been located in the Improper Marketing Act (*Lag om otillbörlig marknadsföring* [*SFS* 1970:412]),[156] later amended to the MA.[157] The central role for enforcement was assigned to the KO.[158] As in the other Nordic countries, marketing law is considered a single branch of law and is not integrated in the law on unfair competition; therefore, a specific system of legal protection is in place (characterised by a special court, the 'Market Court').[159] In addition, options for self-regulation are available. The Group Proceedings Act (LOG) governing group litigation was introduced in 2002 and group litigation is also possible through the ARN. Legal aid is excluded for individual cases in which the claim value does not economically justify the legal expenses, as discussed.

Adjudicative Function of the KO As discussed, the KO may in some limited circumstances take own action and issue orders and injunctions, according to the MA and subject to the acceptance of the trader (immediately or within a certain period).[160] This also applies in relation to misleading advertising. The KO also may use its investigative powers (see Sections 42 and 45 MA) in relation to prohibition and information orders.[161] Therefore, for instance, digital investigations in cases of *mala fide* traders would be possible.

According to Section 28 of the MA, the KO may issue those orders in cases of 'minor importance', when there is an established practice or the law is clear.[162] Legal action is taken primarily if a trader does not want to accept an order, when

155 See Treis (1991), p. 6.

156 See *Lag (SFS 1970:412) om otillbörlig marknadsföring* (Improper Marketing Act).

157 Access the latest translation into English from 2010 (SFS 2008:486) at http://www.sweden.gov.se/content/1/c6/05/03/14/6c7aa374.pdf. Misleading marketing is dealt with as of Section 8.

158 This act was amended by the 1975 Marknadsföringslagen (Marketing Practices Act).

159 See J. Stuyck, 'Public and Private Enforcement in Consumer Protection: General Comparison EU-USA', *New Frontiers of Consumer Protection – The Interplay between Private and Public Enforcement*, eds F. Cafaggi and H-W. Micklitz (Antwerp; Oxford; Portland: Intersentia, 2009) 63–90, p. 77.

160 See Section 28 MA. Related: a prohibition order can also be issued by the KO according to the Consumer Contracts Act, Section 7, 8 and 8 b give the KO the same investigative powers as Section 42 and 45 MA. Legal action is likewise possible in relation to the Consumer Contracts Act.

161 See personal email communications with Gabriella Fenger-Krog, litigator KO/KOV (22 November 2011).

162 See also Table 3, Faure, Ogus and Philipsen (2008), p. 368 and see interview with Market Court (Stockholm, 24 August 2009).

a precedent case is required or if there is a question of evidence in a MA case (a trader has to prove her claims).[163]

These orders are subject to a conditional financial penalty. Once the order has been accepted, it applies as a final judgment without appeal option. If the orders are violated, the KO may start proceedings in the competent district court or (always possible) the Stockholm District Court specifically for the imposition of the fine as a prosecutor (criminal case).

In 2012, KO issued 16 orders that were accepted by the trader (10 in 2011).[164] The average fine was between 400,000kr and 500,000kr.[165]

Judicial Enforcement of Misleading Advertising Judicial proceedings in the area of misleading advertising are primarily litigated at the Market Court and the district courts. KO is the primary enforcer of the MA. Individuals and organisations are important players in remaining alert to marketing actions,[166] but the agency need not wait for a complaint order to act against a trader.[167] It can act on an own motion. KO investigative powers are crucial in cases of *mala fide* traders. Indeed, if a trader is investigated in relation to the MA (due to a complaint by consumers or market surveillance), investigative powers established in Section 42 and 45 of the MA may be implemented,[168] including tracking down traders through IP addresses.

When the KO defends an individual in court, investigative powers are not directly at its disposal. The same is true for procedures before the ARN or when filing an action in line with LOG. As explained in the previous case study, they might still be available in a more indirect way.

At the market court

The Market Court (*Marknadsdomstolen*) is the main forum for violations of the Swedish MA. The Market Court is a special court constituted by a chairman and a

163 If one of the legal sections has investigated a trader due to a consumer complaint or as a result of surveillance action, the case will be reported before the KO with a proposal for action. Subsequently, one of the legal advisers of the KO's secretariat issues an order or takes legal action.

164 See Annual report KO/KOV 2012, p. 18.

165 See personal email communications with Gabriella Fenger-Krog, litigator KO/KOV (23 November 2011). These numbers cover the overall numbers, not just the cases issued according to the MA.

166 See interview with Gunnar Larsson, Swedish Consumer Ombudsman and Head of Consumer Authority (Stockholm, 25 August 2009).

167 See personal email communications with Konsument Europa/ECC Sweden (29 November 2010).

168 See personal email communications with KO/KOV (17 November 2011); see personal email communications with KO/KOV (25 October 2011).

vice-chairman who are legally qualified and have judicial experience.[169] The court includes five special members: one is legally qualified and has experience as a judge and four are economic experts. The court hears cases brought by the KO; a trader affected by the marketing in question; or an association of consumers, traders or employees.[170] The KO's primary role was abolished in 1995.[171] Following this, the KO's involvement in cases at the Market Court has decreased from, for instance, 17 in 1991 to an average of four or five.[172] The court acts upon request of a competitor in 60 to 70 per cent of the cases and in the rest upon the KO's request.[173] Individual consumers do not have standing at this special court. Even though consumer associations are empowered to act, they have not yet taken any action.[174] The fact that consumer associations currently are not involved in law enforcement is not very surprising because historically they have played only a very limited role.[175]

According to the MA, remedies may consist of injunctions, damages and a so-called 'market disruption charge' (*marknadsstöringsavgift*), basically an especially calculated fine.[176] Since 1993, the MA has provided for a two-instance judicial procedure that is closer to ordinary court procedures in composition and procedure.[177] The Market Court is the first and final instance concerning prohibition of certain marketing, orders to provide information and orders to provide technical aids.[178] All three are subject to a financial penalty (Section 26), unless it is regarded as unnecessary.[179] The Stockholm District Court is the first instance concerning the 'market disruption charge'. This remedy is decided upon in an especially composed division including economic experts. Also when damages are granted

169 See Lindell (2004), p. 41. In simple matters the chairman is competent to decide the case. Otherwise it can be judged by the chairman and three members. See §§ 3 Market Court Act 197: 417. See personal email communications with Market Court judge (11 October 2011).

170 See Section 47 MA.

171 See Bakardjieva Engelbrekt (2003), p. 586. See today's Section 47 MA.

172 In terms of coordination: following § 61 the KO should be informed of any court proceedings under the MA and the Market Court should be informed if a proceeding for a market disruption charge is instituted.

173 See interview with Market Court (Stockholm, 24 August 2009).

174 Ibid.

175 See K. Viitanen, 'Enforcement of Consumers' Collective Interests by Regulatory Agencies in the Nordic countries', *Collective Enforcement of Consumer Law Securing Compliance in Europe through Private Group Action and Public Authority Intervention*, eds W.H. Van Boom and M.B.M. Loos (Groningen: Europa Law Publishing, 2007) 83–103, p. 83. See interview with Gunnar Larsson, Swedish Consumer Ombudsman and Head of Consumer Authority (Stockholm, 25 August 2009).

176 The imposition of both the market disruption charge and the claim for damages are not possible for violations regarding the general clause on fair marketing.

177 See Bakardjieva Engelbrekt (2003), p. 591.

178 See Section 23 MA.

179 Normally it constitutes 750,000kr. It can go below or above, but this is unusual.

or conditional financial penalties imposed on traders, these claims are brought at the competent district court or the Stockholm District Court.[180]

For example, the market disruption charge is applicable if the trader intentionally or negligently contravenes the requirements on fair advertising.[181] When the market disruption charge was introduced in 1996, the criminal sanctions previously available were abolished.[182] Apparently, criminal sanctions were never used.[183] Such an action must be initiated by the KO or in cases of the KO's inaction by 'an individual trader affected by the marketing in question or an association of traders'.[184] Subsidiarity applies.[185] The KO's action is primary. Consumer associations do not have the ability to initiate an action for a market disruption charge.[186] The KO has used the market disruption charge only few times, for example once in a case against a repeat offender that concerned advertising for a weight-loss pill heavily exaggerating its effects.[187] Here the Stockholm District Court imposed a fine of 500,000kr. Another case concerned a promotional offer for travels that did not fulfil certain information requirements.[188]

Although cases do not come up often, traders may view the market disruption charge as a threat and most companies would obey the law to avoid such a fee.[189] The market disruption charge, which is paid to the government, amounts to no less than 5,000kr and no more than 5kr million and may not exceed 10 per cent of the trader's annual turnover.[190] Influential determinants for the ultimate amount of the charge are the seriousness and duration of the violation.[191] Therefore, the sanction may be increased, providing a deterrent effect for *mala fide* traders for whom the probability of detection and conviction may be low.

180 See Sections 49 and 50 MA.

181 See Section 29 MA.

182 See Viitanen (2007), p. 90.

183 See personal email communications with Market Court judge (16 November 2010).

184 See Section 48 MA. Guidance as to when and who is to initiate this remedy can, for instance, be found in the Bill to the present Marketing Act, where an expansion of the field of application of the fee was decided (see p. 115 of the Proposition 2007/08:115).

185 See personal email communications with Market Court judge (11 October 2011).

186 Confirmed by personal email communications with Market Court judge (16 November 2010).

187 See Stockholms Tingsrätt, avd. 8:1, dom 14.4.1997, KBA Internationell Medicinkonsult.

188 See Bakardjieva Engelbrekt (2003), p. 579; MD 1998:7: KO v Fritidsresor. The Market Court imposed a fine of 200,000kr.

189 Following personal email communications with Stockholm District Court judge (13 March 2011) who expresses her personal opinion: 'I think that the market disruption charge has a deterrent effect on traders and makes traders want to be in compliance with the Unfair Marketing Act'.

190 See Section 31 MA.

191 See Section 32 MA.

Claims for damages are assessed at the Stockholm District Court.[192] Only traders and consumers, not the KO, may take action against misleading advertising, including damage claims.[193] The district court's judgment can be appealed before the Market Court, according to Section 52 and claims for damages may 'appear' in the Market Court in this way.[194] However, this provision is rarely used.[195]

Individual consumers hardly ever bring cases for damages suffered from misleading advertising in the district courts.[196] If such a case came up, the individual claimant in the damage case could rely on the judgment of the Market Court regarding the very same advertisement; however, the judgment is not formally binding on another court.[197]

Indisputably, consumers are hardly motivated to make such claims for damages because of rational apathy.[198] Individual consumers cannot seek injunctions in the Market Court themselves while traders can and damage cases due to misleading advertisement involving traders are a reality.[199] Typically in a MA damage case, the plaintiff claims that the respondent has violated an injunction or a ruling of the Market Court and thereby caused damages. Likewise, damages may be claimed for respondent's actions during the time period before the Market Court's injunctions. Approximately five to ten such cases a year are initiated at the Stockholm District Court.

The LOG (described in the next section) has extended the procedures to recover damages in mass cases.

---

192 Such is the case according to Sections 47 and 50 in case of a single damage claim or a claim connected to an order or prohibition (23, 24, 25).

193 See Proposition 1994/95:123, p. 107. See personal email communications with Gabriella Fenger-Krog, litigator KO/KOV (1 November 2011).

194 See personal email communications with Market Court judge (11 October 2011).

195 Bernitz in response to my intervention at the Conference 'Empowering the European Consumer in Old and New Market: The Place for EU law' (Stockholm, 11 November 2010).

196 See personal email communications with KO/KOV (25 October 2011); see personal email communications with Stockholm District Court judge (13 March 2011). These cases would be initiated independently of the MA according to which individual consumers do not have standing.

197 See personal email communications with Professor Per Henrik Lindblom, Professor Emeritus of Civil and Criminal Procedure, University of Uppsala (7 November 2010).

198 See Bakardjieva Engelbrekt (2003), p. 581.

199 See personal email communications with Stockholm District Court judge (18 February 2011 and 7 October 2011) By way of example: See case T 822-08: The judgment was given on 18 February 2011 by the Stockholm District Court and was appealed to the Market Court – but settled by the traders during the process in the Market Court. Originally the case involved over five million Swedish Crowns.

Interim decisions seem to make the system work.[200] As set out in Section 27, the court may order that a prohibition under Section 23 or an order under Section 24 or 25 shall apply until further notice if (1) the applicant demonstrates probable cause for her claim, and (2) it can be reasonably assumed that the defendant, by taking or by omitting to take a specific action, can reduce the effectiveness of a prohibition or order.[201] The decision may be implemented with immediate effect. An interim decision prohibiting a certain measure is issued in approximately 5–10 per cent of the cases.[202]

The procedure at the Market Court is adversarial and not inquisitorial.[203] Therefore, parties must provide the evidence although the Market Court also may gather evidence on its own to a certain extent. The Market Court deals with *indispositiva* civil cases, which means there are some inquisitorial elements available. In practice, the Market Court does not use its investigative powers, and, therefore, there is no difference from a 'normal' civil case.[204]

No court fees are charged. Litigation costs arise when a lawyers gets involved. Some years ago the 'no-cost' rule was applicable with the Market Court and all parties bore their own litigation costs, but this has changed.[205] Nowadays the 'loser-pays' principle applies.[206] The judge may still rule that both parties pay for their own costs in proceedings for an injunction (prohibition or information orders; see Section 64 MA).[207] The old system was regarded as one reason for the unwillingness of consumer associations to take up a complaint, but the new system does not seem to have changed anything. This situation was partly justified with the fact that the KO often would take up a complaint to clarify the law, not necessarily expecting to be successful. In this instance, a loser-pays rule would be very discouraging.

An effort is made to decide on a case within a year.[208] The average duration of cases concerning the MA in 2012 was 12 months.[209] Companies can withdraw from the proceedings and still come to an agreement. In 2012, two cases concerning the

---

200 See interview with Market Court (Stockholm, 24 August 2009); personal email communications with Professor Ulf Bernitz, Professor Emeritus of European Integration Law, University of Stockholm (31 October 2011): in misleading advertising cases interim injunctions are possible and used in certain cases, but with a certain caution.

201 The provisions of Chapter 15, Section 5, §§ 2–4 and Sections 6 and 8 RB apply to orders under the first paragraph.

202 See personal email communications with Market Court judge (16 November 2010).

203 See ibid.

204 See personal email communications with Market Court judge (11 October 2011).

205 See Viitanen (2007), p. 91; Treis (1991), pp. 80; Bakardjieva Engelbrekt (2003), p. 576.

206 See personal email communications with Market Court judge (16 November 2010).

207 See personal email communications with SRF (13 September 2011).

208 See interview with Market Court (Stockholm, 24 August 2009).

209 See Annual report Market Court 2012, p. 9.

MA were brought forth by the KO (three in total) and 23 by traders.[210] In one case the KO sought for a market disruption charge. The involvement of the KO is decreasing. Throughout 2010, for instance, the KO brought 11 legal actions, in three of which it was seeking a market disruption charge at the Stockholm District Court.[211]

Group litigation at the district court

LOG representative actions in the general courts were introduced in 2002.[212] Private, public and organisation group actions are now permitted under the act for any area of law. Actions may involve petitions for injunctive relief (such as prohibitions and changes), declaratory judgments and also for damages. Hence, Sweden has a special form of private group (class) action.[213] These actions may be initiated by a member of the group, who may be a natural or legal person. The plaintiff must have standing to be a party to the proceedings with respect to at least one of the causes. Consequently, according to the LOG, a case for any remedy could be brought as a private group action, which is not possible before the Market Court; also the KO's competences and representative actions were expanded in relation to aggregate litigation. This procedural tool can be used to claim damages in line with the MA.

As stated, a member of an affected group – either a natural or legal person – may initiate an action.[214] The plaintiff is a member of the group. Organisation actions were introduced in consumer law and environmental law.[215] In consumer law, actions may be initiated by nonprofit organisations of consumers or wage earners against traders concerning goods, services or other utilities offered in the course of business to consumers, primarily for personal use. All nonprofit organisations with adequate stated objectives have the right to initiate group actions. There are no restrictions concerning authorisation by the government and *ad hoc* associations are permitted if their financial affairs are in good order and the court regards them as an adequate representative of the group.[216] An authority suitable to represent the members of the group, considering the subject matter of the dispute, may initiate public group action. The government has granted this power to the KO (and to the Swedish Environmental Protection Agency for environmental law

210 See Annual report Market Court 2012, p. 11.

211 See Annual report KO/KOV 2011, p. 19.

212 See Lindblom (2007a), p. 8.

213 This was not specifically considered in the model.

214 See Lindblom (2007a), p. 11.

215 See § 5 LOG.

216 See personal email communications with Professor Per Henrik Lindblom, Professor Emeritus of Civil and Criminal Procedure, University of Uppsala (17 October 2011). Regarding LOG's actions, the plantiff must (with a very restrictive exception) be represented by a member of the Bar, see § 11 LOG.

matters).[217] As for individual civil cases, the KO cannot directly use its special investigative powers.

Any action has to be based on one or several matters of law that are common or similar with respect to the claims of the group members.[218] Damages are then assessed and calculated as in an individual case.[219] Legal representation is required, but the court may relax this requirement.[220] The group representative has the power to settle on behalf of the group. Group members are not bound by the settlement unless approved by the court. In all cases the loser-pays rule applies. It is unusual for group members to intervene or appear personally at group proceedings.[221] So-called risk agreements are possible that reduce plaintiffs' risks under the loser-pays rule. Group representatives and lawyers can reach a fee agreement that takes the extent to which group members' claims feel satisfied as a basis. Fees are thus conditional on liability and are based on a customary hourly rate and a set formula. This agreement is not binding on the defendant. In fact, if the defendant is ordered to compensate the plaintiff for litigation costs, but fails to do so, the members of the group affected are liable to pay those costs. There is a limit in terms of liability for each member of the group regarding the amount that each has gained through the proceedings. The risk agreements are binding upon group members if approved by the court. There are no other state or private funds that may potentially reimburse plaintiffs.

The court must send out notices to every group member who has joined an action and bear the costs for this.[222] Nonprofit organisations have appeared as plaintiffs and provided support to plaintiffs.[223] Organisations and other legal persons are ineligible for public legal aid or private legal insurance.[224] Other financing possibilities under consideration are private fundraising among group members, public appeals or coverage under multiple legal insurance policies if the action is specifically designed.

The Swedish LOG is an opt-in scheme, as a result of lobbying pressure from big companies during the legislative process. One weakness of the LOG includes the fact that pretrial discovery (*strictu sensu*) does not exist in Swedish courts

217 See § 6 LOG.

218 See § 8 LOG.

219 See personal email communications with Professor Per Henrik Lindblom, Professor Emeritus of Civil and Criminal Procedure, University of Uppsala (7 November 2010).

220 See Bakardjieva Engelbrekt (2006), p. 34.

221 See Lindblom (2007a), p. 16.

222 See P.H. Lindblom, *Global Class Action – National report: Group Litigation in Sweden*, update paper sections 2.5 and 3 (2008), p. 11.

223 See cases Grupptalan mot Skandia v Försäkringsaktiebolaget Skandia (T 97, 2004, Stockholm District Court), Pär Wihlborg v The Swedish State through the Chancellor of Justice (T 1286, 2007, Nacka District Court) and Carl de Geer et al. v The Swedish Airports and Air Navigation Service (M 1931, 2007, Nacka District Court, Environmental Court).

224 See Lindblom (2009), p. 9.

and as a result it is often difficult for the plaintiff to define the members of the group.[225] Another weakness is the lack of a post-trial calculation mechanism and standardised computation of damages. Fears expressed by businesses regarding legal blackmailing and an adverse impact on the business climate in Sweden do not seem to be justifiable.[226] A judgment that is binding on every member of the group reduces the risk of repeat litigation.[227] Overall, the biggest problem of group litigation is financing, despite experimenting with creative solutions.[228]

Statistics show that the LOG has been used less frequently than expected. No organisation action has been initiated and only one public group action has been brought, which was by the KO in *Kraftkommission*.[229] There have been media reports on a dozen cases that have not gone to trial, sometimes because the parties have settled.[230] The most active representative have been private parties. Case examples include group proceedings against a travel agency for selling tickets which did not exist;[231] against a company for advertising and insurance questions; against a company that arranges and sells tickets for concerts. Various cases have involved very large aggregate claims, even billions.[232]

The example of a 2008 effectiveness study can be used to assess how large the damage must be to initiate a misleading advertising case.[233] According to the case 'Group proceedings v Skandia' an individual could pay €15 to join the action against the insurance company.[234] The LOG thus seems to enhance access to justice for scattered damage cases up to some threshold. The damage in the case at hand might potentially still be too small to justify this procedure. Damage cases that involve a considerable amount of damage per consumer certainly have a fair chance of being formed.

225 See Lindblom (2008b), p. 11.

226 These are the main results of a 2007 report evaluating the Act (JU 2007/5800/P). In individual cases KO's actions brought before the ARN have led to the company that lost the case to file for bankruptcy.

227 See Lindblom (2008b), p. 18.

228 Note that Lindblom disagrees with the report (JU 2007/5800/P), see Lindblom (2009), p. 34.

229 See Konsumentombudsmannen v Kraftkommission (T 5416, 2004, Umeå District Court).

230 See Lindblom (2009), p. 9; Persson (2008), p. 15.

231 See Persson (2008), p. 15.

232 See Lindblom (2008b), p. 8.

233 See Persson (2008), p. 22, the basis for her report are interviews with the Ministry of Justice, the Swedish Consumer Agency, the Confederation of Swedish Enterprises, one Lawyer involved in collective redress and one Judge of Appeal involved in collective redress. Date of interviews: December 2007 and January 2008.

234 Another example of a case involving low damage would be 'Konsumentombudsmannen vs S' as mentioned in Persson (2008).

The biggest problem with group litigation remains funding.[235] Practitioners indicated that a group proceeding involving either a lot of individuals or a lot of money would cost 500,000kr to 1,000,000kr. If the case is complicated, the costs may be much higher. Also appeals would increase costs further.[236] According to the KO, the one group action it initiated required approximately 300 work hours before it even started.[237]

As an intersection between individual and group litigation, a case may be initiated as an individual case and become group litigation. For instance, during litigation, it may become apparent that a group action would be a more appropriate procedural alternative. At that time, the plaintiff may make a special application to the court requesting that an individual suit be enlarged to a group action.[238]

Since 1948 (Chapter 14 RB), it has been possible to handle several similar cases together (so called joinder of parties or consolidation of cases), in addition to the mentioned options for grouping.[239]

The Swedish ADR Body Since 1997, the KO has been able to represent consumers in group litigation before the ARN.[240] As a secondary option, a consumer or wage earners organisation may initiate group proceedings – in case of inaction of the KO.[241] Thus, all but private group actions are possible before the ARN. If the KO does not want to represent consumers in a group action before the ARN, the KO makes a (formal) decision allowing the consumer organisation to take action instead.[242]

As consumer associations do not have a prominent role, the KO currently has been the only initiator of actions before the ARN.[243] In cases where the ARN has received several private individual complaints against the same business operator, the board may ask the KO if it wants to bring a group action in the matter. A precondition in collective claims is that consumers are presumed to have a claim against the trader based on broadly similar grounds.[244] Furthermore, the examination of the disputes must be in the public interest.

235 See Viitanen (2007), p. 97 and Lindblom (2007b), p. 17.

236 See Persson (2008), p. 22.

237 See interview with Gunnar Larsson, Swedish Consumer Ombudsman and Head of Consumer Authority (Stockholm, 25 August 2009).

238 See Lindblom (2009), p. 13.

239 See Lindell (2004), p. 96, see Chapter 14:1–2 RB: Plaintiffs can join additional claims against the same defendant if supported on essentially the same grounds and likewise are scenarios with various defendants or various plaintiffs imaginable, again on the precondition of 'essentially the same grounds'.

240 See *Förordning – Regulation (SFS 1997:9) om försöksverksamhet med grupptalan vid Allmänna reklamationsnämnden* (ARN Group Litigation Regulation).

241 See Lindblom (2009), p. 26.

242 See personal email communications with KO/KOV (22 November 2011).

243 See Lindblom (2009), p. 26.

244 See Swedish Ministry of Justice (2011), p. 4.

The board may then issue a decision requiring the trader to compensate all consumers who are in a similar situation and who have not personally complained to the board.[245] It is unclear how compliance in these cases has been controlled when consumers were unknown to the trader. The willingness to settle seems to rise dramatically once the KO gets involved.[246] The KO's investigative powers are crucial for effective action against *mala fide* traders who try to hide. But the KO cannot make use of the respective sections in the MA during an ARN procedure, as when representing a single individual in the district court.[247] Again, this restriction is valid unless an investigation was carried out before the KO already obtained this information.

The procedure before the ARN is opt-out, while the LOG calls for an opt-in procedure.[248] Therefore the KO is confronted with a choice when considering initiating a public group action under the LOG in a general court, but would chose the ARN option, most likely, to avoid the notice and opt-in requirements imposed by the act. The KO also believes it would be easier to gain acceptance of standardised calculations of damages at the ARN than in a general court. The case *Kraftkommission* actually started in the ARN, but because the trader refused to comply with the ARN's decision, the KO brought a public group action in the Umeå District Court. This is hence a clear weakness of the ARN procedure. Proceedings started late in 2009. In January 2010, the Municipal Court of Umeå ruled that 2,300 customers of the company *Stävrullen* (previously *Kraftkommission*) were entitled to damages. The ruling was appealed before the Court of Appeal (*Hovrätten för övre Norrland*) and is currently pending before the Supreme Court.[249] As with individual cases, the ruling of a court is independent of the ruling by the board.[250] The ARN judgment may have some persuading effect, but is not binding.[251] Both institutions in their separate proceedings evaluate the same evidence.

These options exist besides the actions that can be initiated before the Market Court in cases of misleading advertising. Since the LOG was passed, the KO has reduced its involvement to cases at the ARN.[252] In 2010, for instance, the KO initiated two cases at the ARN, one dealing with general contract terms of an energy company and one concerning compensation in air transport.[253] The KO is the only player to use these provisions.

---

245 See Viitanen (2007), p. 98.

246 See Persson (2008), p. 11.

247 See personal email communications with KO/KOV (23 November 2011).

248 See Persson (2008), p. 9.

249 See Lindblom (2008b), p. 11. See personal email communications with Konsument Europa/ECC Sweden (March 2013).

250 See personal email communications with ARN (26 January 2011).

251 See personal email communications with Professor Per Henrik Lindblom, Professor Emeritus of Civil and Criminal Procedure, University of Uppsala (7 November 2010).

252 See interview with Lotty Nordling, at the time director of the ARN (Stockholm, 24 August 2009).

253 See Annual report KO/KOV 2011, p. 25.

An individual who wants to bring an individual action for €15 in damages to the ARN is prevented from doing that by the minimum value requirements, which go down to 500kr.[254] Generally, an ARN procedure would only be effective concerning *bona fide* traders.

The Role of Self-regulation The International Chamber of Commerce (ICC) Codes on Advertising Practice enjoy wide popularity in Sweden.[255] In January 2009, the two existing complaint boards (the Trades Ethical Council Against Sexism in Advertising and the Council on Market Ethics) were merged into a new body: the *Reklamombudsmannen* or Advertising Ombudsman (RO). The founders and, therefore, board members, are the Association of Swedish Advertisers, the Confederation of Swedish Enterprise, the Swedish Advertising Association, ICC, the Swedish Direct Marketing Association and the Swedish Newspaper Publisher Association. The RO, an independent organisation set up as a foundation reviews complaints from the public to determine if an advertisement is compliant with the Consolidated ICC code of Advertising and Marketing Communication Practice. If there is a precedent for the case, the ombudsman (currently Elisabeth Trotzig) may decide the case herself. The RO jury reviews advertisements that are complicated or have never been reviewed. This jury consists of six members and the chairman. RO decisions, called 'opinions', are nonbinding, but authoritative. Decisions made by the ombudsman may be appealed to the jury within four weeks; jury decisions cannot be appealed. In 2011, two cases were appealed to the jury.

Controversial advertisements, such as a website that invites people to cheat on their partners, may lead to a high number of complaints (over about 200) and also raise awareness concerning the RO. Consumers make most of the complaints – about 95 per cent – rather than traders. The body also may act on its own motion; however, the number of complaints received is so high that there are almost no resources left to do that.[256] A complaint must be in writing; a template is available on the website. The complaint also must include explanations for why a particular advertisement goes against ethical marketing. In cases of misleading print advertisements, a copy must be attached. The RO reaches decisions within an average of one to three months.[257] The service is free to consumers; however, in some cases, if a special investigation is carried out the complainant may be charged with these costs (if she consents). While a consumer might not have these resources, this provision is meant for companies, public organisations or other entities.

The jury is open for all stakeholders in the media sector, such as advertisers, media and agencies. Representation from the business and consumer side is not required, but it is preferable to have a representative of the consumer side when the

254 See http://www.arn.se/English/English/, last accessed: 31 March 2013.

255 See Bakardjieva Engelbrekt (2006), p. 5.

256 See personal telephone communications with RO (24 March 2011).

257 See http://www.reklamombudsmannen.org/anmal_reklam.aspx, last accessed: 31 March 2013.

jury decides a case.[258] The overall impression is that few traders do not comply, but no records are kept.[259] Apparently, if a trader does not comply, the claimant is able to contact the RO again who may then contact the noncompliant trader.

The financial means of an entity such as the RO can be problematic.[260] Currently, the RO system is funded through voluntary contributions from the market players.[261] After two years, the number of financiers has steadily increased to approximately 300.[262] This was achieved by employing a dedicated salesperson working with phone calls and personal meetings to engage all market players to join in, stand behind and contribute financially to the self-regulatory body RO.

The RO applies different laws than the Market Court, and, therefore, its decisions can vary. Swedish traders reportedly care a lot about reputation and publishing the RO's opinions on its website can be an effective means to gain further compliance. An underlying threat to increase compliance is the prospect of involving the KO in the next step. This step is possible only in questions of taste and decency and when a violation of the law is at stake. The KO refers a lot of cases to the RO.

Traders may complain to the RO as well. In a next step, they may bring a case against a competitor before the Market Court (where individual consumers do not have standing). The judicial procedure might work as a threat to compliance with RO opinions.

Regarding possibilities of an *ex ante* preclearance, there is a nonformalised means for traders to ask for advice.[263] The RO can enlighten them about the type of complaints that may be registered, based on past experience. Following RO's advice is no guarantee that no complaint will be lodged against the advertisement. Therefore, this can be a helpful device for the *bona fide* trader as she can ascertain herself about the law and avoid fines and possible damage payments. She will not get a guarantee. In Sweden traders will usually enlist legal advice, perhaps from a specialised law firm.[264] In none of the sectors is there an obligatory *ex*

---

258 Only one of the jury members listed on the website is an official consumer representative, http://www.reklamombudsmannen.org/eng/about/the-jury-ron, last accessed: 31 March 2013.

259 See personal telephone communications with RO (24 March 2011).

260 See interview with Lotty Nordling, at the time director of the ARN (Stockholm, 24 August 2009).

261 See interview with Elisabeth Trotzig, Advertising Ombudsman (Stockholm, 28 August 2009).

262 See personal telephone communications with RO (24 March 2011).

263 See interview with Professor Ulf Bernitz, Professor Emeritus of European Integration Law, University of Stockholm (Stockholm, 11 November 2010); see personal telephone communications with RO (24 March 2011).

264 See interview with Professor Ulf Bernitz, Professor Emeritus of European Integration Law, University of Stockholm (Stockholm, 11 November 2010).

ante mechanism in place. The KO's giving *ex ante* advice would be considered to conflict with the freedom of speech/press.[265]

In 2011 just over 1,000 complaints were received, with 275 ending in procedures; in 2010, there were 500 complaints and 283 procedures.[266] Thirty-four per cent of the cases were upheld in 2011. In 103 cases the jury was involved. Sixty-five per cent of the cases were decided within three months and three cases were passed on to the KO in 2010; nine in 2009.

This mechanism is not effective against *mala fide* traders, and the existence of traders who will not comply with the code is confirmed.[267] But most advertisers are believed to comply and follow the outcome of decisions from the RO and RO Jury, although no statistics of compliance exist.

Criminal Law Enforcement in Advertising Individual criminal proceedings can be taken against someone who intentionally or negligently infringes the rules concerning advertising – the corporate veil can be pierced. When there is more than one victim, the claims for damages are presented by the public prosecutor.[268] There are provisions for the court to order the action to be managed in the manner prescribed for civil actions. The first private group action under the new Swedish LOG (*Bo Åberg* v *Kefalas Elfeterios*) actually originated from a criminal case.[269]

There have been times when a case before the Market Court against a trader was also pending before the district court (as a criminal case), initiated, however, by traders and not by the KO.[270] This could be the case when rogue traders are convicted of fraud, for example. There seems to be no detailed regulation on how to combine these proceedings.

When a trader has breached a prohibition or information order issued by the KO or as a result of a judgment by the Market Court, the KO can bring proceedings for imposition of conditional fines, acting as a prosecutor (criminal cases) at the district court (or specifically at the Stockholm District Court). Criminal cases concerning the imposition of fines are processed as other criminal cases by the civil courts, but with the KO acting as the prosecutor, according to Section 49 MA.[271] There is no police involvement. KO's burden of proof consists of proving the violation of the order or injunction by presenting copies of the ads or TV commercials.

265 See personal email communications Gunnar Larsson, Swedish Consumer Ombudsman and Head of Consumer Authority (21 October 2011).

266 See Annual report RO 2011.

267 See personal email communications with Elisabeth Trotzig, Advertising Ombudsman (19 October 2011).

268 See Chapter 22 RB.

269 See Lindblom (2007a), p. 6, Bo Åberg v Kefalas Elfeterios (Case No. T 3515-03, Stockholm District Court).

270 See interview with Market Court (Stockholm, 24 August 2009).

271 See personal email communications with KO/KOV (5 March 2012).

Assessment and Conclusion

The second part of this analysis focuses on trifling and widespread harm that again requires a 'public law element' for cases of high information asymmetry, according to the design suggestions.

For individual small damage claims at the ARN, the minimum value requirement of 500kr (higher with some of the boards) applies and a case cannot be brought. Besides, the KO can theoretically step in and take up the case for an individual consumer in court if the legal requirements are fulfilled. In this case, the findings mentioned above apply. Rational apathy is likely to prevail among consumers considering pursuit of individual cases of €15 in court despite the very low monetary investments in Swedish litigation.

For the *bona fide* traders, a self-regulation mechanism is in place that gives some informal *ex ante* advice. This advice is without prejudice to a procedure later on, as in the Netherlands. Some consumer involvement in the procedures is encouraged, but not obligatory. Cases in which traders (*mala fide* traders) do not comply with the RO's opinion can be reported to the KO, which is important as an underlying and actual threat. The KO gives no *ex ante* advice and to do so would be considered in conflict with the freedom of speech/press. Therefore, the Swedish enforcement landscape aligns with the optimal design suggested regarding the voluntary nature of *ex ante* actions. The advantage that people in the industry are known by a self-regulatory entity can be exhausted. The RO allows potentially for some cross-financing of more costly enforcement responses in cases of *mala fide* traders.

It is noteworthy that there is almost no role in the enforcement landscape available for consumer associations, although they are empowered to bring actions.[272] The KO/KOV may act in relation to any trader in various ways, which is particularly important for the *mala fide* traders: it can use the internal fining powers it has in accordance with the MA, bring legal action before the Market Court or, for mass damage suits, before the district court or the ARN.

In line with the findings from above, in cases with a *mala fide* trader, the KO/KOV's additional investigative powers can be very beneficial and necessary. Powers may be used directly according to the MA to investigate a trader (due to surveillance or a consumer complaint) and indirectly if the KO is representing an individual or a group of consumers in a civil case or a group of consumers at the ARN. In certain circumstances, the KO acts as a prosecutor. These are ways, in which the public element can be exploited to convict *mala fide* traders.

The court element, which is almost always present in KO procedures, is very positive, as concluded previously and particularly in scenarios with substantial harm to society. An important player is the Market Court. Only in few cases of minor importance – and, importantly, under the condition that the trader agrees – can the KO take its own internal action. As an underlying threat to these actions, the KO can bring contravention to the orders as a criminal case to court as a

272 For instance before the ARN or according to the LOG.

prosecutor. This involves the court element being present again, but delays the process to some extent, an aspect that could be abused by *mala fide* traders who may only pretend to give their consent to the KO's action.

Furthermore, before the Market Court, single traders or trade associations are granted standing to bring cases against their competitors for certain types of remedies. For damage cases, they would have to go to the Stockholm District Court, which happens in actual practice. A trader cannot address the ARN.

Also consumers can be granted damages in accordance with the provisions of the MA. The KO is empowered to bring actions for damages in this setting by the LOG. Currently, there has been only one such incident. Consumers can free ride on traders' actions to some extent if the actions involve injunctions or generate other information that can be used in follow-on damage claims. Granting standing to traders can lead to a reduction of information asymmetries, as these generally exist less between competitors and more between consumers and traders. Furthermore, the KO can carry out collective action for damages in the district court and before the ARN (and, theoretically, if the KO does not take action, associations may do so).

Although it was assumed that there is a high resistance to class action-like procedures in Europe (which is why it was not specifically considered in Part I), in Sweden such procedures exist by means of the LOG – an opt-in action more specifically. The LOG not only empowers the KO, but also associations (including *ad hoc* associations) and allows private group (class) actions. Among the possible remedies are actions for damages. To my knowledge, the case with the lowest consumer contribution was 'Grupptalan v. S' in which an individual could join the action by paying €15. Therefore, there is potentially a role for small and widespread harm cases such as the scenario at hand. For example, the current KO argued that cases of small and widespread harm remain undetected.[273] The financing of group litigation for small and widespread harm is crucial.

Aside of actions for damages, overall cost/benefit considerations might go in favour of using other remedies than distribution of damages. Other remedies are available in the Swedish system, most prominently the market disruption charge in relation to procedures of the MA, which is basically a sanction that belongs to the 'fining' remedies. Here, the role of the KO is vital, there is no possibility for consumer associations to make a claim and traders are given only a subsidiary role. Therefore, frivolous lawsuits from traders who want to damage another trader's business are unlikely. Then again, a court is always involved in deciding. Considering the deterrence effect and the sanction's potential to outweigh low probabilities of detection and conviction, the existence of this sanction is to be seen very positively. In terms of speed, particularly crucial for *mala fide* traders, interim decisions can be a quick and powerful instrument. These are used in 5 to 10 per cent of the cases at the Market Court.

273 See interview with Gunnar Larsson, Swedish Consumer Ombudsman and Head of Consumer Authority (Stockholm, 25 August 2009).

From the perspective of *the bona fide* traders, it is to be welcomed that over-deterring can be prevented within the Swedish enforcement response. *Bona fide* traders have to be targeted differently from the *mala fide* traders. The market disruption charge, for example, allows for some special conditions like the intention that in a way may act as a safeguard to the *bona fide* traders. Then, as mentioned, there is a possibility to go to the RO. As in the Netherlands, the advice offered *ex ante* could be given a stronger value and the procedure also could be more formalised, which would raise awareness.

The best possibilities to deter a *mala fide* trader like in the second scenario are primarily available through mass actions for damages and the market disruption charge, combined with some investigative powers. The KO/KOV and the powers available in the various procedures are crucial. The KO may act as a prosecutor under certain conditions. Finally, a criminal trial involving the police would generate the most investigative powers and might be the right response to *mala fide* traders.

Note that most of the considerations for the KO are also available for a case involving package travel advertisement that conflicts with MA. If a package travel issue harms more than one consumer, the other mass litigation solutions as outlined are applicable.

Thus, the Swedish legal system provides various remedies for relevant players, but some fine-tuning is still desirable in order to tackle both types of traders. Improvements concerning speedy reactions and reducing risks of capture can be suggested. Also, empowerment of consumer associations could be considered, although *ad hoc* associations and nonprofit organisations have emerged to some extent to cure the lack of action by consumer associations. This nourishes hope that a working format for collective actions may be found and funding issues remedied. In the case of very small and widespread damage, alternative remedies to compensation are crucial and a variety of them already exist.

The positive aspect of separating powers is of no importance if the KO brings the case before the Market Court, the ARN or the District Court because a separate body will always be addressed. The ARN is certainly the weakest decision-maker because the risk of capture is the largest and the risk of error costs is comparably high, due to low procedural requirements. Error costs in this case would be spread to an entire group, which can be considered a disadvantage and a reason why traders generally dislike this approach.[274] Then again, there are no underlying business guarantees like in the Netherlands and a trader could potentially avoid compliance, although doing so would be detrimental to the trader's reputation. Also may experts be involved in the procedure before the ARN. When deciding whether to bring a damage case before the ARN or the court (district court or Market Court), the KO reportedly seeks the ARN option most likely to avoid the

274 See personal email communications with SRF (17 November 2011): 'As regards class actions I am not sure that we are much happier than our Dutch colleagues that they are brought to an ADR body. They should rather be brought to a civil court'.

notice and opt-in requirements imposed by the act. The KO also believes it would be easier to gain acceptance of standardised calculations of damages before the ARN than before a general court. However, the *Kraftkommission* case showed that the KO is equally powerless if the trader does not follow the ARN recommendation and the only recourse is to initiate a case before the district court, which is a potential underlying threat. The duration of the procedure may cast some doubts regarding the power of this threat.

Therefore, the scenario involving the *mala fide* trader could not be handled before the ARN and, in this instance, having an alternative is a positive situation. A duplication of enforcement costs may occur. Overall the optimal design suggestions entail that ADR bodies should not be involved in mass litigation because of the named weaknesses. Therefore, one suggestion to improve the enforcement landscape in Sweden would be to avoid mass litigation in the ARN and focus on a court element for these cases. This suggestion is made despite ARN's positive effects, a potential positive influence on funding and the fact that the availability of the procedure ensures competition between various bodies. In practice, and this can be appreciated, few cases of group litigation come to the ARN.

Another crucial suggestion is to make the current indirect use of the KO/KOV's investigative powers direct and provide an explicit legal provision to ensure that this information can enter certain types of procedures, particularly for *mala fide* traders.

The cautionary use of the market disruption charge (traders are only granted a subsidiary right of action and consumer associations no right of action, as consumers have no standing at the Market Court, anyway) provides a welcome protection from over-deterrence among other players in the market. This structure also prevents strategic use of the sanction. Then again, where the proceeds of this remedy go may be fine-tuned. In addition, criminal law enforcement may not be necessary because the effect of a market disruption charge, even if it is not labelled 'criminal', is essentially the same as a criminal fine and provides a high deterrence value.

For some cases of trifling and widespread harm, intervention of a representative that is funded by someone other than the victims might be needed. Therefore, the multiple options that Swedish law allows for group litigation by various claimants and the various remedies available are a positive sign in terms of deterrence and alignment with the optimal mix of enforcement mechanisms. These are not necessarily all exhausted currently. A mechanism might still be desirable to challenge the KO's nonaction in case there is no alternative body to take up a case. Consumer associations even though empowered in various regards are never a realistic alternative.

General Conclusion

Sweden scores high according to the suggested optimal law enforcement mixes. The public element may be introduced to various procedures and could still be expanded. An advantage for focusing on the KO for further improvements is that the Swedish population knows this system and the tendency to resort to the KO if help is not available elsewhere is certainly well embedded in the culture. Criminal law enforcement of consumer protection laws is rare, however. Under certain circumstances, the KO may act as prosecutor. The KO may potentially have a role in individual cases and mass cases. In the latter, various possibilities exist for a variety of players to sue for mass damages, as an alternative means to uphold the deterrent effect. The market disruption charge is a valuable alternative, where damage to individuals is not quantifiable and likewise serves as a deterrent.

Mala fide traders face a powerful enforcement response, although it may be desirable to fine-tune and secure the public law element for more civil law case scenarios. The fact that a court element is involved in almost all procedures, where representatives that may face a risk of capture are part of the procedure, is a positive design. In particular the Market Court is an interesting player with a specialised set of cases that can be brought before it. Some critical thoughts regarding mass procedures before the ARN are expressed.

Sweden provides a variety of ways to differentiate a response to *bona fide* and *mala fide* traders. The involvement of the ARN and the RO serve as potential cross-financing mechanisms. Options are available to ensure deterrence for cases where pure damage cases fail. A speedy interim action is also possible.

Traders are given many remedies and avenues, but their incentives are considered when giving them only a secondary right of action with the market disruption charge. There is no role for consumer associations and no apparent need to strengthen such a role in general. Some way to challenge the KO's failure to take action in a particular case may be warranted, potentially by consumer associations.

Chapter 8
England

Introduction

England[1] emphasises public law enforcement and typically state agencies issue and enforce regulations.[2] The Department for Business, Innovation and Skills (BIS) has overall policy responsibility for consumer issues. The main players in consumer law are the Office of Fair Trading (OFT) and the local Trading Standards Services (TSS).[3] OFT, the most important central government agency and a well-known consumer enforcement regulator,[4] is a nondepartmental government body and both the competition and consumer protection authority.[5] OFT is the national consumer protection body responsible for enforcement at the national level. Its tasks include encouraging businesses to comply with competition and consumer law and to improve their trading practices through self-regulation; acting to stop hard-core or

1 It will be referred to England throughout this chapter, but the wide majority of the findings applies to England and Wales. Their legal systems are widely aligned.

2 See Hodges (2009), pp. 151, 157. 'Governmental policy documents may include rhetoric on empowerment of consumers and consumer bodies, but the reality of enforcement rests firmly on public structures'.

3 TSS are funded by local governments mainly. This funding is expected to decline from an estimated £213 million in 2009 to an estimated £140–170 million in 2014, see BIS, Empowering and Protecting Consumers, Consultation on Institutional Changes for Provision of Consumer Information, Advice, Education, Advocacy and Enforcement (June 2011), http://www.bis.gov.uk/assets/biscore/consumer-issues/docs/e/11-970-empowering-protecting-consumers-consultation-on-institutional-changes.pdf, last accessed: 31 March 2013, p. 10. TSS are funded by and accountable to their individual local authority, some of whose funding is raised by local Council Tax (about 25 per cent), but most of which is provided by central government. A small amount of the central government money goes directly to fund specific local government services (such as animal health), but the vast majority goes into a general account, to allow maximum flexibility to local authorities in how they deliver their services to meet a range of national and local priorities, set by central and local government respectively, see Biennial Report of the UK Member State on the Application of the Regulation on Consumer Protection Cooperation (EC) 2006/2004 (January 2009), http://ec.europa.eu/consumers/enforcement/docs/united_kingdom_report_en.pdf, last accessed: 31 March 2013, p. 11.

4 See G. Howells, 'Enforcing Consumer Interests by Regulatory Agencies – the British Experience; A Case Study of the Office of Fair Trading', *Collective Enforcement of Consumer Law Securing Compliance in Europe through Private Group Action and Public Authority Intervention*, eds W.H. van Boom and M.B.M. Loos (Groningen: Europa Law Publishing, 2007) 65–81, p. 66.

5 See Howells (2007), p. 69.

flagrant offenders; carrying out market studies and empowering consumers. OFT is the single liaison office designated in accordance with the Regulation on CPC, responsible for coordinating initial requests for information and referrals of cases. TSS, which are funded mainly through local authorities, carry out the majority of consumer law enforcement. Their annual budget varies between £240,000 and £6,000,000.[6] Furthermore, England leads in effective models of self-regulation.[7] The Advertising Standards Authority (ASA) operates on the national level. Unlike the Netherlands and Sweden, there is no centralised ADR body available for consumer disputes, but many special business-to-consumer ADR schemes exist in individual sectors, along with a range of ombudsmen.[8] One of those special out-of-court dispute resolution schemes is also available in the package travel sector.

In contrast to the countries previously discussed, criminal law enforcement has traditionally been important in England within consumer law.[9] However, overall, injunctions are becoming more important compared with criminal law sanctions.[10] Another development that marks a move away from criminal law enforcement is the Regulatory Enforcement and Sanctions Act (RESA) 2008, which empowers regulators to exercise a new category of civil sanctions (including compliance requirements) to target violations more specifically.[11] However, noncompliance with these new remedies may still lead to a criminal law response. In private law enforcement, an interesting power of consumer associations is to issue super-complaints to challenge OFT's nonaction.

A difference compared with Sweden and the Netherlands is that England's legal system stems from the so-called common law tradition with a strong emphasis on judge-made law. While the importance of codified law has steadily increased, precedents (the doctrine of *stare decisis*) continue to play a very important role.[12] Laws governing both package travel and unfair commercial practices are available in codified form, and, therefore, the importance of case law in these fields is minor. Changes to the consumer landscape are imminent.[13]

---

6 NAO, Department for Business, Innovation and Skills, the Office of Fair Trading and Local Authority Trading Standards Services Protecting consumers – the system for enforcing consumer law (2011), p. 4.

7 See interview ASA (London, 23 February 2011); I. Bartle and P. Vass, *Self-Regulation and the Regulatory State – A Survey of Policy and Practice* (Centre for the Study of Regulated Industries, University of Bath School of Management, 2005), p. 1.

8 See Hodges (2008), p. 1. See also Hodges (2009), p. 152.

9 See Faure, Ogus and Philipsen (2008), p. 379 referring to interviews carried out with English enforcers in the ambit of their study.

10 See Howells (2007), p. 66.

11 See Hodges (2011b), p. 8. As will be outlined the fate of the RESA 2008 is currently doubtful.

12 See A. Zuckerman, *Zuckerman on Civil Procedure Principles of Practice*, 2nd ed. (London: Sweet & Maxwell, 2008), p. 22.

13 See interview with Consumer Focus (London, 22 February 2011); BIS (2011).

Case 1 – Package Travel

How would the package travel case be handled in England (damage of €2,000; a *bona fide* trader scenario [1] and a *mala fide* trader scenario [2])? Particular attention is paid to the *mala fide* trader, an online merchant who tries to hide his identity.[14]

Summary of Legal Rules

English package travel law[15] is set out in the Package Travel, Package Holidays and Package Tours Regulations (PTRs).[16] An ADR body in the travel sector exists aside of ordinary responses via courts. The security mechanisms for cases of insolvency are included.

Consumers may get advice at various institutions: consumer associations such as Which? or Consumer Direct, a publicly funded national telephone and online advice service managed by OFT and delivered in partnership with TSS. Between 1 April 2011 and 31 March 2012, Consumer Direct received 1,151 complaints regarding package holidays in the UK and 6,455 regarding package holidays overseas.[17]

Individuals also may get information at the Citizens Advice Bureau Service,[18] which maintains around 400 bureaus across England and Wales. These are registered charities, with government funding for building maintenance, volunteer training and so on. As this system is very costly, British authorities have instituted a virtual advice system.[19]

Another player is Consumer Focus,[20] which acts on behalf of consumers by looking at markets, carrying out surveys and formulating policies for markets that do not work well.[21] Consumer Focus may investigate general interest complaints from consumers and initiate super-complaints (outlined below).

---

14 Similarly 'Bogus holiday club scams cost the UK public an estimated £1.17 billion a year. An estimated 400,000 adults fall victim to these scams every year. The mean loss per victim is £3,030, (the median loss was £601)', see OFT (2006), p. 65.

15 See European Commission's working paper on Enforcement of European Consumer Legislation, 27 March 1998, SEC (98) 527, p. 40.

16 The Package Travel, Package Holidays and Package Tours Regulations, S.I. 3288 of 1992, Reg. 16–26.

17 Consumer Direct Data from Annual report OFT 2011, Annex F Complaints to Consumer Direct – summary and comparison with 2010/11, http://www.oft.gov.uk/shared_oft/annual_report/2011/annexe-f-comps.pdf, last accessed: 29 February 2012, p. 10.

18 See http://www.citizensadvice.org.uk/, last accessed: 31 March 2013, see interview with Consumer Focus (London, 22 February 2011).

19 See http://www.adviceguide.org.uk/, last accessed: 31 March 2013.

20 It was formed in October 2008 by a merger of the National Consumer Council, Postwatch and Energywatch. It receives funding from the government and from the energy and postal industries.

21 See interview with Consumer Focus (London, 22 February 2011).

Alternatively, individuals increasingly complain to their Members of Parliament (MPs).[22] A standard procedure is for MPs to open their doors to constituents approximately once every two weeks. Traditionally lodging a complaint with an MP was a measure of last resort, but recently it has become one of the first things to do. The actions that the MP can undertake may be writing to TSS, raising the question in Parliament or involving an ombudsman if it is a sector in which an ombudsman is active.

As with all EU Member States, England has a local contact of the ECC network for cross-border situations.[23]

At the Civil Court England is a common law country where civil procedure is traditionally characterised by an adversarial process in which the judge is the neutral arbiter between the parties.[24] In England, the major reformed court rules called the Civil Procedural Rules (CPR) were introduced in 1999. They stipulate that the role of the judge is to take the initiative and proactively direct 'the intensity and pace of the litigation process'.[25] The process of discovery is applicable to gather evidence in the pretrial stage. Each party is obliged to produce for inspection by the other party all relevant documents or information they possess, independent of whether these support their claim or not. The parties have a right to obtain all the information from the other party, which differs from civil law countries. Discovery of documents can be extensive and costly.[26] The 1999 reforms led to greater judicial control through case management (such as limiting numbers of experts or appointing a single expert; limiting documentary evidence and oral argument and encouraging settlement).[27] As said, codified law prevails in travel law. The CPR is intended to provide predictable and proportionate costs;[28] however, predictability remains a concern.[29] Furthermore, the system is particularly disproportionate

22 See interview with Consumer Focus (London, 22 February 2011).

23 See http://www.ukecc.net/, last accessed: 31 March 2013.

24 The differences of adversarial and inquisitorial procedures have become less in practice.

25 See Zuckerman (2008), p. 32 referring to Section 1.4 (1) CPR on active case management.

26 See Hodges (2008), p. 1.

27 Inquisition, examination of witnesses and instruction of experts in common law countries is under the control of the court within the ambit of the case management. The costs to do so initially are with the litigant, see J. Peysner, 'England and Wales', *The Costs and Funding of Civil Litigation – A Comparative Perspective*, eds C. Hodges, S. Vogenauer and M. Tulibacka (Oxford and Portland, Oregon: Hart Publishing, 2010) 289–302, p. 289.

28 See Peysner (2010), p. 290. Lord Justice Jackson (2010) shows the methods are ineffective, see C. Hodges, 'England and Wales: Summary of the Jackson Costs Review', *The Costs and Funding of Civil Litigation*, pp. 303–12.

29 See Peysner (2010), p. 302.

regarding low-value claims.[30] The most recent among various reform initiatives is the Jackson Report of 2010,[31] which recommended fixed and predictable costs for low-value cases and stressed the value of other types of dispute resolution.

Every claim is allocated to a track: the multitrack (complex and high value cases), the fast track (a procedurally rationed track for most cases) or the small claims track.[32] The small claims track is likely to be the most relevant route for a consumer law case such as the case study at hand.

Small claims procedures take place in the county court.[33] The simplified procedure known as 'small claims arbitration' applies to consumer claims of less than £10,000 (£1,000 in the case of personal injury and disrepair).[34] These procedures are informal, judges are active, lawyers are not necessary and a special rule on fee shifting applies (similar to Sweden, the 'loser-pays' rule does not apply, but the no-cost rule does, according to CPR Rule 27.14).[35] This method of recovery is fairly well used among consumers because of its relatively modest court fees, savings on lawyers' fees and the loser is not exposed to the risk of paying the other parties' legal costs. Consumers are often defendants rather than claimants.[36] Although a solicitor[37] is not necessary, legal representation is allowed, even by so-called 'lay representatives'. Initiating civil proceedings against traders who cannot be traced is like in the previously discussed countries impossible in English law and the *mala fide* trader cannot be tried in the civil court.[38]

---

30 See Creutzfeldt-Banda, Hodges and Benöhr (2012), p. 255. Among the important reports is the Woolf report: Lord Woolf, Final Report to the Lord Chancellor on the civil justice system in England and Wales (1996).

31 See Lord Justice Jackson (2010).

32 See Hodges (2009), p. 152: The fast-track procedure is meant for cases above the small claims limit and up to £25,000. It allows for extended settlement opportunities. Some standard actions are to be undertaken by the parties to facilitate establishing and verifying the facts and evidence. Appeal is only possible with the court's permission. Claim values above £25,000 are processed in the multi-track procedure, in which strong judicial case management applies. See Part 27–9 CPR.

33 See G. Howells, *United Kingdom National Report – Study: An Analysis and Evaluation of Alternative Means of Consumer Redress other than Redress through Ordinary Judicial Proceedings* (2006), p. 2. See now Part 27 CPR.

34 See Part 27 (1) CPR.

35 See Howells (2006), p. 2.

36 See Howells (2008), p. 40; Ogus, Faure and Philipsen (2006), p. 45 'the numbers enforcing their rights are likely to be small'.

37 A solicitor is a lawyer who advises clients on matters of law, draws up legal documents, prepares cases for barristers and so on and who may represent clients in certain courts. A barrister, also called barrister-at-law, in turn, is a lawyer who has been called to the bar and is qualified to plead in the higher courts.

38 Online registry: see whois.co.uk, last accessed: 31 March 2013. See concerning the requirements to identify the defendant: Zuckerman (2008), p. 142; see interview OFT (London, 22 February 2011).

Regarding unmeritorious litigation, two restraints are possible:[39] on the application of the Attorney-General, the High Court may order (Section 42 Supreme Court Act 1981) a restraint against a vexatious litigant from issuing proceedings without permission of the court for an indefinite period. Under CPR, the court may make three types of civil restraint orders.[40]

Claim fees for originating a claim of less than £300 are £30 and £1,530 for a claim of £300,000 or unlimited value, for example. For this scenario, the fee would be £95 (claim range of £1,500.01–£3,000).[41] The hearing fee in the range applicable to this scenario is £165. The system is supposed to be self-supporting.[42] Hourly rates for lawyers amount to £150–£200.[43]

Conditional fees, which are quite similar to contingency fees, for lawyers are the rule.[44] The conditional fee agreement (CFA) contains two elements,[45] a 'no-win-no-fee' provision and a fee increase if the case is dealt with successfully. Therefore, a successful lawyer will obtain the 'normal' basic fee, calculated on an hourly rate and additionally the uplifted success fee (a proportion of the basic fee).

Legal aid is stipulated in the recent Legal Aid, Sentencing and Punishment of Offenders Act (LASPO) 2012. Primarily, this act abolished the Legal Services Commission, which had granted legal aid since 1999. Day-to-day administration of legal aid was transferred to the Lord Chancellor, which, in practice, is handled by civil servants in an executive agency of the Ministry of Justice. Legal aid was intended to be widely available, but the service has been deconstructed and private funding and insurance have become the primary funding mechanisms,[46] a trend that continued with the recently enacted act.[47] There has been a rise during the last 10 years in first party insurance (Legal Expenses Insurance, also known as before-the-event [BTE]), an add-on insurance.[48] The insurer has a say in deciding the direction

39 See Zuckerman (2008), p. 67.

40 See CPR 3.11, practice direction 3c – Civil restraint orders and CPR 2.3.1.

41 See HM Courts & Tribunals Service, Civil and Family Court Fees 2013, http://hmctscourtfinder.justice.gov.uk/courtfinder/forms/ex050-eng.pdf, last accessed: 31 March 2013.

42 See Peysner (2010), p. 295.

43 Estimated by Howells (2008) for small and widespread damage cases.

44 Contingency fees as such are illegal in England. They might be used in pre-litigation settlements. They are furthermore common in employment tribunals, see Peysner (2010), p. 294.

45 See Conditional Fees Agreements Regulations 2000. Section 58 of the Courts and Legal Services Act 1990 (conditional fee agreements) was last amended by LASPO 2012.

46 See Hodges (2008), p. 26; see also R. Moorhead, 'Cost Wars in England and Wales: The Insurers Strike Back', *Cost and Fee Allocation in Civil Procedure*, ed. M. Reimann (Dordrecht; Heidelberg; London; New York: Springer, 2012) pp. 117–25.

47 List of excluded services, see in particular in its schedule 1 civil legal services, part II.

48 See Peysner (2010), p. 293: Generally bundles into products such as house or car insurance at low or no costs.

of the case. Trade unions may be involved in funding civil litigation.[49] There are public NGOs or charity-funded provider(s), such as Law Centres, Citizens' Advice Bureaux, Shelter (housing) or JUSTICE. The CFA system was changed with cuts to legal aid and was extended in 1999 to guarantee access to justice in compensation for less availability of legal aid.[50] Under the CFA, a party is required to have insurance to pay for the winner's costs if the party loses. Some claimants are left only with the option to seek after-the-event (ATE) policies from insurers, which are rather expensive. Overall the interaction of CFAs and ATE insurance is complex; if managed well, basic fees, success fees and reasonable insurance premiums are recoverable from losing defendants.[51]

In 2011, there were a total of 52,660 trials and small claims hearings, a decrease of 13 per cent from 2010 and a number lower than in any year from 2006 onwards.[52] A 2008 study showed that consumers would refrain from suing through ordinary courts if damages were estimated to be between £50 and £250.[53] Some package travel cases are dealt with as small claims in the courts, unlike in Sweden or the Netherlands.[54] In the Eurobarometer Study 2011, 28 per cent of interviewees reported that they encountered a problem worthy of a legitimate complaint during the past 12 months.[55] As a result of these problems, 37 per cent reported no loss and, for instance, 14 per cent reported a loss of €1–20, for an overall average loss of €239. Therefore, for a small percentage of consumer claims, special low-cost devices are needed to trigger consumers' incentives to sue.

Furthermore, the study showed that 78 per cent of the interviewees in the UK said they would complain if they experienced a problem. Seventeen per cent of interviewees said they would have to have a loss of €101–200 to involve a court,[56] a different top group compared with Sweden or the Netherlands. This is a sign that the court is involved in more cases of lower value than in the other countries under investigation. Fifteen per cent set the threshold for a lawsuit at €201–500 and 14 per cent at €501–1,000. Eight per cent set the threshold at €20 or less, which is comparably more than in the other two countries.

---

49 See Hodges (2008), p. 26.

50 Access to Justice Act 1999, s 27, substituting new ss. 58 and 58A in the Access to Justice Act 1990.

51 Access to Justice Act 1999, s. 29.

52 Judicial Court Statistics 2011, p. 6.

53 See Howells (2008), p. 40.

54 See interview ABTA (London, 22 February 2011). See for an illustration of some package travel cases A. Saggerson, *Travel Law and Litigation*, 4th ed. (ST Albans: XPL Publishing, 2008), p. 335.

55 See European Commission, Special Eurobarometer n°342 (2011), p. 170.

56 See European Commission, Special Eurobarometer n°342 (2011), p. 217.

The Role of ADR ADR systems in England are not centralised as in the Netherlands and Sweden. The existing systems can be divided into three types:[57] in-house complaint mechanisms, formal schemes requiring membership and leading to binding decisions and *ad hoc* schemes (including mediation and arbitration). Consumer awareness of ADR is low in England and Wales.[58] OFT supervises the development of codes of practice and their monitoring[59] and can arrange for approval and withdrawal of consumer codes.[60] The OFT approval is a two-step process: first, a promise has to be made to meet the core criteria; second, the criteria must be met in practice.[61] Only then will the code be approved and the use of the OFT-approved logo be permitted. OFT can be, but does not have to be involved in the code approval. With the changes in the consumer landscape, the Code of Conduct Approval Scheme (CCAS) was suspended in 2010 and from April 2013 onwards the Trading Standards Institute (TSI) will operate a successor scheme.[62]

In England, court resolution is a measure of last resort.[63] Judges are incentivised by economic sanctions like adverse cost orders to encourage settlements.[64] However, it is well established that the court has no power to force settlements and does not even have an immediate power to direct parties to participate in settlement negotiations, in line with Article 6 ECHR.

The Code of Conduct available in the travel sector originally was an OFT-approved code (approved in 2005). The Travel Association (formerly the Association of British Travel Agents and still known as ABTA) was established in 1950 and is in charge of monitoring ABTA's code of conduct. Today ABTA's membership includes 5,000 travel agencies and more than 900 tour operators.[65] ABTA members account for around 90 per cent of package holidays sold in the UK. Not all small companies are members, as there are restrictions regarding membership criteria.[66] ABTA voluntarily withdrew its code from the CCAS on 1 September 2006, deciding to change its financial protection arrangements in a way

57 See UK PermRep, answer to consultation on ADR issued by the European Commission (2011), p. 3.

58 See Consumer Focus, answer to consultation on ADR issued by the European Commission (2011), p. 4.

59 See Howells (2007), p. 73.

60 The latter is set out in Section 8 II of the Enterprise Act 2002.

61 See Howells and Weatherill (2005), p. 586.

62 See http://www.oft.gov.uk/OFTwork/ccas/;jsessionid=78DEA92DAE6475968CBCBFC9BDBE145F#.UXEAvrXwmSo and http://www.tradingstandards.gov.uk/advice/ConsumerCodes.cfm, last accessed: 31 March 2013.

63 See Zuckerman (2008), p. 45, CPR 1.4(2)(e) and (f).

64 See Zuckerman (2008), Chapter 26.

65 See Creutzfeldt-Banda, Hodges and Benöhr (2012), p. 328.

66 See interview with ABTA (London, 22 February 2011). Those tour operators often belong to the Association of Independent Tour Operators (AITO) and their travel agent counterparts to the National Association of Independent Travel Agents (NAITA), see Saggerson (2008), p. 11

that did not comply with the CCAS requirements, according to the OFT.[67] However, the OFT expressed that this one area of noncompliance did not mean ABTA's code was unlawful because in the remaining respects it fulfilled the benchmark.[68]

All travel agents and tour operators who join ABTA automatically agree to adhere to ABTA's ADR.[69] On the one hand, ABTA operates a code of conduct in self-regulation,[70] and on the other, consumers may get redress via the arbitration scheme in case of breach of contract and/or negligence of ABTA members.

The ABTA Code of Conduct Committee has various sanctions available for enforcing the Code of Conduct: accepting a member's undertaking, issuing a reprimand, imposing a fine or terminating membership. Fining is regularly used,[71] ABTA is considered to be tough on its own people.[72] There is a fixed financial penalty of £400 for certain clauses of the code.[73] For a breach of the other clauses, the Code of Conduct Committee decides on the fine and it has an unlimited discretion to reprimand, fine or terminate membership of the member.[74] Fines vary in size depending on the seriousness of the offence and the member's previous record of conduct. These bigger cases amount to about 50 to 60 per year. ABTA lists sanctioned business on its website.[75] Referrals to an independent appeal board are possible.[76] The money paid in fines goes back to ABTA.

A consumer seeking to file a complaint against an ABTA member to be decided upon in arbitration must first try to settle the issue informally with the trader, as in the previously analysed countries. At first instance, customers send their complaint directly to the ABTA member and the trader is required to send a full response within 28 days or risk a £400 fixed-penalty fine. Only as a next step may the

67 See OFT press release, 'OFT: ABTA withdraws from OFT Consumer Codes Approval Scheme' (31 August 2006), http://www.oft.gov.uk/news-and-updates/press/2006/127-06, last accessed: 31 March 2013.

68 See interview with OFT (London, 22 February 2011).

69 See ABTA, answer to consultation on ADR issued by the European Commission (2011). The Code makes the arbitration scheme compulsory on members (at clauses 5F and 5G).

70 See interview with ABTA (London, 22 February 2011) for the following.

71 See interview with ABTA (London, 22 February 2011). Note that the OFT originally had proposed that sanctions be dealt with by an independent body because trade associations at times face difficulties to go against their own members and the failure to have this external supervision in place is regarded as a weakness of the system, Howells and Weatherill (2005), p. 590.

72 See personal communications with Professor Christopher Hodges, Head of the Centre for Socio-Legal Studies, University of Oxford/Professor of the Fundamentals of Private Law, Erasmus University Rotterdam. (23 March 2011).

73 See for the cases of Section 7 of the ABTA Code of Conduct.

74 See personal email communications with ABTA (15 December 2011).

75 See Creutzfeldt-Banda, Hodges and Benöhr (2012), p. 329.

76 See interview with ABTA (London, 22 February 2011), See Section 7k ABTA Code of Conduct.

consumer complain to ABTA. An online complaint process was established that encourages settlements. The complaint must be submitted within 18 months of the date of return from the holiday. The Arbitration Scheme for the Travel Industry is entirely private and is administered independently by CEDR Solve. ABTA emphasises in-house solutions. When a complaint is filed, the Consumer Affairs Team sends the claim form to the consumer and to the company and sends it to the ADR provider only if an amicable settlement cannot be reached. Traders and consumers might be induced to settle because fees are lower.[77] If a compensation claim includes an element of minor illness or personal injury, the arbitrator cannot award more than £1,500 per person.[78] Serious personal injury, serious illness, nervous shock, death or the consequences of any of these are outside the scope of the scheme. For these cases, a consumer may utilise the Personal Injury Mediation Scheme for the Travel Industry in which a third party helps to resolve the dispute.

The arbitration process is purely a written one; there is no oral hearing.[79] The arbitrator issues an award, including a summary of the facts and a reasoned conclusion. This decision is legally binding on both parties and directly enforceable through the courts. The trader agrees not to go to court in the first place.[80] The consumer may choose either the court or the arbitration route.

Both parties have limited possibilities to review the arbitrator's decision under the ABTA Arbitration Scheme Appeals Procedure.[81] A reasoned application must be made within 14 days. A very limited judicial review is possible in the courts. An appeal is possible through the High Court, within 28 days of receiving the award. Appeals will normally require evidence of a serious error in law or misconduct on the part of the arbitrator. For the High Court to consider an appeal, a solicitor is required.

While consumers typically play a role in the arbitration procedure, they also may (only or combined with arbitration) bring a complaint for a breach of the code of conduct.[82] Awareness appears to be rising among consumers regarding the code of conduct procedure, although it is generally instigated by a trader or by ABTA. The two procedures can be interrelated. An obligation for the trader to compensate consumers may be included in the committee decisions, but details will be fixed only in the arbitration board decision.[83]

---

77 See N. Creutzfeldt-Banda, C. Hodges and I. Benöhr, 'United Kingdom', *Consumer ADR in Europe*, eds C. Hodges, I. Benöhr and N. Creutzfeldt-Banda (Oxford and Portland, Oregon: Hart Publishing, 2012) 253–353, p. 266.

78 See interview with ABTA (London, 22 February 2011).

79 See interview with ABTA (London, 22 February 2011).

80 See the ABTA Arbitration Scheme – rules & appeal procedure, rule 1.3.

81 See the ABTA Arbitration Scheme – rules & appeal procedure, rule 8.1 and see specifically the ABTA arbitration appeal procedure.

82 See interview with ABTA (London, 22 February 2011).

83 See interview with ABTA (London, 22 February 2011).

Lawyers are generally not involved in the procedure, except for large companies at times.[84] However, in larger claims suppliers' insurers may get involved.[85] Independent consumer representatives sit in ABTA's committees.[86] Trading Standards officials sit on the Code of Conduct Committee.

The consumer must pay a fee to register an arbitration claim. The fee is £108 for claim values of £1–£2,999.99, £180 for claim values of £3,000–£7,499.99 and £264 for claim values of £7,500–£25,000. Therefore, £108 would be the applicable fee in the case scenario here. Arbitration is concluded within eight to 12 weeks.[87] Both consumers and members have lodged cases. The loser-pays rule is generally applicable regarding the registration fee (and for claimants, is restricted to the claimant's registration fee).[88] Each party must bear its own costs of preparing and submitting the case, including the costs of legal representation. If the consumer wishes to appeal an arbitrator's decision, the review fee is £350 plus VAT. This fee is not reimbursable, regardless of the outcome.[89] The fees are fixed at a similar level to the fees payable in the courts' small claims track and at a level intended to discourage frivolous cases. There is no underlying sector guarantee if a member refuses to pay the compensation.[90] In practice, they always pay. If they did not pay and tried to leave membership, ABTA could sue them, but this has never happened to date.

In 2010, the average amount claimed through arbitration was £1,750, compared with an award ceiling of £25,000. The average award was £630.[91] In 2010, 12,702 case files were opened; 1,216 were sent a pre-arbitration notice and ultimately 255 progressed to an award being issued (2 per cent of cases opened). The overwhelming majority of complaints (perhaps 90 per cent) were settled by the mediation stage.[92] The introduction of the pre-arbitration notice was considered a reason for why the number of cases fell.

In 2009, 78 per cent of the cases were decided in favour of the consumer.[93] ABTA members have to pay an annual fee to ABTA as well as a fee for every arbitration that ABTA carries out for the member's company; thus, members who do not use the system do not pay.[94] To prevent the consumer from forecasting the amount for which a company may settle, this amount is kept secret.

84 See interview with ABTA (London, 22 February 2011).

85 See Creutzfeldt-Banda, Hodges and Benöhr (2012), p. 334.

86 See interview with ABTA (London, 22 February 2011).

87 See ABTA Arbitration Scheme – general notes and frequently asked questions.

88 See ABTA Arbitration Scheme – rules & appeal procedure, rule 5 – with an exception if the appeal takes place in court.

89 See ABTA Arbitration Appeal Procedure, rule 3.c. and rule 8.1.

90 See interview with ABTA (London, 22 February 2011).

91 See Creutzfeldt-Banda, Hodges and Benöhr (2012), p. 334.

92 See Creutzfeldt-Banda, Hodges and Benöhr (2012), p. 333.

93 See ABTA (2011).

94 See interview with ABTA (London, 22 February 2011).

ABTA carries out a regulatory function and is able to identify problems from its oversight.[95] The government is reported to appreciate the ABTA system.[96] The ABTA legal team grants the members legal advice regarding the code. The ABTA Code of Conduct has a high reputation and is generally well observed among the members. The logo conveys quality and in the few examples of a fraudulent use, public authorities intervened with criminal enforcement. Consumers and traders like the arbitration scheme. Consumer awareness of this special arbitration scheme is very high.[97] Some at OFT argued that a trader who is not a member of ABTA should 'keep quiet' about it.[98]

Frivolous lawsuits are not an issue.[99] However, there are cases in which unsatisfied consumers have continued to write to all possible email addresses they can find. Bundling claims for arbitration is not possible.[100] The system is apt to dealing with multiple and similar individual claims, processing them through existing channels. According to the recent EU Barometer, British consumers would involve ADR for losses of €20 or less in eight per cent of the cases overall.[101] The majority considered the limit at €101–200 (16 per cent), which is the same limit for court action. Fourteen per cent set the limit at €201–500 and 12 per cent at €501–1,000.[102]

ABTA views the small claims track as a competition for its board and a certain number of cases are decided there.[103] According to ABTA, the court system has a number of hidden costs, despite the initial fees being similar. For example, if the case is not decided in the first instance, other costs may apply. However, the court route – even via county courts – is very rare. Apparently these few cases lead to very 'curious' decisions because judges have little experience in the travel sector.[104] Two different cost rules apply in court and in ABTA arbitration.

The necessity of hiring a lawyer if an appeal is sought before the court (relating to an arbitration award) is a disincentive to go to the courts at that stage.

---

95 See Creutzfeldt-Banda, Hodges and Benöhr (2012), p. 329.

96 See interview with Consumer Focus (London, 22 February 2011).

97 See interview with OFT (London, 22 February 2011); an Ipsos MORI survey in 2008 found that 74 per cent of consumers recognised the ABTA brand: OFT Business leadership in consumer protection. A discussion document on self regulation and industry-led compliance (2009), http://www.oft.gov.uk/shared_oft/reports/consumer-policy/oft1058.pdf, last accessed: 31 March 2013, p. 37.

98 See interview with OFT (London, 22 February 2011). It is named as an example of a sector where the public do look out for membership of the trade association, see Howells and Weatherill (2005), p. 590.

99 See interview with ABTA (London, 22 February 2011).

100 See interview with ABTA (London, 22 February 2011).

101 See European Commission, Special Eurobarometer n°342 (2011), p. 217.

102 These numbers are not specific to the travel sector.

103 See interview with ABTA (London, 22 February 2011).

104 See Creutzfeldt-Banda, Hodges and Benöhr (2012), p. 329. 'Industry stories circulate about solicitors objecting to companies seeking to contact their customers with settlement offers after the solicitors had not passed on offers to their clients'.

If a trader is not an ABTA member, a complaint may be made before the ordinary court.[105] CEDR Solve operates a separate scheme for claims against travel companies that are not ABTA members.[106] Therefore, *bona fide* traders can be successfully dealt with in this system.

ABTA does not consider a centralised ADR as an improvement to the system.[107] Regarding the necessity of mandatory ADR schemes in a recent European Commission consultation, the government reported, 'There is evidence to support an ADR scheme being made mandatory in certain sectors where there is oligopoly or information asymmetry. Where there are asymmetries of information consumers cannot easily assess the quality and/or price characteristics of the goods and services they are buying and particularly when the item being purchased is a one-off, long-term and/or expensive item and there are few repeat purchases, the market may be less effective in sanctioning poor quality – the firm has less incentive to satisfy the individual consumer'.[108] Package travel was subsequently named as one of those sectors.

Security Mechanisms According to the PTRs, all providers of package travel must provide financial securities in cases of insolvencies. There are three options for complying with this provision.[109] The first option is a bond that is entered into by an authorised institution (Reg. 17), amounting to 25 per cent of the trader's annual turnover or the maximum amount of all payments the operator expects to hold at any time, whichever is smaller. If the authorised institution has a reserve fund or insurance cover, the minimum amount of the bond falls to 10 per cent of the annual turnover (Reg. 18). The second option is to take out insurance (Reg. 19). No minimum insurance sum is required, which suggests that the insurer must assume unlimited liability. The third option is to turn over all money paid by a consumer for a package travel deal to a trustee until the contract is fully performed (Regs. 20 and 21). ABTA does not consider the trust option to be safe.[110] As only traders not registered with ABTA may provide for a trust, the combination may be particularly dangerous. The Commission Implementation Report of 1998 also mentioned that the trusteeship system provided only a partial refund of money and expenses for the repatriation of the consumer, in some cases.[111] Furthermore,

105 See interview with ABTA (London, 22 February 2011).

106 See ABTA Arbitration Scheme – rules & appeal procedure rule 7.5.

107 See ABTA (2011), p. 3.

108 See UK PermRep (2011), p. 10.

109 See Report on the Implementation of Directive 90/C on Package Travel and Holiday Tours in the Domestic Legislation of EC Member States, 27 March 1998, SEC (98) 527, p. 40.

110 See interview with ABTA (London, 22 February 2011).

111 See Report on the Implementation of Directive 90/314/EEC on Package Travel and Holiday Tours in the Domestic Legislation of EC Member States, 27 March 1998, SEC (98) 527, p. 40.

Regulation 20 is silent on the nature of the trustee, a requirement of independence or an official approval for trustees.

Therefore, ABTA allows for only two out of the three options mentioned in the package travel directive. However, in comparison with Sweden and the Netherlands, additional security mechanisms are in place. ABTA asks travel agents to contribute to the Travel Agents' Bond Replacement Scheme (TABRS), a low-cost alternative to bonding. Furthermore, in exceptional circumstances, ABTA also may ask the agent to contribute to the Retail Fund.[112] This guarantee for members is obligatory for the package travel scenarios.[113] However, if the company so desires, it can be expanded to all other products as well.

As soon as flights are part of the package deal, the situation changes.[114] Here a different system is in place – the Air Travel Trust (ATT). The Civil Aviation Authority (CAA) administers the Air Travel Organisers' Licensing (ATOL) Scheme, which provides financial protection to those taking flight-based holidays. Businesses pay £2.50 for each booking into a fund to cover the cost of refunds and repatriations. When an air flight is included in a package deal, the compensation works via this mechanism and the other securities remain untouched for the whole package. This system currently has a huge deficit (£42 million), but is supported by a government-backed guarantee.[115] A reform that aims at eliminating the deficit within three years went into effect in January 2012.[116]

The scheme is not expanded to any damage claims outside of the scope of the cases mentioned in the Directive for instance regarding the quality of the accommodation,[117] which is also the case in Sweden; the Netherlands is the exception. However, in the Netherlands damage claims constitute only a small share of the compensation payments.

Involvement of Regulators TSS are responsible for enforcement of the package holiday law.[118] Failure to provide for securities in case of insolvency is stipulated to be an offence and persons are liable (a) on summary conviction to a fine not exceeding Level 5 on the standard scale[119] and (b) on conviction on indictment to a fine.[120] The same liability is incurred in cases of contraventions on the requirements

112 See Creutzfeldt-Banda, Hodges and Benöhr (2012), p. 328.

113 See interview with ABTA (London, 22 February 2011).

114 See interview with ABTA (London, 22 February 2011).

115 See https://www.gov.uk/government/publications/reforming-the-air-travel-organisers-licensing-atol-scheme, last accessed: 31 March 2013.

116 See The Civil Aviation (Air Travel Organisers' Licensing) Regulations 2012.

117 See interview with ABTA (London, 22 February 2011).

118 See Regulation 23 (Schedule 3 enforcement) PTRs: 1-(1) Every local weights and measures authority in Great Britain shall be an enforcement authority for the purposes of Regulations 5, 7, 8, 16 and 22 of these Regulations ('the relevant regulations'), and it shall be the duty of each such authority to enforce those provisions within their area.

119 £5,000.

120 See Regulation 16 (3) PTRs.

of brochures (Reg. 5), information to be provided before contract is concluded (Reg. 7), information to be provided in good time (Reg. 8) or in particular breaches related to trusts (Reg. 22). (TSS's role as prosecutor is described under the next heading.)

TSS consider their role to include proactively ensuring compliance with security requirements, and, therefore, visit all tour operators in the UK to discuss any breaches that consumers may report.[121] This proactive enforcement ensures that regulating the industry does not rely on penalising minor breaches of the legislation. Since the implementation of the Consumer Protection from Unfair Trading Regulations (CPRs) 2008, trading standards also review misleading pricing of holidays as well as inaccuracies (Reg. 5 PTRs). (Misleading advertising is withheld until the next case study.)

Throughout the UK, there are more than 200 TSS, each with different priorities, governed by the councils who employ them. Therefore, approaches may vary, which is presumably the reason why ABTA reported that TSS involvement is infrequent overall.[122] ABTA does refer nonmembers to the OFT/TSS when it comes to providing financial securities. In contrast with the Netherlands and Sweden, England's national enforcer (OFT) has no role to play, in practice.[123] ABTA does not see a role for the OFT in fining ABTA members.[124] While the OFT has a variety of competences in package travel, so far it has clearly not been the priority of the enforcer.[125]

ABTA acknowledges that there is scope for abuse by traders. Under government-introduced changes to the consumer landscape, the local authorities TSS will have a greater role in the enforcement of consumer protection law at national level beginning 1 April 2013. OFT will retain all of its current consumer enforcement powers, but will tend to use them where breaches of consumer protection law point to systemic failures in a market. Therefore, cases will more often be taken against a number of firms in a market rather than individual firms, unless changing the behaviour of one firm would set a precedent or have other marketwide implications.

Generally, the pursuit of private rights can be aided if there is prior public law enforcement by TSS or OFT, notably where the evidence of the contravention is used in the civil proceedings.[126]

OFT currently does not have the ability to fine traders for violations of consumer protection laws; the RESA 2008 might change this. OFT has been active in relation to misleading advertising cases, which is why its powers are set out more in detail in the next case study. OFT's code of conduct scheme and its imminent abolishment has been discussed.

121 See personal email communications with TSS (21 February 2012). He calls the monitoring approach robust.

122 See interview with ABTA (London, 22 February 2011).

123 See interview with ABTA (London, 22 February 2011).

124 See interview with ABTA (London, 22 February 2011).

125 See interview with OFT (London, 22 February 2011).

126 See Ogus, Faure and Philipsen (2006), p. 45.

Criminal Law Enforcement in the Travel Sector A lot of travel law is formulated in terms of criminal offences, including provisions regarding information requirements, fraudulent uses of logos or the failure to provide financial securities in case of insolvency.[127] Consumers may report suspected criminal offences to the respective enforcing authority.[128] The offences are categorised as 'regulatory crimes'. They are offences of strict liability,[129] the due diligence offence applies and the burden of proof rests upon the accused. A defense of 'innocent publication' may apply in relation to misleading brochures.[130] The offence can be committed by the officers and managers of corporate organisations may be pursued in the criminal courts as well as the guilty corporation if they 'connived' at an offence or if the offence is 'attributable' to them.[131]

Criminal prosecution is an important part of TSS's enforcement.[132] In their formal enforcement role, officers are required to operate according to the same rules and standards as police officers and must comply with the provisions of the Police and Criminal Evidence Act 1984, the Criminal Procedure and Investigations Act 1996 and the Regulation of Investigatory Powers Act 2000. According to the explanatory schedule for Regulation 23 in the PTRs, English enforcement authorities have various powers when carrying out a prosecution regarding the production of books, documents, taking copies and entry (with a warrant) or inspection of any good. People obstructing officers can be guilty of an offence. In fact, TSS may prosecute cases in the 'holiday sector' leading to fines and/or compensation.[133] The cases' subject matter cannot be extracted from the OFT annual reports, which summarise TSS actions in the field.

TSS may undertake their own prosecutions, but may link with the police if the investigation reveals serious fraud issues, such as tour operators' failure to protect consumers' money, collapsing the company and disappearing.[134] OFT has a role, but not day-to-day involvement, for example if Enterprise Act action is required on a matter of national importance (for example, all airlines' excluding taxes in their headline prices).

Criminal prosecutions may be brought either to the magistrates court or the Crown Court, for more serious cases.[135] In the magistrates court, the regulator undertakes the prosecution, the case is tried summarily and a maximum fine may

---

127 It is more specifically Regulations 5, 7, 8, 16 and 22 of the PTRs.

128 See Saggerson (2008), pp. 380, 551.

129 With the exception of Regulation 5 (2) PTRs.

130 See Regulation 25 (5) PTRs.

131 See Regulation 25 PTRs; Saggerson (2008), p. 552.

132 See European Commission's working paper on Enforcement of European Consumer Legislation, 27 March 1998, SEC (98) 527, p. 40.

133 See as examples of the activity of TSS the respective annexes to the annual reports of the OFT that reflect TSS's action.

134 See personal email communications with TSS (21 February 2012).

135 See Faure, Ogus and Philipsen (2008), p. 388, based on interviews with enforcers in 2006.

be imposed. However, a case brought to the Crown Court must involve the Crown Prosecution Service, which decides whether it is appropriate for the prosecution to proceed. Fines and imprisonment are possible penalties for breaches of consumer protection laws.

According to English criminal law, the court may both fine a business and award compensation orders to consumers. Criminal courts in England have a general power to order a person convicted of an offence to pay compensation for loss or damage resulting from that offence and for any personal injury or for any other offence that is taken into consideration by the court in determining the sentence.[136] If damages are also claimed in civil proceedings, these are assessed without regard to the compensation order; however, the claimant may recover only an amount equal to the aggregate of any amount that exceeds the compensation order and any portion of the compensation that was not recovered. Although the compensation order is not often used,[137] it recently has received more attention. The LASPO 2012 gave courts an express duty (rather than the current power) to consider making compensation orders when victims have suffered harm or loss, the effects of which remain to be seen.[138] This might be an interesting route against *mala fide* traders.

In the past, there have been problems with *mala fide* traders and cases of fraud have occurred.[139] This has been tackled by involving the police, for instance to check traders' identities. Some people in this instance even have gone to prison. The problem appears to be more under control now. ABTA also regularly checks websites of nonmembers.

Assessment and Conclusion

Comparing the English law enforcement system with the optimal design suggestions, the following conclusions may be drawn. As in the previously discussed countries, a low-cost mechanism is in place for easy, clear-cut cases to cross-finance. There are numerous ways to receive low-cost or free advice on consumer issues throughout the country from government-financed institutions. The arbitration offered within the travel sector is regularly used and the county courts seem to play more of a role in these case scenarios than in Sweden and the Netherlands. In contrast to the Netherlands, England like Sweden has no official system of an underlying business guarantee to secure the ADR awards. In practice, however, ABTA does not report problems with members that would not comply with the arbitration board's awards. This situation may be due to the fact that awards granted are binding and enforceable through the

136 See Hodges (2009), p. 157; Powers of Criminal Courts (Sentencing) Act 2000, ss. 130, 134.

137 See personal email communications with TSS (21 February 2012) concerning travel law.

138 Section 63 of LASPO 2012 suggests this change to the Section 130 of the Powers of Criminal Courts (Sentencing) Act 2000.

139 See interview with ABTA (London, 22 February 2011).

courts. In this sense, the value is similar to that of a court judgment. It may furthermore be related to the underlying threat of criminal law enforcement that is more imminent in England than in the other two countries. Furthermore, threats include internal sanctions like the termination of ABTA membership or fines. The £400 fine in case of a late reply to a consumer is a new element. Statistics on compliance are not available. Strikingly, few cases reach the award stage at all. Again, the problematic candidates are those that are not members of the trade association, although ABTA monitors them to some extent. There is no role of OFT in securing traders' adherence to the security mechanisms for insolvency situations. TSS are empowered with the enforcement of travel law. The evidence is inconclusive regarding how far they engage in proactive monitoring because approaches seem to vary. The prosecutions that are carried out result mostly in fines and some in compensation although overall few prosecutions are reported (examples are fraudulent uses of logos). Incidents of police involvement to ensure that traders adhere to security mechanisms were reported. This involvement is a solution to *mala fide* traders.

The *bona fide* trader case scenario can be handled through ABTA arbitration. But this system could not deal with a nonmember of ABTA who may be unlikely to agree to arbitration. Nonmembers can agree to *ad hoc* arbitration, which is also offered by the same provider for any trader. A *mala fide* trader is unlikely to agree to arbitration because of the rational suspicion that the consumer probably will not follow up with a court procedure because of the unpredictable and disproportionate court fees as well as uncertainties and 'hidden costs' involved. (Then again, initial court fees in a procedure in the county court are almost as modest as the costs involved in arbitration.) In addition, to appeal an ABTA procedure in court requires a lawyer to be involved. According to ABTA, some cases are indeed handled by the county courts, which poses a certain threat.

In striking contrast, ABTA arbitration applies the loser-pays rule to some extent and the county court has a no-cost rule. Also, in the county court, legal representation in general is not required, which reduces expected costs. Then again, *mala fide* traders may not be dealt with in the ordinary civil procedure because of a lack of information on their whereabouts that cannot be verified. So the court cannot act as an underlying threat for the ADR solution. Criminal law enforcement though is more readily available in England than in the other two countries and might induce compliance with private law enforcement solutions. Compensation is generally possible in English criminal law enforcement and might become more common with recent legislation.

More ADR proceedings end in the consumer's favour than in trader's favour. Fees are higher than in Sweden, but still potentially remedy rational apathy issues. Expertise seems to be with the ADR body. Furthermore, the pre-arbitration form may help to reduce the number of cases by inducing parties to settle their issues. Most cases are solved through mediation, which can be desirable because of lower administrative costs, provided that no party is pressured into this. Unlike Sweden, traders alone finance the ADR system in England. (The Netherlands provides a middle way, as traders are increasingly financing the ADR system). Basically, traders pay each time they use the system, which may be another reason why case numbers have decreased. If having none of the affected parties as funders of a board is a guarantee of unbiased decision-making, then the Swedish system must be preferred. There, the ARN is financed entirely by the government. The court system is almost completely financed by public funding in Sweden, by users in England and by a mix of the two in the Netherlands. It is noteworthy that in the European study, the financial threshold for consumers to bring cases to courts is lower in England than in Sweden and the Netherlands, which seems to suggest that the county court procedure is actually working, although the data does not allow firm conclusions.

There is a particularity with ADR and the lack of further development of the law in this common law country in contrast to civil law countries. This loss could be substantial in countries that strongly rely on case law.[140] ADR enhances future conflict resolution and behaviour modification. The guidelines regarding substantive law that are achieved in a civil court cannot be formulated here, the less the more non-legal players take part in the process.[141] This is particularly severe in legal systems where the value of precedents is high. However, it is doubtful that this is applicable in the travel case, in which the important legal provisions are codified as a consequence of implementing European legislation.

Again, the insolvency mechanisms do not cover situations of damages like a ruined holiday, which is like Sweden, but unlike the Netherlands. Contraventions to the legal requirement to provide for insolvency mechanisms count as criminal offences.

Applying the suggestions for optimal law enforcement mixes for cases of *mala fide* traders, an institution is needed that can both make use of investigative powers and grant damages. Such an institution would guarantee incentives for the consumers to file a suit and sufficient information to carry out this lawsuit. In addition, cross-financing of this costly mechanism must be provided, and, in fact, many traders are ABTA members who take part in the system. Is the required public law element also available in England? The crucial point is the way in which the public law element is added to the procedure. In contrast to Sweden and the Netherlands, a role for criminal law was reported more often in England. Compensation may be obtained through or thanks to a criminal procedure. It was not reported if individuals would actually seek this route, as data is unavailable. Currently OFT is not significantly involved in the travel sector regarding securing traders identities. TSS engage in monitoring to some extent, as described, but the approach seems to vary with the different regulators. They also act as prosecutors, and, interestingly, will involve the police when they reach the limits of their investigative powers as prosecutors. The police apparently have wider investigative powers. The case example reported was a fraud issue regarding precisely such a *mala fide* trader (tour operators not protecting consumers' money, collapsing the company and disappearing). Here the problem of missing investigative powers was clearly mitigated and the potential for tracing the trader increased. ABTA agreed that there is currently still some scope for abuse.

140 See Lindblom (2008a), p. 73.

141 See Lindblom (2008a), p. 72.

While the police are occasionally involved, a stronger role for TSS or a role for OFT can be advocated. This involvement may be either *ex ante*, such as ensuring security mechanisms for insolvencies (which some TSS already seem to do), or *ex post*, such as compensation for damage caused by *mala fide* traders. Remember, pure private law enforcement would fail due to a low degree of information that can be generated in the system.

In terms of signalling, traders who are not members of ABTA could be primarily targeted as ABTA monitors its own members (and incidentally nonmembers). ABTA is said to be tough on its members and by their involvement information can be generated at low cost because they know the market. Attention must be paid to incentives that might not always align with social-welfare criteria.

OFT/TSS do not seem to guarantee *ex ante* the comprehensive availability of information regarding a trader's whereabouts to the extent that the CA or the KO do; therefore, a focus on the *ex post* level may be welfare enhancing. Ways for the consumers to be granted damages in follow-on claims can be fine-tuned by involvement of public regulators or within or through a criminal trial.

Empowering the regulators with other remedies can be considered. The next case study can be indicative here.

Case 2 – Misleading Advertising

Within misleading adverting, a *bona fide* (scenario 3) and a *mala fide* (scenario 4) trader scenario are assessed. This time, the damage to the individual is small, even trifling (€15), but widespread. The competitor is a new actor, whose damage from a misleading advertisement may amount to €100,000. Alternatively, solutions are discussed in which the competitor has no interest in the case. Again, a particular focus is the behaviour of the *mala fide* trader in online transactions.

Summary of Legal Rules

Misleading advertisement is stipulated in the Consumer Protection from Unfair Trading Regulations (CPRs) 2008, which replaced the Trade Descriptions Act 1968 and the provisions of Part 3 of the Consumer Protection Act 1987, among others. The CPRs apply to businesses that deal directly with consumers. (Practices that occur higher up in the supply chain also are covered when they directly affect consumers or are likely to do so.) OFT and TSS enforce the CPRs, with powers given to the authorities under the CPRs and under the Enterprise Act 2002, including criminal sanctions and enforcement orders. ASA plays a role in self-regulation.

Damage from rogue traders engaging in unfair marketing practices is estimated at £6.6 billion.[142] A recent National Audit Office (NAO) report concluded that £4.8

142 See BIS (2011), p. 6.

billion (73 per cent) of consumer detriment from unfair and rogue practices was a result of threats that span more than one local authority area.[143]

Individual Actions The CPRs do not include provisions to grant consumers or traders an individual right to claim compensation for harm from misleading advertising. Consumers may claim compensation according to the provisions of English misrepresentation law if they can show they entered into a contract based on false assurances given to them.[144] Consequently, this law allows for rescission of the contract. However, the law of misrepresentation seems to be a complex combination of common law, equity and statute law that leaves gaps in access to justice.[145] Consumer advisers find it difficult to guide consumers in this area of the law, particularly if the misrepresentation does not constitute a breach of contract. Damage claims are possible along the lines of the common law tort of negligent misstatement in which a contract is no precondition. However, the claimant must show some sort of 'special relationship'. This is a limited right.[146] In the case study at hand, the modest damage suffered would not induce an individual to sue. From the competitor's viewpoint, an injunction could be an interesting remedy, but in reality, these actions are not happening in the courts.[147] Therefore, the Law Commission

143 See NAO (2011).

144 See OFT 'Response to the Law Commission and the Scottish Law Commission Consultation on Consumer Redress for Misleading and Aggressive Practices (July 2011), http://www.oft.gov.uk/shared_oft/reports/oft_response_to_consultations/oft1355.pdf, last accessed: 31 March 2013. For the provisions regarding B2B advertising, see Business Protection from Misleading Marketing Regulations (BPRs) 2008.

145 See Law Commission and Scottish Law Commission, 'Misrepresentation and unfair commercial practices – some initial questions' (2011), http://www.lawcom.gov.uk/misrepresentation_commercial.htm, last accessed: 31 March 2013, p. 1.

146 See Hedley Byrne & Co Ltd v Heller and Partners Ltd [1964] AC 465 regarding the 'special relationship'. It will be found to exist only where the claimant relies on the negligent statement of the representator, and the representator knew or ought to have known that the claimant was likely to rely upon the statement. Aside, the representator must know that the claimant will rely on it in entering a particular transaction or type of transaction, see Caparo Industries plc v Dickman [1990] 2 AC 605.

147 See personal communications with Professor Christopher Hodges, Head of the Centre for Socio-Legal Studies, University of Oxford/Professor of the Fundamentals of Private Law, Erasmus University Rotterdam (23 March 2011). See on interim injunctions in England more generally: N. Andrews, 'Injunctions in Support of Civil Proceedings and Arbitration', *Comparative Studies on Enforcement and Provisional Measures*, eds R. Stürner and M. Kawano (Tübingen: Mohr Siebeck, 2011) 319–44, p. 330.

suggested new legislation covering consumer rights of private redress in relation to misleading advertising and aggressive business practices.[148]

Regulatory Enforcement of Misleading Advertising (Civil Law Enforcement Side) Regulatory enforcement is divided between OFT and TSS: TSS enforce the provisions on misleading advertising at the local level and OFT takes cases of national concern.[149] OFT chooses the 'high-impact' cases, those relevant for clarifying the law, setting a precedent or having a major deterrent effect.[150] OFT (and not TSS) generally would act in cases of Internet enforcement or where the source of the problem had no clear local connection, such as a *mala fide* trader advertising online.[151] In fact, OFT has a special 'Internet enforcement team'.[152] A precondition for regulatory involvement is harm caused to the general interest.[153] This notion in the OFT Guidance is defined as 'must affect, or have the potential to affect, consumers generally or a group of consumers'.[154]

Consumer complaints play an important role in law enforcement, as do proactive monitoring and market studies.[155] Regulators extract information on consumer complaints mainly from the data that Consumer Direct collects.[156] Public regulators have various investigative powers. According to the Enterprise Act (Part 8, 'Enforcement of Certain Consumer Legislation', §§ 224), OFT and other enforcers are granted powers to obtain information, to enter premises without warrant, powers exercisable on the premises, power to enter premises with warrant and retention of documents and goods.

Regulators' actions may promote compliance, for example, through education, giving advice or guidance.[157] But regulators are also empowered to take civil

---

148 The final report of the Law Commission was issued in March 2012: see http://lawcommission.justice.gov.uk/publications/Consumer-redress.htm, last accessed: 31 March 2013.

149 See Howells (2007), p. 66; Howells and Weatherill (2005), p. 576. See personal email communications with OFT (7 October 2011).

150 Confirmed in interview with OFT (London, 22 February 2011).

151 See OFT 'Criminal Enforcement of the Consumer Protection from Unfair Trading Regulations 2008 – OFT Policy' (2010), http://www.oft.gov.uk/shared_oft/policy/OFT1273.pdf, last accessed: 31 March 2013, p. 6.

152 See http://www.oft.gov.uk/OFTwork/consumer-enforcement/internet-enforcement/#.UYOuoGdIj2k, last accessed: 31 March 2013.

153 Part 8 of the Enterprise Act does not deal with individual cases.

154 See OFT 'Enforcement of Consumer Protection Legislation – Guidance on Part 8 of the Enterprise Act' (2003), http://www.oft.gov.uk/shared_oft/business_leaflets/enterprise_act/oft512.pdf, last accessed: 31 March 2013, p. 8.

155 See Faure, Ogus and Philipsen (2008), p. 383, according to interviews carried out with officials in 2006.

156 See personal email communications with OFT (7 October 2011).

157 See OFT/BERR 'Consumer Protection from Unfair Trading – Guidance on the UK Regulations (May 2008) implementing the Unfair Commercial Practices Directive'

enforcement action in case of a breach of the CPRs, under Part 8 of the Enterprise Act 2002.[158] This action can be taken by applying to a court for an enforcement order (an injunctive or 'cease and desist' form of preventive control[159]), and a breach of any order could result in up to two years' imprisonment and/or an unlimited fine. The CPRs also stipulate criminal offences that may be prosecuted by OFT and TSS. The penalty on summary conviction is a fine not exceeding the statutory maximum (£5,000) and on conviction on indictment, is an unlimited fine or imprisonment for up to two years or both.[160] (These powers are discussed under the criminal law section.)

Therefore, in a misleading advertising case, the public regulators have enforcement powers through the civil court. Normally an attempt to solve the case through a voluntary undertaking by the trader must be made first; only if 'urgent action' is needed may the enforcement order be made immediately. For this order, the enforcement authority has to satisfy the civil burden of proof. An enforcement order by the civil court directs someone to comply, by not continuing or repeating the conduct, not engaging in such conduct in the course of any business or not consenting to or colluding in the carrying out of such conduct by a company. Instead of seeking an order, an undertaking by a person not to engage in or repeat the conduct that constitutes an infringement can be accepted.[161] While there is no penalty attached to an enforcement order, a breach of the order can lead to proceedings for contempt of court with, as said, an unlimited fine and/or imprisonment up to two years in cases of noncompliance.[162]

Upon application of the public regulator, the court may issue an injunction on terms considered fit to secure compliance with the CPRs. OFT routinely publishes details of orders or undertakings relating to consumer enforcement investigations.[163]

In OFT's capacity in consumer law (unlike its capacity in competition law), it cannot fine a company directly, despite some companies' beliefs.[164] In a 2006 survey, OFT considered its powers to deal with rogue traders in consumer law as inadequate[165] and officials regarded the inability to impose financial penalty as the deficiency.[166]

The RESA 2008 introduced a framework for new civil powers for regulators. This set of powers consists of fixed monetary penalty notices for up to £3,000,

---

(2008), http://www.oft.gov.uk/shared_oft/business_leaflets/cpregs/oft1008.pdf, last accessed: 31 March 2013, p. 53.

158 See Section 26 CPRs 'Application of Part 8 of Enterprise Act 2002'.

159 See M. Koutsias and C. Willett, 'The Unfair Commercial Practices Directive in the UK', *Erasmus Law Review* 5.4 (2012): 237–51, p. 238.

160 See Section 13 CPRs.

161 See Sections 219 and 217 (9) Enterprise Act.

162 See Ogus, Faure and Philipsen (2006), p. 43.

163 See personal email communications with OFT (7 October 2011).

164 See interview with OFT (London, 22 February 2011).

165 See Howells (2007), p. 75.

166 See Faure, Ogus and Philipsen (2008), p. 386. Officials interviewed in 2006 regarded the possibility of an introduction of a financial penalty as very positive, however not if it led to the removal of the power to, in appropriate cases, undertake a criminal prosecution.

discretionary requirements (a variable monetary penalty up to the lesser of £500,000; a compliance notice with a £2,000 penalty for failure to comply; or a restoration notice), stop notices and enforcement undertakings. Among others, this new law includes fining powers. For breaches of CPRs, empowering TSS and OFT with the listed civil law sanctions as a pilot scheme is envisaged. The scheme was originally to start in April 2011, but was put on hold to await the restructuring of the English consumer law enforcement landscape.[167]

Currently, while a speedy reaction is regarded as crucial, interim measures that would be fast are less common.[168] Injunctions are not obtained in a remarkably fast way.

Generally the public law enforcement dimension can aid the pursuit of private rights, as previously expressed, where the evidence of the contravention is used in the civil proceedings. OFT can bring cases to court, for instance test cases.[169] In terms of interrelations between the two case studies, OFT took action in relation to misleading advertisements in the travel sector.[170] Various other cases in which OFT became involved concerned unfair commercial practices.[171]

Available Forms of Group Litigation In a case of widespread damage, joining individual claims is crucial and England provides various forms of group claims.[172] Individual claims may be consolidated via an opt-in procedure, as established in

167 See OFT/LBRO (Local Better Regulation Office) 'Civil Sanctions Pilot Joint consultation by the OFT and LBRO on the operation of the BIS Civil Sanctions Pilot' (2010), http://www.oft.gov.uk/shared_oft/consultations/OFT1296.pdf, last accessed: 31 March 2013.

168 See interview with OFT (London, 22 February 2011).

169 See Hodges (2009), p. 152. Please access the OFT Consumer enforcement case archive, http://www.oft.gov.uk/OFTwork/consumer-enforcement/consumer-enforcement-archive/#.UfC9W43wmSo, last accessed: 31 March 2013.

170 See 'OFT secures enforcement orders against holiday club companies' (6 May 2011), http://www.oft.gov.uk/news-and-updates/press/2011/58-11, last accessed: 31 March 2013; Final Enforcement Order against Martin White, Jonathan Daniels, Mark Gales, Robert Knight and Lily Alderson sealed by the High Court of Justice on 19 April 2011.

171 See the overview available on the OFT homepage. An example concerning small and widespread damage: 'OFT stops misleading premium rate scratchcard promotion' (1 March 2006), http://www.oft.gov.uk/news-and-updates/press/2006/41-06, last accessed: 31 March 2013, around £9 damage per consumer, responses: nearly 45,000.

172 See Loos and Van Boom (2010), p. 188. See Response of the Bar Council of England and Wales to the EU Commission's public consultation 'Towards a coherent European approach to collective redress' (2009), http://ec.europa.eu/competition/consultations/2011_collective_redress/bcew_en.pdf, last accessed: 31 March 2013, p. 5.

the Group Litigation Order (GLO), to have representative actions, test cases and consolidation of claims.[173]

The GLO, the most popular group litigation mechanism (19.11 [2] and [3], CPR[174]),[175] serves for cases of common or related questions that must be answered in a comparable case ('a number of claims giving rise to common or related issues of fact or law').[176] The GLO is not regarded as representative litigation despite the possibility of bringing individual test or lead cases during the procedure.[177] A GLO provides for case management of claims that give rise to common or related issues of fact or law. Any party to a claim (claimant or defendant) or the court itself may initiate the procedure.[178] A lead solicitor is selected.[179] The individual claims become part of a bigger centrally organised procedure via an opt-in procedure and are registered in the GLO register.[180] As mentioned, the court has the discretion to select one or some test/lead cases; for instance, all cases may be stayed except for one, or a small number of test case(s). In addition, the loser in these procedures incurs significant costs because the lawyers' fees are considerable and the special knowledge required for these cases is shared among a small number of judges and lawyers. Therefore, the law firms involved are familiar players ('steering groups' are put together for complex cases).[181] The court will normally divide orders for costs between the individual costs and the common costs of the group.[182] Cases where media interest was considerable reportedly have led to many people gathering, which may sometimes introduce a fraudulent element.

The GLO has been used in a number of cases, including damage cases.[183] Since 2000, more than 70 GLOs have been made. However, the procedure is not very successful and is used only in cases of substantial claims.[184] The major problem is the funding.[185] There are no special arrangements for trifling and widespread harm, which reduces the GLO's suitability for the case scenario at hand. These procedures are reserved for high-value claims with complex procedures, which

173 See Hodges (2008), p. 2.

174 See Practice Direction 19B – Group litigation. This practice direction supplements Section III of Part 19.

175 See Howells (2006), p. 3.

176 See Loos and Van Boom (2010), p. 188.

177 See Hodges (2008), p. 2.

178 See Hodges (2009), p. 153.

179 See Section 2.2. Practice Direction 19B.

180 See Section 6.1. Practice Direction 19B.

181 See Hodges (2008), p. 11. The practice that has emerged, certainly in the product liability GLOs, has overwhelmingly been that of test cases.

182 See Howells (2008), p. 22.

183 See Hodges (2009), p. 154 for some examples.

184 See Hodges (2008), p. 35. See for a list of the GLO procedures that have been initiated: also his annex on p. 37.

185 See Hodges (2009), p. 154.

generally would be personal injury claims.[186] Some judges may lack experience in applying this mechanism.[187]

GLO matters have broadened lately beyond product liability cases to include abuse in childcare homes, holiday disasters and transport crashes.[188] Another area in which GLOs have been brought is against the government regarding tax issues. Despite substantial detriment to society, the GLO procedure is not a rational choice in cases with small and widespread harm,[189] such as the case scenarios.

These types of cases would typically not be allocated to the small claims track.[190] This has important costs implications because in the small claims track the 'loser-pays' rule would not apply. Courts fees can be substantial, and, therefore, do not decrease rational apathy.[191] Lawyers' fees can be estimated at £750,000 (assuming 3,000 hours at £250 per hour). Litigation costs are at least the same in a GLO as in individual redress. Despite a GLO, some individual aspects might still have to be litigated (or negotiated) individually such as damage levels. CFAs might be a financing possibility.

The representative action was developed in case law (now stipulated in Section 19.6 CPR) and can be employed when more than one person has the same interest in a claim. The requirement of a 'same interest' is interpreted strictly.[192] The representative must also have an interest in the case. If the conditions of same interest are met, a judgment in a representative action will be binding on all persons represented in the claim. The judgment may be enforced by or against a person who is not a party to that claim only with the court's permission. Therefore, representative action would not typically be used in consumer cases. Again, the fact that damages are based on separate contracts complicates matters. Outcomes that are declaratory in nature are more easily achievable with this procedure. Public funding is unlikely to be available (except for serious product liability claims), but CFAs are a possibility. Overall representative actions are used very rarely.[193]

As appears from the descriptions above, test cases may be litigated under any of these collective action procedures[194] and are matter for case management. Test cases are not a separate form of action and do not have specific rules under the CPR. 'Consolidation' is a phenomenon that allows the judge to use discretion in order to combine procedures. However, this is rarely used in practice. One explanation for why these procedures are rarely used is that the English courts' wide

186 See Howells (2006), p. 1.
187 See Howells (2006), p. 3.
188 As summarised by Hodges (2008), p. 20.
189 See Hodges (2008), p. 35.
190 See Howells (2008), p. 24.
191 See Howells (2008), p. 20.
192 See Hodges (2008), p. 2; Howells (2008), p. 27.
193 See Hodges (2009), p. 153.
194 See Response of the Bar Council of England and Wales (2009), p. 5.

case management powers render these procedures to a certain extent unnecessary.[195] Having said this, any court claim involving private enforcement will be slow and costly, which is true for individual and mass litigation.[196] Collective damage actions are basically nonexistent for small and widespread harm.[197]

Role of Consumer Associations The focus of the current consumer policy is on 'consistent and expert oversight by public authorities' more than on a large amount of private litigation.[198] The primary enforcement powers rest firmly with public authorities; however, consumer associations also have been granted certain rights to bring collective actions.[199] The availability of Legal Aid during the 1980s and 1990s has had a significant impact on the development of the group action phenomenon.[200] Legal actions may be brought by approved consumer representative bodies, rather than an *ad hoc* group of individuals who join forces. There is no single official definition or criterion in England for determining what a consumer organisation at the national level is. The most powerful consumer association is 'Which?'.[201] With around 700,000 members in the UK, it is the largest consumer organisation in Europe and is independent of government and industry.

Which? could have a role in seeking injunctions against misleading advertising, but in practice it does not.[202] Likewise, it is empowered for cross-border actions. The organisation rarely gets involved with test cases[203] and in practice its role is very limited.[204] Consumer associations reportedly have little enthusiasm for taking a wider or more significant role in enforcement, although cooperation between them and OFT is good.[205] Rather than litigation, consumer associations have seen their role as providing primarily advisory services and a lobbying function.[206] The

195 See personal email communications Professor Christopher Hodges, Head of the Centre for Socio-Legal Studies, University of Oxford/ Professor of the Fundamentals of Private Law, Erasmus University Rotterdam (January 2012). See C. Hodges 'The Buncefield Litigation', book contribution (forthcoming 2013).

196 See Creutzfeldt-Banda, Hodges and Benöhr (2012), 253–353.

197 See Loos and Van Boom (2010), p. 188.

198 See Hodges (2008), p. 20.

199 See Hodges (2008), p. 4.

200 See Hodges (2008), p. 26.

201 See interview with OFT (London, 22 February 2011). See http://www.which.co.uk/, last accessed: 31 March 2013.

202 See Hodges (2008), p. 20.

203 See personal communications with Professor Christopher Hodges, Head of the Centre for Socio-Legal Studies, University of Oxford/ Professor of the Fundamentals of Private Law, Erasmus University Rotterdam (23 March 2011).

204 See Hodges (2008), p. 6.

205 See interview with OFT (London, 22 February 2011).

206 See personal email communications Professor Christopher Hodges, Head of the Centre for Socio-Legal Studies, University of Oxford/ Professor of the Fundamentals of Private Law, Erasmus University Rotterdam (January 2012).

primary enforcement body is a public body, OFT.[207] Consumer associations are involved as watchdogs, compensating deficiencies in resources of the regulator in market surveillance.

Which? was active in a follow-on damage case in competition law, not consumer law, according to the Competition Act 1998. The organisation used this procedure once in a case with various companies that were involved in cartel price fixing of replica football T-shirts.[208] The case revealed various procedural weaknesses and was settled in 2008.[209] Which? is reportedly reluctant to bring such claims in the future because there is no public support for such cases and the specified body bringing the case is potentially liable for costs on the usual basis.[210]

BTE and trade union insurance are unlikely to cover group cases.[211] Collective CFAs are permitted for trade unions, commercial organisations and others providing or purchasing legal services for groups.[212] An impact might be felt by an increasing involvement of commercial third-party funders.[213]

Therefore, considering this case scenario with a small and widespread claim, a solution that includes compensation is highly unlikely. There is a gap stated between successful enforcement action and adequate consumer compensation.[214] A higher impact is possible when it comes to injunctive actions.

Interrelationship between Regulators and Consumer Associations Some cooperation and monitoring occurs between consumer associations and public regulators. Regular discussions take place between OFT and consumer associations to identify future priorities.[215] Which? may seek injunctions, but it generally does not, preferring to bring matters to OFT. Associations cooperate with the public authorities in providing information.[216] In the OFT-administered forum 'Consumer Concurrencies Group' regulators may exchange information. Also, close liaisons exist between OFT and Citizens Advice and Consumer Focus.[217]

Consumer associations play a real role in the super-complaint mechanism, which allows a private body to act as the watchdog of the public authority when

207 See Hodges (2007), p. 216.

208 The legal action followed a Decision of the Office of Fair Trading, No CA98/06/2003, Competition Act 1998, Price-fixing of Replica Football Kit.

209 See Hodges (2009), p. 162.

210 See Howells (2008), p. 36.

211 See Hodges (2008), p. 26.

212 See Hodges (2008), p. 26.

213 Third party funding is a recent phenomenon, see Peysner (2010), p. 294.

214 See J. Peysner and A. Nurse, 'Representative Actions and Restorative Justice: A Report for the Department for Business, Enterprise and Regulatory Reform (BERR)' (2008), http://www.bis.gov.uk/files/file51559.pdf, last accessed: 31 March 2013.

215 See interview with OFT (London, 22 February 2011).

216 The OFT can lodge a formal request via Section 9 Enterprise Act. This is generally not necessary. Associations would normally give prior notice and pass on the information.

217 See Annual report OFT 2010, p. 38.

a market feature or a combination of features may significantly harm consumer interests.[218] This power was first given to consumer associations in the 2002 Enterprise Act.[219] When a super-complaint is filed, OFT has 90 days to publish a response stating how it proposes to deal with the complaint.

The Secretary of State designates the empowered consumer associations.[220] Any body that is not empowered can still make complaints to OFT. Once a complaint is received, the super-complainant is acknowledged and within five working days someone within OFT or the relevant regulator is designated to be the main contact during the 90-day period. This assigned official and supporting team examines the complaint in detail and determines if all requirements are met (Section 11). Next, the team assesses the quality of information and evidence supplied and decides if the information is sufficient or if further evidence or clarification is required. At the same time, the team evaluates if the super-complaint is frivolous or vexatious, which would lead to a rejection of the complaint. Cooperation with other regulators that should be involved is also possible throughout the procedure. Further information may be requested from the complainant if the team considers the complainant competent to obtain this information. Alternatively, the public authority may gather the information itself if it is in a better position to investigative. The 90-day period may be extended under special circumstances, such as the complainant cannot provide further information in time. In a meeting between the team and the super-complainant, the evidence submitted and the continuation of the inquiry may be discussed. Further investigations, decided on a case-by-case basis, may include internal research, public requests for information and approaching trade associations, consumer organisations, TSS, government departments and/or other public bodies for information.

The public response that is given must include information on the action that the regulator proposes to take on the issue, such as enforcement action by OFT's competition or consumer regulation divisions, launching a market study into the issue or referrals to competent bodies to take further action. OFT may also find that the complaint requires no action because it was unfounded, frivolous or vexatious.

Several organisations have brought super-complaints on issues such as private dentistry, doorstep selling, the care homes market, postal services and doorstep credit. The role of the designated authorities is mainly to alert and provide information to regulators, which reflects the British approach that regulators should carry out enforcement and consumers and consumer associations should be the watchdogs ('biting is reserved for the public authority').[221] Note that some

218 See for a short description also Hodges (2009), p. 161 and see the OFT 'Super-complaints: Guidance for designated consumer bodies' (2002), http://www.oft.gov.uk/shared_oft/business_leaflets/enterprise_act/oft514.pdf, last accessed: 31 March 2013.

219 See Section 11 Enterprise Act.

220 See Section 11 of Enterprise Act. For instance: The Consumers' Association (Which?).

221 See Hodges (2008), p. 9.

consumer associations may find it burdensome to provide the necessary evidence for such a proceeding.

The Role of Self-regulation England is considered a leading example of effective self-regulation within Europe.[222] Self-regulation in advertising, administered by ASA, has gradually evolved since 1961[223] and after a period of decline it has had a resurgence in the past two decades.[224] Self-regulation is designed to be independent from both the government and the advertising industry. One finds a mixture of self-regulation for non-broadcast advertising and co-regulation for broadcast advertising. Overall ASA today regulates all TV and radio advertisements under the Broadcast Committee of Advertising Practice (BCAP) TV Advertising Standards Code and the BCAP Radio Advertising Standards Code. Advertisings in non-broadcast media (such as print, posters, cinema, direct marketing and pop-up ads) are under the British Code of Advertising, Sales Promotion and Direct Marketing (the CAP Code). The CAP, BCAP and ASA operate independently, but share the same secretariat.[225] Members of these committees are advertisers, media owners and agencies (including individual broadcasters).

Office of Communications (Ofcom), the communications regulator established in 2003, contracted out the responsibility for broadcast (TV and radio) advertising to the ASA system in a co-regulatory partnership. In 2009, this scheme was expanded when ASA entered into a co-regulatory partnership with Ofcom to regulate advertisings accompanying video-on-demand (VOD) services.[226] With the ASA digital remit extension in March 2011, regulation of companies' own websites and other space under an advertiser's own control, like Facebook, was included.

The codes of the advertising industry go beyond what the law requires; they reflect the law, but are stricter and regularly updated with every new law.[227] When setting up or updating codes, wide public consultations are held. While legal rules may sometimes allow circumventing the wording of the law, in the codes the spirit of the law must be observed, which renders this practice impossible.

The majority of claims concern misleading advertising.[228] Anyone can complain (anonymously); traders bring about 5 to 10 per cent of complaints and consumers bring the rest, the clear majority.[229] The procedure is free of charge for

222 See OFT 'Policy statement – The role of self-regulation in the OFT's consumer protection work' (2009), http://www.oft.gov.uk/shared_oft/reports/consumer-policy/oft1115.pdf, last accessed: 31 March 2013, p. 4.

223 See for the history of the ASA, http://www.asa.org.uk/, last accessed: 31 March 2013.

224 See Hodges, Draft Note on ASA (2011) (on file with the author).

225 See Hodges, Draft Note on ASA (2011).

226 See Hodges, Draft Note on ASA (2011).

227 See interview with ASA (London, 23 February 2011).

228 See interview with ASA (London, 23 February 2011).

229 See personal email communications with ASA (23 February 2011).

the complainant and must be initiated within three months of the airing. While ASA can act upon just one complaint, a higher number of complaints has an impact, for example, in questions of taste and decency. The adjudication takes place within ASA's council whose members are independent of the advertising industry (two-thirds) and industry experts (one-third).[230]

Upon reception of a complaint, the Complaints Reception Team establishes whether it falls within ASA's remit. If so, the complaint is passed on to the Complaints Team that contacts the advertiser and asks for comments. The advertiser must produce evidence, if required, without delay. Among the types of action that ASA can take when assessing an ad against the codes are: no case to answer; no case to answer after council discussion; informal resolution or formal investigation. An informal resolution of complaints is possible if the advertiser accepts the complaint and/or offers to amend or remove it.[231]

If a breach occurs, ASA expects advertisers to adapt their advertisement to the code as quickly as possible.[232] Media and media owners play an important role in blocking advertisements. Directories are published only yearly and direct action is impossible. Only a few advertisers fail to comply with ASA's rulings. In cases of noncompliance, cooperation from media owners is necessary, and a 'name and shame' technique (weekly publications of adjudications) is used, which is effective in an industry relying on reputation. Adverse publicity is said to be the most potent sanction available to ASA.[233] Another type of sanction is the refusal by media owners to feature ads that break the codes and through a cooperative arrangement with Royal Mail, traders may lose their discounts.[234]

Both sides have 21 days to ask the Independent Reviewer of ASA Adjudications to review the case for any apparent substantial flaw of process or adjudication or if additional relevant evidence becomes available. If the Independent Reviewer accepts the case, the other parties will be informed and invited to comment. The process ends with a recommendation to the ASA Council which may ask for the council to reconsider its ruling. The council's adjudication on reviewed cases is final.

There are wide provisions of preclearance that are different for broadcast and the non-broadcast areas. The vast majority of TV and radio ads are precleared. For non-broadcast advertisers, help is found through the so-called Copy Advice team. For broadcast advertisers, Advertising Codes require that all claims be substantiated before being published or aired, which leads to most of them being precleared. In accordance with their licenses, broadcasters must ensure that the

230 The Nolan Principles for public appointments are observed. See Hodges, Draft Note on ASA (2011).

231 See Hodges, Draft Note on ASA (2011). In these cases the ASA nevertheless publishes a decision, stating that the matter has been resolved informally.

232 See interview with ASA (London, 23 February 2011).

233 See Howells and Weatherill (2005), p. 423, referring as an example to the case British Airways v Ryanair [2001] FSR 541.

234 See interview with ASA (London, 23 February 2011).

advertisings they broadcast are compliant with the TV and Radio Advertising Codes, and broadcasters are obliged by a condition of their broadcast licenses to enforce ASA rulings. If they persistently run advertisements that breach the advertising codes, broadcasters risk being referred by ASA to Ofcom. Ofcom can impose fines and even withdraw their broadcasting license. If ASA upholds a complaint (against the BCAP Code), the broadcaster is responsible for ensuring the ad does not reappear.[235] There are two 'preclearance centres': Clearcast for television commercials and the Radio Advertising Clearance Centre (RACC) for radio ads. This is very interesting from the point of view of giving guidance to the *bona fide* trader, but seems to almost pressure the *mala fide* trader, too, because of the underlying threat of revocation of the broadcaster's license.

For non-broadcast advertising, which entail a mass amount of ads, complete control is impossible.[236] The volume is estimated at more than 30 million press advertisings and 100 million pieces of direct marketing each year. The CAP Copy Advice, financed by the industry, provides some guidance, and, therefore, the *bona fide* trader may ask for help. The team generates free prepublication advice for traders to guide them in creating advertisements that align with the CAP Code. Copy Advice maintains a searchable online database available to check current laws and publishes a free quarterly email newsletter. Tailored advice on individual campaigns is provided. Seeking advice or even receiving preclearance is no guarantee that a complaint might not be substantiated against the advertisement because until an ad is aired, the consumer's reaction cannot be forecast.[237]

On very few occasions ASA has been taken to court for judicial review and although it lost the first case, it has won on all occasions ever since.[238] Therefore, this outcome may signal that the courts tend not to interfere with ASA decisions. The situation described in 2005 indicated that most matters were dealt with by ASA and those that progressed end at OFT.[239] Litigation is very uncommon. A relationship can be seen between the court's attitude of not squashing ASA rulings and allowing ASA a margin of discretion.[240] Furthermore, court injunctions have no role to play because when an individual compares court costs to those of the

235 See personal email communications with ASA (12 October 2011).

236 See interview with ASA (London, 23 February 2011).

237 See interview with ASA (London, 23 February 2011).

238 See interview with ASA (London, 23 February 2011).

239 See Howells and Weatherill (2005), p. 426.

240 As compiled by G. Howells: in the case R v ASA, ex parte SmithKline Beecham plc [2001] EMLR 23, no danger of bias in the ASA procedure was acknowledged despite involving advice from an individual whose negative views on the health aspects of the product were already known as the decision-making process had been kept separate from this advice. The judicial review of the ASA decision was therefore very limited, similarly in R v ASA, ex parte Vernons [1992] 1 WLR 1289 and R v ASA, ex parte Charles Robertson (Developments) Ltd, The Times 26 November 1999. In Director-General of Fair Trading v Tobyward Ltd [1989] 2 All ER 266 an injunction at the OFT was granted that backed ASA's findings.

ASA procedure, the individual will always prefer the latter.[241] Indeed the ASA services are sufficient for the *bona fide* trader.[242]

ASA is entirely funded by advertisers through a voluntary levy on advertising spending: 0.1 per cent on display advertising expenditures and airtime and 0.2 per cent of the Royal Mail's Mailsort contract. No government funding is received. Two separate bodies collect the levies, the Advertising Standards Board of Finance (Asbof) and the Broadcast Advertising Standards Board of Finance (Basbof). Each year, ASA pitches to Asbof and Basbof for its funding for the following year. ASA does not know which advertisers choose to fund the system or the amount they contribute.

In 2012, ASA handled 31,298 complaints, of which 3,700 ads were changed or withdrawn.[243] Compliance surveys revealed that more than 94 per cent of the advertisements were in line with the codes. There were 6,979 requests for copy advice in 2012. Overall, complaints to ASA account for less than one per cent of total ads seen each year. The independent reviewer received 66 complaints and recommended that the ASA Council reconsider 17. In 2009, complaints were resolved within an average of 13 working days. Nearly half of all complaints to ASA concern misleading advertising claims.[244]

ASA can and does refer non-broadcast advertisers that persistently breach the codes to OFT for legal action (under the CPRs and the Business Protection from Misleading Marketing Regulations [BPRs] 2008); similarly, ASA refers broadcast advertisers to Ofcom, which is empowered to fine them or even revoke their licenses. Such referrals are rarely necessary. Between 2005 and 2010, ASA referred only three cases to OFT.[245] Referrals to OFT have been possible since 1988 and the first referral in 1989 resulted in an injunction to prevent misleading claims for Speedslim. In addition, Ryanair was among the approximately 30 referrals made in the last ten years.[246] ASA sees little scope left for *mala fide* traders.[247] In cases of foreign advertisers and direct mailing, the cooperation through EASA is helpful. According to OFT, ASA is normally the first instance, even though there is no obligation.[248] OFT takes legal action in cases of national importance or when ASA fails to achieve progress. TSS, which are responsible for local advertising, back up ASA.[249] ASA believes industry sanctions – negative publicity, withholding media

241 See personal communications with Professor Christopher Hodges, Head of the Centre for Socio-Legal Studies, University of Oxford/Professor of the Fundamentals of Private Law, Erasmus University Rotterdam (23 March 2011).

242 See interview with OFT (London, 22 February 2011).

243 See Annual report ASA 2012, pp. 27, 29.

244 See Annual report ASA 2009. See for the standard performance 2012 Annual report ASA 2012, p. 31.

245 See Hodges, Draft Note on ASA (2011).

246 See personal email communications with ASA (23 February 2011).

247 See interview with ASA (London, 23 February 2011).

248 See interview with OFT (London, 22 February 2011).

249 See interview with OFT (London, 22 February 2011).

space and so on – are effective. The threat of referral to OFT for misleading non-broadcast advertising or to Ofcom for any noncompliant broadcaster, is a powerful incentive for advertisers to comply,[250] although a minority of rogue traders resists these enforcement efforts.[251] OFT infrequently refers cases to ASA.[252] Self-regulation is suggested to work best if there is a strong governmental supervisory body involved.[253] As mentioned, cooperation for a self-regulatory body with Internet media owners is a challenge. ASA argues that they cope well with the recent expansion of its remit to a wide amount of Internet advertisement.

TSS have asked ASA to provide evidence for court procedures.[254] As far as using outcomes of ASA decisions for damage cases in courts is concerned, there do not seem to be any cases involving consumers.[255] The weaknesses in the current English law when it comes to granting individual damages are outlined above. Furthermore, criminal law enforcement has a role to play. Obscure shop window advertising was given as an example for police involvement.[256]

Criminal Law Enforcement in Advertising The CPRs define criminal offences that may be prosecuted by OFT and TSS, as well as providing an independent role for the police and criminal courts. While TSS have traditionally had criminal enforcement powers in relation to misleading advertising,[257] OFT was given these only with the CPRs: Article 13 reads, 'A person guilty of an offence under regulation 8, 9, 10, 11 or 12 shall be liable (a) on summary conviction, to a fine not exceeding the statutory maximum; or (b) on conviction on indictment, to a fine or imprisonment for a term not exceeding two years or both'.

Both bodies may enforce the 2008 CPRs and may bring criminal prosecution regarding the various offences stipulated.[258] The CPRs apply to commercial practices before, during and after a contract is formed; misleading advertising falls under Regulation 9. It is a strict liability offence and due diligence[259] and innocent

250 See personal email communications with ASA (12 October 2011).

251 See Howells and Weatherill (2005), p. 423.

252 See personal email communications with ASA (12 October 2011).

253 See Hodges (2007), p. 224.

254 See interview with ASA (London, 23 February 2011).

255 See interview with ASA (London, 23 February 2011).

256 See interview with ASA (London, 23 February 2011).

257 See for instance the Trade Descriptions Act 1968 in Section 18 combined with 26 (enforcer). The act also sets out TSS investigative powers.

258 See Regulation 2: 'enforcement authority' means OFT, every local weights and measures authority in Great Britain (within the meaning of Section 69 of the Weights and Measures Act 1985(1)) and the Department of Enterprise, Trade and Investment in Northern Ireland.

259 The defendant can 'prove that commission of the offence was due to a mistake, reliance on information supplied, the act or default of another, an accident or some other cause beyond the defendant's control and that all reasonable precautions were taken and all due diligence exercised to avoid the commission' (See Regulation 17).

publication[260] (catalogue, circulars and price-lists advertising) are possible defenses. Again, the corporate veil may be pierced.[261]

As outlined above, compensation orders are applicable as part of the ordinary criminal law. The CPRs do not contain any provisions on accelerated procedures, and, therefore, the general court rules apply that allow for expedited interim injunctions.[262] This order will prevent publication of the offending advertising until the case can be fully argued in court, after which a court order may prevent further publication. The regulations provide that the injunction can be granted without proof of actual loss or damage or without proof of intention or negligence on the part of the advertiser. Those who fail to follow court orders are held in contempt of court.

Regulators do not necessarily have to await a complaint to take action, but can act on an own motion. OFT took a criminal consumer case to conclusion in 2012 in which the accused went to prison.[263] Compensation to consumers was possible, but was not awarded in this case.

OFT must make the decision to prosecute a case under criminal law in accordance with the two-stage test established in the Code for Crown Prosecutors, which include the evidential sufficiency test and the public interest test.[264] Like TSS, OFT may involve the police if necessary[265] and in the case mentioned, the police arrested the accused.

Despite criminal measures being those of last resort, TSS brought 3,929 prosecutions in 1999–2004 under the Trade Descriptions Act.[266] However, in 2010, no specific evidence appeared to indicate that criminal law is currently being used as the primary means to enforce consumer protection.[267] The ability to pursue criminal enforcement has enhanced OFT's powers, assessed as inadequate in 2006. In discussions for the RESA 2008, it was generally expressed that criminal powers should be reserved for more serious breaches, real rogue traders and failures to comply with civil sanctions.[268] This reasoning reflects the

---

260 See Regulation 18 CPRs.

261 See Regulation 15(1) CPRs.

262 See European Commission Unfair Commercial Practices (UCP) portal, https://webgate.ec.europa.eu/ucp/public/index.cfm?event=public.country.showCountry&countryID=UK, last accessed: 31 March 2013.

263 See CRE-E/26641 OFT investigation into Colin Michael Ogle t/a Swindon Decodes.

264 See OFT (2010), p. 12; see Code for Crown Prosecutors.

265 See personal email communications with OFT (15 December 2011).

266 See Chartered Institute of Public Finance, compiled data 2005 that was made available to Faure, Ogus and Philipsen (2008).

267 See OFT 'Criminal Liability in Regulatory Contexts Response to the Law Commission consultation' (2010), http://www.oft.gov.uk/shared_oft/consultations/OFT1285res.pdf, last accessed: 31 March 2013, p. 8: Only 1.5 to 2 per cent of defendants tried in the Crown Court are tried for offences arising out of regulatory contexts.

268 See OFT (2010), p. 8.

deterrence approach adopted in this book. Criminal enforcement powers should be reserved for *mala fide* traders.[269]

Again, public law enforcement is superior to private enforcement in its investigative powers. The CPRs[270] provide OFT and TSS with investigation powers that are a modernised version of those granted under the Trade Descriptions Act 1968 and wider than those under the Enterprise Act.

Enforcement officers have the power to check compliance with the CPRs by purchasing or securing the provision of products. Under certain circumstances they also may enter premises and seize or detain goods or documents.[271] In practice, effective remedies appear to result from coordination with other regulators, such as providing information or taking action when it comes to disconnecting telephone lines, for example.[272] OFT has powers under criminal and civil legislation to request information from others in relation to an enforcement issue, which could include ISPs or communications providers for details of an IP address. The powers are enforceable by a court if needed, and, therefore, are better than that of an individual:[273] for example, in a 2010 investigation of unauthorised traders selling Fédération Internationale de Football Association (FIFA) World Cup tickets, OFT communicated with the Internet service provider for the traders' websites.[274] As mentioned, the police may be involved when OFT acts as a prosecutor and the police have a wider range of powers, such as covert surveillance, that are superior to those of regulators.[275]

Public regulators are not obligated to carry out an investigation into a consumer complaint. OFT cannot intervene or provide details for individual consumers who seek to take action on their own to find a trader. OFT has investigative powers only for cases it is investigating and not on the behalf of consumers.[276] The wide investigative powers also do not apply to market studies.[277] According to Section 5 of the Enterprise Act 2002, OFT may commission research, but has no real information-gathering powers equivalent to those it has relating to cases.

---

269 This can increase investigative powers. See OFT (2008), p. 9.

270 See Part 4 of the CPRs.

271 See OFT 'Guidance for the use of on-site inspection powers under the Consumer Protection Cooperation Regulation' (2009), http://www.oft.gov.uk/shared_oft/business_leaflets/general/oft884.pdf, last accessed: 31 March 2013.

272 See interview with OFT (London, 22 February 2011). Regulators cooperate via official cooperation agreements.

273 See personal email communications with OFT (15 December 2011).

274 See OFT 'Investigation into sales of 2010 FIFA World Cup tickets by unauthorised traders' (Case reference: CRE-E-24580) (2010), http://www.oft.gov.uk/OFTwork/consumer-enforcement/consumer-enforcement-completed/fifa/#.UfDDVI3wmSo, last accessed: 31 March 2013.

275 See personal email communications with OFT (15 December 2011).

276 See personal email communications with OFT (27 October 2011).

277 See personal email communications with OFT (15 December 2011).

Assessment and Conclusion

As in the two previous country analyses, England has a mixed system that includes a public authority and self-regulation in advertising. Whereas this analysis focuses on cases with trifling and widespread harm that require a 'public law element' for high information asymmetry, the individual competitor's damage from misleading advertising may be substantive. Consumer damage cases related to misleading advertising do not appear in the courts. Possible remedies are currently not feasible and reforms are suggested.

Unlike in Sweden and the Netherlands, England has no general ADR board where the case can be brought, a mechanism that could in some cases potentially remedy rational apathy. ADR bodies are available in some sectors, however. In advertising, the self-regulatory body ASA is a low-cost player, which does not grant damages. To some degree, the body allows for a cross-financing of cases with high information asymmetry. The body may act upon one complaint, but a high number of complaints may have greater impact, for instance in questions of taste and decency.

Collective damage actions are basically nonexistent for small and widespread harm. The various procedures for joining claims within the ambit of case management currently depend a lot on the judge's abilities. Even when claims can be joined, substantial problems arise from the different methods for calculation of damages among slightly different scenarios. The GLO provides some potential for joint damage claims; however, as is typically the case, the biggest problem is lack of funding. Then again, courts are said to be very flexible when utilising case management. Aggregate solutions for alternative remedies, like injunctions, might work. Therefore, there is potential for improvement in enabling claims for small and widespread damage as an alternative threat for regulators' action or to actions for injunctions.

Regulators have a number of powers for alternative legal responses, and reforms that would expand them are currently discussed. OFT/TSS and their investigative powers can be efficient in relation to *mala fide* traders, particularly when joined with the powers of the police in criminal prosecutions. Likewise, following the approach of responsive regulation, regulators target *bona fide* and *mala fide* traders differently. In other words, remedies/sanctions may be tailored to the offence and the mind-set of the trader. In OFT self-initiated investigations, OFT employees may use the available investigative powers (including tracking IP addresses and getting in touch with Internet address providers). Internet enforcement, as in this case scenario where no location is given, falls generally within the competence of OFT and not the local TSS; OFT has a special 'Internet enforcement team'. The investigative powers are more limited in market studies than in legal actions. In a criminal procedure, wide investigative powers are available to search for *mala fide* traders. Within ASA, the information that can be generated by people involved in the sector can be absorbed and incentives are high for competitors, consumer associations or even single consumers to bring cases because of the low investment needed. OFT sometimes refers cases to ASA.

In terms of *ex post* and *ex ante* action, England has the most sophisticated system of preclearance of advertising among the countries investigated. The *bona fide* trader may play it rather safe through *ex ante* advice, although the guidance does not preclude litigation on the matter. For broadcast advertising, preclearance is basically the rule. The close cooperation with broadcasters, who can be pressured with possible loss of their licenses, is a key element. *Mala fide* traders cannot be threatened by ASA, although they must participate in the preclearance for broadcast advertising. The question is how far a threat for the *mala fide* trader may extend. Smooth cooperation between ASA and Ofcom and OFT is crucial in ensuring this. In rare cases, this underlying threat has been used. Furthermore, ASA's rulings are rarely successfully challenged in court. In terms of aligning incentives, the source of ASA's funding is kept anonymous.

The public law element can be provided through the involvement of public regulators – particularly, if they act as prosecutors in the criminal courts – and possibly through further police involvement. Often there is a court element involved when it comes to legal action (civil and criminal). In both scenarios here, OFT/TSS have a range of investigative powers at their disposal, which may be enhanced if the police are involved. Extending these powers is under discussion.

The underlying stronger importance of criminal law aligns with the optimal mix of law enforcement mechanisms. A welcome change has been the additional criminal law enforcement powers that were granted to OFT through the CPR 2008 (which TSS have made use of for quite some time), for cases of national concern, such as Internet enforcement. Criminal actions also may lead to court-ordered damage payments, which are crucial for deterrence. Fines or imprisonment are additional sanctions. Indeed, an OFT consumer criminal case in 2012 led to imprisonment of the accused.

The effectiveness of remedies depends on the nature of the traders and indeed some traders value reputation and others do not.[278] Regulators would have been given the power to levy fines under a pilot scheme, but that is adjourned. As mentioned, a speedy reaction is crucial, but interim measures that would be fast are less common and injunctions also are not remarkably fast (if action is initiated by OFT). Therefore, interim injunctions, which may provide for a fast reaction to stop illegal gains of *mala fide* traders, need some fine-tuning, particularly when wrongdoers try to delay enforcement responses. Responsive regulation distinguishes between responses to *bona fide* and *mala fide* traders. The proposed pilot project on targeted remedies would introduce even more targeted civil law sanctions and also injunctive relief. Note that some traders already attribute a fining power to OFT, which it currently has only for competition law purposes. This leads to a certain degree of deterrence.

278 See interview with OFT (London, 22 February 2011). There is no direct evidence on deterrence effects of injunctions available. See OFT, 'The OFT's approach to promoting business compliance with consumer protection law' (2011), http://www.oft.gov.uk/shared_oft/policy/OFT1292.pdf, last accessed: 31 March 2013 regarding OFT's vision on increasing impact (including deterrence).

The new remedies/sanctions have a potential to increase the speed of the procedure, but the loss of the court element should not be underestimated. Appeal possibilities for traders have to be ascertained, as provided by administrative procedural law.

From a deterrence perspective, the British government made an interesting advance with suggested legislation to give the courts the power to prohibit traders (individuals or companies) who persistently breach their obligations from carrying on business with consumers.[279] A 'Fighting Fund' to tackle specifically rogue traders[280] is available to TSS under certain conditions, for example if there is a serious risk to consumer safety or an element of fraud. The sanction of imprisonment certainly comes with a high value in terms of deterrence.

Some report a lack of coordination between OFT and TSS, which involves a potential loss of resources and duplication of enforcement efforts.[281] This data needs to be examined with caution because the government's interest is a serious restructuring of the consumer law enforcement landscape and no strong conclusions may be drawn from it.

Consumer associations play a minor role in law enforcement. At most, they signal cases to OFT that should be taken up. Then again, an interesting relation that does not exist in the other two countries examined is the super-complaint mechanism. Super-complaints from consumer associations that are considered frivolous are rejected. If the consumer associations refer cases to OFT, they refer to a body with more investigative powers than they have. From this point of view, the inactivity of the consumer associations is not unreasonable. If the consumer association or even OFT refers a case to ASA, this can be beneficial because the self-regulatory body knows its members well. It is furthermore a low-cost mechanism.

An increase in using ASA or OFT rulings on injunctions for follow-on damage cases is imaginable because these currently formally exist only for the competition law case (OFT rulings only). This change would certainly increase consumers' incentives to get involved in acting against social harms. Current alternative deterrent sanctions are criminal prosecutions by public regulators that can lead to compensation. In this light, enabling mass damage cases might not be an immediate necessity, particularly for cases of trifling and widespread harm where social welfare may be adversely affected by high administrative costs in damage calculation and distribution. If damage is substantial and widespread, the ratio might look different, but setting this threshold is outside the scope of this book.

A study has shown that a publicly funded advocate may be needed to strengthen consumer enforcement, which would be in line with the optimisation of the enforcement process.[282] A proposal – which has been dropped[283] – was discussed to develop an ombudsman (like in Scandinavia) with powers to take legal action

279 See BIS (2009), p. 54. No action seems to have been taken in this respect yet.

280 See BIS (2009), p. 56; see interview with OFT (London, 22 February 2011).

281 See NAO (2011).

282 See Peysner and Nurse (2008).

283 See interview with Consumer Focus (London, 22 February 2011).

for a group of consumers, if other routes for obtaining compensation had been exhausted or judged inappropriate. The ombudsman would also have distributed compensation to consumers from ill-gotten gains seized by overseas enforcement agencies and would have tackled unfairness in consumer credit agreements.[284] This suggestion aligns itself with the suggestions for efficient designs. Alternatively the existent regulators could implement this action. Since consumer associations are already active and well known in England, empowering them may be more likely than in Sweden, for instance where the branch of consumer associations has almost dried out. Then again, consumer associations will always be more limited in terms of investigative powers than a public authority and the associations' watchdog function in its current form may be desirable.

Available sanctions include compensation, fines, imprisonment and punitive damages. The latter are available in theory under conditions made by the Supreme Court in old cases, but would never be awarded in a consumer case.[285] Therefore, the discussion on available remedies does not differ from the other two countries. Fines are possible as remedies and fulfil a similar function, basically taking wealth from the wrongdoer.

To exploit consumers' potential to free ride on traders' actions (although traders may not always have an incentive to take action), strengthening the traders' ability to seek compensation is crucial. There is no private right of action against traders by businesses or consumers emanating from the CPRs. Individuals currently only have defective legal avenues at their disposal. Public regulators are under no obligation to investigate consumer complaints and an additional right to seek compensation for another market player may enhance deterrence. Limits of over-deterrence might have to be carefully considered because traders apparently have a high interest in using the law strategically against competitors. A court element is crucial to start with and, potentially, sanctions for frivolous suits. The section below describes the current, drastic reform proposal of the enforcement landscape in consumer law.

General Conclusion

As part of the reforms in the consumer law enforcement landscape, plans are underway to abolish Consumer Focus by April 2013 and merge it with Citizen's Advice.[286] Consumer law enforcement will primarily be channelled to

284 See BIS (2009), p. 60.

285 See personal email communications with Professor Christopher Hodges, Head of the Centre for Socio-Legal Studies, University of Oxford/Professor of the Fundamentals of Private Law, Erasmus University Rotterdam (January 2012).

286 See interview with Consumer Focus (London, 22 February 2011); interview with OFT (London, 22 February 2011). See BIS (2011); BIS, 'Empowering and Protection Consumers, Government Response to the Consultation on Institutional Reform' (2012),

TSS. A National Trading Standards Board (NTSB) is planned to be operative as of April 2013 as a coordinating unit. By October 2013, OFT will merge with other existing regulatory bodies into a new Competition and Markets Authority (CMA) to be fully operative by April 2014. In addition to the competition law enforcement, CMA will take over some of OFT's current consumer law enforcement responsibilities. Thus, TSS will be a key player with national funding to provide a more integrated approach to national and cross-boundary threats under the heading of NTSB. As mentioned, the OFT's CCAS will be shifted to TSI at the lower regulatory level. OFT will retain all of its current consumer enforcement powers, but will tend to use them where breaches of consumer protection law point to systemic failures in a market.

These changes have to be critically judged from a deterrence perspective. The final outcome of the restructuring must be awaited to clarify this aspect. Some important questions to consider include: Are enforcement gaps prevented? Is duplication of enforcement efforts mitigated? What is the role of OFT in providing an underlying threat in ASA rulings? In other words, is the response for *mala fide* traders tough enough, or if not, will the necessary bigger threat radiate from these changes? What will be the effect on the various regulators' investigative powers and the ability to cooperate in investigations?

For the first-case scenario, an important question is whether there is an impact on the ADR system. Since the ABTA scheme has already worked without OFT approval for the past years, little impact may be felt. Until now TSS rather than OFT have been active regarding package travel laws.

OFT seemed well suited for Internet enforcement cases with no clear local connecting factor, particularly because of OFT's wide investigative powers as a prosecutor for criminal cases and the ability to coordinate with the police. An impact could be felt in this regard depending on how active the new CMA will be in this respect and on the effectiveness of NTSB's role.

---

http://www.bis.gov.uk//assets/biscore/consumer-issues/docs/e/12-510-empowering-protecting-consumers-government-response.pdf, last accessed: 31 March 2013; BIS, 'Empowering and Protection Consumers, Consumer Landscape Review: Impact Assessment on Enforcement, Advocacy and Information, Advice and Education' (2012), https://www.gov.uk/government/uploads/system/uploads/attachment_data/file/31398/12-637-empowering-protecting-consumers-impact-assessments.pdf, last accessed: 31 March 2013.

PART III
Conclusions

Chapter 9
Conclusions

Introduction

Enforcement of consumer law can be problematic. According to research in consumer law enforcement in law and economics, optimal enforcement mixes should be created that draw upon the strengths and weaknesses of the various enforcement systems. In order to design optimal enforcement mixes, the existing mechanisms must be combined and hybrid solutions should be considered. This will vary for different sectors in consumer law and for different case scenarios.

This is the point at which this book stepped in and refined economic insights on the economic strengths and weaknesses of different enforcement systems, demonstrating what combinations for different case scenarios should look like. The research question was: 'Provided that the goal of enforcement is optimal deterrence how should an optimal mix of public and private enforcement look like within consumer law?'

To approach this challenging task, first existing economic criteria were systematised into a three-stage efficiency analysis and existing standardised enforcement mechanisms were assessed within this framework. The three stages were (1) optimal risk allocation, (2) the optimal provision of incentives and (3) administrative costs. The various existing economic criteria such as rational apathy, free riding, or principal-agent issues were allocated to the categories to which they fit best. Although there is already a sizeable body of research on strengths and weaknesses of various enforcement mechanisms, this book refines the criteria and places them within this comprehensive framework. Where the interrelations between certain criteria and certain mechanisms were not discussed in previous literature, this analysis filled the gap. This analysis identified and discussed the crucial factors related to incentives and deterrents for players to sue and carry out the optimal level of law enforcement and administrative costs of enforcement mechanisms.

Next, the framework was applied to specific consumer law cases and the characteristics of 'optimal mixes' for these representative scenarios were presented in a context, that reflects the common core of European procedural law.

The research does not stop at the theoretical level. Findings on the optimal mixes were used as a benchmark for a discussion of comparative law and economics. Real-life situations in three countries (Sweden, the Netherlands and England) with different enforcement traditions were illustrated in detail with a focus on various enforcers' roles in the selected scenarios and the interrelationship between the mechanisms. This comparison made it possible to conduct a critical assessment of the consumer law enforcement landscapes in these countries and to present reform suggestions from an efficiency perspective.

This concluding part summarises the main findings regarding the roles that various players have and should have in the selected case studies and contrasts the three investigated countries. The results of the comparative law and economics part are explained by summarising insights on the degree to which legal realities, particularly the roles of the players, conform with the suggested mixes and recommendations for welfare-enhancing changes derived from this comparison. Finally, by way of a personal point of view based partly on the analysis and partly on anecdotal evidence, a general lesson for policy advice to Europe is formulated.

Two Sets of Design Requirements

Two typical consumer law matters were used as sector studies – one in the field of package travel and one in the field of misleading advertising. A significant variety of contingencies were discussed. The selections made have the potential to capture various important features. First, one scenario was structured to lead to substantial individual harm (package travel) and one to lead to trifling and widespread harm (misleading advertising). Thus, the flow of argumentation was facilitated because only solutions of individual litigation were discussed in the travel sector and group litigation only for the advertising sector. The economic analysis (explained in the results section below) confirmed the logical, but so far not thoroughly founded suspicion that these different scenarios must trigger different mechanisms for an efficient response.

The figure of the trader was tackled in various ways. Information asymmetries between two parties were identified as an important trigger of litigation, particularly when the consumer lacks information regarding the location of the trader (aggravated by Internet trade), and this information asymmetry can lead to current failures in enforcement. Each sector study included a scenario involving a *bona fide* and a *mala fide* trader, the latter being the one who intends to hide within (or possibly outside of)[1] the country and who potentially may cause significant societal harm. At this point, the crucial question was, what was the potential of each law enforcer to generate the missing information and thus enable a lawsuit, which is a crucial aspect for deterrence? Each enforcement body was analysed for its ability to remedy the information asymmetries and further analysis looked at how the mechanisms could be combined to cure each other's weaknesses, while paying attention to overall social-welfare considerations.

The trader was also considered in a second way – as a competitor who incurred damage from the actions of the other trader, apart from that incurred by the consumer. In the misleading advertising example, the scenario was constructed

1 For the case study the trader was assumed to be hiding within the country. At some instances throughout the book, reference was nevertheless made to cross-border enforcement.

so that the competing trader's business was (potentially) severely damaged; however, the package travel example was an individual damage case and did not considerably harm a competitor's business. Therefore, the misleading advertising case provided an opportunity to assess the role of the competitor to step in and initiate law enforcement instead of consumers, and, consequently, the consumer's potential to free ride and society to benefit from this intervention.

The studies were chosen to allow a wide illustration of contingencies of consumer law cases, and, therefore, a rather complete description of a country's consumer law enforcement landscape.

From the conclusions drawn in the package travel examples, it was evident that public law solutions are needed to back up private law solutions, which was primarily shown in the case of *mala fide* traders who try to hide. Here, private law enforcement as currently structured has its limits. Due to insufficient information in the system, lawsuits are not initiated. The response has to differ for *mala fide* and *bona fide* traders. For cases against *bona fide* traders, using a Consumer ADR system is superior to the civil court. The basis of these suggestions is that an ADR system for the *bona fide* traders may potentially cross-finance the more costly enforcement responses against *mala fide* traders. A particular advantage of the ADR is that costs to file a complaint are low, and principal-agent problems between clients and lawyers are avoided because the consumer pursues the procedure herself. Administrative costs are low. The lack of a further development of the law as a loss to society is not present with easy, clear-cut cases. ADR personnel are experts (which seems realistic in the travel sector), when the case does not concern a complex application of law, but just the facts. Generally, ADR involves a voluntary element on the part of the trader. *Mala fide* traders cannot be dealt with.

Overall, it is crucial in these scenarios to provide the individual with an incentive to sue (with the prospect of compensation clearly given) and to guarantee a public law element to generate the necessary information in cases against *mala fide* traders, whenever in the societal interest. Special powers vested in public authorities or involvement of criminal law can fulfil this role. The different contingencies were discussed throughout the book; one option would be empowering public agencies to grant damages under certain conditions (a hybrid solution). Whenever public authorities are involved, incentives must be given to individuals to report. The use of criminal law can be suggested only for a few cases, primarily because of high administrative costs. Undoubtedly criminal law as a legal branch involves the widest investigative powers. Furthermore, trade associations have a role to play to facilitate a targeted, resource-saving approach if they, for instance, monitor the market. A working format of small claims tribunals might induce parties to consider the ADR system. Informing consumers upfront, the use of quality hallmarks through logos and so on may be warranted approaches and a role can be seen here for consumer associations.

In the misleading advertising examples, the findings described above also apply in an adapted way to an injured competitor's taking action. As a result, a consumer may be able to free ride to some degree and profit from the competitor's suit, and society may also reap benefits. In a competitor-initiated case, fewer information asymmetries arise because competitors work in the same sector and there would presumably be less need for a public law element to generate information. However, because a competitor's intervention is not certain (for instance, in cartel-like situations), a consumer-triggered enforcement response is also needed. In cases against *mala fide* traders, again the public law element is crucial. Individuals may not be induced to sue individually for their small harm, and, therefore, mass litigation is important and different representatives for such cases come into play. Depending on the nature of the trader, those enforcers who generate more information must be favoured whenever it is in the social interest. Then, the enforcer's intervention must be optimally coordinated in terms of the incentives that remedies provide. A definition must exist regarding which players are empowered to bring lawsuits and where to mitigate frivolous lawsuits, aggravated agency and capture problems. In terms of where these actions are to be brought, a court element is favoured because mass ADR cases are not optimal from the overall social-welfare perspective. Self-regulatory solutions, if supported by the underlying threat of stronger enforcement responses, can be welfare enhancing and allow for some cross-financing. As currently structured, self-regulation is more crucial than ADR bodies for terminating certain advertisements or requesting changes. The information that is available within the market can be absorbed in this way.

In relation to *mala fide* traders the speed of procedures is a crucial factor and *ex ante* actions were discussed in detail. On a voluntary basis, preclearance may protect the *bona fide* trader and to some extent help identify *mala fide* traders. With some products that may cause very high societal harm, obligatory preclearance can be effective.

For some violations the social harm does not justify an enforcement system response. An example of such an efficient breach is a case of small individual harm that is not widespread. Here, any enforcement response might come at a cost to society that far surpasses the emanating benefits.

An 'information generator' (how, by whom, by which combination of actors) may play an important role especially in the *mala fide* trader scenario where high information asymmetries are present, and may potentially cause large societal harm. A particularly interesting way to generate a lot of information, and avoid duplication of enforcement efforts, seems to be for public entities to act as prosecutors, with the option of involving the police as required. The analysis assessed which enforcement body could best remedy the information asymmetry and how mechanisms could be combined to eliminate each other's weaknesses while paying attention to the overall social welfare. For the *bona fide* trader, ADR and self-regulatory systems respectively should be fine-tuned and cases successfully filtered. Furthermore, if mass litigation is involved a court element is desirable. Capture is more likely with institutions like public agencies or ADR bodies than with courts and is inherent to self-regulation. Structures that are susceptible to capture and error costs are to be avoided in particular if a mass procedure is at stake to avoid spreading errors.

Regarding incentives for players to initiate a lawsuit, various enforcement mechanisms may remedy rational apathy, including having a representative take action (involving an association or a public agency) or a competitor. The potential for frivolous lawsuits or a strategic use of the law must be considered in particular regarding mass scenarios or whenever the competitor is involved.

Apparently, the various package travel and misleading advertising scenarios appear in parallel in reality and indeed the various described sets of design requirements have to be captured by a country's consumer law landscape to allow responses to the respective cases. The enforcement response has to be differentiated according to the amount of damage, the number of victims involved and the type of trader, in particular. In fact the case scenarios may be interrelated as misleading advertising issues also may be at stake in the package travel scenarios. Finally, the country under investigation is crucial.

These are the general guidelines regarding the ingredients that are needed, the competences that one or the other body must provide and which role it is to play. Various possibilities were at times presented that led to similar outcomes. Therefore, strictly speaking this research did not identify one economic optimal model, but rather a set of design requirements that need to be adhered to when creating an optimal enforcement response. Different priors in countries will lead to different solutions.

Consumer law enforcement landscapes show different designs and the solution to this analysis was not expected to be one optimal mix of enforcement mechanisms in consumer law, a one-size-fits-all solution that could be transplanted into any country as desired. Apparently, countries are not dark horses as this book confirms. A crucial factor in a country's potential to implement an optimal solution in a low-cost, welfare-enhancing way is to consider the importance of path dependency. Path dependency positively explains why countries' legal enforcement systems are shaped the way they are. The literature on path dependency discusses how disregarding 'context variables' of certain countries may lead to inefficient institutions or systems.[2] This concept is regularly applied when it comes to harmonisation of European Member States' laws.[3] Suggesting new institutions to a country – by legal borrowing, for example – as part of recommendations for legal reforms may have adverse effects. The origin of these differences in the institutional setting and related macroeconomic factors is not based on coincidences, but to

---

2 See Legrand (1996); Heine and Kerber (2002); Ogus (2002).

3 The problem of legal transplants has also been analysed on a world-wide scale, see M.G. Faure, M. Goodwin and F. Weber, 'Bucking the Kuznets Curve: Designing Effective Environmental Regulation in Developing Countries', *Virginia Journal of International Law* 15 (2010): 95–157. See also the approach by Bakardjieva Engelbrekt (2009), p. 95; see D. North, *Institutions Institutional Change and Economic Performance* (Cambridge: Cambridge University Press, 1990).

some extent reflects varying circumstances and, in particular, different legal traditions and cultures'.[4] Of course, a country need not confine changes only to the path it has taken, but the current system certainly must be considered when suggesting changes. The more innovative and alien the reform, the higher the potential cost of change and that cost must be weighed against the long-term social benefits that may be derived. Also, the relative strengths and weaknesses of a country have to be considered in design suggestions. Suggestions have to consider the roles that bodies play in the current legal setting and how flexible the country is in allowing for innovative solutions that diverge from the existing path. The specific analyses describe more concretely the role and nature that the different enforcement mechanisms play in the three selected countries, how they differ from the benchmark and where the system potentially may compensate for the difference. Suggestions for improvements are also presented.

Results of the Comparative Law and Economics Analysis

What do the enforcement mixes in the selected countries look like and how do they score in comparison to the design suggestions for optimality? The comparative law and economics analysis provides the answers to this second set of research questions. What is the legal solution to a consumer law problem? How do the legal systems of the selected countries compare to the insights from the economic analysis? Drawing upon the optimal mixes, what improvements can be suggested for each country?

This research approach allowed comparison of various countries individually with the design suggestions for optimal mixes, but comparing countries directly with each other may be done only as an illustration to describe the role and nature of different enforcement mechanisms in the countries. These comparisons are not meant to suggest that one country is better than another; rather, the findings may be used in relation to countries with similar traditions and enforcement bodies.

The Netherlands

The Netherlands traditionally has relied on private law enforcement and the introduction of the *Consumentenautoriteit* (CA) in 2007 (soon to be merged into a new public body) marked an historical change towards a stronger public law element in the law enforcement system. Overall, adding the CA to the enforcement landscape in the Netherlands has had positive effects that align with the design suggestions by providing a public law element in both types of case scenarios.

A sophisticated ADR system, the *Geschillencommissie* (GC), exists for 53 different branches of consumer law, including travel cases. This is where package travel cases are handled. The ADR board is financed primarily by traders and only

4 See Faure, Ogus and Philipsen (2008), p. 400.

partly by the state. Cases may be brought only against a trader who is registered with the body, either independently or through a trade association. The CA is active in ensuring traders' security mechanisms in case of insolvencies and has engaged in various civil court proceedings. For insolvencies the fund *Stichting Garantiefonds Reisgelden* (SGR) is an interesting institution, same as some newly established smaller funds. Hardly any cases regarding package travel end up in the court. Even the procedure before the subdistrict judge seems to be no competition to the ADR board. Lower fees with the ADR body are one crucial reason. The expertise for travel matters is clearly found with the GC. Criminal law enforcement is extremely rare. Priority is normally not given to consumer law matters. Only incidents of fraudulent abuses of the SGR logo were reported. The private association, *Consumentenbond* (CB), is an information provider for individual travellers. The ANVR is regarded as a well-working trade association in the sector.

Regarding misleading advertising, the CA and the self-regulatory body *Stichting Reclame Code* (SRC) have roles to play. The CA has heavily fined some traders through a system of administrative fining, with the possibility of judicial review. The fines available to the CA for unfair commercial practices, which includes misleading advertising, are higher than those normally available (€450,000 as opposed to €74,000 per violation). Although the CA has both private and administrative law enforcement powers, the powers are purely administrative in misleading advertising cases. At the RCC, a generic copy advice procedure is available; for some sectors preclearance is obligatory. In cases of widespread harm, the CB pursued mass cases, seeking declaratory or injunctive actions. The *Wet Collectieve Afwikkeling van Massaschade* (WCAM) procedure – a special procedure according to which mass settlements can be declared binding by the courts – was used in six occasions involving cases of misleading advertising. However, this procedure is feasible only in relation to substantial individual and widespread harm. It has a minor deterrent role in cases of trifling and widespread damage, and seeking other remedies in court or through CA intervention are more powerful. Competitors are generally empowered to seek actions against B2B and B2C advertising that harms them. Criminal law action has been reported in exceptional cases for particularly fraudulent cases.

Overall in both case scenarios, there is a mechanism with a potential to cross-finance more costly enforcement related to *mala fide* traders. In the travel sector, this mechanism is the ADR board, and in advertising, the self-regulatory body SRC. Both serve to cross-finance the involvement of the CA for *mala fide* traders or the possible, but rare, involvement of criminal law. In line with the design suggestions, a mass procedure at the ADR body is generally unavailable. The public authority's investigative powers are in between those of the police and the civil judge; it indeed has powers that the CB, which previously was the main consumer rights defendant, does not have. The CA actions to secure insolvency guarantees in the travel sector add a public element to the system to secure traders' whereabouts. Indicative, but inconclusive as to the nature of the trader might be the nonmembership in ANVR and related participation in the SGR (and the newly established funds). A non-registration at the ADR body (via ANVR or individually) is another indicator. The consumers' responsibility for checking on traders is regarded as important. In misleading advertising, a signal might be non-participation in the foundation SRC. A procedure that allows for claiming and distributing trifling and widespread harm is not available, but alternative enforcement options are given that may uphold the deterrent effect. Duplication of enforcement costs because of lack of coordination between the CA and the CB is not evident.

Improvements are suggested regarding the speed of CA proceedings. Currently, speed can be an issue in both civil and administrative law proceedings. In terms of administrative law enforcement, the expedient administrative order under penalty has proven an effective and fast sanction on various occasions when infringements were imminent. The CA's powerful capabilities to intervene have to be weighed against the danger of capture and the likelihood of error. The underlying appeal system may mitigate these dangers. Likewise, a means to challenge the CA's inaction may be beneficial, such as a complaint of the CB, which currently does not exist.

The *mala fide* trader has a valid expectation that a consumer will not easily take action at the civil court because of rational apathy. This reluctance seems to be true even for the subdistrict judge. Therefore, the public law element is particularly important for *mala fide* trader cases.

The position of *bona fide* traders could still be strengthened in misleading advertising by giving more value to the outcome of a pre-copy advice. Overall the Dutch system has considerably strengthened the deterrent threat of the ADR body's awards, apparently without an impeding increase in administrative costs.

Sweden

The Swedish legal system is characterised by a strong public law element. The Swedish Consumer Ombudsman/Consumer Agency (KO/KOV) has played a role in various sectors of consumer law enforcement for decades. For historical reasons, the Swedish population is not afraid of government intervention or the government carrying out tasks for the people, in strong contrast to some countries that in the aftermath of World War II avoided empowerment of government bodies and favoured empowering private parties.[5] Consequently, Sweden had no necessity of an evolvement of 'the principles of law-bound administration and an independent judiciary' as crucial safeguards against 'despotic arbitrariness' and means to secure individual freedom. Since the Middle Ages, an emphasis has been on parliamentarism with a relatively broad-based representation.[6] Private law,

5 See personal communications with Professor Antonina Bakardjieva Engelbrekt, University of Stockholm (Stockholm, August 2009).

6 See Bakardjieva Engelbrekt (2003), p. 122.

less than in other countries, is regarded as an important guarantor of individual autonomy[7] and the distinction between private and public law is less crucial.

Based on the analysis, Sweden scores high in terms of players whose involvement in the package travel case is as suggested. The ADR body, *Allmänna reklamationsnämnden* (ARN), and potentially the local consumer advisors may serve to cross-finance cases that would require a public law element. The ARN is solely financed by the state and may generally address any trader. The public law element is provided in various ways, by the involvement of the KO or even criminal law. KO, which merged with the Swedish consumer agency KOV, has various monitoring, negotiation and litigation powers. Like the Netherlands, Sweden provides a role for the public body in securing the traders' adherence to security mechanisms, and, therefore, indirectly knowledge about traders' whereabouts. Some police involvement is mentioned, too. *Kammarkollegiet* coordinates financial guarantees for companies and centrally organises them. In exceptional circumstances, the KO may represent one individual in court, relieving the person of costs of the court procedure.

For the misleading advertising case, the KO scores highly. According to the Marketing Act, investigative powers can be used to find traders or information about them. In limited circumstances, the KO also may directly fine traders, using its investigative powers in the process. There are costly sanctions available as deterrents, like the 'market disruption charge'. Under certain conditions, the KO may act as a prosecutor. A rather strong role is given to traders. Their incentive to damage a competitor's business is considered, and, therefore, traders are, for instance, given only a subsidiary right to bring action for the market disruption charge. Under the *Lag om grupprättegång* (LOG) 2002, collective actions, including for damages, are widely available as alternative deterrence options. Funding possibilities are being tested. The KO may sue damages for a group of consumers. In addition to the market disruption charge and compensation, injunctions and some interim measures are available as deterrent sanctions. Also, the LOG established private and organisation group actions and the criminal court may be called upon.

For *bona fide* traders, the *Reklamombudsmannen* (RO) provides *ex ante* advice in an unregulated form. The system of preclearance is very informal. The RO uses the threat of transferring cases to the KO. It is mainly available to cross-finance cases. *Ex ante* action by the KO, except for providing guidelines, is not available. These actions align with the suggestions for optimality because voluntary *ex ante* action may provide some signalling.

Overall, a cross-financing possibility is given and a public law element is present in various procedures. In most procedures, a 'court element' also is available. Only in very limited circumstances can the KO make its own decisions. The main suggestions for improvement are to expand the cases in which the KO may represent an individual for *mala fide* trader scenarios and facilitate use of the

7 See Bakardjieva Engelbrekt (2003), p. 120.

KO's investigative powers, which currently are only available in an indirect way for representation in civil cases. The KO is actually not different from a lawyer (in civil and ARN procedures). The KO may use additional information about a matter only if it was obtained through an unrelated investigation it carried out, which is far from certain. In other instances, such as when investigating traders, wide investigative powers are currently at the KO's disposition. Also, investigative powers should be ensured for mass cases if they are of a civil nature. The KO's role as a prosecutor is interesting and there may be a necessity to allow for a procedure to challenge the KO's inaction.

The necessity to use criminal law might be mitigated by the fact that a market disruption charge, even if the case is not labelled 'criminal', has basically the same high-deterrent effect that would emanate from a criminal fine. Another suggestion to strengthen deterrence concerns the ADR body, which has a weak mechanism to ensure the trader's compliance with awards. Here deposit systems could potentially increase the effects on traders' behaviour. The *ex ante* element at the RO also may be strengthened.

Mass litigation at the ARN may be deficient when compared to the optimality suggestions because of capture issues and spreading of error cost in particular. The set of efficiency requirements suggests disabling this feature. A stronger role for consumer associations does not seem to be warranted, particularly because they would not add to the investigative powers available in the system. Alternatives for collective actions have developed in the ambit of private group actions.

Overall, because the KO may step in for single individuals, the public law element may potentially be nicely intertwined with the consumer's interest in compensation.

England

The Office of Fair Trading (OFT) has been an important player in the enforcement landscape for a long time. The underlying concept to the regulatory approach in England is the *Ayres and Braithwaite* pyramid that sets out the concept of responsive regulation with measures like advice, persuasion and education at the broad bottom and the criminal sanctions, suspensions and licensing towards the top.[8] OFT is a nondepartmental government body and both the competition and consumer protection authority. Despite the similarity with Sweden's focus on public law enforcement, England has the particularity of making a comparably stronger use of criminal law, also within the ambit of administrative agencies.[9] Changes to the British consumer law enforcement landscape are imminent.

---

8 See Ayres and Braithwaite (1992).

9 See Faure, Ogus and Philipsen (2008), p. 376. With the RESA the focus of the sanctioning system was shifted to a considerable extent towards civil law sanctions. As mentioned the act has found little implementation.

In the package travel scenario, cross-financing is provided via an arbitration scheme administered by The British Travel Association (ABTA) and organised by an independent provider. Here cases of ABTA members, and, if desired, of non-ABTA members can be solved. Procedures in the county courts seem to offer more competition than in other discussed countries. ABTA as a trade association is considered to be tough on its members. Despite the nonexistence of a system of an underlying business guarantee or the like, no problems were reported with the compliance of the members. ABTA is active in self-regulation to discipline its members; *mala fide* traders would not use arbitration. Here, the public law element is available through Trading Standards Services (TSS), which are the local regulators that enforce travel law via criminal prosecutions, particularly the requirement to provide for financial securities in case of insolvencies. Most violations in travel law are formulated as criminal offences. TSS involvement goes as far as proactive monitoring, but cannot be confirmed for all of the more than 200 TSS. OFT currently does not seem to have a role in package travel issues as discussed in these scenarios. An instance of police involvement in a fraud case concerning traders' identities was reported. When acting as a prosecutor, TSS also may coordinate with the police and investigative powers may be used. A court element is generally present.

In advertising, a very sophisticated self-regulatory system is present with wide possibilities and requirements of *ex ante* action, which serves the *bona fide* traders' interests as well. For the *mala fide* traders, the cooperation between the Advertising Standards Authority (ASA) and OFT may be a deterrent. OFT is indeed active in civil law enforcement, and, newly, in criminal prosecution of misleading advertising. TSS traditionally have carried out criminal prosecutions. The regulators' involvement may be a deterrent, along with fines and compensation and imprisonment. A pilot project expanding the set of regulators' powers by various remedies, including fines and injunctions which may also serve deterrence demands, is pending. However, the court element for the first step in the procedure may get lost.

The route of mass damage litigation as a deterrent in cases with trifling and widespread damage seems problematic. While there are various potential routes, particularly via the courts' own case management, these options are not practical for trifling and widespread damage. Aggregate solutions for alternative remedies, like injunctions, might work. The role for consumer associations overall is limited, although they have an interesting competence in challenging OFT's potential inaction.

Therefore, suggestions for welfare-enhancing improvements include strengthening the role and coordination of the public regulators. An underlying guarantee system may have value for ensuring traders' compliance in the arbitration scheme in the travel sector. Ways to facilitate mass damage litigation can be explored, particularly in conjunction with an OFT/TSS decision. Coordinating the action of the various TSS and aligning their approaches seems to be a particular challenge. For cases of Internet enforcement, the main addressee would be

OFT. When acting as a prosecutor a public regulator's coordination with the police is a highly interesting route against *mala fide* traders. Indeed initiating the pilot project could be an interesting add-on in terms of costly remedies/sanctions. In terms of making the county court procedure a real competitor, it stands out that the costs in the county court are still higher and less predictable than, for instance, the ABTA arbitration scheme. Improvement could hence be warranted. Furthermore, both types of procedures follow different cost rules and the effects of these are unclear in terms of optimality.

General Policy Advice

As explained, the influence of the EU has traditionally been stronger in countries' substantive law provisions rather than their enforcement. However, some convergence is occurring within the union regarding the players involved in consumer law enforcement, not least because the European Commission has taken a stronger stance on advocating public law enforcement. As outlined, additional legislation that may impact enforcement landscapes is being prepared.

What are the general lessons that EU policy can learn from this research? Suggestions emerge from the contrast of the countries' various enforcement traditions and the optimal mixes, which may be applicable for these selected countries and others with similar legal traditions. These suggestions may also inform the European Commission's policy.

As a personal comment, I advocate for the public law element in particular, a stand that is partly based on the analysis undertaken and partly on anecdotal evidence. Independent of a country's law enforcement path, this research singled out economic reasons why a public law element is a warranted addition to a country's enforcement response, not least of which is an emergence of Internet trade that facilitates traders' being able to hide. As established, *mala fide* traders potentially cause substantial harm to society and information asymmetries between them and consumers regarding the traders' location lead to a failure of law enforcement in a purely private law setting. The investigative powers could be vested in various authorities, apart from public entities, such as a consumer association or the civil judge. Likewise, a larger role for criminal law enforcement would guarantee a high level of investigative powers. Vesting investigative powers in a public authority is just one option and allows countries that newly establish an authority to reap the benefits from best practices. As said, a particularly interesting route for generating a lot of information and avoiding duplication of enforcement efforts seems to be the power of public entities to act as prosecutors, with the option to involve the police as required. Very high administrative costs of criminal law enforcement impede its frequent use. Experiences in the Netherlands seem to signal that the establishment of a public authority for certain well-defined cases of consumer law can be an efficient add-on to private law enforcement traditions. Interestingly, the CA follows a dual approach: it has some private law and some public law enforcement powers depending on the case. Therefore, in terms of following path dependency, the Netherlands has not directly made a full turn to public law enforcement. In a way, a gradual change from purely private law enforcement to more public law enforcement is occurring, which might be just the right speed, by which a country's path may actually be changed. Overall satisfaction and no contraindication seem to show that the public body could indeed be well integrated in the Netherlands.

Germany also has a private law enforcement tradition. However, with the enactment of the Regulation on CPC, a public authority with some competences was established.[10] An enhancement of that authority's powers is under discussion because consumer associations that carry out enforcement activity in various instances refer the cases back to the public authority for more appropriate handling.[11]

Similarly, Austria has a strong private law enforcement tradition. Collective actions in criminal cases were suggested as a necessity for tackling cases of *mala fide* traders who cannot be located.[12] 'Criminal collective action' also would guarantee the public law element for certain consumer law cases. Common to all options, costs are low for individual consumers because the state funds the action, thus remedying potential rational apathy.

The scientific reasons for using a public law element to cure information asymmetries are timely when *mala fide* traders hide their identities and capitalise on gaps in the current enforcement response to avoid legal consequences. The discussions in the countries with private law enforcement traditions in particular confirm that investigative powers (and subsidising individual's enforcement responses to some extent) are necessary in *mala fide* trader cases. The increase in Internet trade creates new challenges.

Having promoted the public law element in general, safeguards in a legal system are likewise desirable, including involving courts, certainly for mass cases or appeal structures to counteract societal costs emerging from captured bodies, a high occurrence of error costs and a lack of a further development of the law.

10 In some Member States, like Germany, the competences of this entity are nevertheless few and the need to cooperate with private actors, such as consumer associations, for the purposes of carrying out the actual enforcement of consumer law cases is stressed, see § 7 EG-Verbraucherschutzdurchsetzungsgesetz (EC Consumer Protection Enforcement Act, VSchDG).

11 See M. Radeideh (Head of Bundesamt für Verbraucherschutz und Lebensmittelsicherheit (Economic Consumer Protection, Federal Office of Consumer Protection and Food Safety (BVL)) 'European consumer protection cooperation and implementation in Germany', presentation, Borderless consumer protection!? Effective enforcement, powerful consumers (Berlin 7 November 2011) and personal email communications.

12 See Expertentagung, 'Wilhelminenberg Gespräche' (2011); R. Enthofer-Stoisser and J. Habersberger, eds, *Catch Me if You can! – Internet „abzocke", „cold calls" und unseriöse Werbeveranstaltungen, Verbraucherrecht – Verbraucherpolitik*, Band 43 (Wien: Verlag Österreich, 2012).

For instance, the establishment of public authorities in some CEE countries, as favoured by the European Commission, may have been a premature step due to a lack of safeguards and resources needed to operate these bodies.[13] In the case of Italy, the public authority responsible for competition and consumer law enforcement (*Autorità Garante della Concorrenza e del Mercato*) started off with very soft procedural rules, leaving the agency with a lot of discretion that was then continuously specified in a variety of appeal procedures.[14]

Conclusion

This book develops a set of requirements for an efficient enforcement design for specific consumer law cases and uses these requirements as a benchmark to compare real-life situations in the Netherlands, Sweden and England. Despite the complexity of the topic, some conclusions were achieved, in particular regarding the economic value of the public law element and to fine-tune it within a legal system. This element must be part of the second best and third best solutions that become valuable whenever the market is not able to self-correct. This analysis has taken a broad approach to reflect the legal realities in different countries appropriately.

The comparative law and economics analysis confirms the importance of designing an enforcement response with adequate investigative powers. Considering a scenario involving one case of substantial damage to a case of small and widespread harm the notion of inducing optimal incentives of the involved gets a different dimension. One result of the analysis is to advocate the involvement of a court in mass proceedings. For cases of trifling and widespread harm, risks and costs involved in litigation must be spread or lawsuits will not be initiated. A variety of enforcers and enforcement mechanisms are crucial in a world with *bona fide* and *mala fide* traders who respond to different deterrents. For *bona fide* players, solutions like ADR or self-regulation that offer some precopy advice are effective. But for *mala fide* players, a public agency with wide investigative powers and deterring fines or even the criminal law branch must be available. Furthermore, emphasis is needed for appeal options and accountability where, for instance, public authorities have wide fining powers of their own (without involving a court). One may tentatively suggest that a particular strong player in the Dutch system is the *Geschillencommissie*. A system to provide an underlying business guarantee, certainly in the travel sector, strengthened the value of the awards this body grants, and in turn, compliance. A particularly convincing design for the demands of consumer law enforcement in Sweden is the KO's ability under special circumstances to represent one single individual in court. Whereas improvements are still imaginable in making investigative powers easily available

13 See Bakardjieva Engelbrekt (2009), p. 111.

14 See Tesauro and Russo (2008) and interview with Francesco Russo, Bonelli Erede & Pappalardo, Rome/Amsterdam Centre for Law and Economics (Rome, 23 April 2010).

in these scenarios (currently as outlined, this is only indirectly possible), KO's representation of a consumer is a way to combine investigative powers, waive litigation costs, cure any rational apathy and obtain damages. Finally, in England, OFT and TSS may act as prosecutors in certain cases and involve the police as necessary. This integration avoids duplication of enforcement costs and may potentially lead to an effective prosecution of *mala fide* traders. As a side aspect, various bodies such as consumer associations may challenge OFT's inaction through a super-complaint.

This book considered four typical case scenarios in consumer law and others may be imagined that leave some scope for future research. One could, in the misleading advertising scenario, also imagine that there are several competitors claiming substantial damage and that they would want to initiate a collective mass claim. The exact implications and welfare considerations of a collective mass action (if individual damage is substantial) in contrast to individual mass actions would have to be analysed.

A threshold needs to be established regarding when collective mass claims become inefficient (also the possibility of an injunction with follow-on damage claims) and for deterrence reasons, one should focus on alternatives such as 'fining'. Another threshold that needs to be established concerns the exact interrelation between the ADR body and the civil court – when would a consumer still use one, but not the other, same as the notion of 'interim measures'.

This research was based on the assumption that the *mala fide* trader hides within the country, but a trader may also hide abroad, of course. Cross-border enforcement mechanisms were referred to in some cases, but more thorough research needs to be done regarding the cross-border situation.

The outcomes of on-going legislative procedures at the European Union level are eagerly anticipated. May this book provide helpful input in such endeavours.

Bibliography

Literature

'Note on 'Shame, Stigma and Crime: Evaluating the Efficacy of Shaming Sanctions in Criminal Law', *Harvard Law Review* 116 (2003): 2186–207.

'The Swedish National Courts Administration', *Scandinavian Studies in Law* 51 (2007): 629–50.

ALI/UNIDROIT *Principles of Transnational Civil Procedure*. Cambridge: Cambridge University Press, 2006.

Akerlof, G. 'The Market for Lemons: Qualitative Uncertainty and the Market Mechanism'. *Quarterly Journal of Economics* 84.3 (1979): 488–500.

Alleweldt, F. et al. (Civic Consulting on behalf of IMCO). *State of Play of the Implementation of the Provisions on Advertising in the Unfair Commercial Practices Legislation*, 2010.

Andrews, N. 'Injunctions in Support of Civil Proceedings and Arbitration'. *Comparative Studies on Enforcement and Provisional Measures*, ed. R. Stürner and M. Kawano. Tübingen: Mohr Siebeck, 2011, 319–44.

Arons, T. and W.H. Van Boom. 'Beyond Tulips and Cheese: Exporting Mass Securities Claim Settlements from the Netherlands'. *European Business Law Review* (2010): 857–83.

Ayres, I. and J. Braithwaite. *Responsive Regulation: Transcending the Deregulation Debate*. New York: Oxford University Press, 1992.

Baggott, R. 'Regulatory Reform in Britain: The Changing Face of Self-Regulation'. *Public Administration* 67.4 (1989): 435–54.

Bakardjieva Engelbrekt, A. *Fair Trading Law in Flux? National Legacies, Institutional Choice and the Process of Europeanisation*. US-AB, 2003 Stockholm.

——. *Sweden National Report – Study: An Analysis and Evaluation of Alternative Means of Consumer Redress other than Redress through Ordinary Judicial Proceedings*, 2006.

——. 'Från Materiella Regler Till Genomföranderegler: En Ny Fas i det Europeiska Rättssamarbetet på Konsumentskyddsområdet?' *Europarättslig Tidskrift* 3 (2007): 568–97.

——. 'Public and Private Enforcement of Consumer Law in Central and Eastern Europe: Institutional Choice in the Shadow of EU Enlargement'. *New Frontiers of Consumer Protection – the Interplay between Private and Public Enforcement*, eds F. Cafaggi and H-W. Micklitz. Antwerp; Oxford; Portland: Intersentia, 2009, 91–136.

Bartle, I. and P. Vass, *Self-Regulation and the Regulatory State – A Survey of Policy and Practice* (Centre for the Study of Regulated Industries, University of Bath School of Management, 2005).

Bebchuk, L.A. and A. Guzman. 'How would you Like to Pay for that? the Strategic Effects of Fee Arrangements on Settlement Terms'. *Harvard Negotiation Law Review* 1 (1996): 53–65.

Bebchuk, L.A. 'Litigation and Settlement under Imperfect Information'. *RAND Journal of Economics* 15 (1984): 404–15.

Beccaria, C. *On Crimes and Punishments, and other Writings*, ed. R. Bellamy. New York: Cambridge University Press, 1995.

Becker, G.S. 'Crime and Punishment: An Economic Approach'. *Journal of Political Economy* 76 (1968): 169–217.

Becker, G.S. and G.J. Stigler. 'Law Enforcement, Malfeasance, and Compensation of Enforcers'. *Journal of Legal Studies* 3 (1974): 1–18.

Bentham, J. 'An Introduction to the Principles of Morals and Legislation'. *The Utilitarians*, ed. Garden City. New York: Anchor Books, 1789 [1973].

Bernitz, U. 'Consumer Protection: Aims, Methods, and Trends in Swedish Consumer Law'. *Scandinavian Studies in Law* 20 (1976): 11–36.

Bingham, L.B. et al. 'Dispute Resolution and the Vanishing Trial; Comparing Federal Government Litigation and ADR Outcomes'. *Ohio State Journal on Dispute Resolution* 24.2 (2009): 225–62.

Bowles, R., M.G. Faure and N. Garoupa. 'The Scope of Criminal Law and Criminal Sanctions: An Economic View and Policy Implications'. *Journal of Law and Society* 35.3 (2008): 389–416.

Bruns, A. 'Provisional Measures in European Civil Procedural Laws – Preservation of Variety or Need for Harmonisation'. *Comparative Studies on Enforcement and Provisional Measures*, eds R. Stürner and M. Kawano. Tübingen: Mohr Siebeck, 2011, 183–91.

CLEF, prepared by Howells, G. and H-W. Micklitz. *Guidelines for Consumer Associations on Enforcement and Collective Redress*, 2009.

Cafaggi, F. and H-W. Micklitz, 'Collective Enforcement of Consumer Law: A Framework for Comparative Assessment'. *European Review of Private Law* 16.3 (2008): 391–425.

——. *New Frontiers of Consumer Protection – the Interplay between Private and Public Enforcement*. Antwerp; Oxford; Portland: Intersentia, 2009.

——. 'Administrative and Judicial Enforcement in Consumer Protection: The Way Forward'. *New Frontiers of Consumer Protection – the Interplay between Private and Public Enforcement*, eds F. Cafaggi and H-W. Micklitz. Antwerp; Oxford; Portland: Intersentia, 2009, 401–45.

Cafaggi, F. *Reframing Self-Regulation in European Private Law*. The Hague: Kluwer, 2006.

——. 'The Great Transformation. Administrative and Judicial Enforcement in Consumer Protection: A Remedial Perspective'. *Loyola Consumer Law Review* 21 (2009): 496–539.

Calabresi, G. *The Costs of Accidents: A Legal and Economic Analysis*. 5th ed. New Haven: New Haven: Yale University Press, 1977.

Calabresi, G. and K.S. Schartz. 'The Costs of Class Actions: Allocation and Collective Redress in the US Experience'. *European Journal of Law and Economics* 32 (2011): 169–83.

Calabresi, G. 'Some Thoughts on Risk Distribution and the Law of Torts'. *Yale Law Review* 70.4 (1961): 499–553.

Carlson, L. *Fundamentals of Swedish Law*. Lund: Studentlitteratur AB, 2009.

Cartwright, P. 'Crime, Punishment, and Consumer Protection'. *Journal of Consumer Policy* 30.1 (2007): 1–20.

Coase, R.H. 'The Problem of Social Cost'. *Journal of Law and Economics* 3 (1960): 1–44.

——. 'Advertising and Free Speech'. *Journal of Legal Studies* 6.1 (1977): 1–34.

Coffee, J.C. JR. 'Class Wars: The Dilemma of the Mass Tort Class Action'. *Columbia Law Review* 95.6 (1995): 1343–465.

Collins, H. *Regulating Contracts*. New York: Oxford University Press, 1999.

Cooter, R. and T. Ulen. *Law & Economics*. 5th ed. Boston: Pearson Addison Wesley, 2008.

Cooter, R. 'Prices and Sanctions'. *Columbia Law Review* 84 (1984): 1523–60.

Creutzfeldt-Banda, N. 'Empirical Findings'. *Consumer ADR in Europe – Civil Justice Systems*, eds C. Hodges, I. Benöhr and N. Creutzfeldt-Banda. Oxford and Portland, Oregon: Hart Publishing, 2012, 367–88.

Creutzfeldt-Banda, N., C. Hodges and I. Benöhr. 'United Kingdom'. *Consumer ADR in Europe*, eds C. Hodges, I. Benöhr and N. Creutzfeldt-Banda. Oxford and Portland, Oregon: Hart Publishing, 2012, 253–353.

Cseres, K.J. 'Consumer Protection in the European Union'. *Regulation and Economics (Vol. 9, Encyclopedia of Law and Economics)*, eds R.J. Van den Bergh and A. M. Pacces. 2nd ed. Cheltenham: Edward Elgar, 2012, 163–228.

De Geest, G. and Van den Bergh, R.J., 'Introduction', *Comparative Law and Economics I,* eds G. De Geest and R.J. Van den Bergh. Cheltenham: Edward Elgar, 2004, pp. ix–xxi.

De Vrey, R.W. 'Handelspraktijken'. *Handboek Consumentenrecht*, eds E.H. Hondius and G.J. Rijken. 3rd ed. Zutphen: Uitgeverij Paris, 2011. 421–40.

Dubois, E., C. Schurrer and M. Velicogna. *The Functioning of Judicial Systems and the Situation of the Economy in the European Union Member States, Report Prepared for the European Commission by CEPEJ*, 2013.

Duggan, A.J. 'Consumer Access to Justice in Common Law Countries: A Survey of the Issues from a Law and Economics Perspective'. *International Perspectives on Consumers' Access to Justice*, eds C.E.F. Rickett and T.G.W. Telfer. Cambridge: Cambridge University Press, 2003. 46–67.

Eide, E. 'Economics of Criminal Behavior'. *Encyclopedia of Law and Economics, Volume I. the History and Methodology of Law and Economics*, eds B. Bouckaert and G. De Geest. Cheltenham: Edward Elgar, 2000, 345–89.

Enthofer-Stoisser, R. and J. Habersberger, eds. *Catch Me if You can! – Internet„abzocke", „cold calls" und unseriöse Werbeveranstaltungen.* Verbraucherrecht – Verbraucherpolitik, Band 43 Wien: Verlag Österreich, 2012.

Epstein, R.A. 'The Independence of Judges: The Uses and Limitations of Public Choice Theory'. *BYU Law Review* (1990): 832–5.

Faure M.G. and J.P.B. De Mot. 'Comparing Third Party Financing of Litigation and Legal Expenses Insurance'. *Journal of Law, Economics and Policy* 8.3 (2012): 743–78.

Faure, M.G., M. Goodwin and F. Weber. 'Bucking the Kuznets Curve: Designing Effective Environmental Regulation in Developing Countries'. *Virginia Journal of International Law* 15 (2010): 95–157.

Faure, M.G., A.I. Ogus and N.J. Philipsen. 'Enforcement Practices for Breaches of Consumer Protection Legislation'. *Loyola Consumer Law Review* 20.4 (2008): 361–401.

——. 'Curbing Consumer Financial Losses: The Economics of Regulatory Enforcement'. *Law & Policy* 31.2 (2009): 161–91.

Faure, M.G. 'Onbegrensd Toezicht?' *Toezicht op Markt en Mededinging (Justitiele Verkenningen)*, ed. WODC. Den Haag: Boom Juridische Uitgevers, 2008, 84–104.

Faure, M.G., F.J. Fernhout and N.J. Philipsen. *Resultaatgerelateerde Beloningssystemen voor Advocaten – Een Vergelijkende Beschrijving van Beloningssystemen voor Advocaten in een Aantal Landen van de Europese Unie en Hong Kong*. Den Haag: Boom Juridische Uitgevers, 2009.

Faust, F. 'Comparative Law and Economic Analysis of Law' *The Oxford Handbook of Comparative Law*, eds M. Reimann and R. Zimmermann. Oxford: Oxford University Press, 2006, pp. 837–65.

Forbes, J.D. *The Consumer Interest: Dimensions and Policy Implications*. London: Croom Helm, 1987.

Friedman, M. and L.P. Savage. 'The Utility Analysis of Choices Involving Risk'. *Journal of Political Economy* 56 (1948): 279–304.

Friehe, T. and A. Tabbach. 'Preventive Enforcement'. *International Review of Law and* Economics 35 (2013): 1–12.

Galbiati, R. and N. Garoupa. 'Keeping Stigma Out of Administrative Law: An Explanation of Consistent Beliefs'. *Supreme Court Economic Review* 15 (2007): 273–83.

Garoupa, N. 'Optimal Law Enforcement when Victims are Rational Players'. *Economics of Governance* 2 (2001): 231–42.

Garoupa, N. and F. Gomez-Pomar. 'Punish Once or Punish Twice: A Theory of the use of Criminal Sanctions in Addition to Regulatory Penalties'. *Harvard Law School John M. Olin Center for Law, Economics and Business Discussion Paper Series*. Paper 308 (2000): 1–30.

Geerts, P.G.F.A. and E.R. Vollebregt, eds. *Oneerlijke Handelspraktijken, Misleidende en Vergelijkende Reclame – Een Bespreking van de Art. 6:193a-6:196 BW*. Deventer: Kluwer, 2009.

Gibbons, T. 'The Utility of Economic Analysis of Crime'. *International Review of Law and Economics* 2.2 (1982): 173–91.

Gunningham, N. and P. Grabowsky. *Smart Regulation: Designing Environmental Policy*. Oxford: Clarendon Press, 1998.

Hadfield, G.K., R. Howse and M.J. Trebilcock. 'Information-Based Principles for Rethinking Consumer Protection Policy'. *Journal of Consumer Policy* 21 (1998): 131–69.

Harel, A. and A. Stein. 'Law and Economics at the Animal Farm: Offering a New Solution to the Class Action Agency Problem' (2001).

Heine, K. and W. Kerber. 'European Corporate Laws, Regulatory Competition and Path Dependence'. *European Journal of Law and Economics* 13 (2002): 47–71.

Heuman, L. 'Objectivity in Swedish Criminal Proceedings'. *Scandinavian Studies in Law* 51 (2007): 213–28.

Hicks, J. 'The Foundations of Welfare Economics'. *Economic Journal* 49. No. 196 (1939): 696–712.

Hodges, C. 'Collectivism: Evaluating the Effectiveness of Public and Private Models for Regulating Consumer Protection'. *Collective Enforcement of Consumer Law*, eds W.H. Van Boom and M.B.M. Loos. Groningen: Europa Law Publishing, 2007, 207–28.

——. *Global Class Actions Project, Country Report: England and Wales*, 2008.

——. 'Developing Approaches to Public and Private Enforcement in England and Wales'. *New Frontiers of Consumer Protection – the Interplay between Private and Public Enforcement*, eds F. Cafaggi and H-W. Micklitz. Antwerp; Oxford; Portland: Intersentia, 2009, 151–69.

——. 'Collective Actions'. *The Oxford Handbook of Empirical Legal Research*, eds P. Cane and H.M. Kritzer. Oxford: Oxford University Press, 2010, 705–28.

——. 'England and Wales: Summary of the Jackson Costs Review'. *The Costs and Funding of Civil Litigation – A Comparative Perspective*, eds C. Hodges, S. Vogenauer and M. Tulibacka. Oxford and Portland, Oregon: Hart Publishing, 2010, 303–12.

——. 'Objectives, Mechanisms and Policy Choices in Collective Enforcement and Redress'. *Mass Justice* eds J. Steele and W.H. Van Boom. Cheltenham: Edward Elgar, 2011, 101–17 (Hodges 2011a).

——. 'Public and Private Enforcement: The Practical Implications for Policy Architecture'. *The Foundations of European Private Law*, eds R. Brownsword et al. Oxford: Hart Publishing, 2011, 437–52 (Hodges 2011b).

Hodges, C., S. Vogenauer and M. Tulibacka, eds. *The Costs and Funding of Civil Litigation – A Comparative Perspective*. Oxford and Portland, Oregon: Hart Publishing, 2010.

Hodges, C., I. Benöhr and N. Creutzfeldt-Banda, eds. *Consumer ADR in Europe*. Oxford and Portland, Oregon: Hart Publishing, 2012.

Hodges, C., I. Benöhr and N. Creutzfeldt-Banda. 'Findings and Conclusions'. *Consumer ADR in Europe – Civil Justice Systems*, eds C. Hodges,

I. Benöhr and N. Creutzfeldt-Banda. Oxford and Portland, Oregon: Hart Publishing, 2012, 339–435.

Hodgson, J. and A. Roberts. 'Criminal Process and Prosecution'. *The Oxford Handbook of Empirical Legal Research*, eds P. Cane and H.M. Kritzer. Oxford: Oxford University Press, 2010, 64–93.

Hondius, E.H. 'Self-Regulation in Consumer Matters on a European Level'. *Reframing Self-Regulation in European Private Law*, ed. F. Cafaggi. The Hague: Kluwer Law International, 2006, 239–47 (Hondius 2006a).

——. *Netherlands National Report – Study: An Analysis and Evaluation of Alternative Means of Consumer Redress other than Redress through Ordinary Judicial Proceedings*, 2006 (Hondius 2006b).

——. 'Public and Private Enforcement in Consumer Protection – A Dutch Perspective'. *New Frontiers of Consumer Protection – the Interplay between Private and Public Enforcement*, eds F. Cafaggi and H-W. Micklitz. Antwerp; Oxford; Portland: Intersentia, 2009, 235–59.

Hood, C., H. Rothstein and R. Baldwin. *The Government of Risk: Understanding Risk Regulation Regimes*. New York: Oxford University Press, 2001.

Howells, G. and S. Weatherill. *Consumer Protection Law*. 2nd ed. Aldershot: Ashgate Publishing, 2005.

Howells, G. *United Kingdom National Report – Study: An Analysis and Evaluation of Alternative Means of Consumer Redress other than Redress through Ordinary Judicial Proceedings*, 2006.

——. 'Enforcing Consumer Interests by Regulatory Agencies – the British Experience; A Case Study of the Office of Fair Trading'. *Collective Enforcement of Consumer Law Securing Compliance in Europe through Private Group Action and Public Authority Intervention*, eds W.H. Van Boom and M.B.M. Loos. Groningen: Europa Law Publishing, 2007, 65–81.

——. *Evaluation of the Effectiveness and Efficiency of Collective Redress Mechanisms in the European Union – Country Report United Kingdom*, 2008.

Huls, N. 'Consumer Bankruptcy: A Third Way between Autonomy and Paternalism in Private Law'. *Erasmus Law Review* 3.1 (2010): 7–21.

Hylton, K.N. and V.S Khanna. 'Toward an Economic Theory of Pro-Defendant Criminal Procedure'. *Discussion Paper No. 318*.3 (2001).

Issacharoff, S. and I. Samuel. 'The Institutional Dimension of Consumer Protection'. *New Frontiers of Consumer Protection – the Interplay between Private and Public Enforcement*, eds F. Cafaggi and H-W. Micklitz. Antwerp; Oxford; Portland: Intersentia, 2009, 47–62.

Issacharoff, S. and G.P. Miller. *Will Aggregate Litigation Come to Europe?*, 2008.

Johnsen, J.T. 'Enforcement of Civil Claims in Criminal Litigation: The Norwegian Example'. *Enforcement and Enforceability – Tradition and Reform*, eds C.H. Van Rhee and A. Uzelac. Antwerp; Oxford; Portland: Intersentia, 2010, 313–26.

Jongbloed, A.W. 'Burgerlijk Procesrecht voor de Individuele Consument'. *Handboek Consumentenrecht*, eds E. Hondius and G.J. Rijken. 3rd ed. Zutphen: Uitgeverij Paris, 2011, 509–34.

Jordan, E.R. and P.H. Rubin. 'An Economic Analysis of the Law of False Advertising'. *The Journal of Legal Studies* 8.3 (1979): 527–53.

Kaldor, N. 'Welfare Propositions in Economics and Interpersonal Comparisons of Utility'. *Economics Journal* 49. No. 195 (1939): 549–52.

Kaplow, L. and S. Shavell. 'Optimal Law Enforcement with Self-Reporting of Behavior'. *The Journal of Political Economy* 102.3 (1994): 583–606.

Karapanou, V. and L.T. Visscher. 'The Magnitude of Pain and Suffering Damages from a Law and Economics and Health Economics Point of View'. *RILE Working Paper No. 2009/02* (2009).

Keser, C. and M. Willinger. 'Experiments on Moral Hazard and Incentives: Reciprocity and Surplus-Sharing'. *The Economics of Contracts Theories and Applications*, eds E. Brousseau and J-M. Glachant. Cambridge: Cambridge University Press, 2002, 293–312.

Keske, S., A. Renda and R.J. Van den Bergh. 'Financing and Group Litigation'. *New Trends in Financing Civil Litigation – A Legal, Empirical and Economic Analysis*, eds M.L. Tuil and L.T. Visscher. Cheltenham: Edward Elgar, 2010, 57–91.

Keske, S. *Group Litigation in European Competition Law: A Law and Economics Perspective*. Antwerp: Intersentia, 2010.

Keulen, B.F. and E. Gritter. 'Corporate Criminal Liability in the Netherlands'. *Electronic Journal of Comparative Law* 14.3 (2010): 1–12.

Keulen, B.F. and G. Knigge, eds. *Strafprocesrecht*. 12th ed. Deventer: Kluwer, 2010.

Kisjes, P. 'Geschillencommissie Reizen, minder klachten, meer betalen', *View*, August 2011.

Klapwijk, A. and M. Ter Voert. *Evaluatie De Geschillencommissie 2009*. Den Haag: Van Boom Juridische Uitgevers, 2009.

Klip, A. *European Criminal Law. An Integrative Approach*. 2nd ed. Cambridge – Antwerp – Portland: Intersentia, 2012.

Kohler, M. *Die Entwicklung des Schwedischen Zivilprozeßrechts*. Tübingen: Mohr Siebeck, 2002.

Koniak, S.P. and G.M. Cohen. 'Under Cloak of Settlement'. *Virginia Law Review* 82 (1996): 1051–270.

Koutsias, M. and C. Willett. 'The Unfair Commercial Practices Directive in the UK'. *Erasmus Law Review* 5.4 (2012): 237–51.

Kramer, X.E. 'Vereenvoudiging van de Geschillenbeslechting in Consumentenzaken: De Europese Small Claims Procedure en Nationale Initiatieven'. *Tijdschrift voor Consumentenrecht* 4 (2007): 111–21.

Landes, W.M. and R.A. Posner. 'The Private Enforcement of Law'. *Journal of Legal Studies* 4.1 (1975): 1–46.

——. 'The Independent Judiciary in an Interest Group Perspective'. *Journal of Law and Economics* 18 (1997): 875–901.

Lave, L.B. *The Strategy of Social Regulation: Decision Frameworks for Policy*. Washington, DC: The Brookings Institution, 1981.

Legrand, P. 'European Legal Systems are not Converging'. *International and Comparative Law Quarterly* 45 (1996): 52–81.

Lewis-Beck, M.S., A. Bryman and T. Futing Liao, eds. *The SAGE Encyclopedia of Social Sciences Research Methods, Vol. 3 (Q-Z)*. Thousand Oaks-London-New Delhi: SAGE Publications, 2004.

Lindblom, P.H. *The Globalization of Class Actions Oxford Conference, December 12–14*, 2007 (Lindblom 2007a).

——. 'The Growing Role of the Courts and the New Functions of Judicial Process – Facts or Flummery?' *Scandinavian Studies in Law* 51 (2007): 281–310.

——. 'ADR – the Opiate of the Legal System? Perspectives on Alternative Dispute Resolution Generally and in Sweden'. *European Review of Private Law* 1 (2008): 63–93 (Lindblom 2008a).

——. *Global Class Action – National Report: Group Litigation in Sweden, Update Paper Sections 2.5 and 3.*, 2008 (Lindblom 2008b).

——. 'Group Litigation in Scandinavia'. *ERA Forum* 10 (2009): 7–35.

Lindell, B. *Civil Procedure in Sweden*. Uppsala: Iustus Förlag, 2004.

——. 'Alternative Dispute Resolution and the Administration of Justice – Basic Principles'. *Scandinavian Studies in Law* 51 (2007): 311–44.

Loos, M.B.M. 'Individuele Handhaving van het Consumentenrecht bij de Burgerlijke Rechter'. *Tijdschrift voor Consumentenrecht* 1 (2011): 1–11.

——. 'Evaluation of the Effectiveness and Efficiency of Collective Redress Mechanisms in the European Union – Country Report Netherlands' (2008).

Loos, M.B.M. and W.H. Van Boom. *Handhaving van het Consumentenrecht – Preadviezen Nederlandse Vereniging voor Burgerlijk Recht 2009*. Deventer: Kluwer, 2010.

Luth, H.A. *Behavioural Economics in Consumer Policy – the Economic Analysis of Standard Terms in Consumer Contracts Revisited*. Antwerp: Intersentia, 2010.

Löfgren, K-G., T. Persson and J.W. Weibull. 'Markets with Asymmetric Information: The Contributions of George Akerlof, Michael Spence and Joseph Stiglitz'. *Scandinavian Journal of Economics* 104.2 (2002): 195–211.

Mahé, C.B.P. 'De Concurrent als "Handhaver" van Consumentenbescherming'. *Handhaving van en door het Privaatrecht*, eds E. Engelhardt et al. Den Haag: Boom Juridische Uitgevers, 2009, 173–89.

Main, T.O. 'ADR: The New Equity'. *University of Cincinnati Law Review* 74 (2005): 329–404.

Mannelqvist, R. 'Compensation for Victims in Public Legislation and as a Civil Right'. *Scandinavian Studies in Law* 50 (2007): 423–34.

Meili, S. 'Consumer Protection'. *The Oxford Handbook of Empirical Legal Research*, eds P. Cane and H.M. Kritzer. Oxford: Oxford University Press, 2010, 176–97.

Menkel-Meadow, C.J. and B.G. Garth. 'Civil Procedure and Courts'. *The Oxford Handbook of Empirical Legal Research*, eds P. Cane and H.M. Kritzer. Oxford: Oxford University Press, 2010, 679–704.

Menkel-Meadow, C.J. 'Dispute Resolution'. *The Oxford Handbook of Empirical Legal Research*, eds P. Cane and H.M. Kritzer. Oxford: Oxford University Press, 2010, 586–624.

Micklitz, H-W. 'Collective Private Enforcement of Consumer Law: The Key Questions'. *Collective Enforcement of Consumer Law – Securing Compliance in Europe through Private Group Action and Public Authority Intervention*, eds W.H. Van Boom and M.B.M. Loos. Groningen: Europa Law Publishing, 2007, 13–33.

Micklitz, H-W. and A. Stadler. 'The Development of Collective Legal Actions in Europe, especially in German Civil Procedure'. *European Business Law Review* 17 (2006): 1473–503.

Micklitz, H-W. and C. Poncibò. *Evaluation of the Effectiveness and Efficiency of Collective Redress Mechanisms in the European Union – Country Report Italy*, 2008.

Micklitz, H-W., N. Reich and P. Rott, eds. *Understanding EU Consumer Law*. Antwerp: Intersentia, 2009.

Miller, G.P. 'Compensation and Deterrence in Consumer Class Actions in the US and Europe'. *New Frontiers of Consumer Protection – the Interplay between Private and Public Enforcement*, eds F. Cafaggi and H-W. Micklitz. Antwerp; Oxford; Portland: Intersentia, 2009, 263–82.

Miller, J.C. 'The FTC and Voluntary Standards: Maximizing the Net Benefits of Self-Regulation'. *Cato Journal* 4.3 (1985): 897–903.

Moewe, J.A. 'Consumers, Class Actions and Costs: An Economic Perspective on Deceptive Advertising'. *UCLA Law Review* 18 (1970): 592–615.

Moorhead, R. 'Cost Wars in England and Wales: The Insurers Strike Back'. *Cost and Fee Allocation in Civil Procedure*, ed. M. Reimann. Dordrecht; Heidelberg; London; New York: Springer, 2012, 117–25.

Mölenberg, L.J.H. 'Reisovereenkomst'. *Handboek Consumentenrecht*, eds E.H. Hondius and G.J. Rijken. Zutphen: Uitgeverij Paris, 2011, 233–56.

Nelson, P. 'Information and Consumer Behavior'. *Journal of Political Economy* 78 (1970): 311–29.

——. 'Advertising as Information'. *Journal of Political Economy* 82.4 (1974): 729–54.

Nikkels, L. et al. *Kennen Consumenten hun Rechten en Plichten? Onderzoek naar het Kennisniveau van Consumenten*, 2008.

North, D. *Institutions Institutional Change and Economic Performance*. Cambridge: Cambridge University Press, 1990.

Ogus, A.I., M.G. Faure and N.J. Philipsen. 'Best Practices for Consumer Policy: Report on the Effectiveness of Enforcement Regimes'. *Report prepared for the UK Department of Trade and Industry and OECD* (2006).

Ogus, A.I. *Regulation: Legal Form and Economic Theory*. Oxford: Clarendon Press, 1994.

——. 'Self-Regulation'. *Encyclopedia of Law and Economics Volume V. The Economics of Crime and Litigation* (1999): 587–602.

——. 'The Economic Basis of Legal Culture: Networks and Monopolization'. *Oxford Journal of Legal Studies* 22.3 (2002): 419–34.

——. 'Enforcing Regulation: Do we Need the Criminal Law?' *New Perspectives on Economic Crime*, eds H. Sjörgen and G. Skogh. Cheltenham: Edward Elgar, 2004, 42–56

——.*Costs and Cautionary Tales: Economic Insights for the Law*. Oxford: Hart Publishing, 2006.

——. 'Shifts in Governance for Compensation to Damage: A Framwork for Analysis'. *Shifts in Compensation between Private and Public Systems*, eds W.H. Van Boom and M.G. Faure. Wien: Springer-Verlag, 2007, 31–42.

Olson, M. *The Logic of Collective Action: Public Goods and the Theory of Groups*. 2nd ed. Cambridge, MA: Harvard University Press, 1971.

O'Connor, K.J.L. et al. 'Interaction of Public and Private Enforcement'. *Private Enforcement of Antitrust Law in the United States – A Handbook*, eds A.A. Foer and R.M. Stutz. Cheltenham: Edward Elgar, 2010, 280–304.

Pareto, V. 'The Maximum of Utility Given by Free Competition'. *Giornale degli Economisti* 67.3 (2008): 387–403.

Parisi, F., ed. *The Economic Structure of the Law the Collected Economic Essays of Richard A. Posner*. Vol. 1. Cheltenham: Edward Elgar, 2000.

Persson, A.H. 'Evaluation of the Effectiveness and Efficiency of Collective Redress Mechanisms in the European Union – Country Report Sweden' (2008).

Peysner, J. 'England and Wales'. *The Costs and Funding of Civil Litigation – A Comparative Perspective*, eds C. Hodges, S. Vogenauer and M. Tulibacka. Oxford and Portland, Oregon: Hart Publishing, 2010, 289–302.

Polinsky, A.M. and D. Rubinfeld. 'A Note on Settlements Under the Contingent Fee Method of Compensating Lawyers'. *International Review of Law and Economics* 22 (2002): 217–25.

Polinsky, A.M. and S. Shavell. 'The Theory of Public Enforcement of Law'. *NBER Working Paper 11780* (2005) (Polinsky and Shavell 2005a).

Polinsky, A.M. and S. Shavell, 'Economic Analysis of Law'. *Discussion Papers 05-005, Stanford Insitute for Economic Policy Research* (2005) (Polinsky and Shavell 2005b).

Posner, R.A. 'The Federal Trade Commission'. *The University of Chicago Law Review* 37.1 (1969): 47–89.

——. 'The Behavior of Administrative Agencies'. *Journal of Legal Studies* (1972): 305–48.

——. 'The Theories of Economic Regulation'. *The Bell Journal of Economics and Management Science* 5.2 (1974): 335–58.

——. 'An Economic Approach to Legal Procedure and Judicial Administration'. *The Economic Structure of the Law: The Collected Economic Essays of Richard A. Posner*, ed. F. Parisi. Cheltenham: Edward Elgar, 2000, 290–349.

——. *Economic Analysis of Law*. 8th ed. New York: Aspen Publishers, 2011.

Priest, G.L. 'Reexamining the Selection Hypothesis: Learning from Wittman's Mistakes'. *Journal of Legal Studies* 14 (1985): 215–43.

Priest, G.L. and B. Klein. 'The Selection of Disputes for Litigation'. *Journal of Legal Studies* 13 (1984): 1–55.

Ramsay, I. 'Consumer Redress and Access to Justice'. *International Perspectives on Consumers' Access to Justice*, eds C.E.F. Rickett and T.G.W. Telfer. Cambridge: Cambridge University Press, 2003, 17–45.

Rasmusen, E. 'Stigma and Self-Fulfilling Expectations of Criminality'. *Journal of Law and Economics* 39 (1996): 519–43.

Renda, A. et al. *Making Antitrust Damages Actions More Effective in the EU: Welfare Impact and Potential Scenarios*. Report for the European Commission/Contract DG COMP/2006/A3/012: 2007.

Rickett, C.E.F. and T.G.W. Telfer. 'Consumers' Access to Justice: An Introduction'. *International Perspectives on Consumers' Access to Justice*, eds C.E.F. Rickett and T.G.W. Telfer. Cambridge: Cambridge University Press, 2003, 1–16.

Rischkowsky, F. and T. Döring. 'Consumer Policy in a Market Economy: Considerations from the Perspective of the Economics of Information, the New Institutional Economics as Well as Behavioural Economics'. *Journal of Consumer Policy* 31 (2008): 285–313.

Rosenberg, D. 'Mandatory-Litigation Class Action: The Only Option for Mass Tort Actions'. *Harvard Law review* 115 (2002): 829–7.

Rosenberg, D. and S. Shavell. 'A Model in which Suits are Brought for their Nuisance Value'. *International Review of Law and Economics* 5 (1985): 3–13.

Sabbatini, P. 'Funding the Budget of a Competition Authority with Fines it Imposes'. (2009).

Saggerson, A. *Travel Law and Litigation*. 4th ed. St Albans: XPL Publishing, 2008.

Schaub, M.Y. 'Handhaving van Consumentenrecht'. *Handhaven van en door het Privaatrecht*, eds E. Engelhardt et al. Den Haag: Boom Juridische Uitgevers, 2009, 149–71.

Schwarze, J., ed. *European Administrative Law*. London: Sweet & Maxwell, 1992.

Schäfer, H-B. 'The Bundling of Similar Interests in Litigation. the Incentives for Class Action and Legal Actions Taken by Associations'. *European Journal of Law and Economics* 9.3 (2000): 183–213.

Schäfer, H-B. and C. Ott, eds. *The Economic Analysis of Civil Law*. Cheltenham: Edward Elgar, 2004.

Segal, I.R. and M.D. Whinston. 'Public vs. Private Enforcement of Antitrust Law: A Survey'. *Stanford Law and Economics Olin Working Paper No. 335* (2006).

Shapira, Z. *Risk Taking: A Managerial Perspective*. New York: Russell Sage Foundation, 1997.

Shavell, S. 'Risk Sharing and Incentives in the Principal and Agent Relationship'. *Bell Journal of Economics, The RAND Corporation* 10.1 (1979): 55–73.

——. 'The Social versus the Private Incentive to Bring Suit in a Costly Legal System'. *Journal of Legal Studies* 11 (1982): 333–9.

——. 'Liability for Harm versus Regulation of Safety'. *Journal of Legal Studies* 13 (1984): 357–74. (Shavell 1984a)

——. 'A Model of the Optimal use of Liability and Safety Regulation'. *The RAND Journal of Economics* 15.2 (1984): 271–80.

——. 'Criminal Law and the Optimal use of Nonmonetary Sanctions as a Deterrent'. *Columbia Law Review* (1985): 1231–62.

——. 'Specific versus General Enforcement of Law'. *Journal of Political Economy* 99.5 (1991): 1088–108.

——. 'The Optimal Structure of Law Enforcement'. *Journal of Law and Economics* 36 (1993): 255–88.

——. 'Alternative Dispute Resolution: An Economic Analysis'. *Journal of Legal Studies* 24 (1995): 1–28.

——. 'The Fundamental Divergence between the Private and the Social Motive to use the Legal System'. *Journal of Legal Studies* 16 (1997): 575–612.

——. 'Economic Analysis of Litigation and the Legal Process'. *NBER Working Papers National Bureau of Economic Research, Inc.* 9697 (2003).

——. *Foundations of Economic Analysis of Law*. Cambridge, Massachusetts: The Belknap Press of Harvard University Press, 2004.

Shleifer, A. et al. 'Courts'. *Quarterly Journal of Economics* 118.2 (2003): 453–517.

Slovic, P., H. Kunreuther and G.F. White. 'Decision Processes, Rationality, and Adjustment to Natural Hazards'. *Natural Hazards. Local, National and Global*, ed. G.F. White. New York: Oxford University Press, 1974, 187–205.

Soderlind, S.D. *Consumer Economics: A Practical Overview*. Armonk, New York/ London, England: M.E. Sharpe, 2001.

Stadler, A. 'Group Actions as a Remedy to Enforce Consumer Interests'. *New Frontiers of Consumer Protection – the Interplay between Private and Public Enforcement*, eds F. Cafaggi and H-W. Micklitz. Antwerp; Oxford; Portland: Intersentia, 2009, 305–28.

Stephen, F.H. and J.H. Love. 'Regulation of the Legal Profession'. *Encyclopedia of Law and Economics Volume III. the Regulation of Contracts*, eds B. Bouckaert and G. De Geest. Cheltenham: Edward Elgar, 2000.

Stigler, G.J. 'The Economics of Information'. *Journal of Political Economy* 69 (1961): 213–25.

——. 'The Optimum Enforcement of Laws'. *Journal of Political Economy* 78.3 (1970): 526–36.

——. 'The Theory of Economic Regulation'. *Bell Journal of Economics and Management Science* 3 (1971): 3–18.

——. 'Free Riders and Collective Action: An Appendix to Theories on Economic Regulation'. *The Bell Journal of Economics and Management Science* 5.2 (1974): 359–65.

Stiglitz, J. 'The Contributions of the Economics of Information to the Twentieth Century Economics'. *Quarterly Journal of Economics* 114 (2000): 1441–78.

Stuyck, J. 'Public and Private Enforcement in Consumer Protection: General Comparison EU-USA'. *New Frontiers of Consumer Protection – the Interplay between Private and Public Enforcement*, eds F. Cafaggi and H-W. Micklitz. Antwerp; Oxford; Portland: Intersentia, 2009, 63–90.

Stuyck, J. et al. 'An Analysis and Evaluation of Alternative Means of Consumer Redress other than Redress through Ordinary Judicial Proceedings – Final Report' (2007).

Sunnqvist, M. 'Loser Pays – but only a Reasonable Amount – Cost and Fee Allocation in Sweden'. *Cost and Fee Allocation in Civil Procedure*, ed. M. Reimann. Dordrecht; Heidelberg; London; New York: Springer, 2012, 267–73.

Svatikova, K. *Economic Criteria for Criminalization: Optimizing Enforcement in Case of Environmental Violations*. Antwerp; Oxford; Portland: Intersentia, 2012.

Tesauro, C. and F. Russo. 'Unfair Commercial Practices and Misleading and Comparative Advertising: An Analysis of the Harmonization of EU Legislation in View of the Italian Implementation of the Rules'. *Competition Policy International* 4.1 (2008): 192–222.

Trebilcock, M.J. 'Rethinking Consumer Protection Policy'. *International Perspectives on Consumers' Access to Justice*, eds C.E.F. Rickett and T.G.W. Telfer. Cambridge: Cambridge University Press, 2003, 68–98.

Treis, M. *Recht des unlauteren Wettbewerbs und Marktvertriebsrecht in Schweden*. Köln Berlin Bonn München: Carl Heymanns Verlag KG, 1991.

Tuil, M.L. 'The Netherlands'. *The Costs and Funding of Civil Litigation. A Comparative Perspective*, eds C. Hodges, M. Tulibacka and S. Vogenauer. Oxford: Hart Publishing, 2010, 401–19.

Tullock, G. 'The Welfare Costs of Monopolies, Tariffs, and Theft'. *Western Economic Journal* 5 (1967): 224–32.

Tversky, A. and D. Kahneman. 'Prospect Theory: An Analysis of Decision Under Risk'. *Econometria* 47.2 (1979): 263–91.

Tzankova, I.N. 'Class Actions, Group Litigation and other Forms of Collective Litigation Dutch Report (Memorandum in the Ambit of the Global Class Action Exchange Project), Report Part 1' (2007).

——. 'Global Class Action Project Country Report the Netherlands – Part 2' (2008).

Tzankova, I.N. and M.A. Gramatikov. 'A Critical Note on Two EU Principles: A Proceduralist View on the Draft CFR'. *The Foundations of European Private Law*, ed. R. Brownsword et al. Oxford: Hart Publishing, 2011.

Ulen, T.S. 'Rational Choice Theory in Law and Economics'. *Encyclopedia of Law and Economics, Volume I. the History and Methodology of Law and Economics*, eds B. Bouckaert and G. De Geest. Cheltenham: Edward Elgar, 2000, 790–818.

Schulte-Nölke, H. 'EC Consumer Law Compendium – Comparative Analysis'. Bielefeld: University of Bielefeld, 2007.

Van Boom, W.H. and M.B.M. Loos. *Collective Enforcement of Consumer Law – Securing Compliance in Europe through Private Group Action and Public Authority Intervention*. Groningen: Europa Law Publishing, 2007.

——. 'Effective Enforcement of Consumer Law in Europe: Synchronizing Private, Public, and Collective Mechanisms'. *Working Paper Series* (2008).

Van Boom, W.H. 'Collective Settlement of Mass Claims in the Netherlands'. *Auf dem Weg zu einer Europäischen Sammelklage?* eds M. Casper et al. München: Sellier, 2009, 171–92.

Van Boom, W.H. *Efficacious Enforcement in Contract and Tort*. Den Haag: Boom Juridische Uitgevers, 2006.

——. 'Effectuerend Handhaven in het Privaatrecht'. *Nederlands Juristenblad* 16 (2007): 982–91.

——. 'Inpassing en Handhaving van de Wet Oneerlijke Handelspraktijken'. *Tijdschrift voor Consumentenrecht en Handelspraktijken* 1 (2008): 4–24.

——. 'De Minimis Curat Praetor: Redress for Dispersed Trifle Losses'. *Journal of Comparative Law* 4.2 (2009): 169–83.

——. *Handhaving Consumentenbescherming – Een Toelichting op de Wet Handhaving Consumentenbescherming*. Zutphen: Uitgeverij Paris, 2010.

Van Boom, W.H. et al. *Handelspraktijken, Reclame en Zelfregulering*, ed. WODC Ministerie van Justitie. Den Haag: Boom Juridische Uitgevers, 2009 (Van Boom et al. 2009a).

Van Boom, W.H., B.J. Drijber, J.H. Lembstra, V.C.A. Lindijer and T. Novakovski. *Strooischade:* Een Verkennend (Rechtsvergelijkend) Onderzoek naar de Mogelijkheden tot Optreden tegen Strooischade (2009), https://zoek.officielebekendmakingen.nl/blg-82770.pdf, last accessed: 31 March 2013.

Van Campen, M.M. 'Privaatrechtelijke Handhaving door de Consumentenautoriteit'. *Privaatrecht Ondersteund – Doelen, Baten, Kosten en Effecten van Bijzondere Ondersteuning door de Overheid van Privaatrechtlijke Handhaving*, eds W.H. Van Boom, S D. Lindenbergh and S.B. Pape. Den Haag: Boom Juridische Uitgevers, 2007, 35–60.

Van Damme, E. 'Toekomst van de Consument Concurrentiebeleid en Consumentenbeleid'. *ESB Dossier* (2007): 36–42.

Van den Bergh, R.J. 'Towards Efficient Self-Regulation in Markets for Professional Services'. *European Competition Law Annual 2004: The Relationship between Competition Law and the (Liberal) Professions*, eds C. Ehlermann and I. Atanasiu. Oxford and Portland, Oregon, USA: Hart Publishing, 2006, 155–76.

——. 'Should Consumer Protection Law be Publicly Enforced?' *Collective Enforcement of Consumer Law*, eds W.H. Van Boom and M.B.M. Loos. Groningen: Europa Law Publishing, 2007, 179–203.

——. 'Enforcement of Consumer Law by Consumer Associations'. *Essays in the Law and Economics of Regulation – in Honour of Anthony Ogus*, eds M.G. Faure and F.H. Stephen. Antwerp; Oxford; Portland: Intersentia, 2008, 279–306.

Van den Bergh, R.J. and L.T. Visscher. 'Optimal Enforcement of Safety Law', *Mitigating Risk in the Context of Safety and Security. How Relevant is a Rational Approach?* ed. R.V. de Mulder. Rotterdam: Erasmus University, 2008, 29–62 (Van den Bergh and Visscher 2008a).

——. 'The Preventive Function of Collective Actions for Damages in Consumer Law'. *Erasmus Law Review* 1 (2008): 5–30 (Van den Bergh and Visscher 2008b).

Van den Bergh, R.J. and S. Keske. 'Rechtsökonomische Aspekte Der Sammelklage'. *Auf dem Weg zu einer Europäischen Sammelklage?* eds M. Casper et al. München: Sellier. European Law Publishers, 2009, 17–40.

Van den Bergh, R.J. and P. Camasasca. *European Competition Law and Economics: A Comparative Perspective*. 2nd ed. London: Sweet & Maxwell, 2006.

Van den Wyngaert, C. ed. (co-editors: Gane, C./ Kühne, H.H./ Mcauley, F.), *Criminal Procedure Systems in the European Community*. London, Brussels, Dublin, Edinburgh: Butterworths, 1993.

Veljanovski, C.G. 'The Economics of Regulatory Enforcement'. *Enforcing Regulation*, eds K. Hawkins and J.M. Thomas. Boston: Kluwer-Nijhoff Publishing, 1984, 171–91.

Verbruggen, P. *Transnational Private Regulation in the Advertising Industry – Case Study Report for the Research Project Constitutional Foundations of Transnational Private Regulation*, 2011.

Verkerk, R. 'The Netherlands'. *European Traditions in Civil Procedure*, ed. C.H. Van Rhee. Antwerp – Oxford: Intersentia, 2005, 281–90.

Viitanen, K. 'The Baltic Model for the Settlement of Individual Consumer Disputes'. *Journal of Consumer Policy* 23 (2000): 315–39.

——. 'Enforcement of Consumers' Collective Interests by Regulatory Agencies in the Nordic Countries'. *Collective Enforcement of Consumer Law Securing Compliance in Europe through Private Group Action and Public Authority Intervention*, eds W.H. Van Boom and M.B.M. Loos. Groningen: Europa Law Publishing, 2007, 83–103.

Visscher, L.T. and T. Schepens. 'A Law and Economics Approach to Cost Shifting, Fee Arrangements and Legal Expense Insurance'. *New Trends in Financing Civil Litigation in Europe: A Legal, Empirical and Economic Analysis*, eds M.L. Tuil and L.T. Visscher. Cheltenham: Edward Elgar, 2010, 7–32.

Weber, F. 'Assessing Existing Enforcement Mechanisms in Consumer Law – the Unavailability of an Allrounder'. *Swedish Journal of European Law (Europarättslig Tidskrift)* 3 (2011): 536–54.

——. 'Abusing Loopholes in the Legal System – Efficiency Considerations of Differentiated Law Enforcement Approaches in Misleading Advertising', *Erasmus Law Review* 5.4 (2012): 289–307.

Weber, F. and W.H. Van Boom. 'Dutch Treat: The Dutch Collective Settlement of Mass Damage Act (WCAM 2005)'. *Contratto e impresa/Europa* 1 (2011): 69–79.

Weber, F. and C. Hodges. 'Netherlands'. *Consumer ADR in Europe*, eds C. Hodges, I. Benöhr and N. Creutzfeldt-Banda. Oxford and Portland, Oregon: Hart Publishing, 2012, 129–65.

Weber, F., C. Hodges and N. Creutzfeldt-Banda. 'Sweden'. *Consumer ADR in Europe*, eds C. Hodges, I. Benöhr and N. Creutzfeldt-Banda. Oxford and Portland, Oregon: Hart Publishing, 2012, 229–52.

Wilson, J.Q. *Bureaucracy – what Government Agencies do and Why they do It*. New York: Basic Books, A division of HarperCollinsPublishers, 1989.

Wittman, D. 'Prior Regulation versus Post Liability: The Choice between Input and Output Monitoring'. *Journal of Legal Studies* 6 (1977): 193–12.

Zuckerman, A. *Zuckerman on Civil Procedure Principles of Practice*. 2nd ed. London: Sweet & Maxwell, 2008.

pro facto (Schol, M.J., J. Nagtegaal and H.B.). Winter. *Evaluatie Wet Handhaving Consumentenbescherming Ervaringen met het Duale Handhavingsstelsel en de Handhavingsbevoegdheid Inzake Massaschade*, 2010.

B. Reports/Studies

'De ANVR op de stoel van de rechter?' (14 January 2011): http://www.reishonger.nl/reisnieuws/anvr-op-de-stoel-van-de-rechter, last accessed: 31 March 2013.

'Consumentenautoriteit: Na actie meer reisaanbieders met garantiestelling' (15 June 2011), http://www.consumentenautoriteit.nl/nieuws/2011/consumentenautoriteit-na-actie-meer-reisaanbieders-met-garantiestelling, last accessed: 31 March 2013.

OFT Business leadership in consumer protection. A discussion document on self regulation and industry-led compliance (2009): http://www.oft.gov.uk/shared_oft/reports/consumer-policy/oft1058.pdf, last accessed: 31 March 2013.

'OFT secures enforcement orders against holiday club companies' (6 May 2011): http://www.oft.gov.uk/news-and-updates/press/2011/58-11, last accessed: 31 March 2013.

'OFT stops misleading premium rate scratchcard promotion' (1 March 2006): http://www.oft.gov.uk/news-and-updates/press/2006/41-06, last accessed: 31 March 2013.

ABTA, answer to consultation on ADR issued by the European Commission (2011).

Annual report ANVR 2010.

Annual report ARN 2012.

Annual report ASA 2009.

Annual report ASA 2012.

Annual report CA 2008.

Annual report CA 2010/11.

Annual report CA 2012.

Annual report Geschillencommissie 2009.

Annual report Geschillencommissie 2010.

Annual report Geschillencommissie 2011.

Annual report Geschillencommissie 2012.

Annual report KO/KCV 2011.

Annual report KO/KCV 2012.

Annual report Market Court 2012.

Annual report OFT 2010.

Annual report OFT 2011.

Annual report RCC 2010.

Annual report RCC 2012.

Annual report Rechtspraak 2011.

Biennial Report of the UK Member State on the Application of the Regulation on Consumer Protection Cooperation (EC) 2006/2004 (January 2009): http://ec.europa.eu/consumers/enforcement/docs/united_kingdom_report_en.pdf, last accessed: 31 March 2013.

BIS, A Better Deal for Consumers Delivering Real Help Now and Change for the Future (2009), http://webarchive.nationalarchives.gov.uk/+/http://www.bis.gov.uk/policies/consumer-issues/consumer-white-paper, last accessed: 31 March 2013.

BIS, Empowering and Protecting Consumers, Consultation on Institutional Changes for Provision of Consumer Information, Advice, Education, Advocacy and Enforcement (June 2011): http://www.bis.gov.uk/assets/biscore/consumer-issues/docs/e/11-970-empowering-protecting-consumers-consultation-on-institutional-changes.pdf, last accessed: 31 March 2013.

BIS, 'Empowering and Protection Consumers, Consumer Landscape Review: Impact Assessment on Enforcement, Advocacy and Information, Advice and Education' (2012): https://www.gov.uk/government/uploads/system/uploads/attachment_data/file/31398/12-637-empowering-protecting-consumers-impact-assessments.pdf, last accessed: 31 March 2013.

BIS, 'Empowering and Protection Consumers, Government Response to the Consultation on Institutional Reform' (2012), http://www.bis.gov.uk//assets/biscore/consumer-issues/docs/e/12-510-empowering-protecting-consumers-government-response.pdf, last accessed: 31 March 2013.

Borg, T. Towards a More Efficient Enforcement of EU Consumer Rights, 2013: http://www.european-consumer-summit.eu/index_en.html, last accessed: 31 March 2013.

Borg T. 'Building a strong political case for a consumer friendly internal market', 18 March 2013, at the European Consumer Summit.

Court Statistics: Official Statistics of Sweden 2012.

Consumentenautoriteit, Agenda 2012/2013: http://www.consumentenautoriteit.nl/sites/default/ files/redactie/consumentenautoriteit-agenda-2012-2013.pdf, last accessed: 31 March 2013.

Consumer Focus, answer to consultation on ADR issued by the European Commission (2011).

Departementsserien 2009:14 Konsumentombudsmannen – en översyn.

Department of Business, Innovation and Skills (BIS), Empowering and Protecting Consumers, Consultation on Institutional Changes for Provision of Consumer Information, Advice, Education, Advocacy and Enforcement (June 2011): http://www.bis.gov.uk/assets/biscore/consumer-issues/docs/e/11-970-empowering-protecting-consumers-consultation-on-institutional-changes.pdf, last accessed: 31 March 2013.

European Business Test Panel (EBTP), Alternative Dispute Resolution (2011): http://ec.europa.eu/yourvoice/ebtp/consultations/2010/adr/report_en.pdf, last accessed: 31 March 2013.

European Commission's working paper on Enforcement of European Consumer Legislation, 27 March 1998, SEC (98) 527.

European Commission, Executive Summary of the impact assessment, accompanying the document proposal for a Directive of the European Parliament and of the Council on alternative dispute resolution for consumer disputes (Directive on Consumer ADR) and proposal for a regulation of the European Parliament and of the Council on online dispute resolution for consumer disputes (Regulation on Consumer ODR) (Commission staff working paper, Brussels, 29.11.2011, SEC(2011) 1409 final), http://ec.europa.eu/consumers/redress_cons/docs/summary_impact_assessment_adr_en.pdf, last accessed: 31 March 2013.

European Commission, Special Eurobarometer n°195, European Union citizens and access to justice (2004), http://ec.europa.eu/consumers/redress/reports_studies/eurobarometer_11-04_en.pdf, last accessed: 31 March 2013.

European Commission, Special Eurobarometer n°342, Consumer Empowerment (2011), http://ec.europa.eu/consumers/consumer_empowerment/docs/report_eurobarometer_342_en.pdf, last accessed: 31 March 2013.

European Commission, The System of Administrative and Penal Sanctions in the Member States of the European Communities (Office for Official Publications of the European Communities, Brussels, Vol. 1 and 2, 1994).

European Consumer Law Group (ECLG), report 2003/4.

European Parliament resolution of 2 February 2012 on 'Towards a Coherent European Approach to Collective Redress' (2011/2089(INI)).

Europe Economics, An Analysis of the Issue of Consumer Detriment and the Most Appropriate Methodologies to Estimate it (Final Report for DG SANCO, 2007), http://ec.europa.eu/consumers/strategy/docs/study_consumer_detriment.pdf, last accessed: 31 March 2013.

Eurostat, Panorama on Tourism (2008), http://epp.eurostat.ec.europa.eu/cache/ITY_OFFPUB/KS-30-08-550/EN/KS-30-08-550-EN.PDF, last accessed: 31 March 2013.

Expertentagung. 'Wilhelminenberg Gespräche', Sozialministerium Österreich (Austrian Ministry of Social Affairs), Catch Me if You Can/Geschäfte an der Grenze des Erlaubten, as reported in 'Die Presse', Internet-Abzocke: Ruf nach kollektiver Rechtsdurchsetzung, (9 October 2011), http://diepresse.com/home/recht/rechtallgemein/699564/InternetAbzocke_Ruf-nach-kollektiver-Rechtsdurchsetzung?_vl_backlink=/home/recht/index.do, last accessed: 31 March 2013.

HM Courts & Tribunals Service, Civil and Family Court Fees 2013, http://hmctscourtfinder.justice.gov.uk/courtfinder/forms/ex050-eng.pdf, last accessed: 31 March 2013.

Judicial Court Statistics 2011.

Kwink Groep BV, Eindrapport Evaluatie Consumentenautoriteit op grond van de Whc (2011), http://www.consumentenautoriteit.nl/sites/default/files/

redactie/eindrapport-evaluatie-consumentenautoriteit.pdf, last accessed: 31 March 2013.

Law Commission and Scottish Law Commission, 'Misrepresentation and unfair commercial practices – some initial questions' (2011), http://www.lawcom.gov.uk/misrepresentation_commercial.htm, last accessed: 31 March 2013.

London Economics, Study on Consumer Detriment in the area of Dynamic Packages (Final report to The European Commission – Health and Consumers DG 2009), http://ec.europa.eu/consumers/rights/docs/study_consumer_detriment_dyna_packages_en.pdf, last accessed: 31 March 2013.

Lord Justice Jackson, Review of Civil Litigation Costs, Final Report (2010).

Lord Woolf, Final Report to the Lord Chancellor on the civil justice system in England and Wales (1996).

NAO, Department for Business, Innovation and Skills, the Office of Fair Trading and Local Authority Trading Standards Services Protecting consumers – the system for enforcing consumer law (2011).

OFT/BERR 'Consumer Protection From Unfair Trading – Guidance on the UK Regulations (May 2008) implementing the Unfair Commercial Practices Directive' (2008), http://www.oft.gov.uk/shared_oft/business_leaflets/cpregs/oft1008.pdf, last accessed: 31 March 2013.

OFT 'Criminal Enforcement of the Consumer Protection from Unfair Trading Regulations 2008 – OFT Policy' (2010), http://www.oft.gov.uk/shared_oft/policy/OFT1273.pdf, last accessed: 31 March 2013.

OFT 'Criminal Liability in Regulatory Contexts Response to the Law Commission consultation' (2010), http://www.oft.gov.uk/shared_oft/consultations/OFT1285res.pdf, last accessed: 31 March 2013.

OFT 'Enforcement of Consumer Protection Legislation – Guidance on Part 8 of the Enterprise Act' (2003), http://www.oft.gov.uk/shared_oft/business_leaflets/enterprise_act/oft512.pdf, last accessed: 31 March 2013.

OFT 'Guidance for the use of on-site inspection powers under the Consumer Protection Cooperation Regulation' (2009), http://www.oft.gov.uk/shared_oft/business_leaflets/general/oft884.pdf, last accessed: 31 March 2013.

OFT 'Investigation into sales of 2010 FIFA World Cup tickets by unauthorised traders' (Case reference: CRE-E-24580) (2010), http://www.oft.gov.uk/OFTwork/consumer-enforcement/consumer-enforcement-completed/fifa/#.UfDDVI3wmSo, last accessed: 31 March 2013.

OFT/LBRO (Local Better Regulation Office) 'Civil Sanctions Pilot Joint consultation by the OFT and LBRO on the operation of the BIS Civil Sanctions Pilot' (2010), http://www.oft.gov.uk/shared_oft/consultations/OFT1296.pdf, last accessed: 31 March 2013.

OFT 'Policy statement – The role of self-regulation in the OFT's consumer protection work' (2009), http://www.oft.gov.uk/shared_oft/reports/consumer-policy/oft1115.pdf, last accessed: 31 March 2013.

OFT press release, 'OFT: ABTA withdraws from OFT Consumer Codes Approval Scheme' (31 August 2006), http://www.oft.gov.uk/news-and-updates/press/2006/127-06, last accessed: 31 March 2013.

OFT, Research on Impact of Mass Marketed Scams, A Summary of Research into the Impact of Scams on UK Consumers (December 2006), http://www.oft.gov.uk/shared_oft/reports/consumer_protection/oft883.pdf, last accessed: 31 March 2013.

OFT 'Response to the Law Commission and the Scottish Law Commission Consultation on Consumer Redress for Misleading and Aggressive Practices (July 2011), http://www.oft.gov.uk/shared_oft/reports/oft_response_to_consultations/oft1355.pdf, last accessed: 31 March 2013.

OFT 'Super-complaints: Guidance for designated consumer bodies' (2002), http://www.oft.gov.uk/shared_oft/business_leaflets/enterprise_act/oft514.pdf, last accessed: 31 March 2013.

OFT 'The OFT's approach to promoting business compliance with consumer protection law' (2011), http://www.oft.gov.uk/shared_oft/policy/OFT1292.pdf, last accessed: 31 March 2013.

Peysner, J. and A. Nurse 'Representative Actions and Restorative Justice: A Report for the Department for Business, Enterprise and Regulatory Reform (BERR)' (2008), http://www.bis.gov.uk/files/file51559.pdf, last accessed: 31 March 2013.

Policy Department Economic and Scientific Policy, Study on Safety and Liability Issues Relating to Package Travel (requested by the European Parliament's Committee on Internal Market and Consumer Protection, 2008), http://www.europarl.europa.eu/meetdocs/2004_2009/documents/dv/999/999000/999000en.pdf, last accessed: 31 March 2013.

Press releases RAPID, No Hiding Place for Rogue Traders: Commission Proposes EU-wide Network of National Watchdogs (22 July 2003), http://europa.eu/rapid/pressReleasesAction.do?reference=IP/03/1067&format=HTML&aged=0&language=EN&guiLanguage=en, last accessed: 31 March 2013.

Protocol Consumentenautoriteit – OM, http://www.consumentenautoriteit.nl/sites/default/files/redactie/samenwerkingsprotocol-procureurs-generaal-consumentenautoriteit.pdf, last accessed: 31 March 2013.

Protocol Consumentenautoriteit – Stichting Reclame Code, http://www.consumentenautoriteit.nl/sites/default/files/redactie/Samenwerkingsovereenkomst%20Consumentenautoriteit-Stichting%20Reclame%20Code.pdf, last accessed: 31 March 2013.

RCC, The Dutch Advertising Code – Information about the working procedures of the Advertising Code Committee and the Board of Appeal (2011), http://www.reclamecode.nl/ bijlagen/20110920_NRC_Engels.pdf, last accessed: 31 March 2013.

Report on the Implementation of Directive 90/C on Package Travel and Holiday Tours in the Domestic Legislation of EC Member States, 27 March 1998, SEC (98) 527.

Response by the Confederation of Netherlands Industry and Employers (VNO-NCW) and the SME lobby organisation MKB-Nederland to the European Commission's consultation document dated 18 January 2011 on the use of Alternative Dispute Resolution, http://ec.europa.eu/consumers/redress_cons/adr_responses/Confederation_Netherlands_Industry_Employers_en.pdf, last accessed: 31 March 2013.

Response of the Bar Council of England and Wales to the EU Commission's public consultation 'Towards a coherent European approach to collective redress' (2009), http://ec.europa.eu/competition/consultations/2011_collective_redress/bcew_en.pdf, last accessed: 31 March 2013.

Scottish Law Commission. 'Multi-Party Actions, Report Under a Reference Under Section 3(1) (E) of the Law Commissions Act 1965'. *Scottish Law Commission No. 154, Edinburgh, HMSO* (1996).

Sveriges Konsumenter, The Swedish Consumer Association, response to the European Commission's consultation document dated 18 January 2011 on the use of Alternative Dispute Resolution.

Swedish Ministry of Justice, response to the European Commission's consultation document dated 18 January 2011 on the use of Alternative Dispute Resolution.

UK PermRep, answer to consultation on ADR issued by the European Commission (2011).

Index

Some of the information is country-specific. This is indicated in brackets by E=England, NL=the Netherlands and SW=Sweden

Printed in Canada

PGCA2024